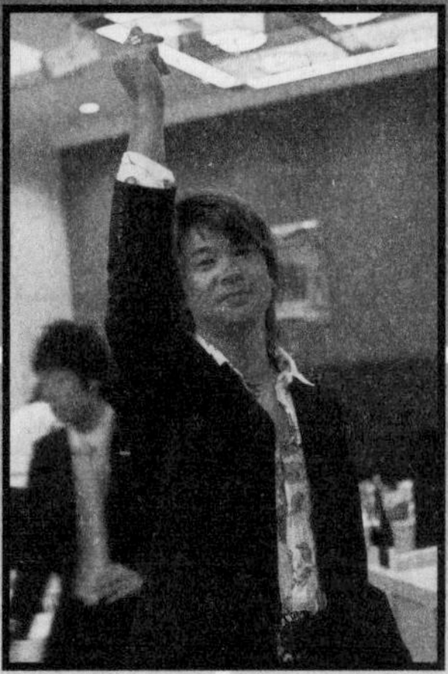

SNAP!

(The photographer forced me to do it.)

— Takeshi Konomi, 2007

About Takeshi Konomi

Takeshi Konomi exploded onto the manga scene with the incredible **THE PRINCE OF TENNIS**. His refined art style and sleek character designs proved popular with **Weekly Shonen Jump** readers, and **THE PRINCE OF TENNIS** became the number one sports manga in Japan almost overnight. Its cast of fascinating male tennis players attracted legions of female readers even though it was originally intended to be a boys' comic. The manga continues to be a success in Japan and has inspired a hit anime series, as well as several video games and mountains of merchandise.

THE PRINCE OF TENNIS
VOL. 36
SHONEN JUMP Manga Edition

STORY AND ART BY
TAKESHI KONOMI

Translation/Joe Yamazaki
Touch-up Art & Lettering/Vanessa Satone
Design/Sam Elzway
Editor/Daniel Gillespie

VP, Production/Alvin Lu
VP, Sales & Product Marketing/Gonzalo Ferreyra
VP, Creative/Linda Espinosa
Publisher/Hyoe Narita

Printed in the U.S.A.

Published by VIZ Media, LLC
P.O. Box 77010
San Francisco, CA 94107

10 9 8 7 6 5 4 3 2 1
First printing, March 2010

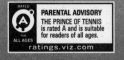

www.viz.com

RATED A FOR ALL AGES
PARENTAL ADVISORY
THE PRINCE OF TENNIS is rated A and is suitable for readers of all ages.
ratings.viz.com

THE WORLD'S MOST POPULAR MANGA
www.shonenjump.com

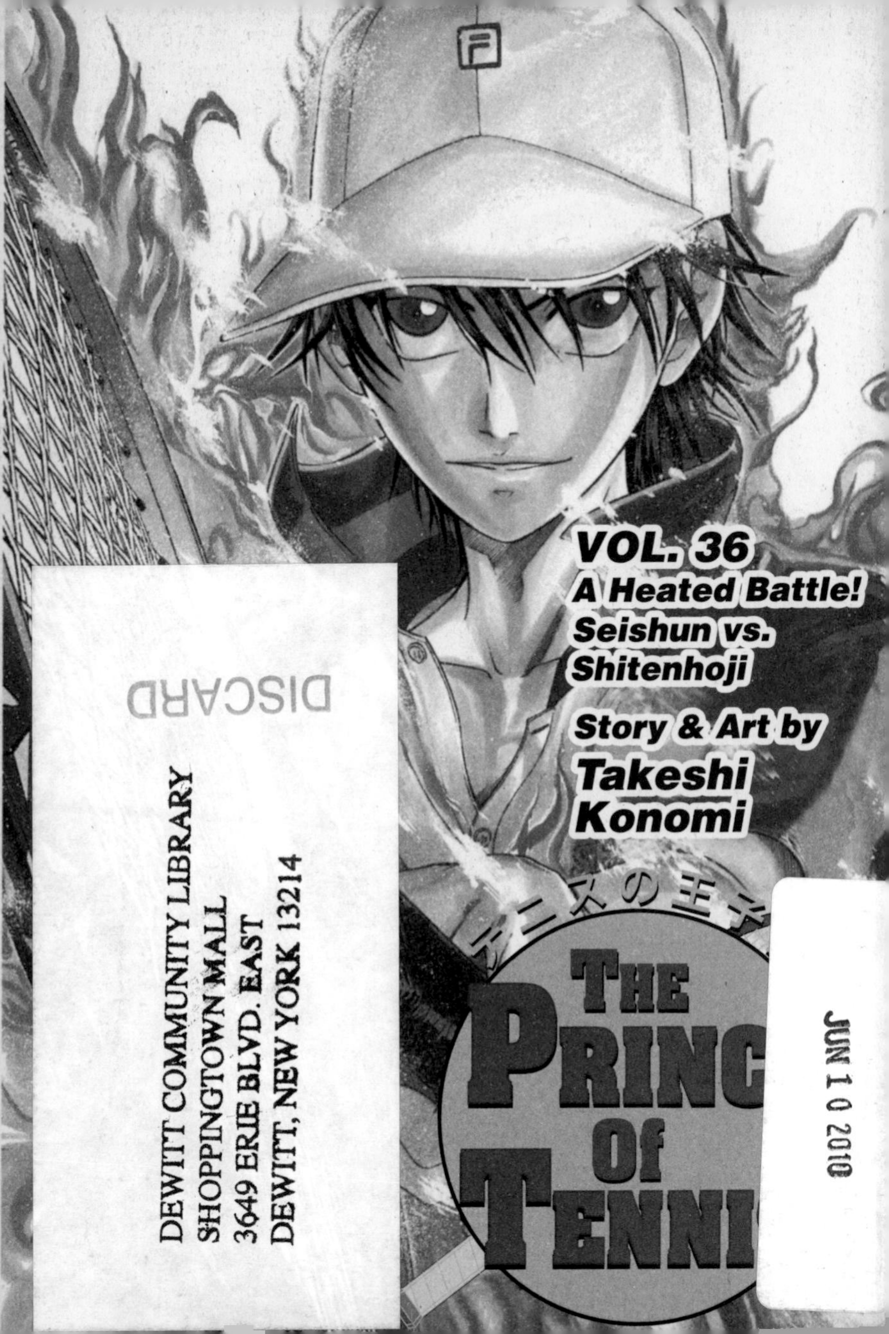
VOL. 36
A Heated Battle! Seishun vs. Shitenhoji
Story & Art by Takeshi Konomi
テニスの王子
THE PRINC[E] OF TENNI[S]

ENNIS CLUB

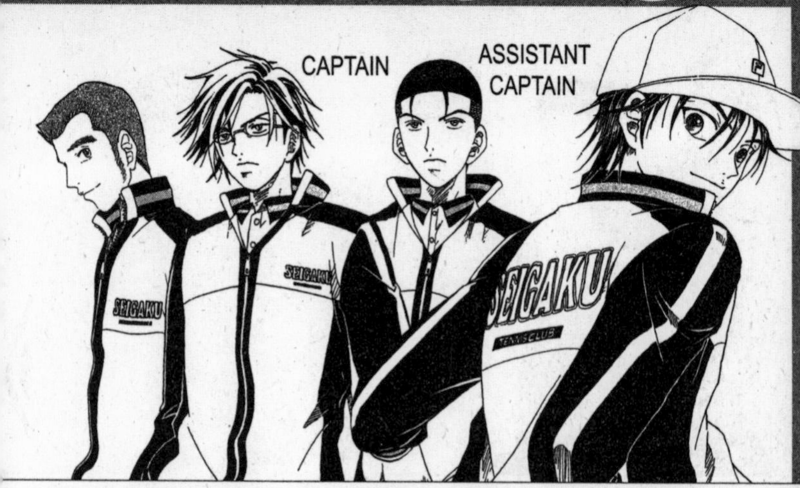
CAPTAIN
ASSISTANT CAPTAIN

• TAKASHI KAWAMURA • KUNIMITSU TEZUKA • SHUICHIRO OISHI • RYOMA ECHIZEN •

STORY & HARACTERS

Sheishun Academy student Ryoma Echizen is a tennis prodigy, with wins in four consecutive U.S. Junior Tennis Tournmants under his belt. He became a starter as a 7th grader and led his team to the District Preliminaries! Despite a few mishaps, Seishun won the District Prelims and the City Tournament, and earned a ticket to the Kanto Tournament. The team came away victorious from its first-round matches, but captain Kunimitsu injured his shoulder and went to Kyshu for treatment. Despite losing Kunimitsu and assistant captain Shuichiro to injury, Seishun pulled together as team, winning the Kanto Tournament and earning a slot in the Nationals!

With Kunimitsu recovered and back on the team, Seishun enter the Nationals with their strongest line-up and defeat Higa Junior High in the opening round to face Hyotei Academy in the semifinals. After a vicious face-off, Ryoma defeats Keigo, and Seishun win the round. Now they'll face Osaka's Shitenhoji in the semifinals! Just how good is last year's top-four team?!

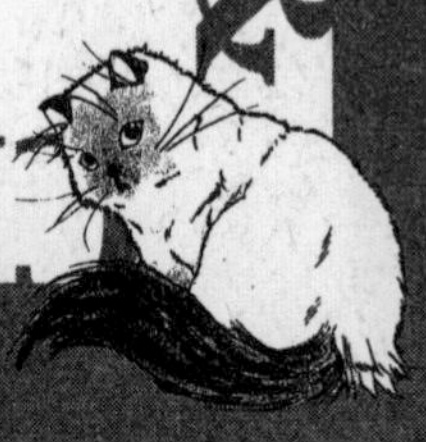

SEIGAKU T

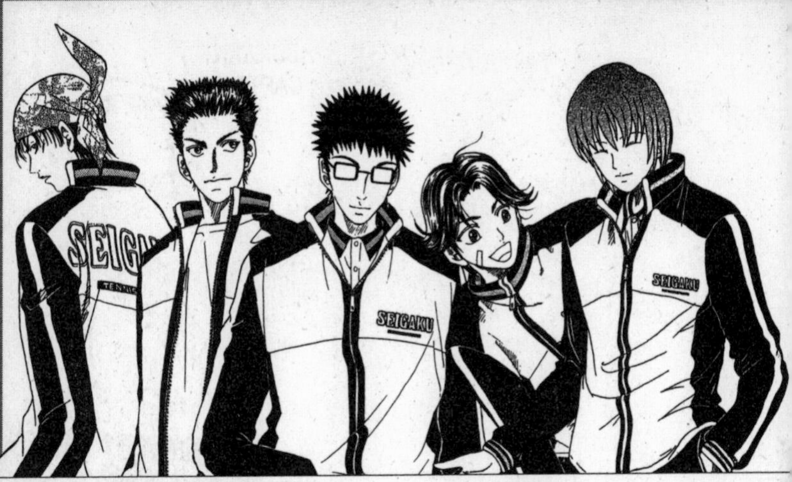

• KAORU KAIDO • TAKESHI MOMOSHIRO • SADAHARU INUI • EIJI KIKUMARU • SHUSUKE FUJI •

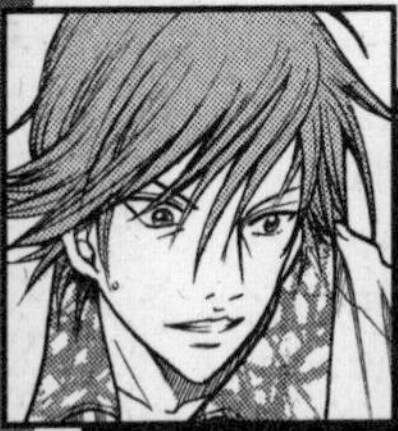

SHITENHOJI

KURANOSUKE SHIRAISHI

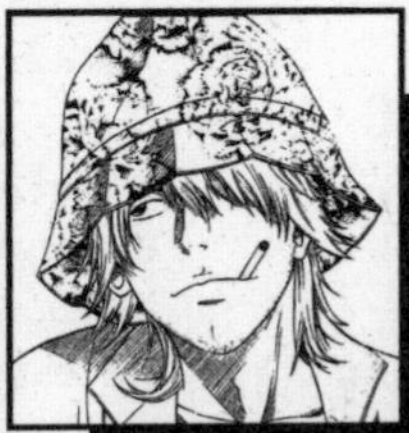

SHITENHOJI

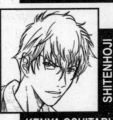

OSAMU WATANABE

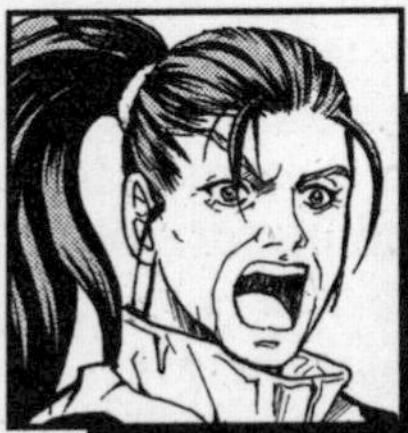

SEISHUN ACADEMY TENNIS COACH

SUMIRE RYUZAKI

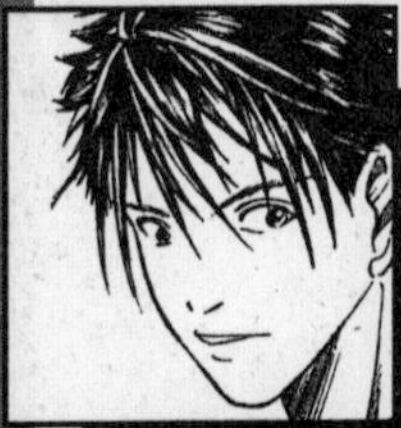

SHITENHOJI

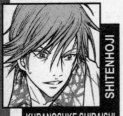

HIKARU ZAIZEN

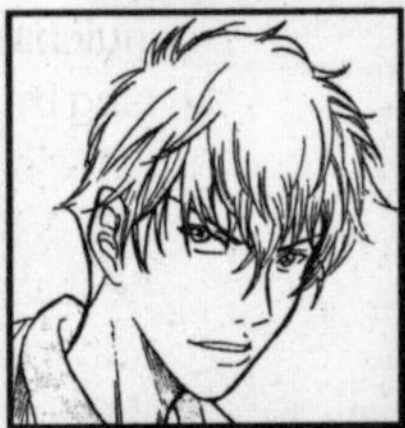

SHITENHOJI

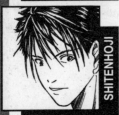

KENYA OSHITARI

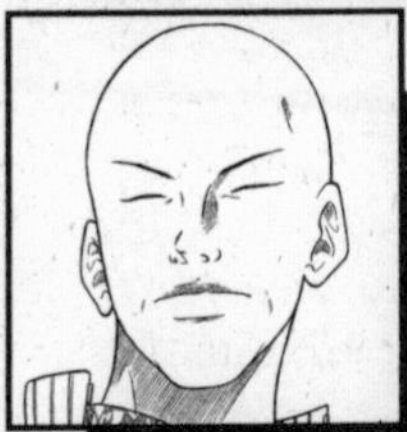

SHITENHOJI

GIN ISHIDA

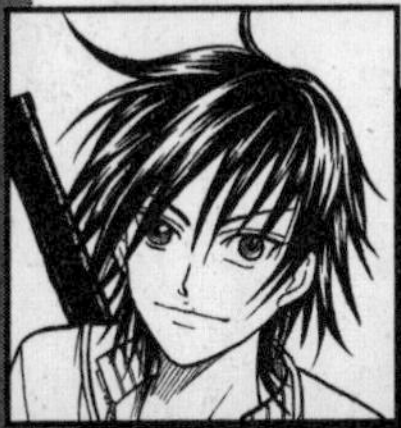

SHITENHOJI

KINTARO TOYAMA

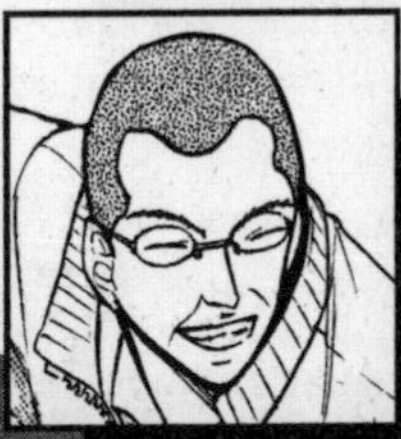

SHITENHOJI

KOHARU KONJIKI

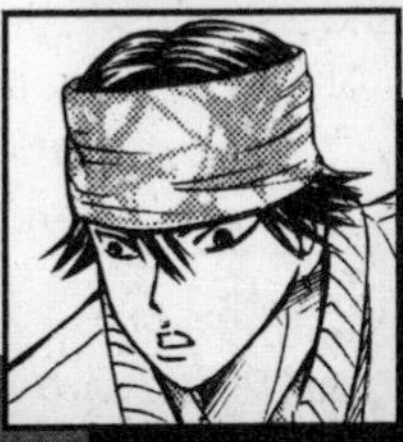

SHITENHOJI

YUJI HITOJI

CONTENTS

Vol. 36
A Heated Battle! Seishun vs. Shitenhoji

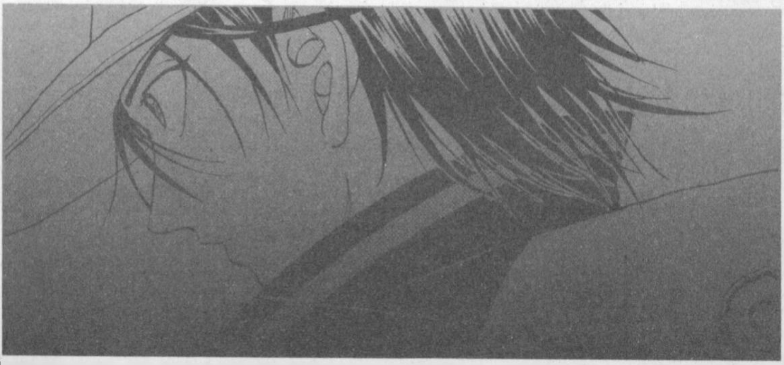

READ THIS WAY

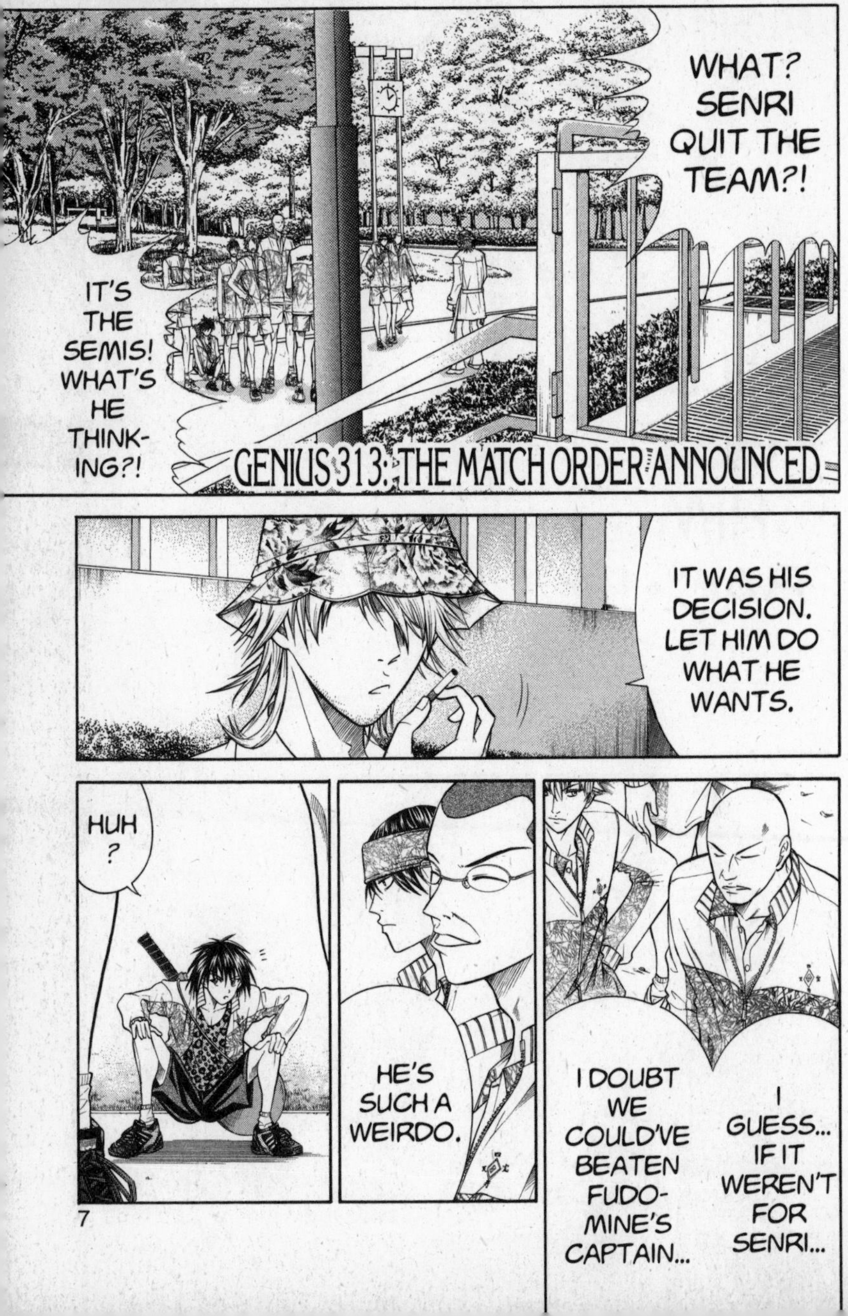
WHAT? SENRI QUIT THE TEAM?!
IT'S THE SEMIS! WHAT'S HE THINKING?!
GENIUS 313: THE MATCH ORDER ANNOUNCED
IT WAS HIS DECISION. LET HIM DO WHAT HE WANTS.
I GUESS... IF IT WEREN'T FOR SENRI...
I DOUBT WE COULD'VE BEATEN FUDOMINE'S CAPTAIN...
HE'S SUCH A WEIRDO.
HUH?

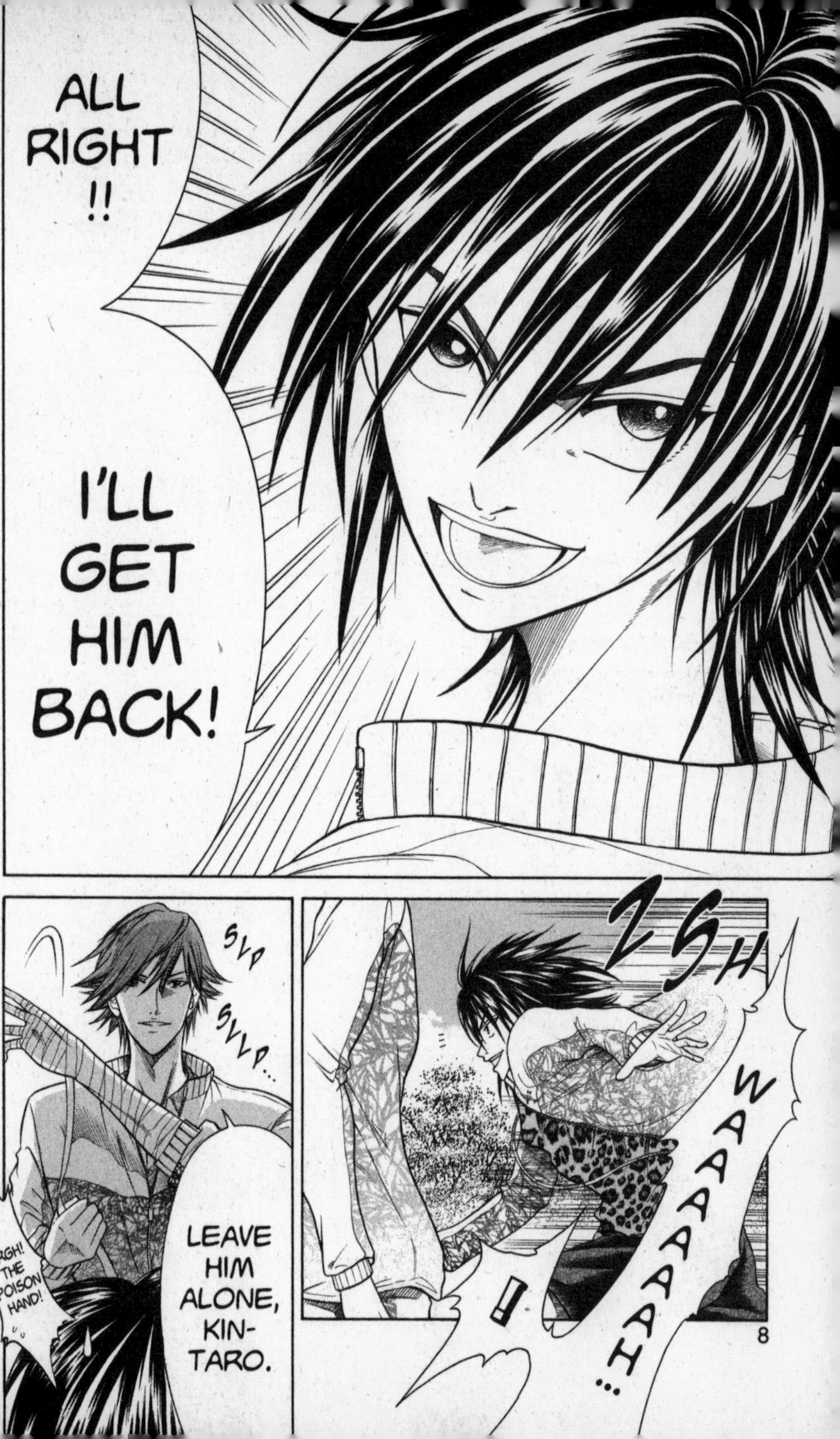
ALL RIGHT !!
I'LL GET HIM BACK!
ZSH
WAAAAAAAAAH..
!
SVP
SVVP...
LEAVE HIM ALONE, KIN-TARO.
ARGH! THE POISON HAND!

GENIUS 313: THE MATCH ORDER ANNOUNCED

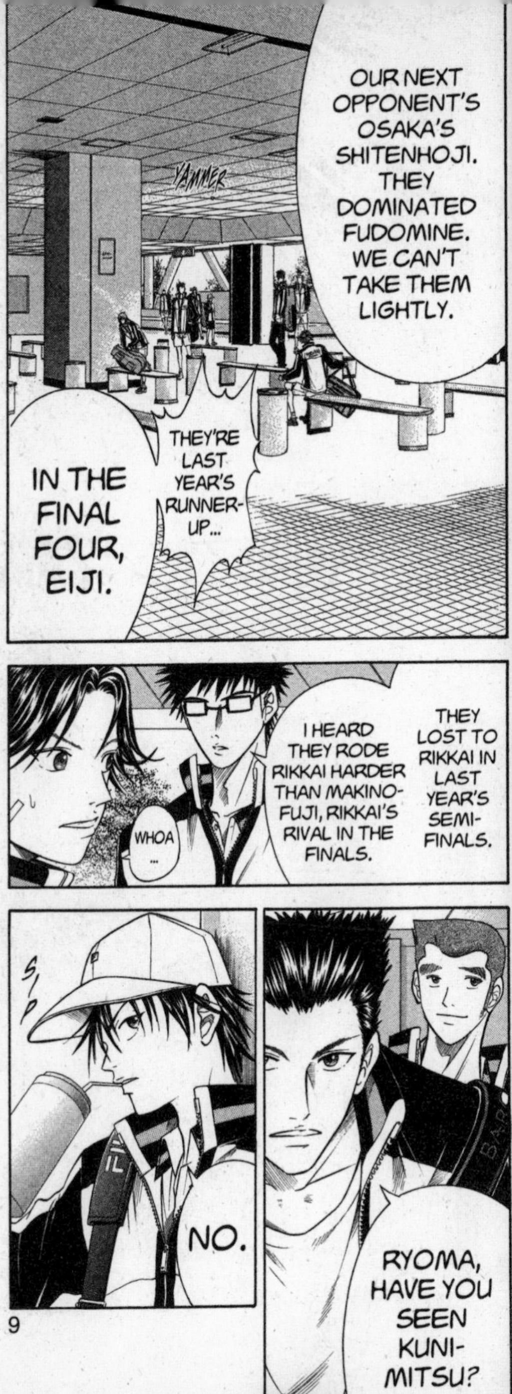
OUR NEXT OPPONENT'S OSAKA'S SHITENHOJI. THEY DOMINATED FUDOMINE. WE CAN'T TAKE THEM LIGHTLY.
YAMMER
THEY'RE LAST YEAR'S RUNNER-UP...
IN THE FINAL FOUR, EIJI.
THEY LOST TO RIKKAI IN LAST YEAR'S SEMI-FINALS.
I HEARD THEY RODE RIKKAI HARDER THAN MAKINO-FUJI, RIKKAI'S RIVAL IN THE FINALS.
WHOA ...
RYOMA, HAVE YOU SEEN KUNI-MITSU?
SIP
NO.

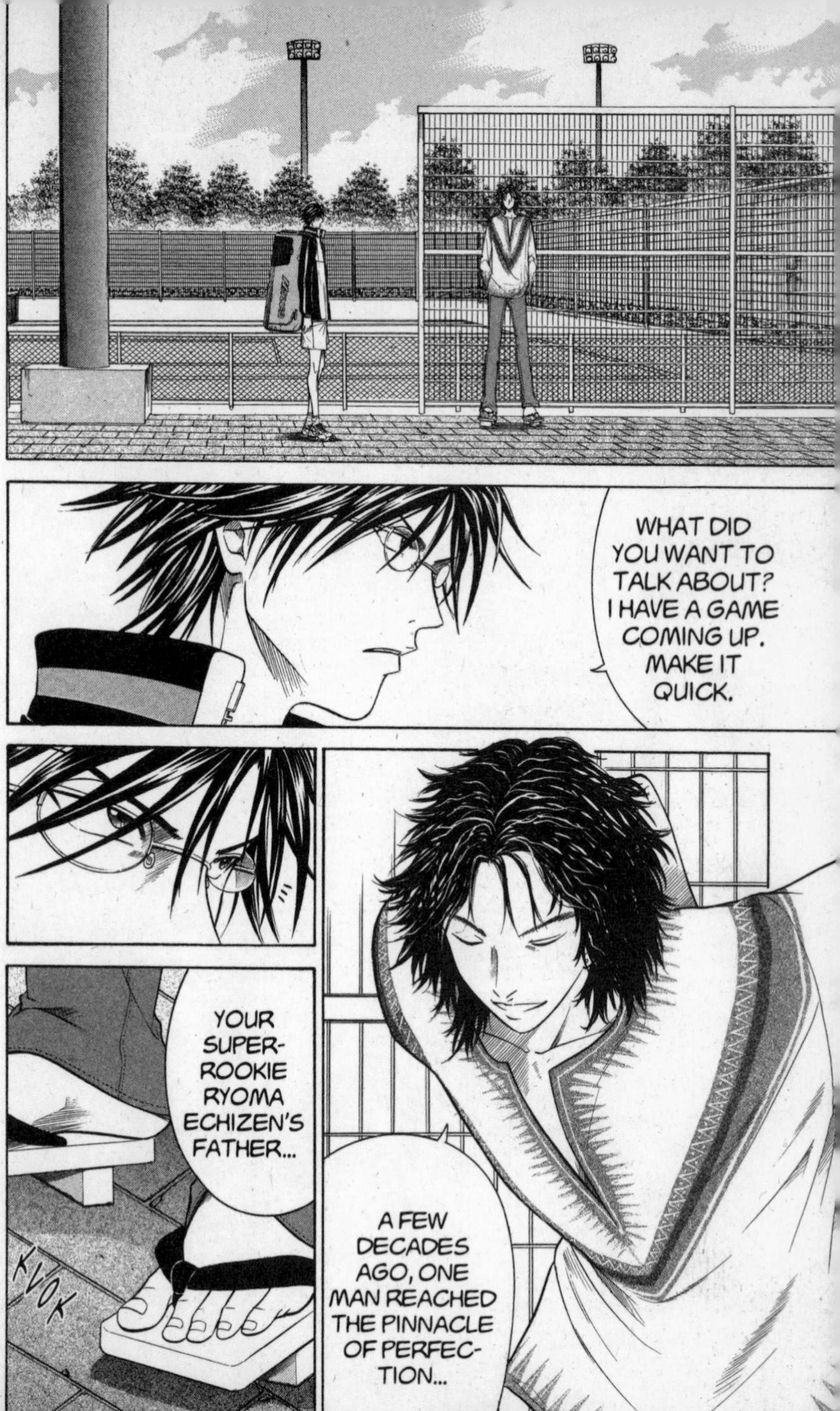
WHAT DID YOU WANT TO TALK ABOUT? I HAVE A GAME COMING UP. MAKE IT QUICK.
A FEW DECADES AGO, ONE MAN REACHED THE PINNACLE OF PERFEC-TION...
YOUR SUPER-ROOKIE RYOMA ECHIZEN'S FATHER...
KVOK

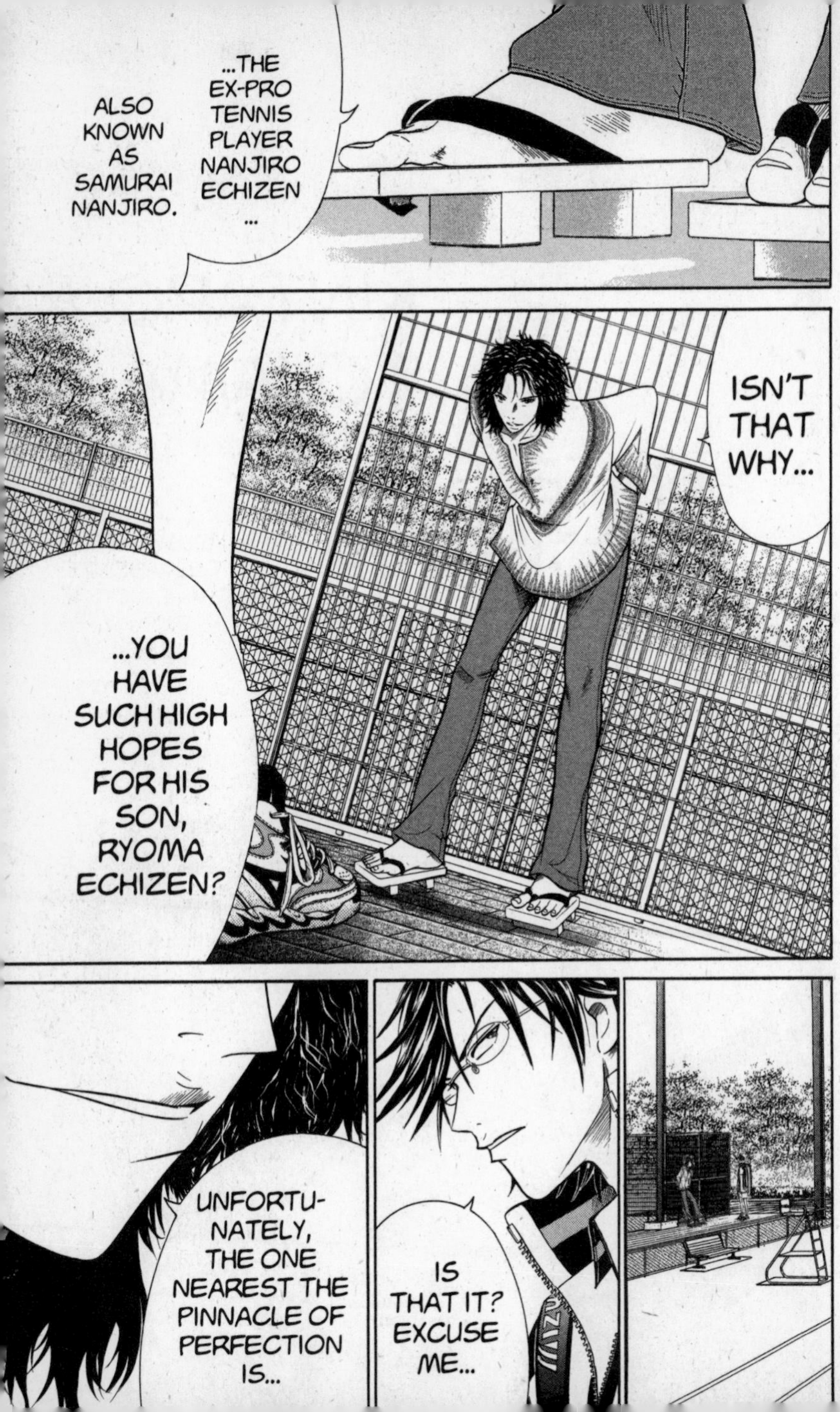
...THE EX-PRO TENNIS PLAYER NANJIRO ECHIZEN ...
ALSO KNOWN AS SAMURAI NANJIRO.
ISN'T THAT WHY...
...YOU HAVE SUCH HIGH HOPES FOR HIS SON, RYOMA ECHIZEN?
IS THAT IT? EXCUSE ME...
UNFORTUNATELY, THE ONE NEAREST THE PINNACLE OF PERFECTION IS...

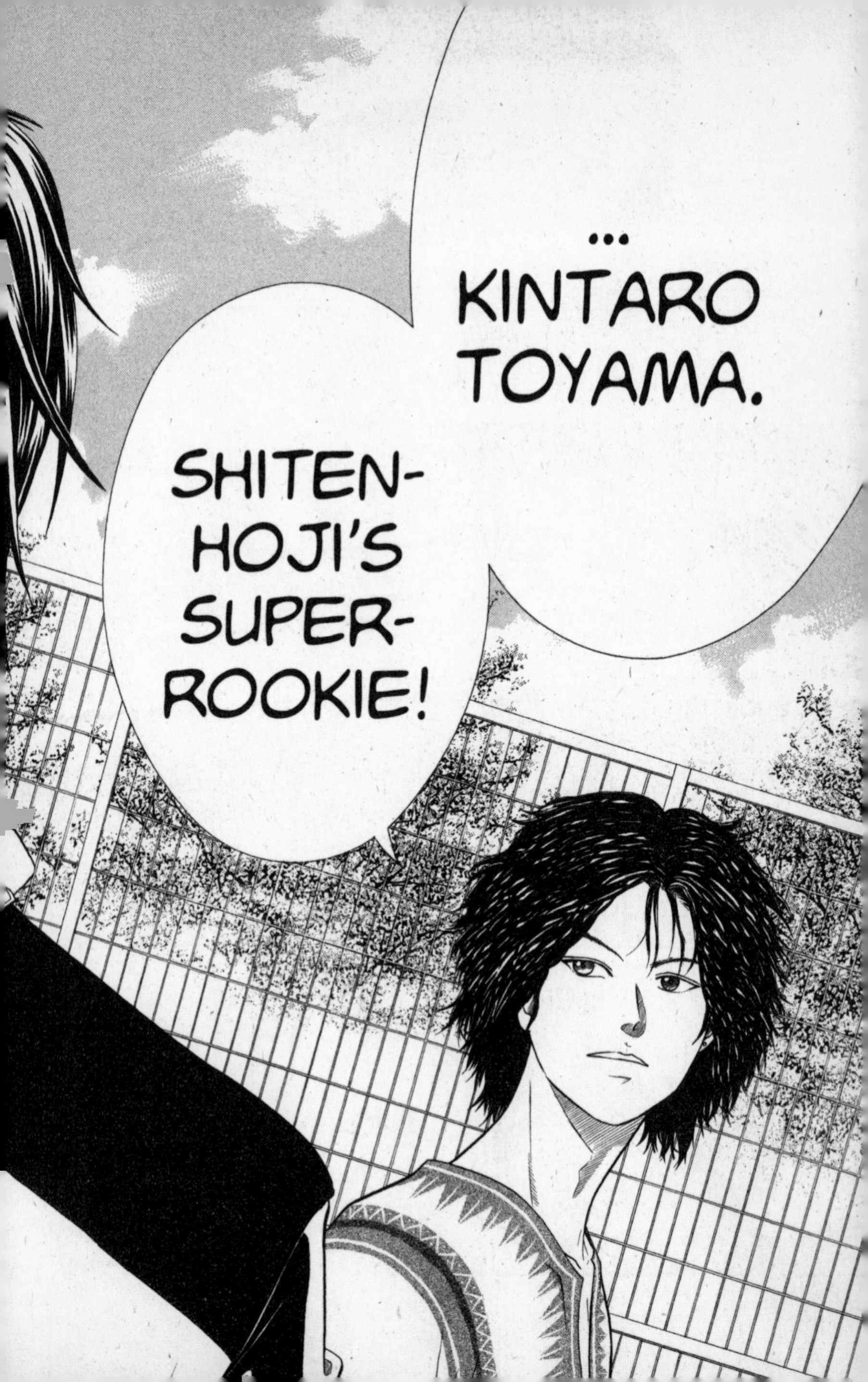
... KINTARO TOYAMA.
SHITEN-HOJI'S SUPER-ROOKIE!

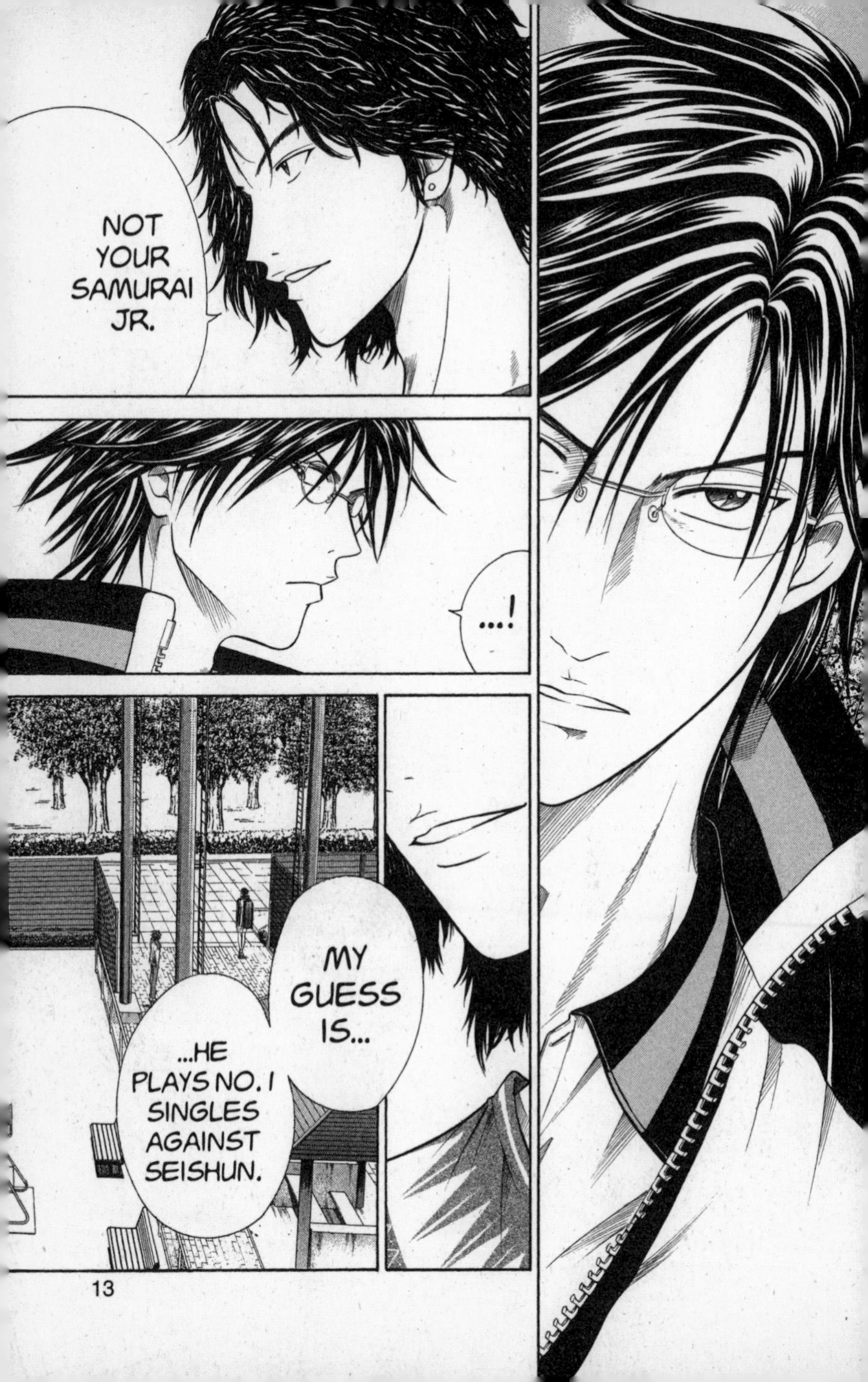
NOT YOUR SAMURAI JR.
...!
MY GUESS IS...
...HE PLAYS NO. 1 SINGLES AGAINST SEISHUN.

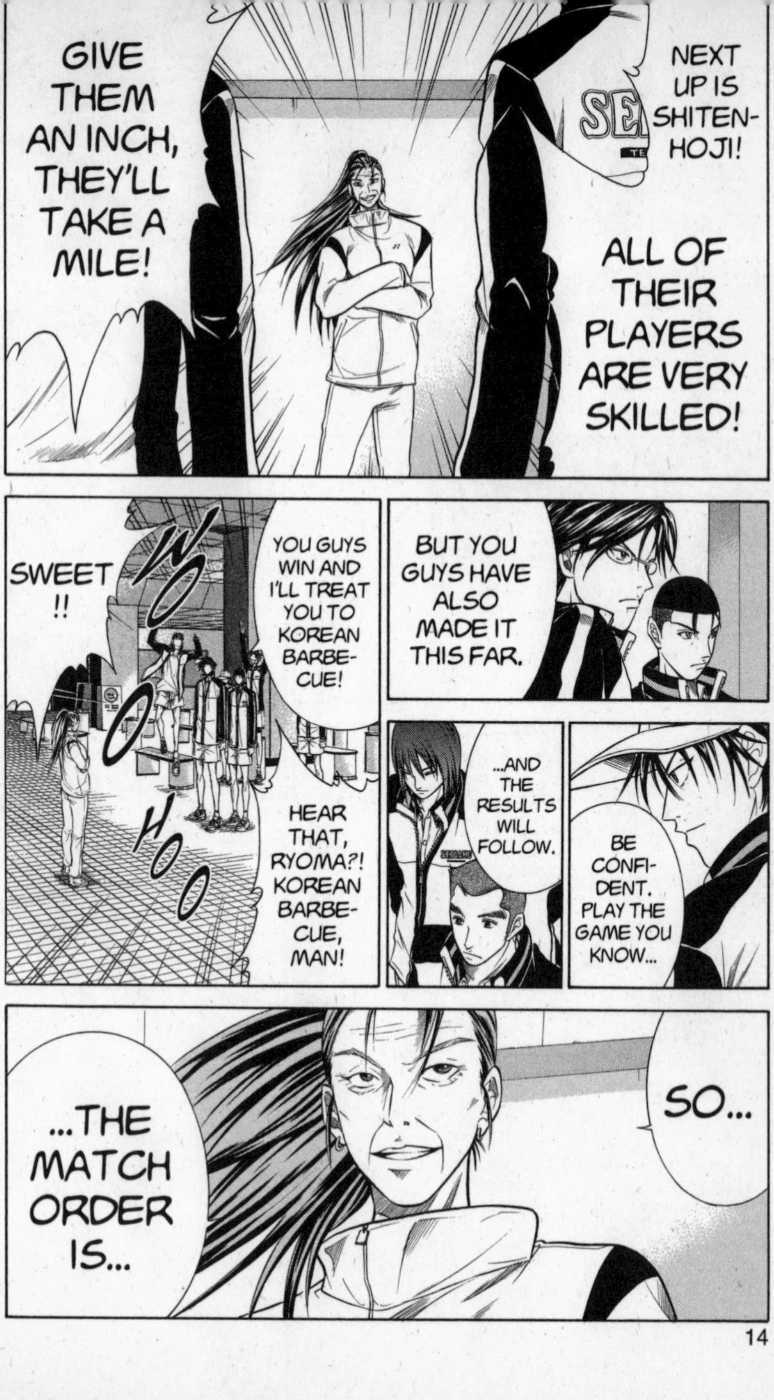
NEXT UP IS SHITEN-HOJI!
ALL OF THEIR PLAYERS ARE VERY SKILLED!
GIVE THEM AN INCH, THEY'LL TAKE A MILE!
BUT YOU GUYS HAVE ALSO MADE IT THIS FAR.
BE CONFIDENT. PLAY THE GAME YOU KNOW...
...AND THE RESULTS WILL FOLLOW.
YOU GUYS WIN AND I'LL TREAT YOU TO KOREAN BARBECUE!
WOOOHOOO
SWEET !!
HEAR THAT, RYOMA?! KOREAN BARBECUE, MAN!
SO...
...THE MATCH ORDER IS...

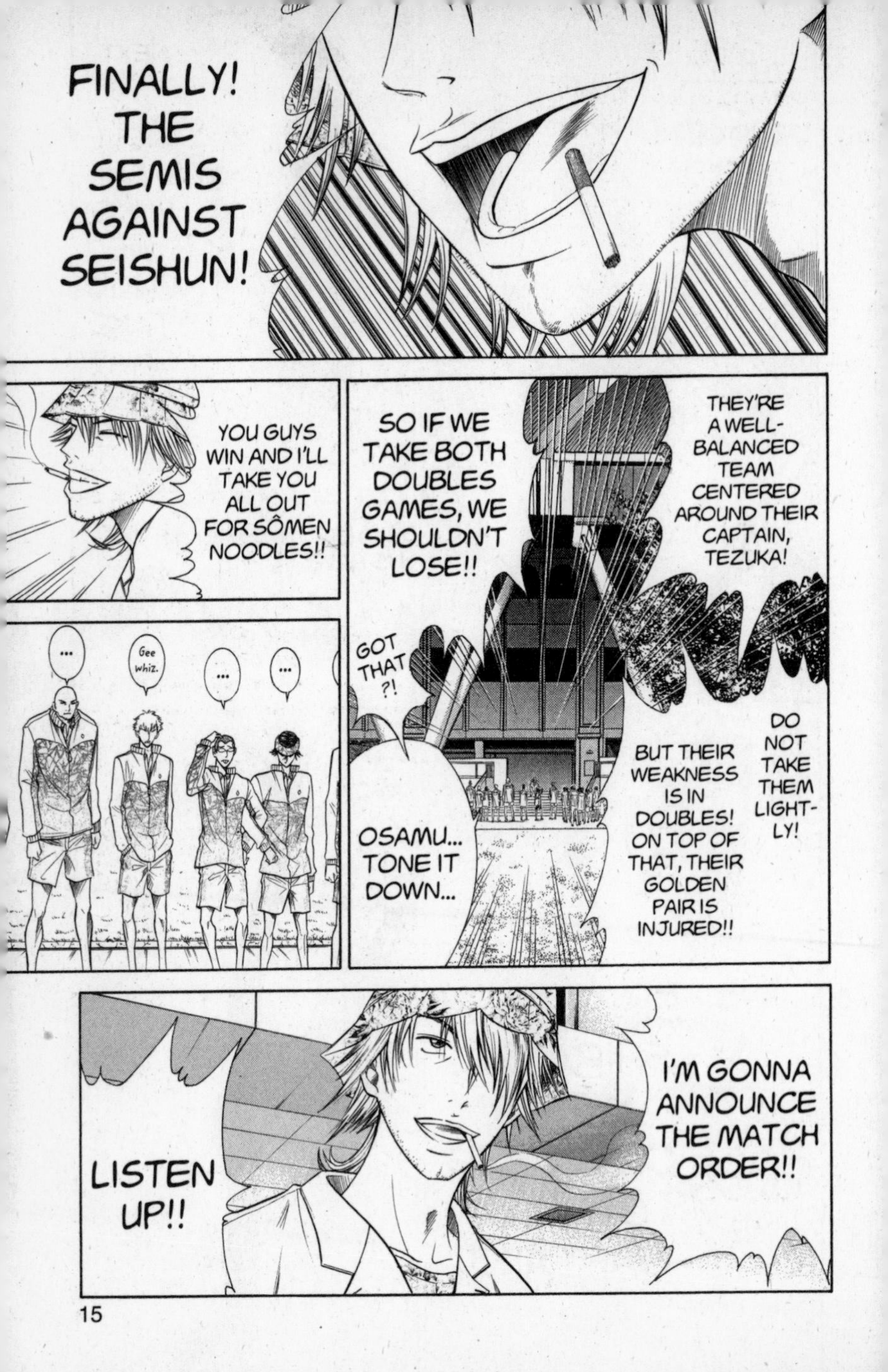
FINALLY! THE SEMIS AGAINST SEISHUN!
THEY'RE A WELL-BALANCED TEAM CENTERED AROUND THEIR CAPTAIN, TEZUKA!
DO NOT TAKE THEM LIGHTLY!
BUT THEIR WEAKNESS IS IN DOUBLES! ON TOP OF THAT, THEIR GOLDEN PAIR IS INJURED!!
SO IF WE TAKE BOTH DOUBLES GAMES, WE SHOULDN'T LOSE!!
GOT THAT?!
OSAMU... TONE IT DOWN...
YOU GUYS WIN AND I'LL TAKE YOU ALL OUT FOR SÔMEN NOODLES!!
...
...
Gee whiz.
...
I'M GONNA ANNOUNCE THE MATCH ORDER!!
LISTEN UP!!

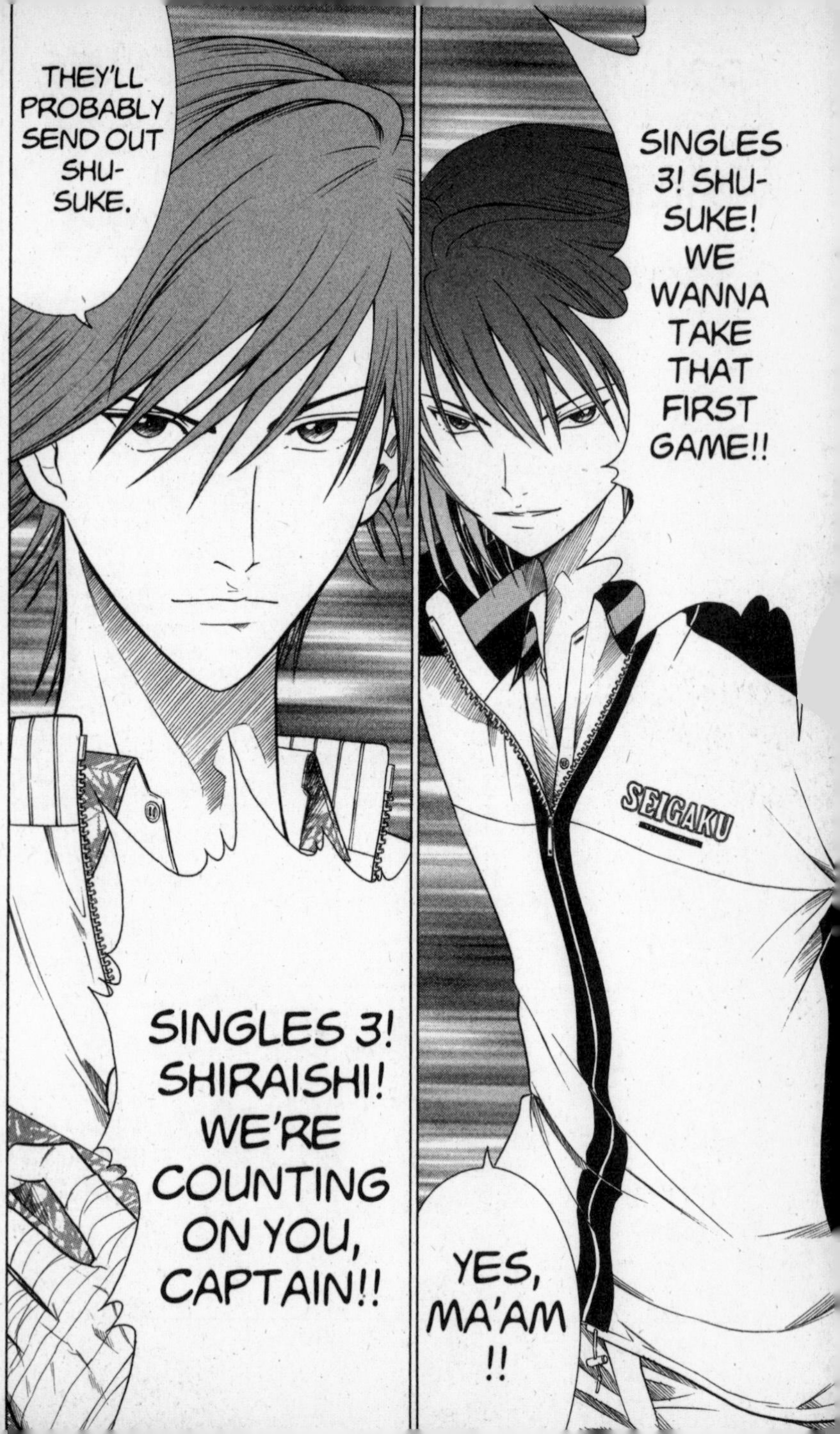
SINGLES 3! SHU-SUKE! WE WANNA TAKE THAT FIRST GAME!!
YES, MA'AM!!
THEY'LL PROBABLY SEND OUT SHU-SUKE.
SINGLES 3! SHIRAISHI! WE'RE COUNTING ON YOU, CAPTAIN!!

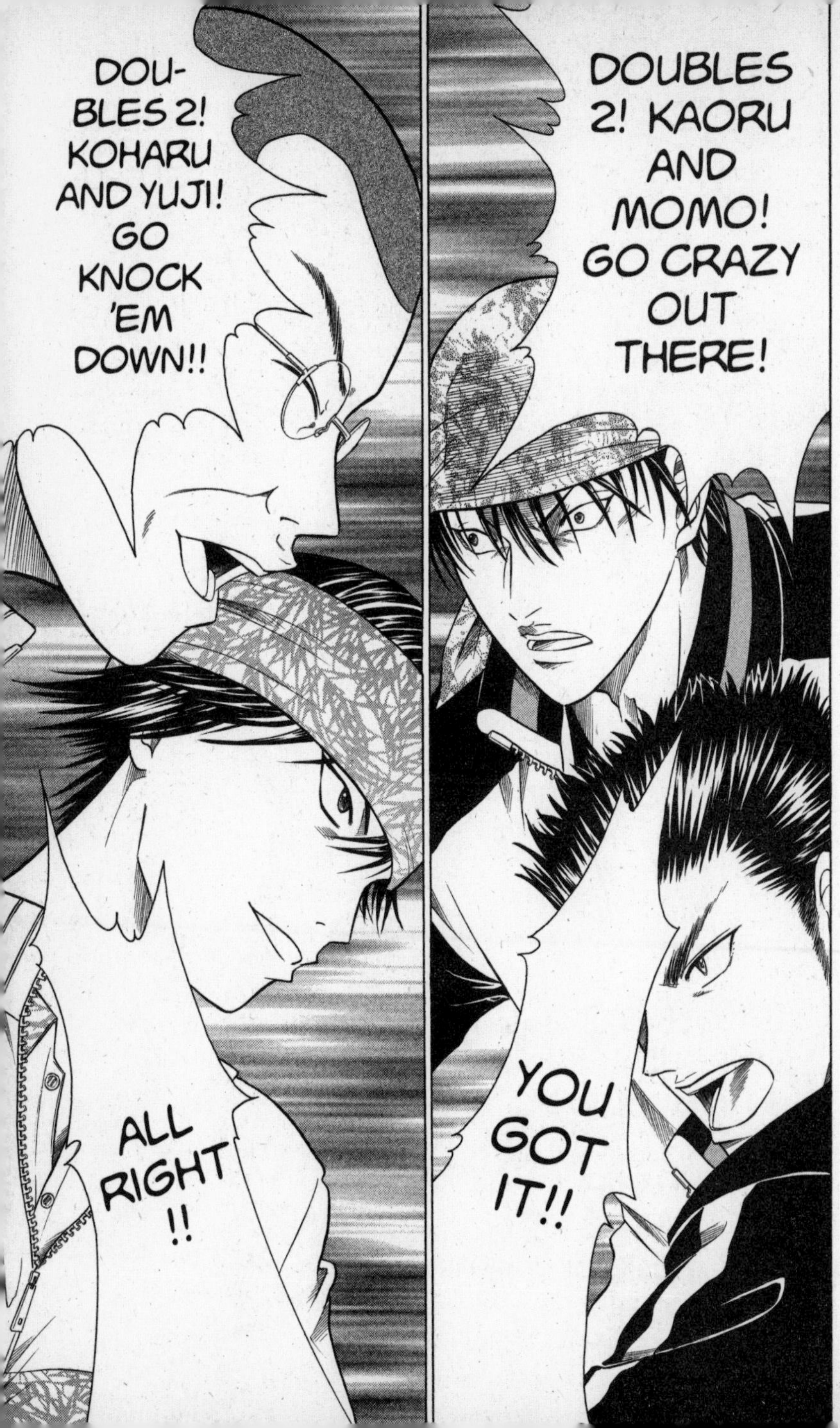
DOUBLES 2! KAORU AND MOMO! GO CRAZY OUT THERE!
YOU GOT IT!!
DOU-BLES 2! KOHARU AND YUJI! GO KNOCK 'EM DOWN!!
ALL RIGHT!!

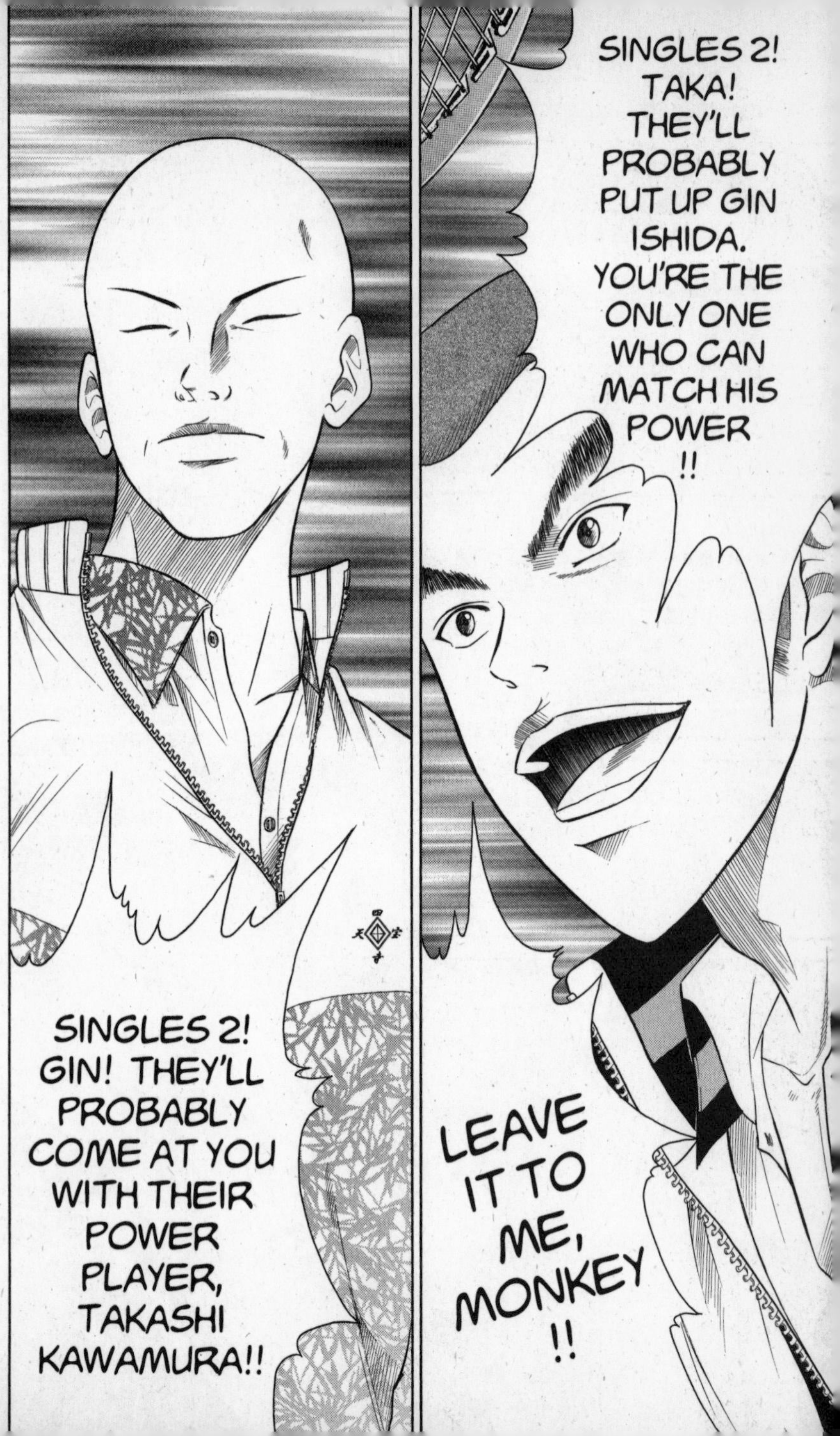
SINGLES 2! TAKA! THEY'LL PROBABLY PUT UP GIN ISHIDA. YOU'RE THE ONLY ONE WHO CAN MATCH HIS POWER!!
LEAVE IT TO ME, MONKEY!!
SINGLES 2! GIN! THEY'LL PROBABLY COME AT YOU WITH THEIR POWER PLAYER, TAKASHI KAWAMURA!!

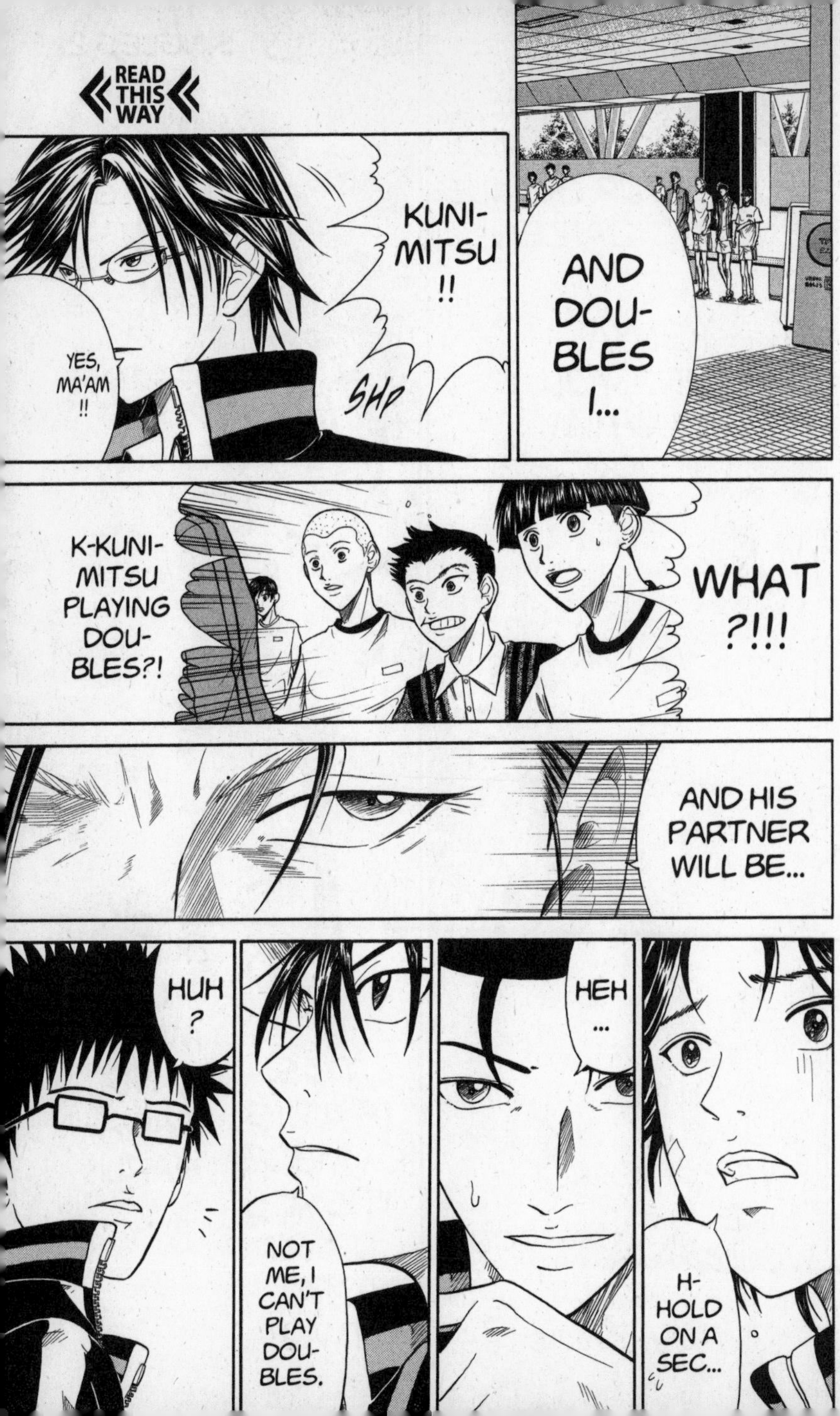
READ THIS WAY
AND DOUBLES I...
KUNIMITSU!!
SHP
YES, MA'AM!!
WHAT?!!!
K-KUNIMITSU PLAYING DOUBLES?!
AND HIS PARTNER WILL BE...
H-HOLD ON A SEC...
HEH...
NOT ME, I CAN'T PLAY DOUBLES.
HUH?

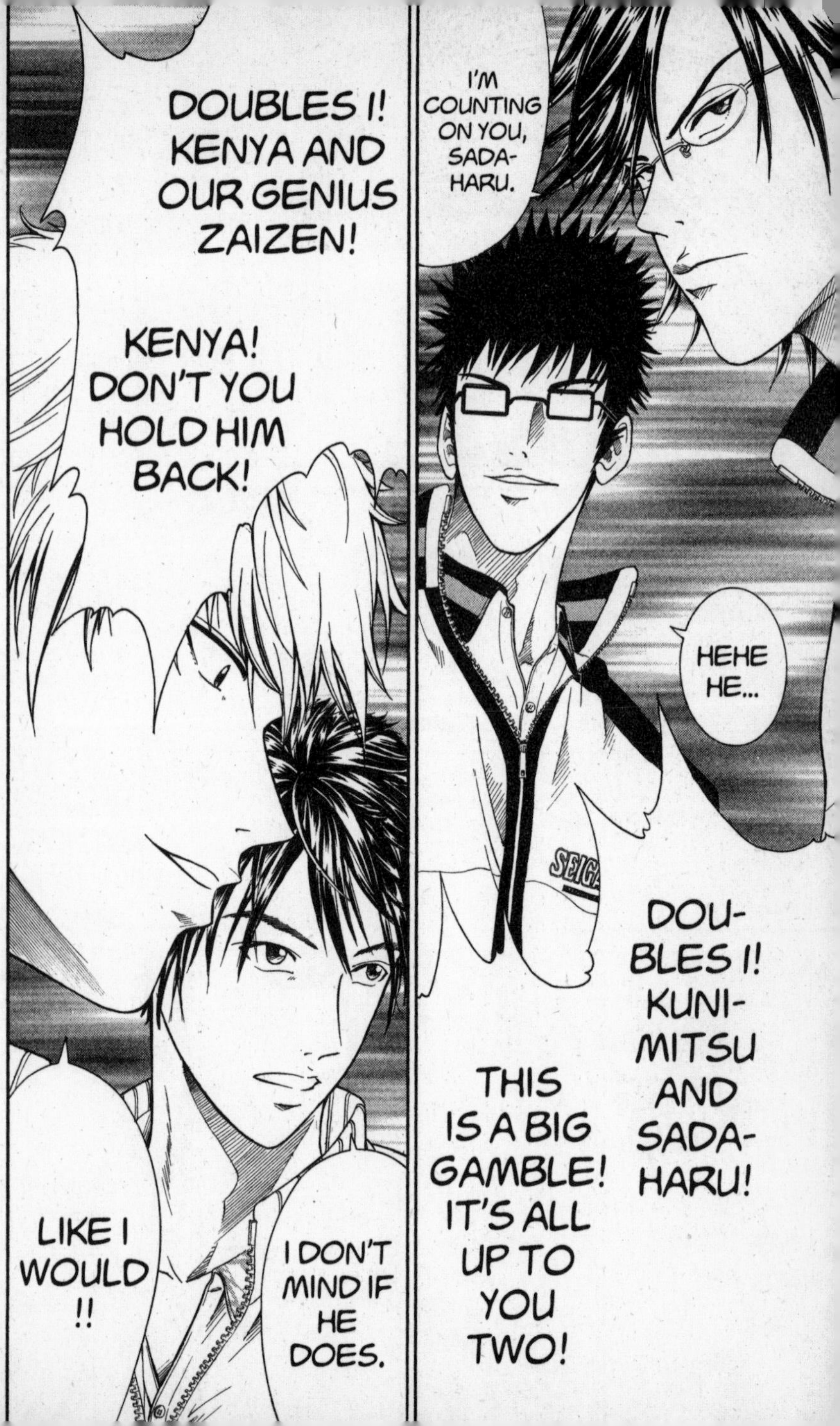
I'M COUNTING ON YOU, SADA-HARU.
HEHE HE...
DOU-BLES 1! KUNI-MITSU AND SADA-HARU!
THIS IS A BIG GAMBLE! IT'S ALL UP TO YOU TWO!
DOUBLES 1! KENYA AND OUR GENIUS ZAIZEN!
KENYA! DON'T YOU HOLD HIM BACK!
I DON'T MIND IF HE DOES.
LIKE I WOULD !!

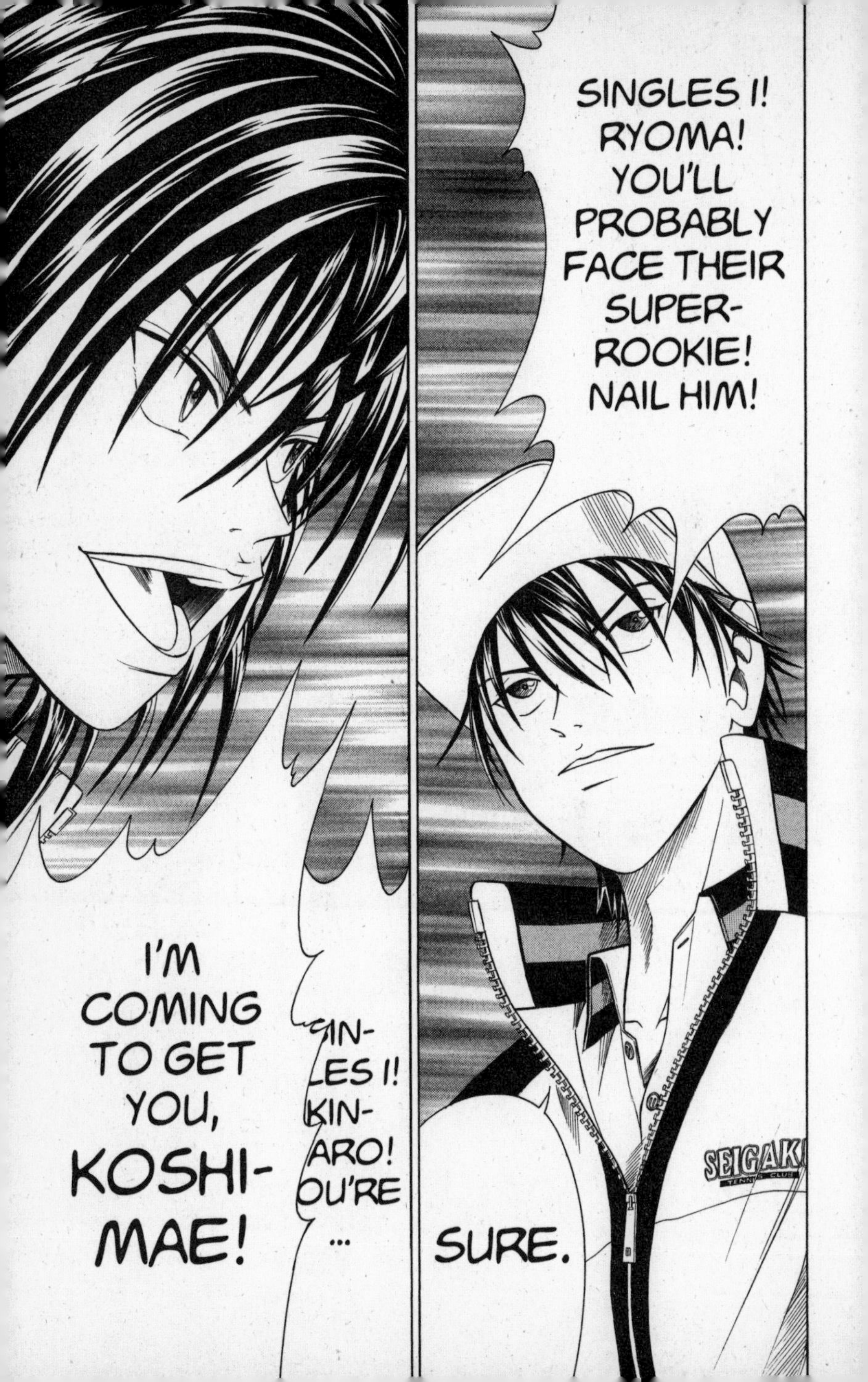
SINGLES 1! RYOMA! YOU'LL PROBABLY FACE THEIR SUPER-ROOKIE! NAIL HIM!
SURE.
SIN- LES 1! KIN- ARO! OU'RE ...
I'M COMING TO GET YOU, KOSHI-MAE!

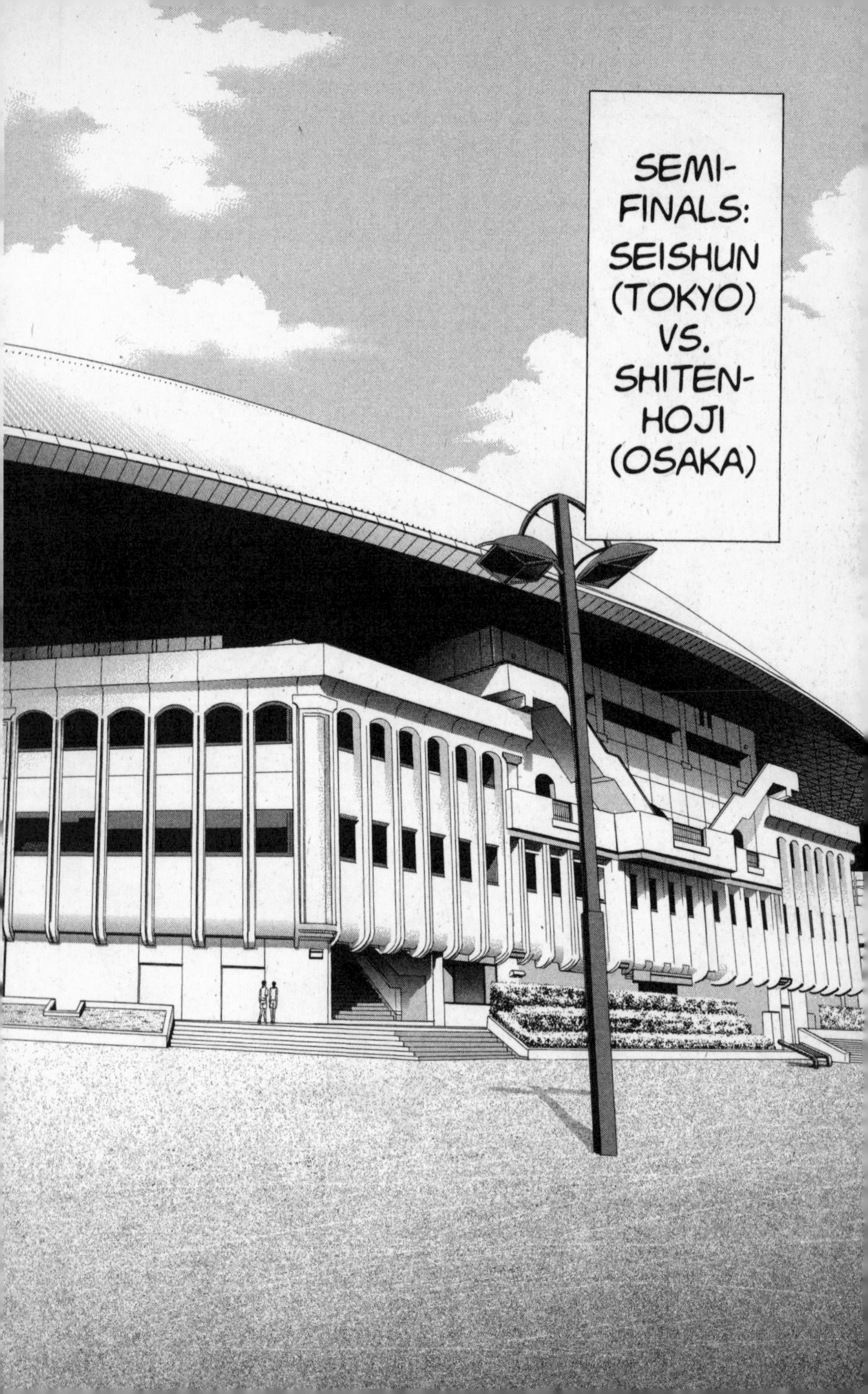
SEMI-FINALS: SEISHUN (TOKYO) VS. SHITEN-HOJI (OSAKA)

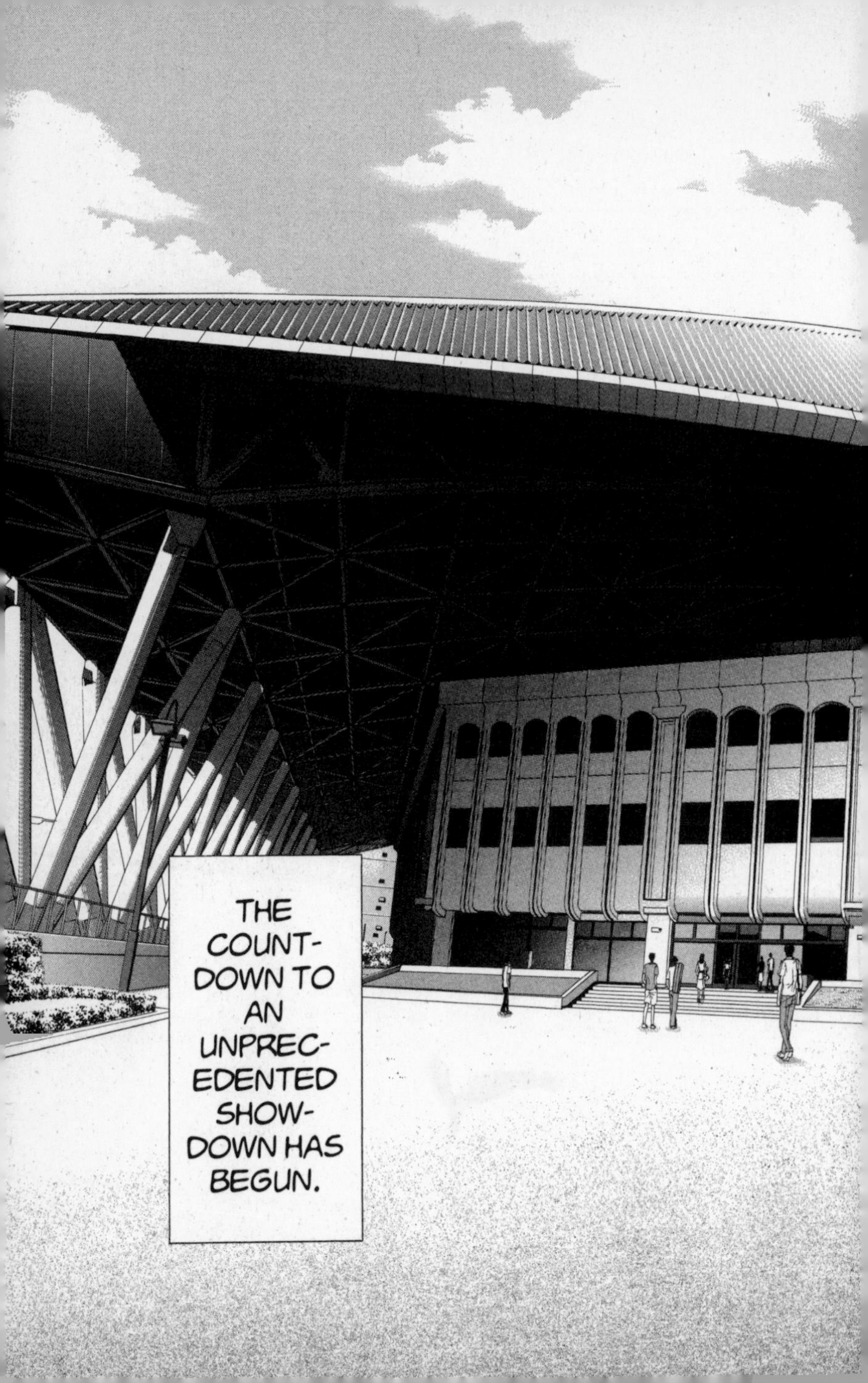
THE COUNT-DOWN TO AN UNPREC-EDENTED SHOW-DOWN HAS BEGUN.

Thank you for reading *Prince of Tennis* volume 36.

Thanks for waiting. The first comic in four months! I'm pretty sure we'll be publishing them on schedule again, so not to worry. \(ᵔ◡ᵔ)/

In March 2007, the OVA (original video animation) of the Nationals story arc will temporarily conclude with the Ryoma/Keigo match. But! There's another big project in the works (just between you and me). Anyway, I plan on working harder than ever, so please keep up the support.

I have a deadline coming up, so that's all for now! I'll see you in the next volume.

KONOMI
2006. 12. 1

Send fan letters to: Takeshi Konomi, *The Prince of Tennis*, c/o VIZ Media LLC, P.O. Box 77010, San Francisco, CA 94107

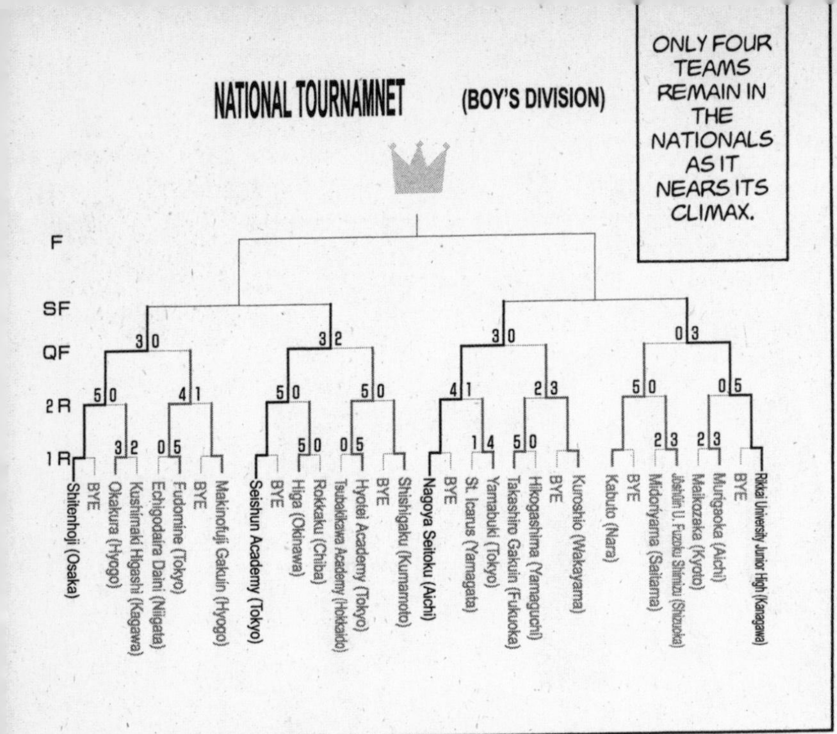
ONLY FOUR TEAMS REMAIN IN THE NATIONALS AS IT NEARS ITS CLIMAX.
NATIONAL TOURNAMNET
(BOY'S DIVISION)
F
SF
QF
2R
1R
Shitenhoji (Osaka)
BYE
Okakura (Hyogo)
Kushimaki Higashi (Kagawa)
Echigodaira Daini (Niigata)
Fudomine (Tokyo)
BYE
Makinofuji Gakuin (Hyogo)
Seishun Academy (Tokyo)
BYE
Higa (Okinawa)
Rokkaku (Chiba)
Tsubakikawa Academy (Hokkaido)
Hyotei Academy (Tokyo)
BYE
Shishigaku (Kumamoto)
Nagoya Seitoku (Aichi)
BYE
St. Icarus (Yamagata)
Yamabuki (Tokyo)
Takashiro Gakuin (Fukuoka)
Hikogashima (Yamaguchi)
BYE
Kuroshio (Wakayama)
Kabuto (Nara)
BYE
Midoriyama (Saitama)
U. Fuzoku Shimizu (Shizuoka)
Maikozaka (Kyoto)
Murigaoka (Aichi)
BYE
Rikkai University Junior High (Kanagawa)

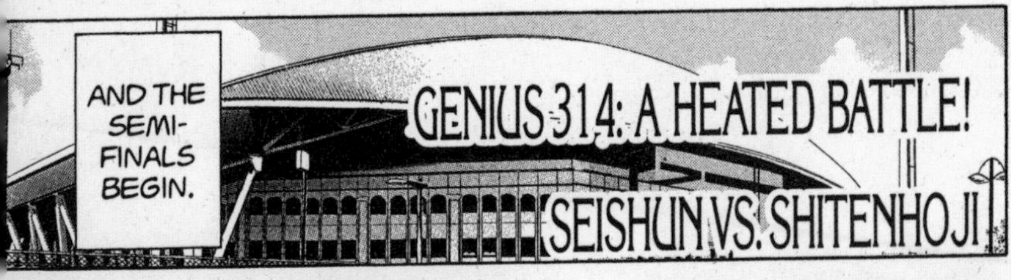
GENIUS 314: A HEATED BATTLE!
SEISHUN VS. SHITENHOJI
AND THE SEMI-FINALS BEGIN.

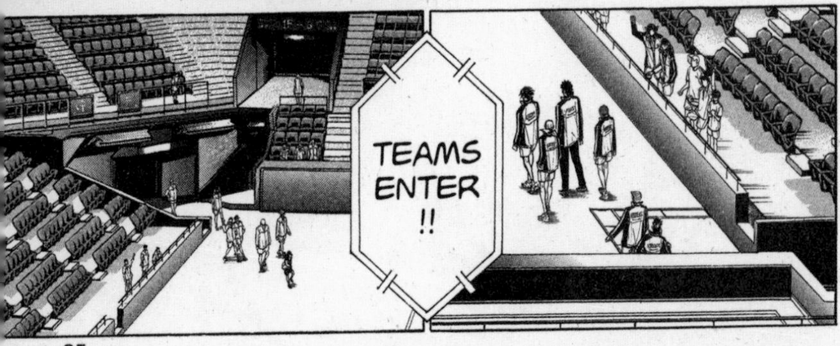
TEAMS ENTER!!

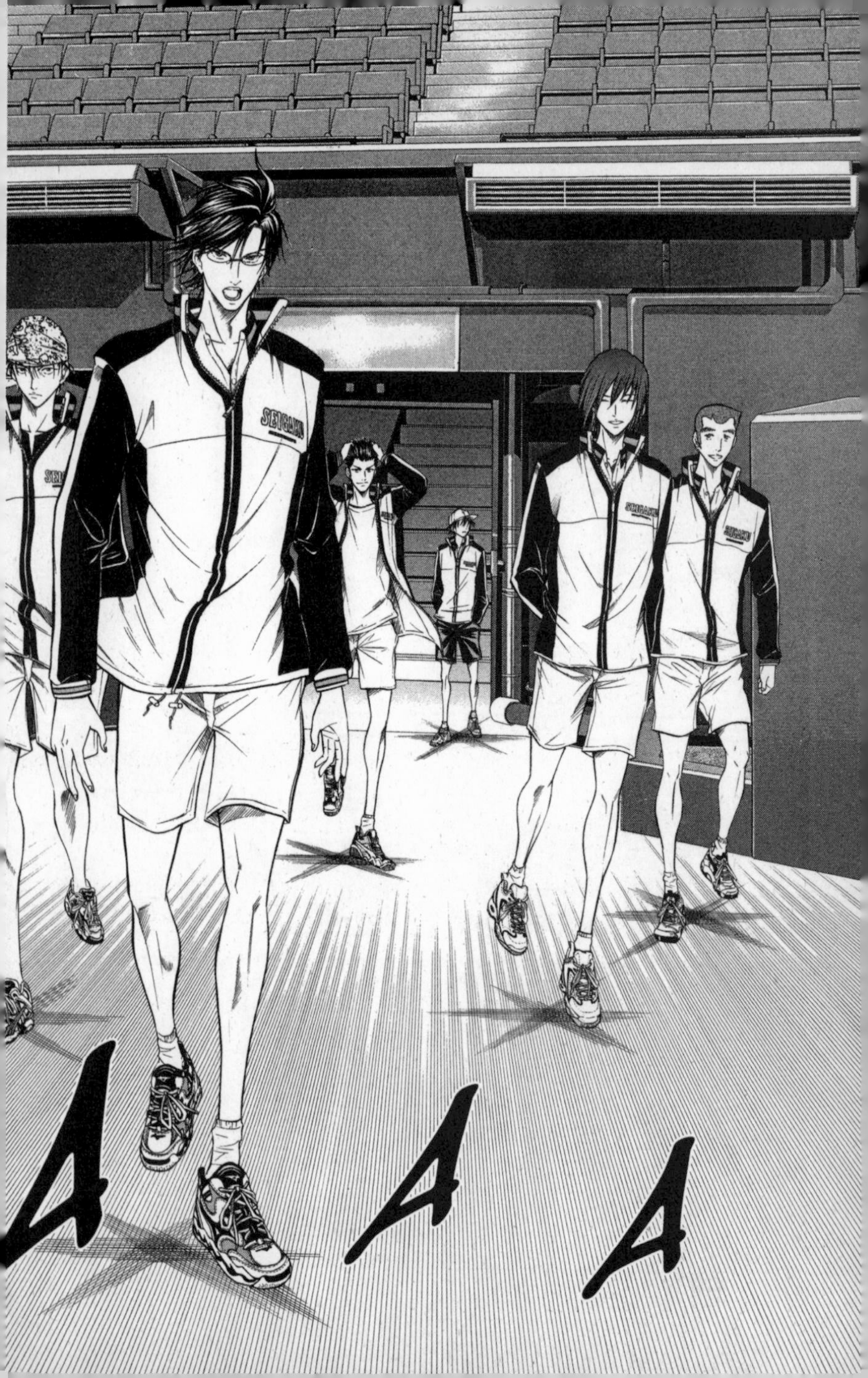
SEIGAKU

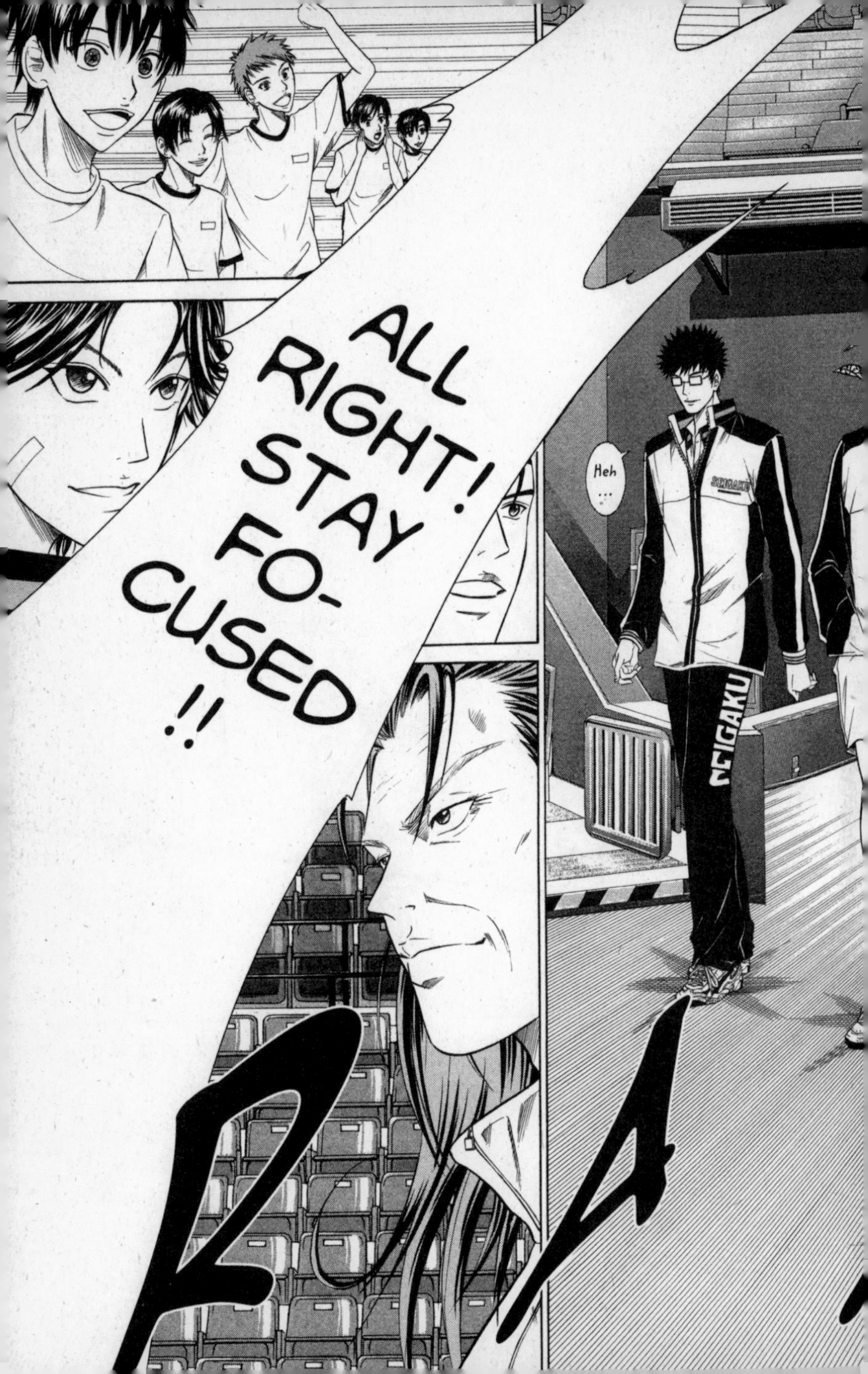
Heh...
ALL RIGHT! STAY FO-CUSED!!

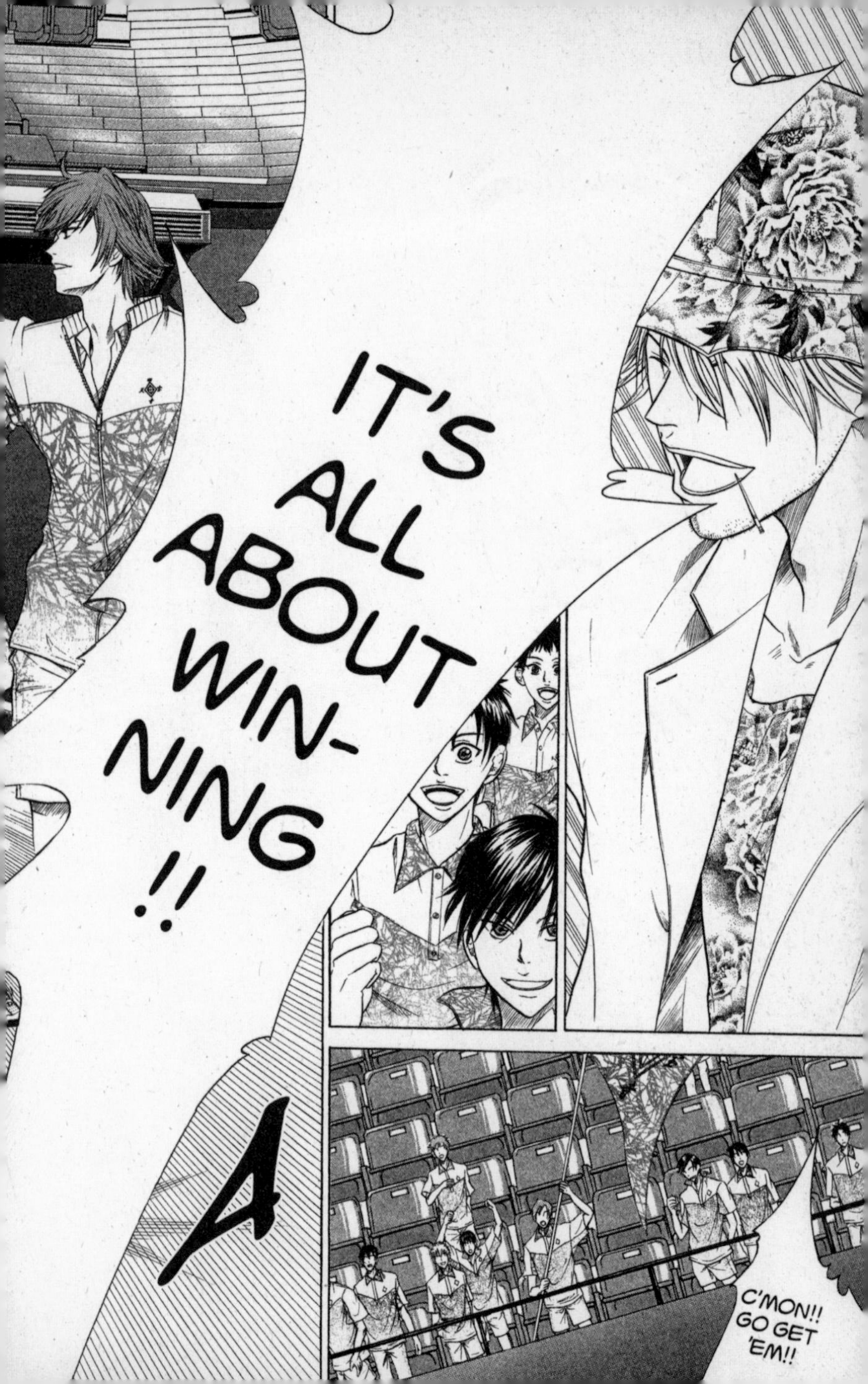
IT'S ALL ABOUT WIN-NING!!
C'MON!! GO GET 'EM!!

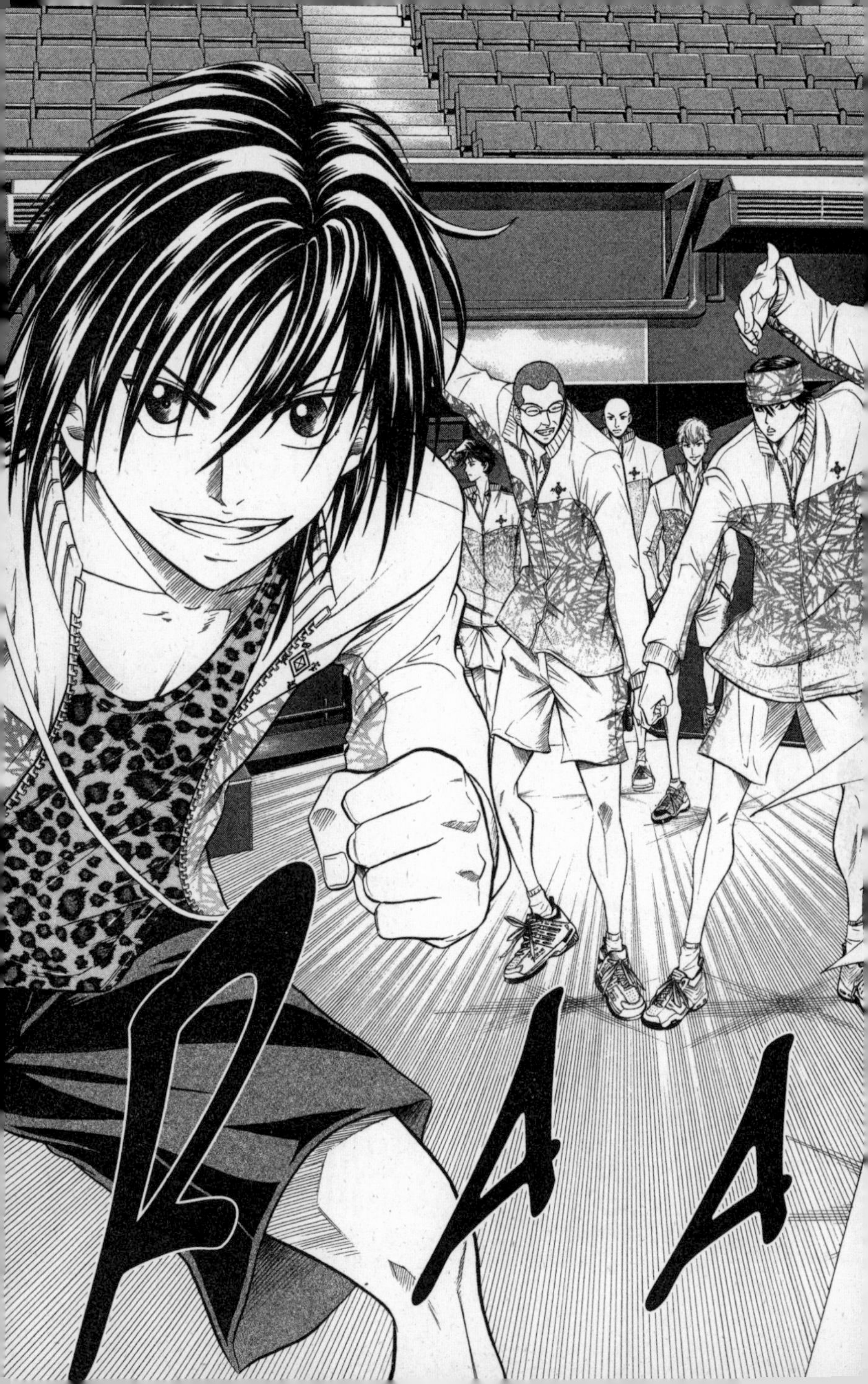

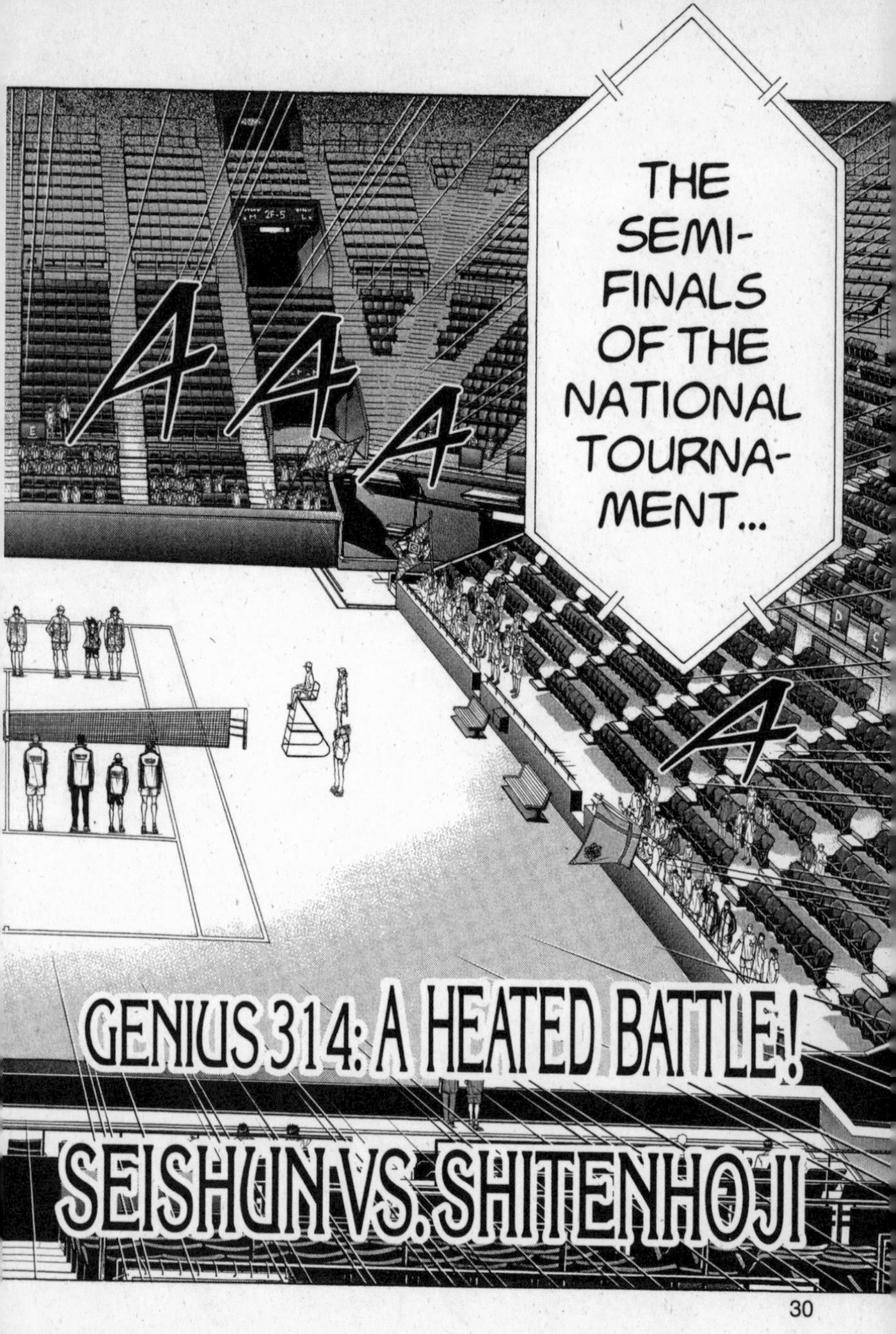
THE SEMI-FINALS OF THE NATIONAL TOURNA-MENT...
AAA
A
GENIUS 314: A HEATED BATTLE!
SEISHUN VS. SHITENHOJI

READ THIS WAY

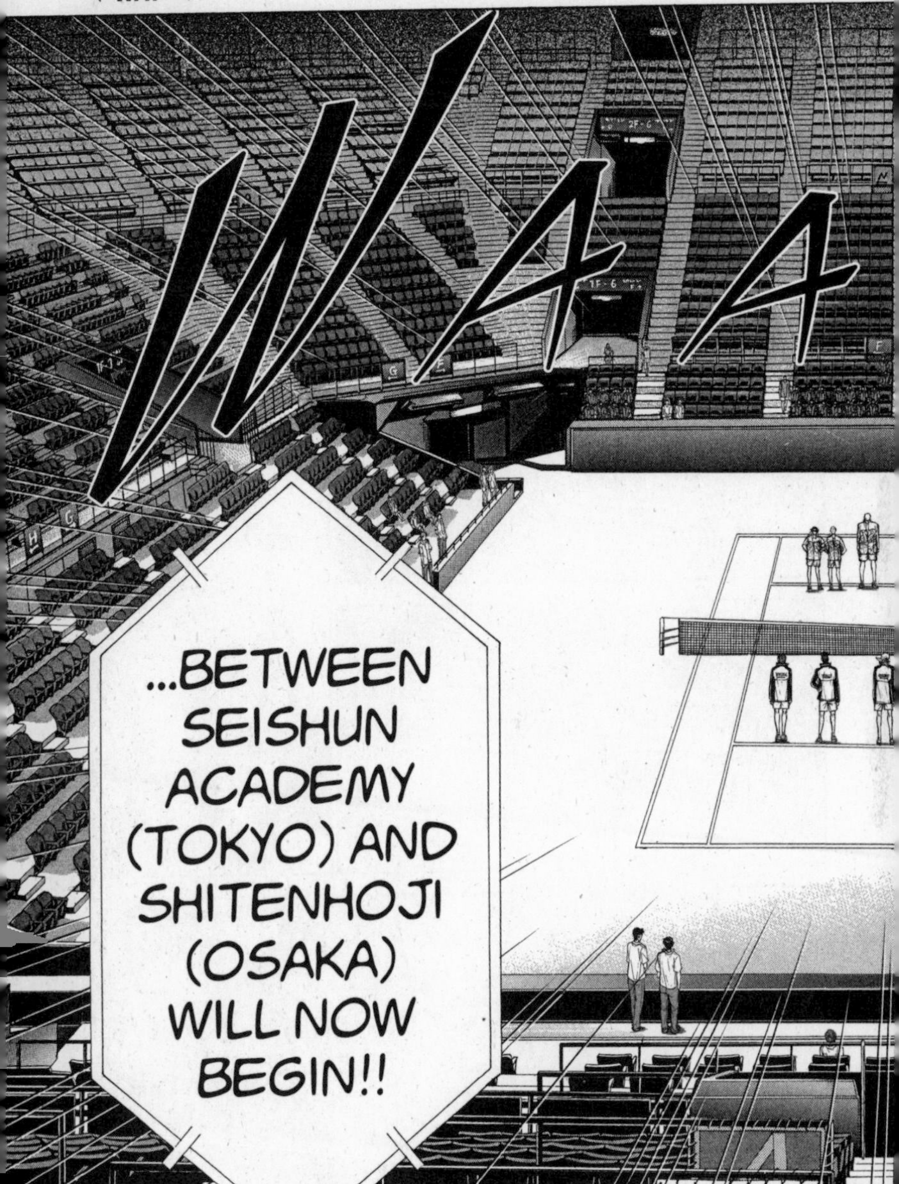
WAA
...BETWEEN SEISHUN ACADEMY (TOKYO) AND SHITENHOJI (OSAKA) WILL NOW BEGIN!!

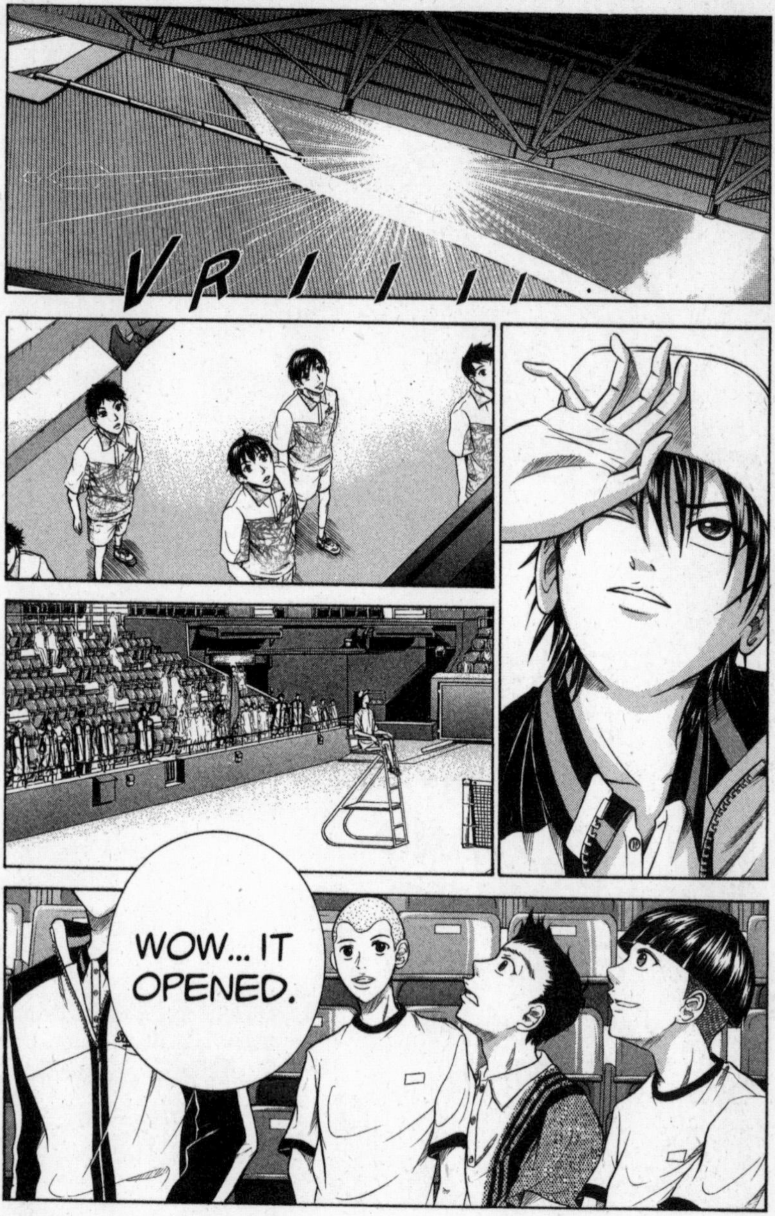
VRIIIII...
WOW... IT OPENED.

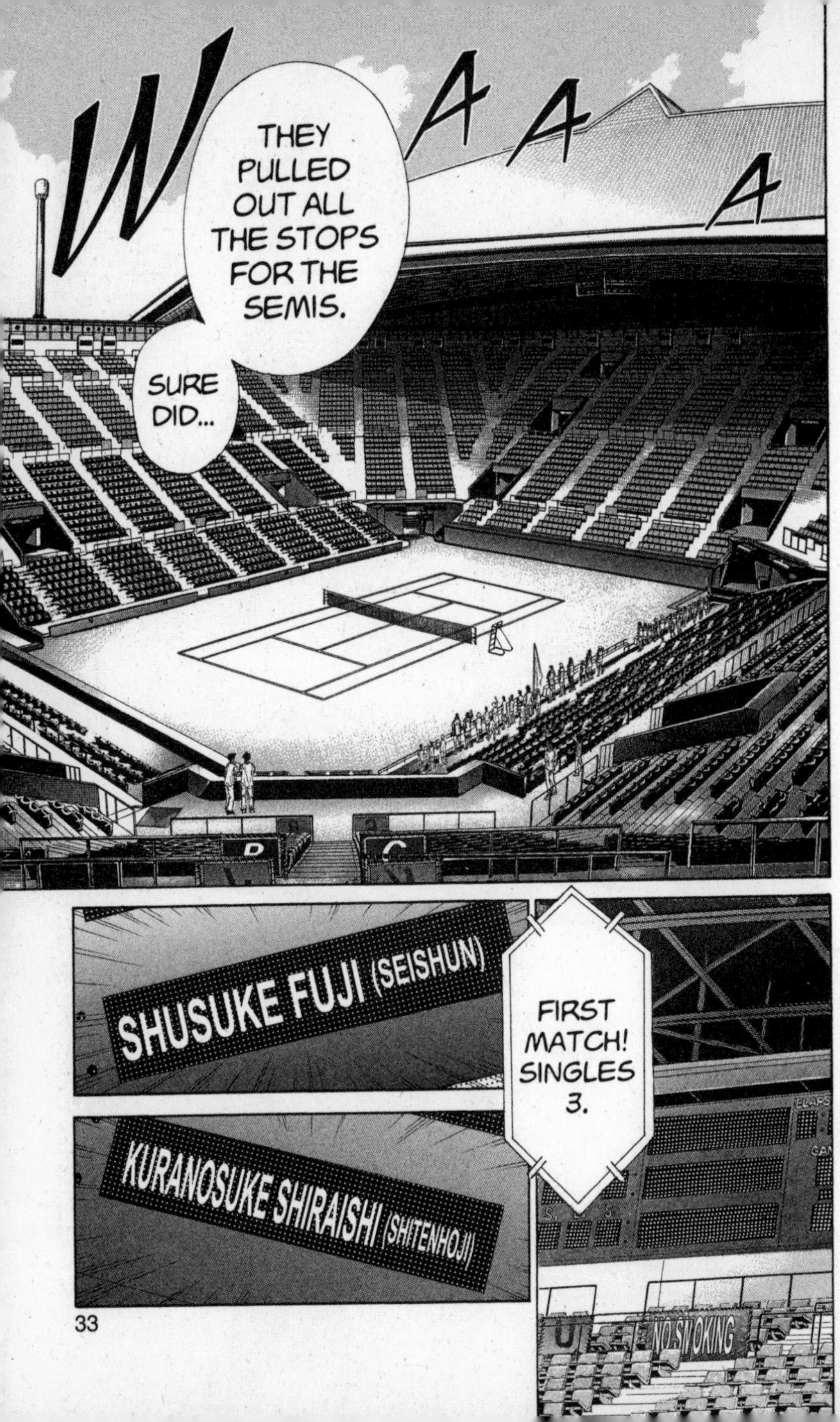
WAAAA
THEY PULLED OUT ALL THE STOPS FOR THE SEMIS.
SURE DID...
D
C
FIRST MATCH! SINGLES 3.
NO SMOKING
SHUSUKE FUJI (SEISHUN)
KURANOSUKE SHIRAISHI (SHITENHOJI)

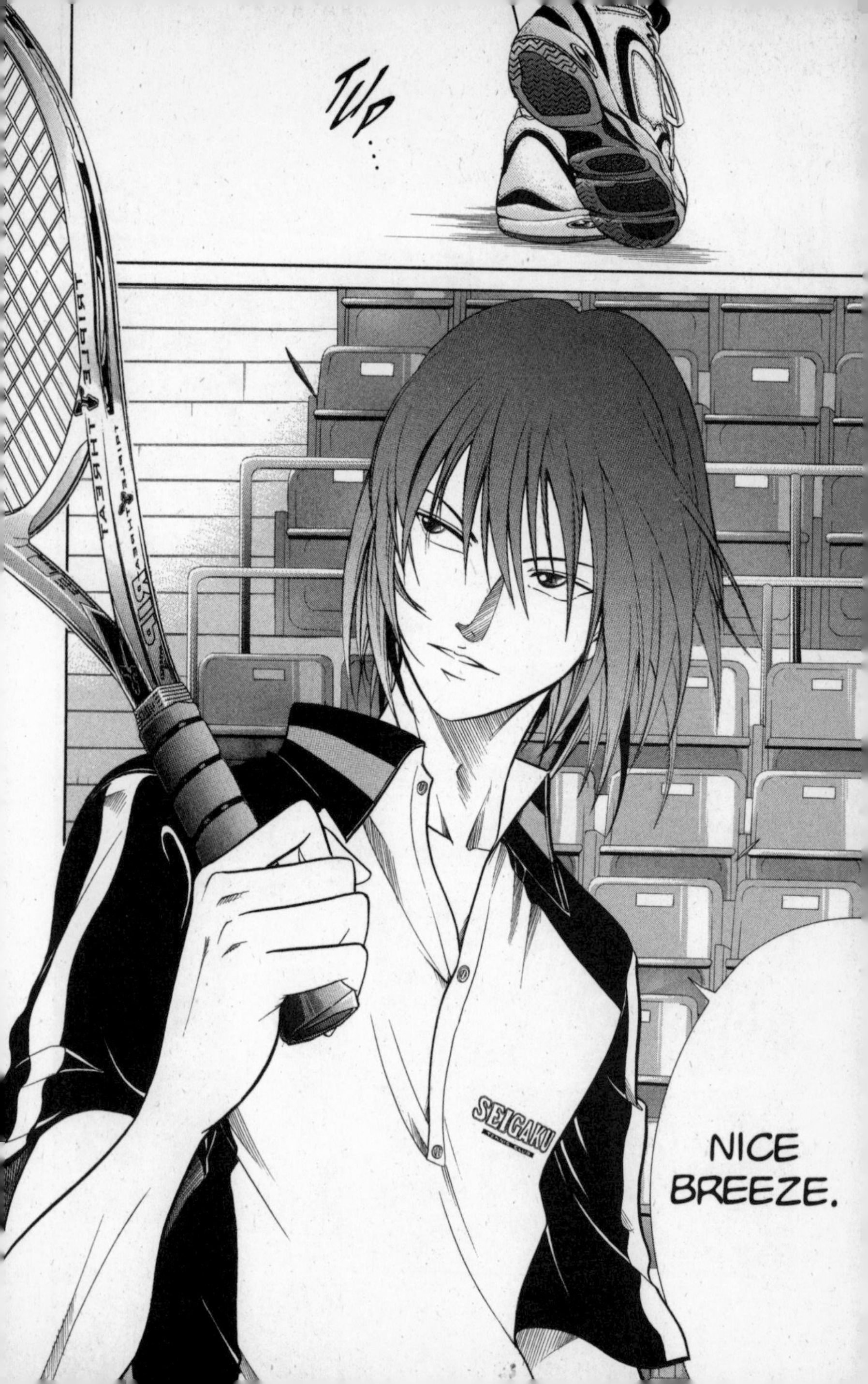
TUD...
NICE BREEZE.

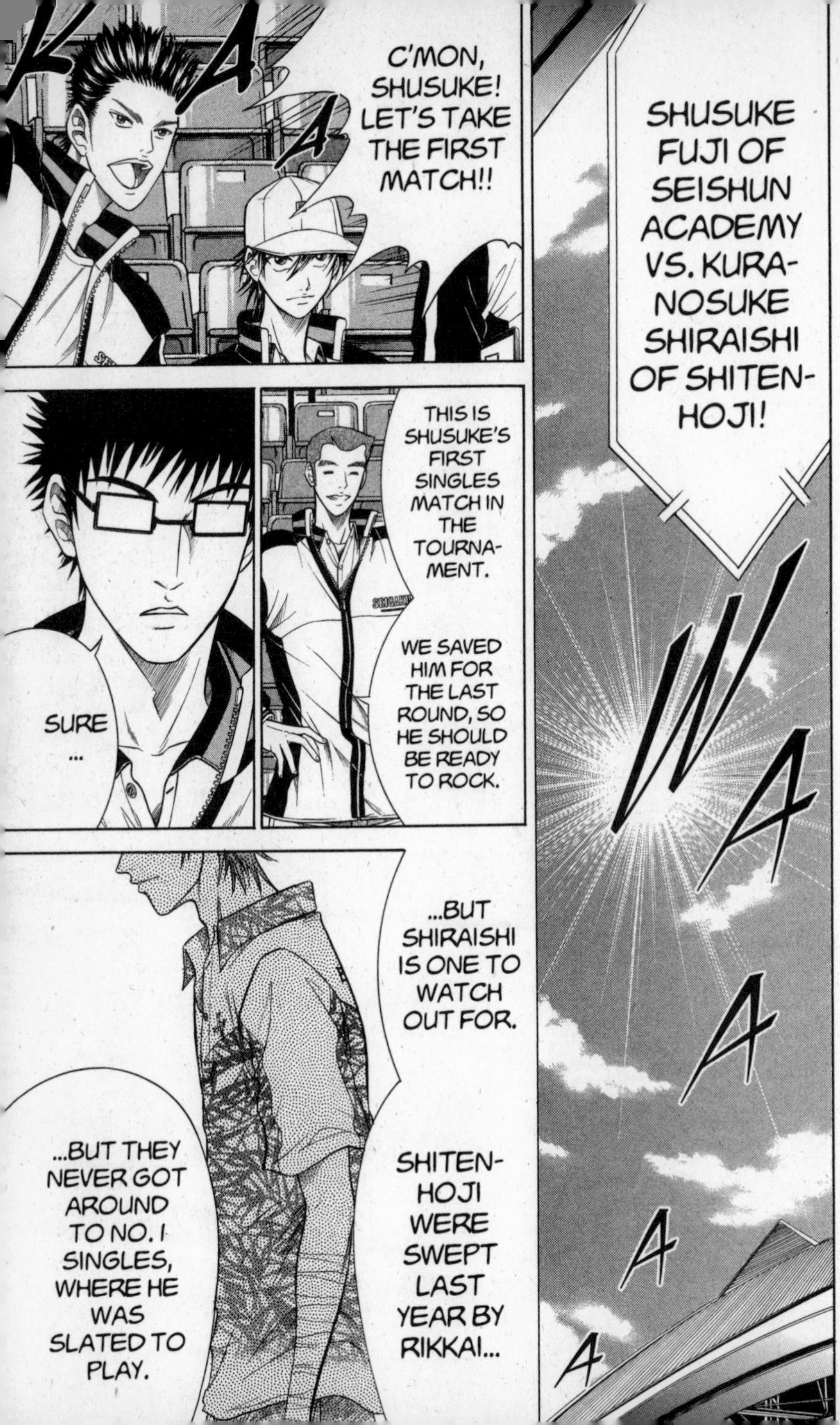
SHUSUKE FUJI OF SEISHUN ACADEMY VS. KURA-NOSUKE SHIRAISHI OF SHITEN-HOJI!
WAAAA
C'MON, SHUSUKE! LET'S TAKE THE FIRST MATCH!!
KAA
THIS IS SHUSUKE'S FIRST SINGLES MATCH IN THE TOURNA-MENT.
WE SAVED HIM FOR THE LAST ROUND, SO HE SHOULD BE READY TO ROCK.
SURE ...
...BUT SHIRAISHI IS ONE TO WATCH OUT FOR.
SHITEN-HOJI WERE SWEPT LAST YEAR BY RIKKAI...
...BUT THEY NEVER GOT AROUND TO NO. 1 SINGLES, WHERE HE WAS SLATED TO PLAY.

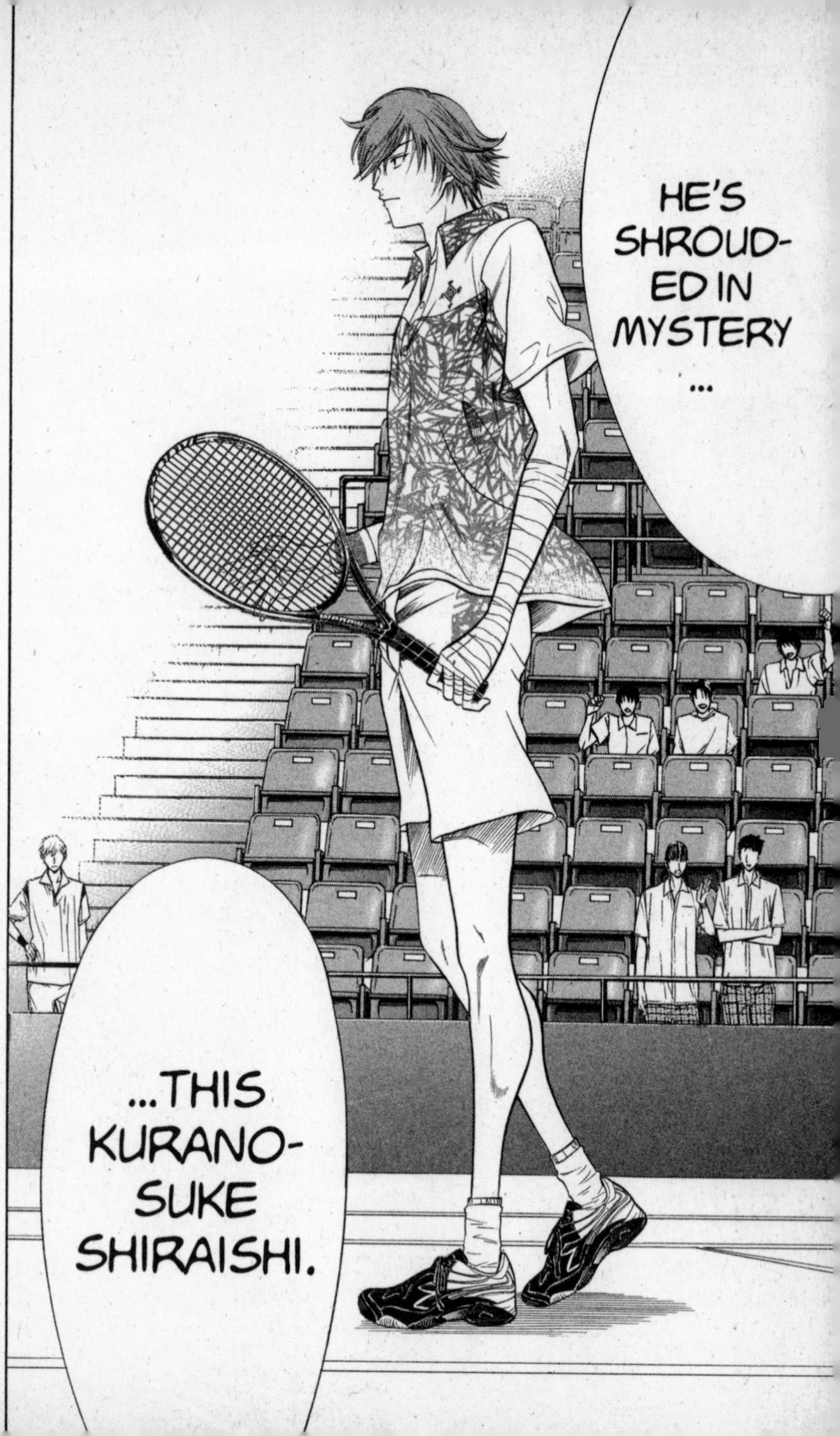
HE'S SHROUDED-ED IN MYSTERY ...
...THIS KURANO-SUKE SHIRAISHI.

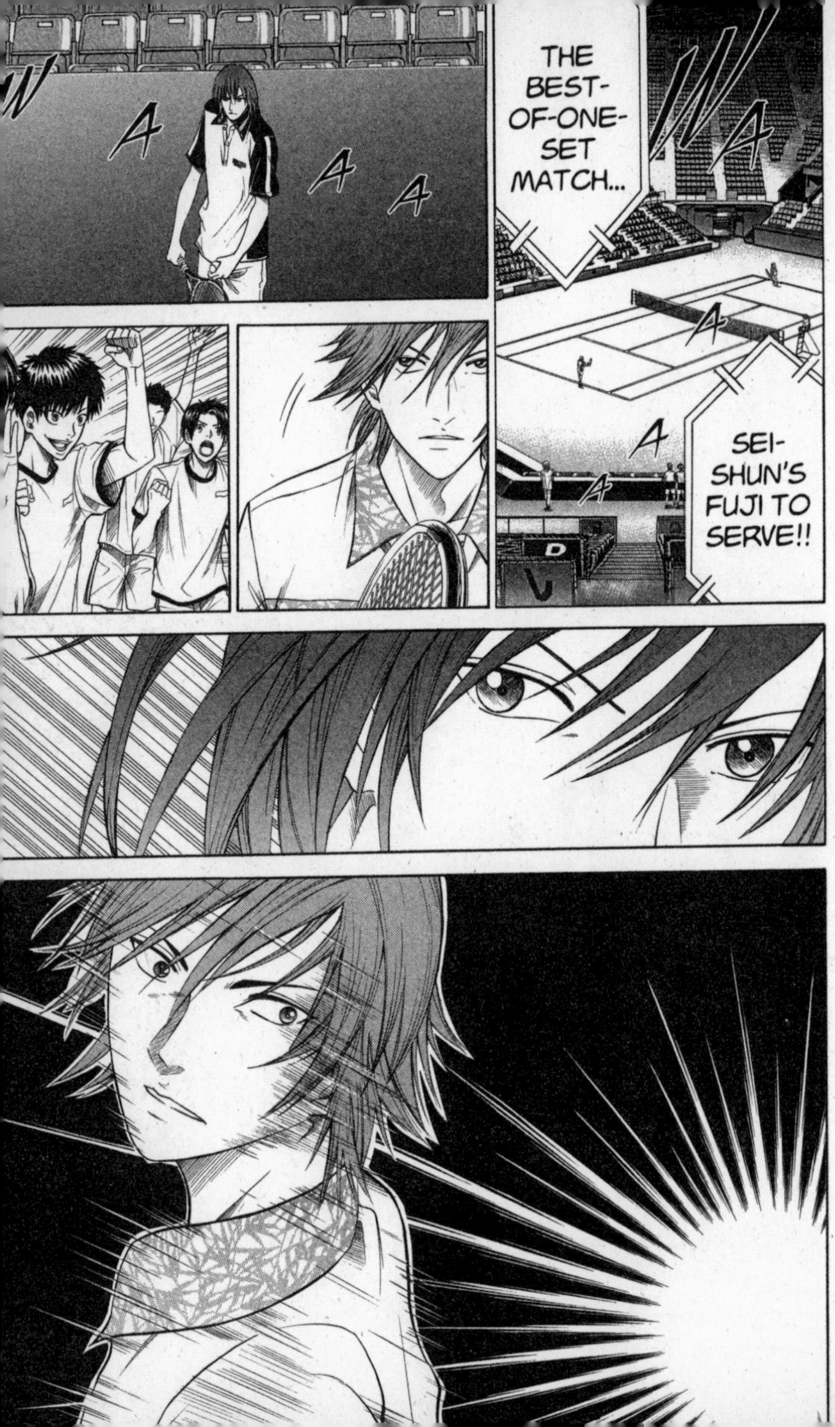
THE BEST-OF-ONE-SET MATCH...
WAAAA
SEI-SHUN'S FUJI TO SERVE!!
WAAA

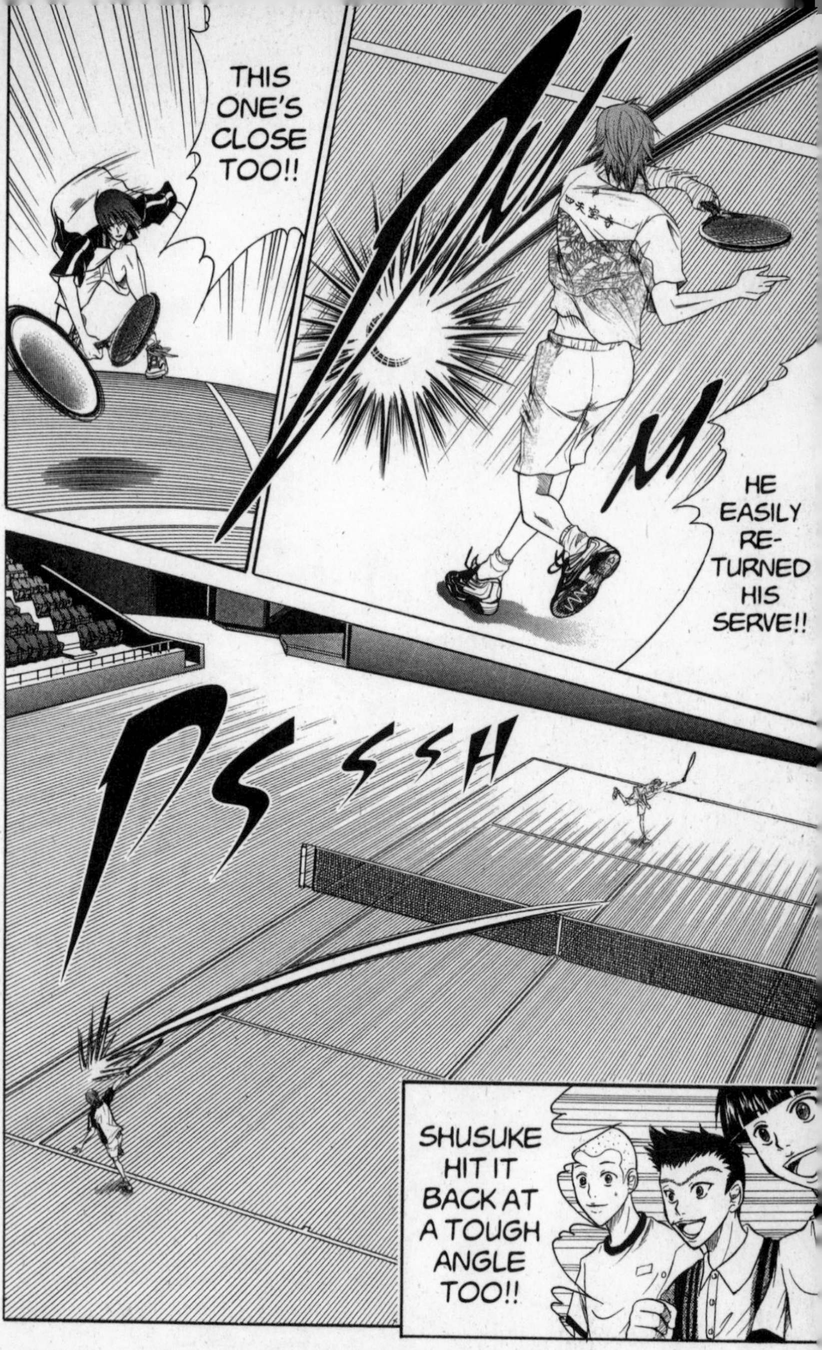
HE EASILY RE-TURNED HIS SERVE!!
THIS ONE'S CLOSE TOO!!
SHUSUKE HIT IT BACK AT A TOUGH ANGLE TOO!!

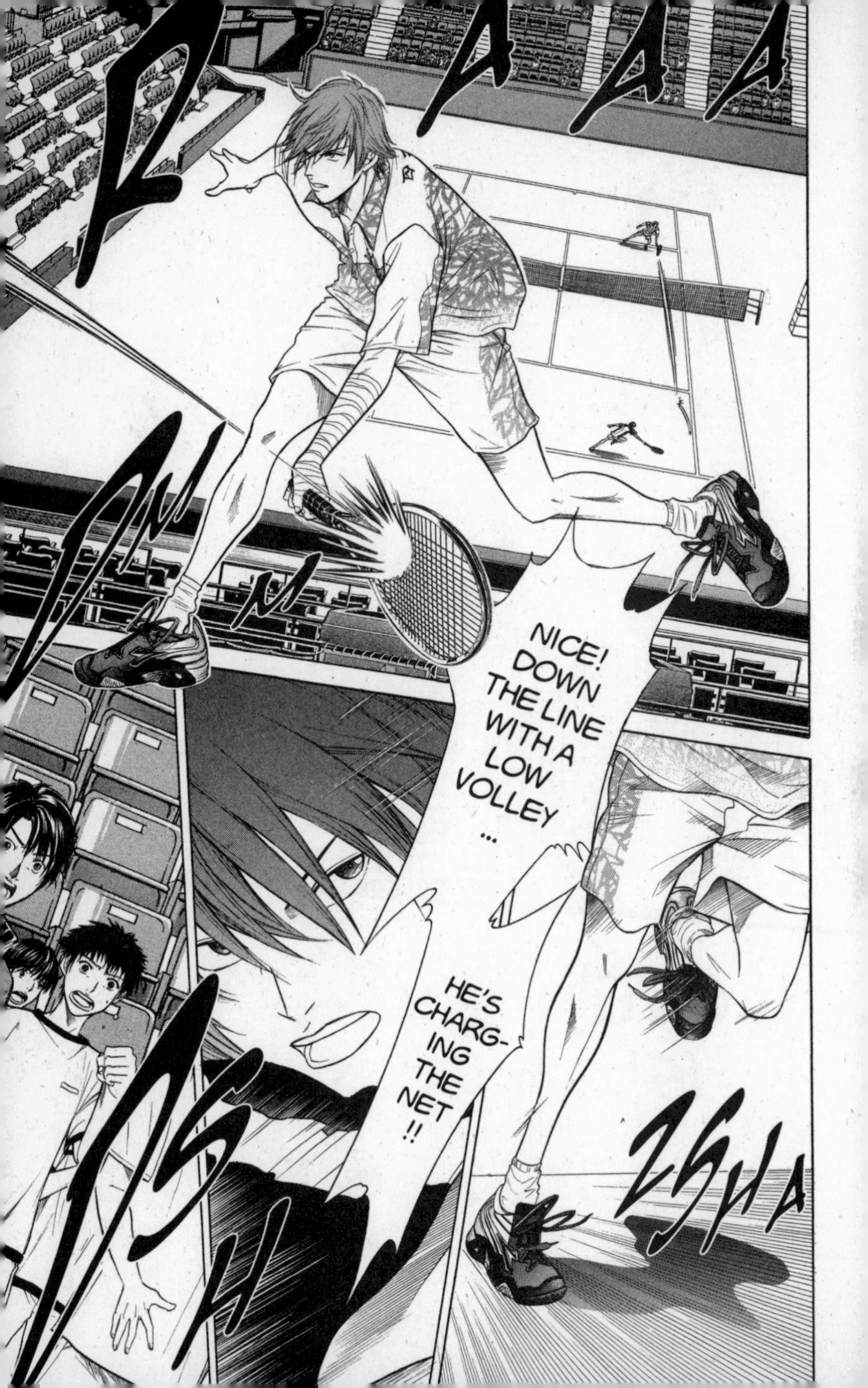
NICE! DOWN THE LINE WITH A LOW VOLLEY ...
HE'S CHARG-ING THE NET!!
ZSHA

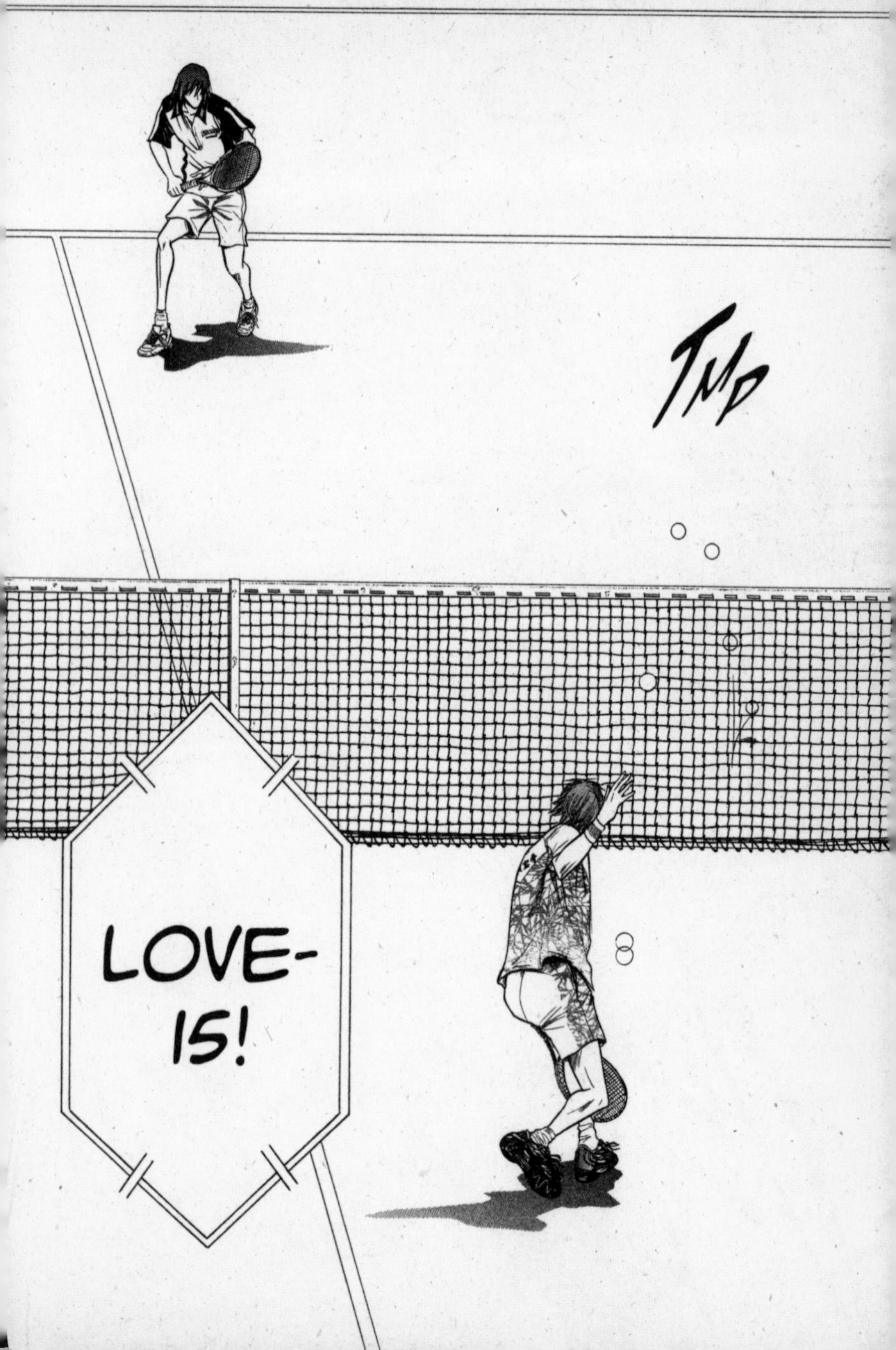
TMP
LOVE-15!

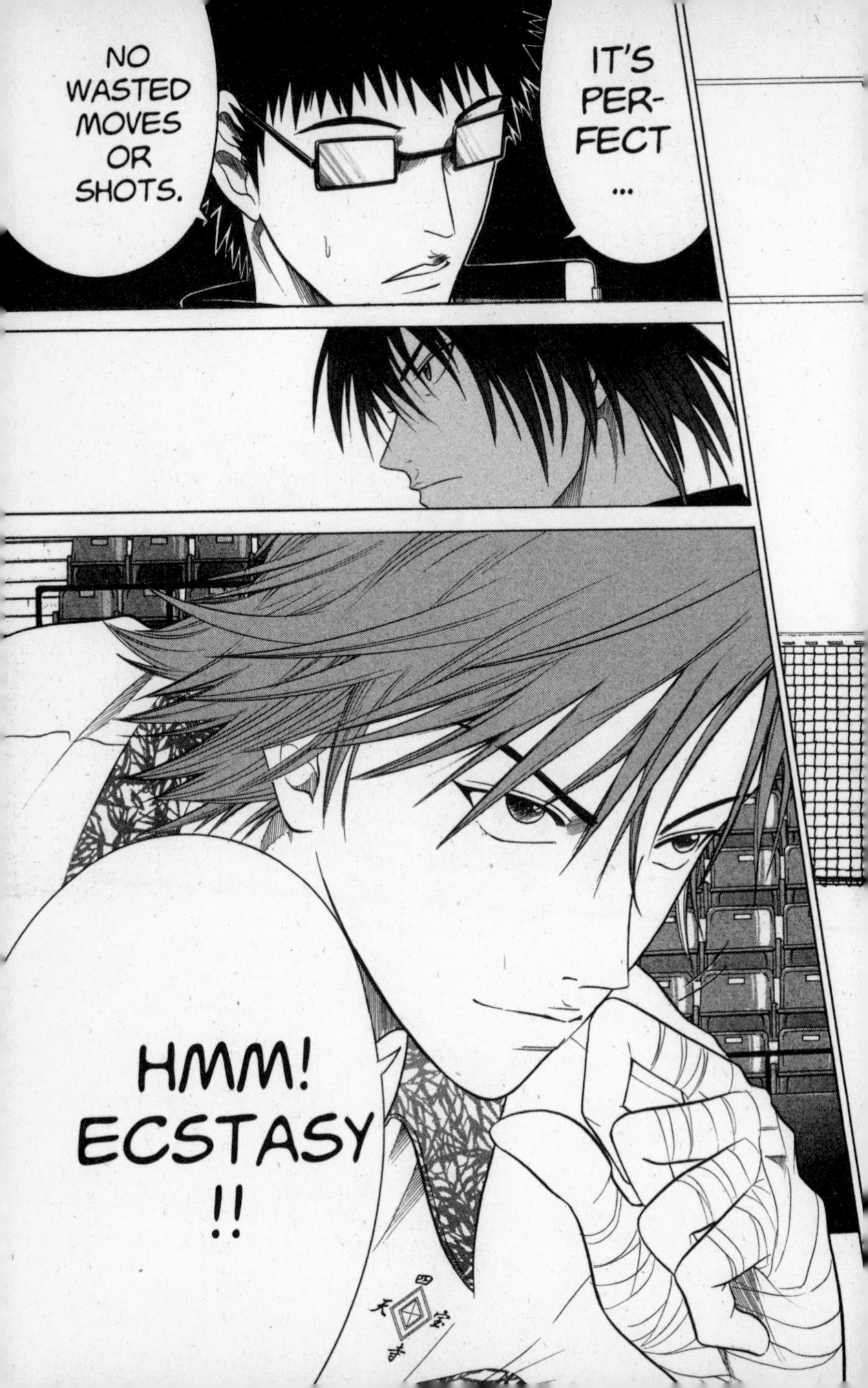
IT'S PER-FECT...
NO WASTED MOVES OR SHOTS.
HMM! ECSTASY!!

テニスの王子様

THE PRINCE OF TENNIS

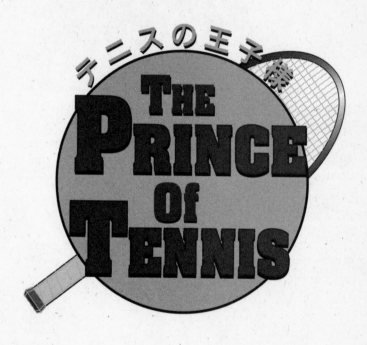

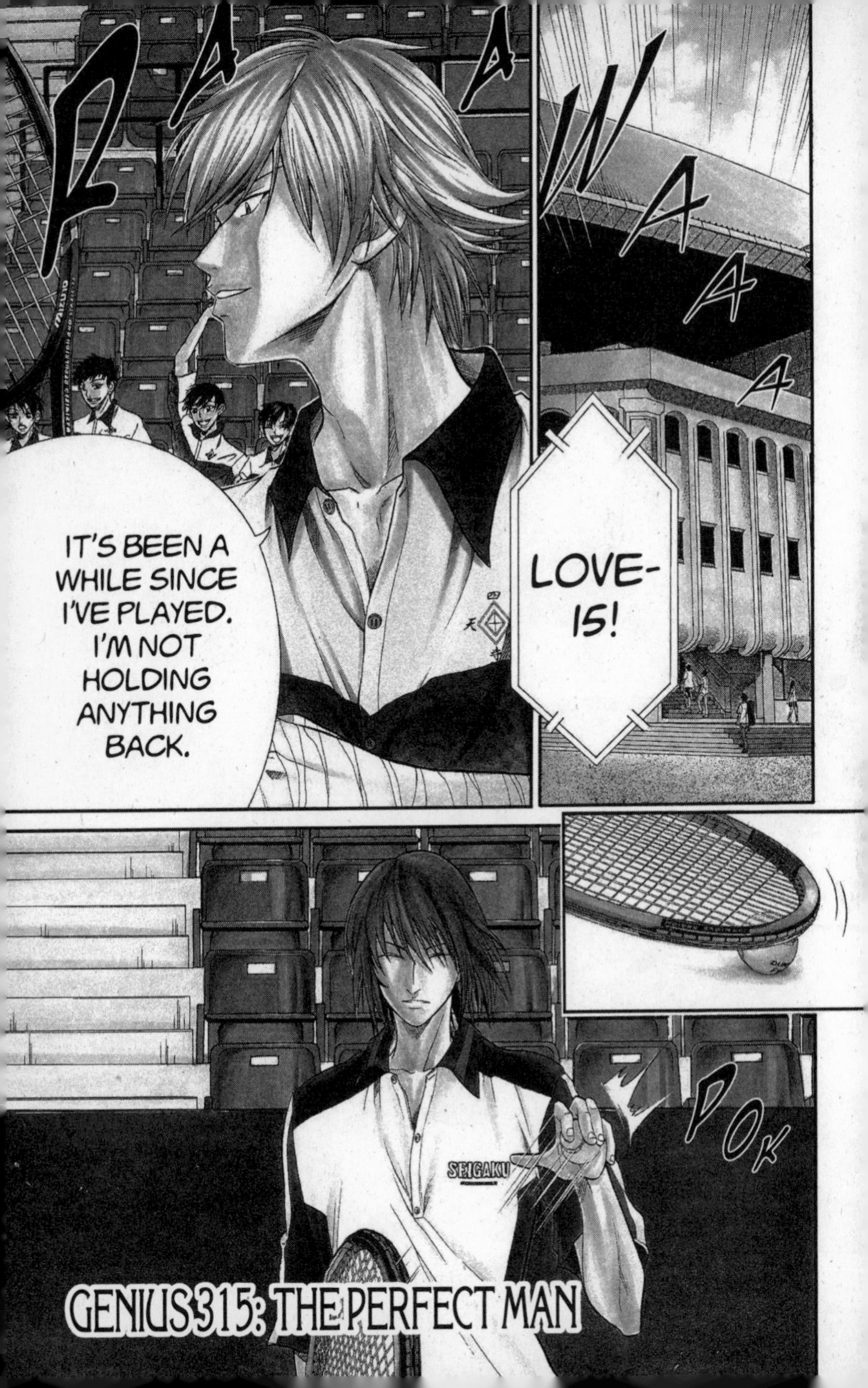
WAAAAA
LOVE-15!
PAAA
IT'S BEEN A WHILE SINCE I'VE PLAYED. I'M NOT HOLDING ANYTHING BACK.
POK
SEIGAKU
GENIUS 315: THE PERFECT MAN

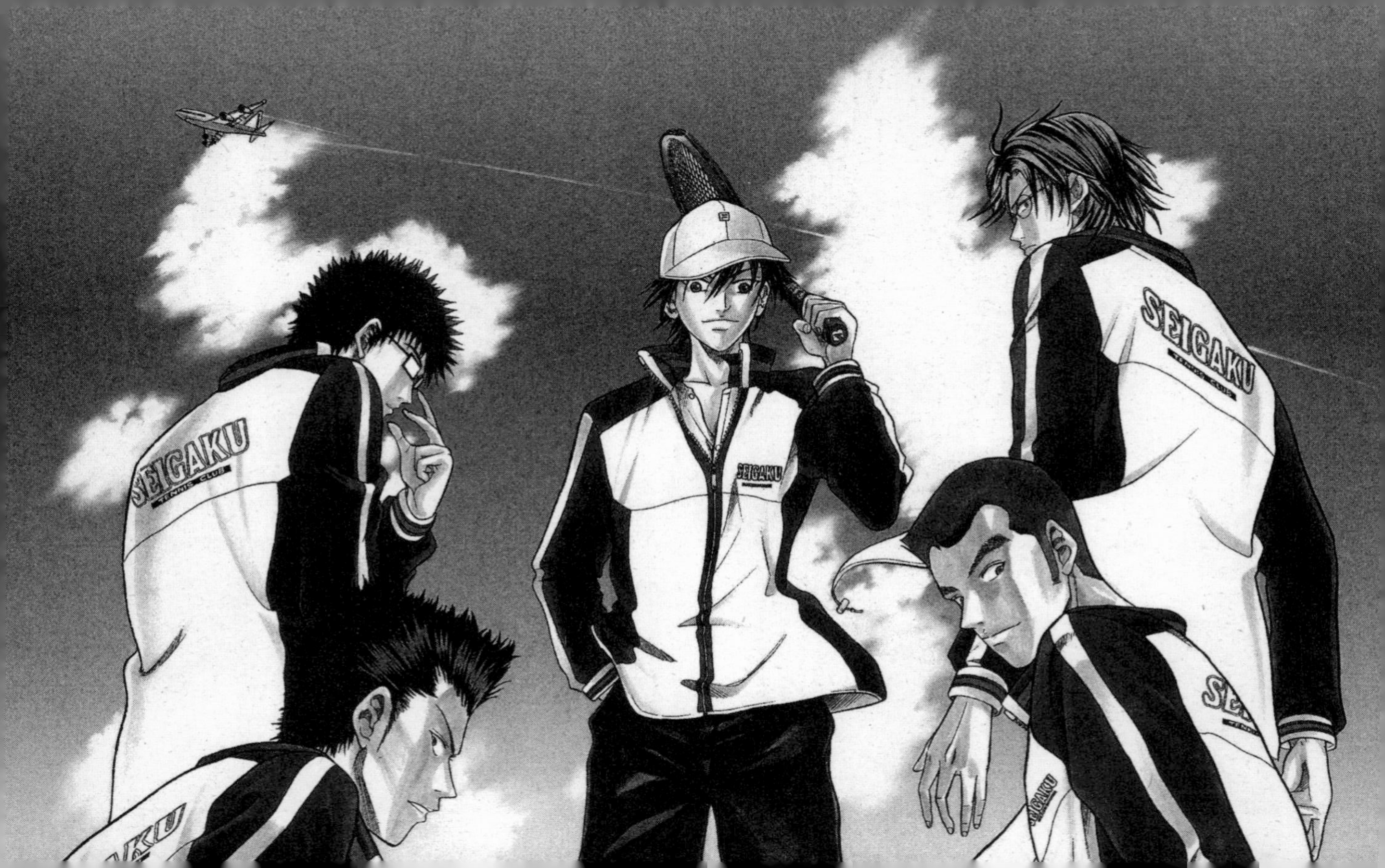
SEIGAKU
TENNIS CLUB
SEIGAKU
SEIGAKU
TENNIS CLUB

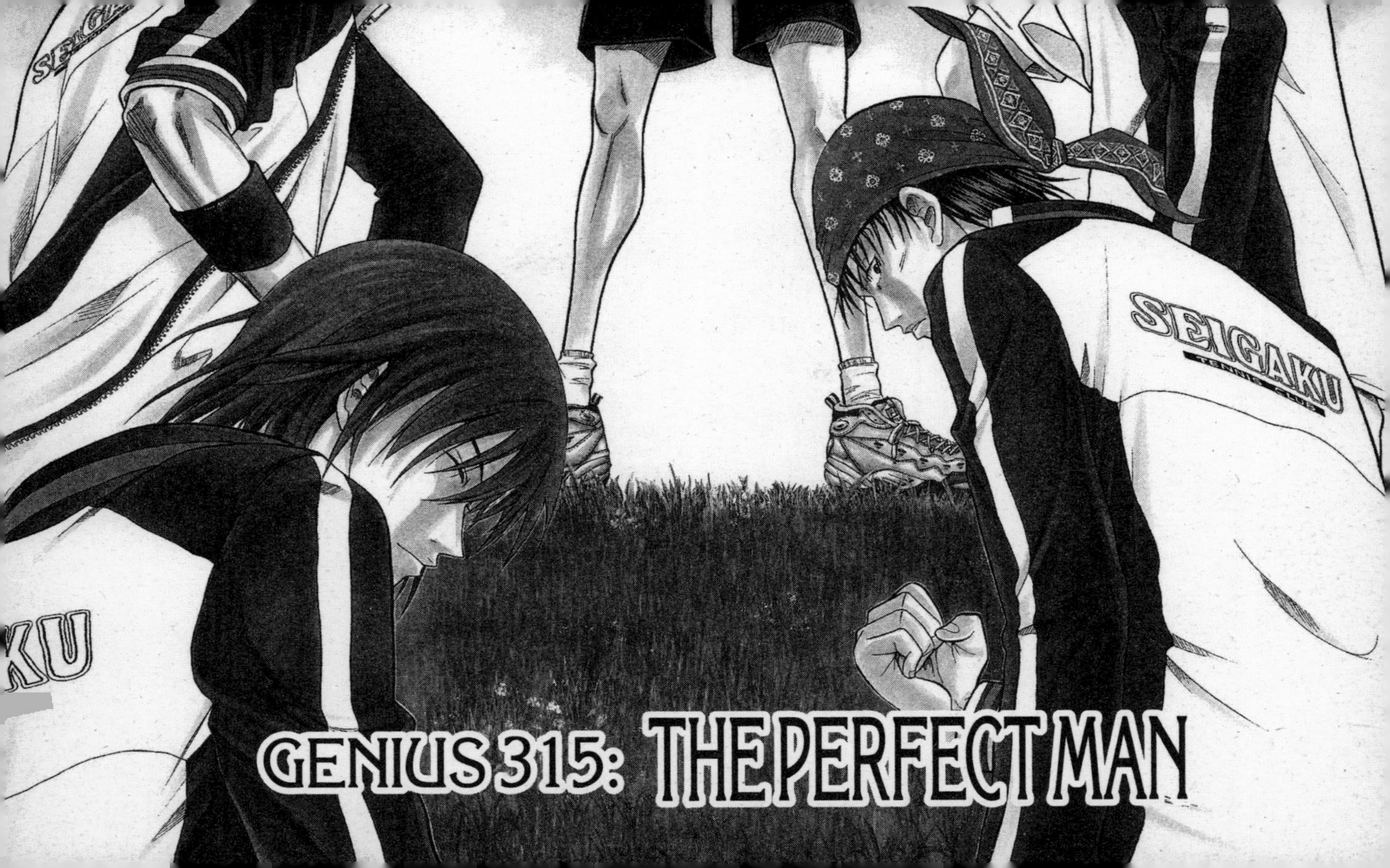

SEIGAKU
TENNIS CLUB
KU
GENIUS 315: THE PERFECT MAN

テニスの王子様

THE PRINCE OF TENNIS

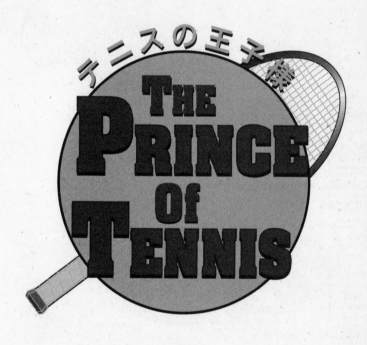

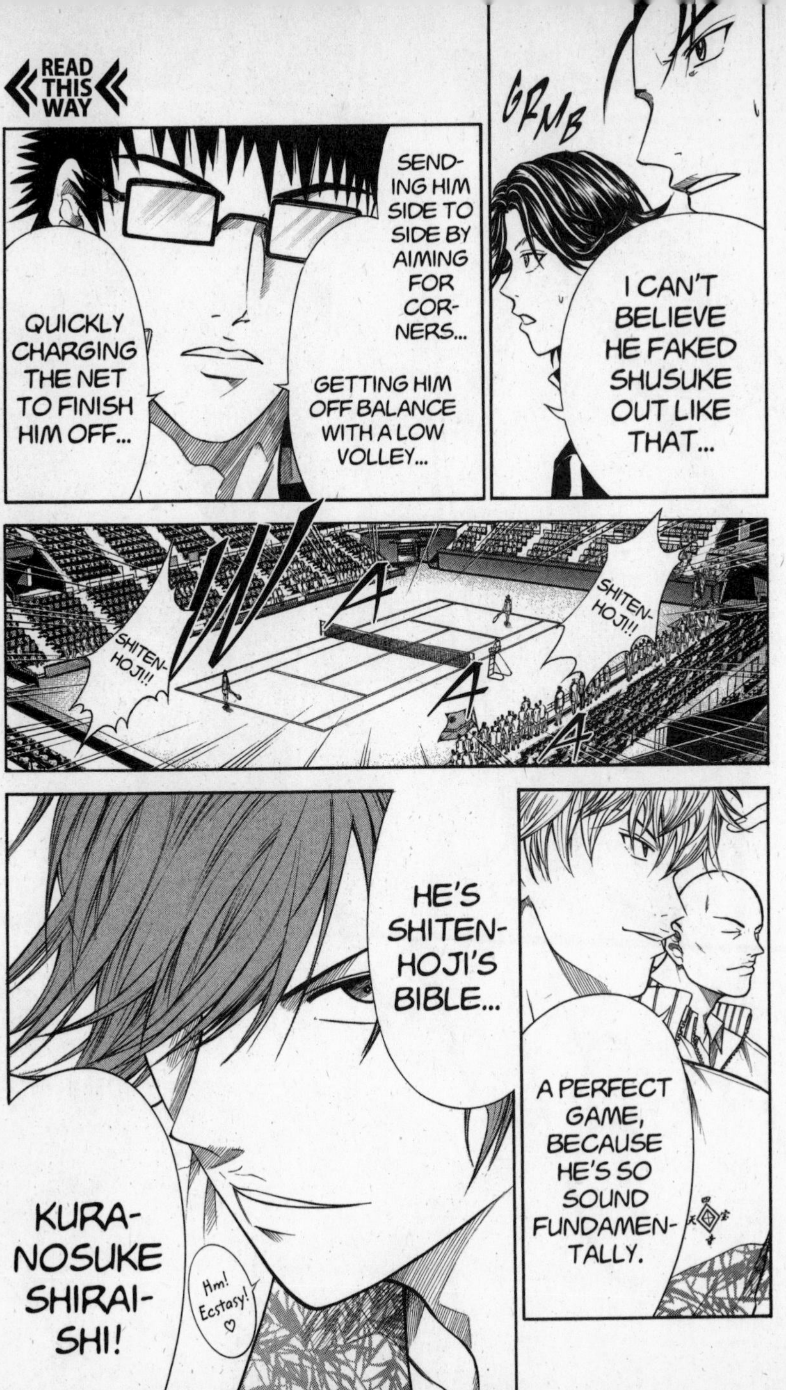
READ THIS WAY
GRMB
I CAN'T BELIEVE HE FAKED SHUSUKE OUT LIKE THAT...
SEND-ING HIM SIDE TO SIDE BY AIMING FOR COR-NERS...
GETTING HIM OFF BALANCE WITH A LOW VOLLEY...
QUICKLY CHARGING THE NET TO FINISH HIM OFF...
SHITEN-HOJI!!!
WAAAA
SHITEN-HOJI!!!
A PERFECT GAME, BECAUSE HE'S SO SOUND FUNDAMEN-TALLY.
HE'S SHITEN-HOJI'S BIBLE...
KURA-NOSUKE SHIRAI-SHI!
Hm! Ecstasy! ♡

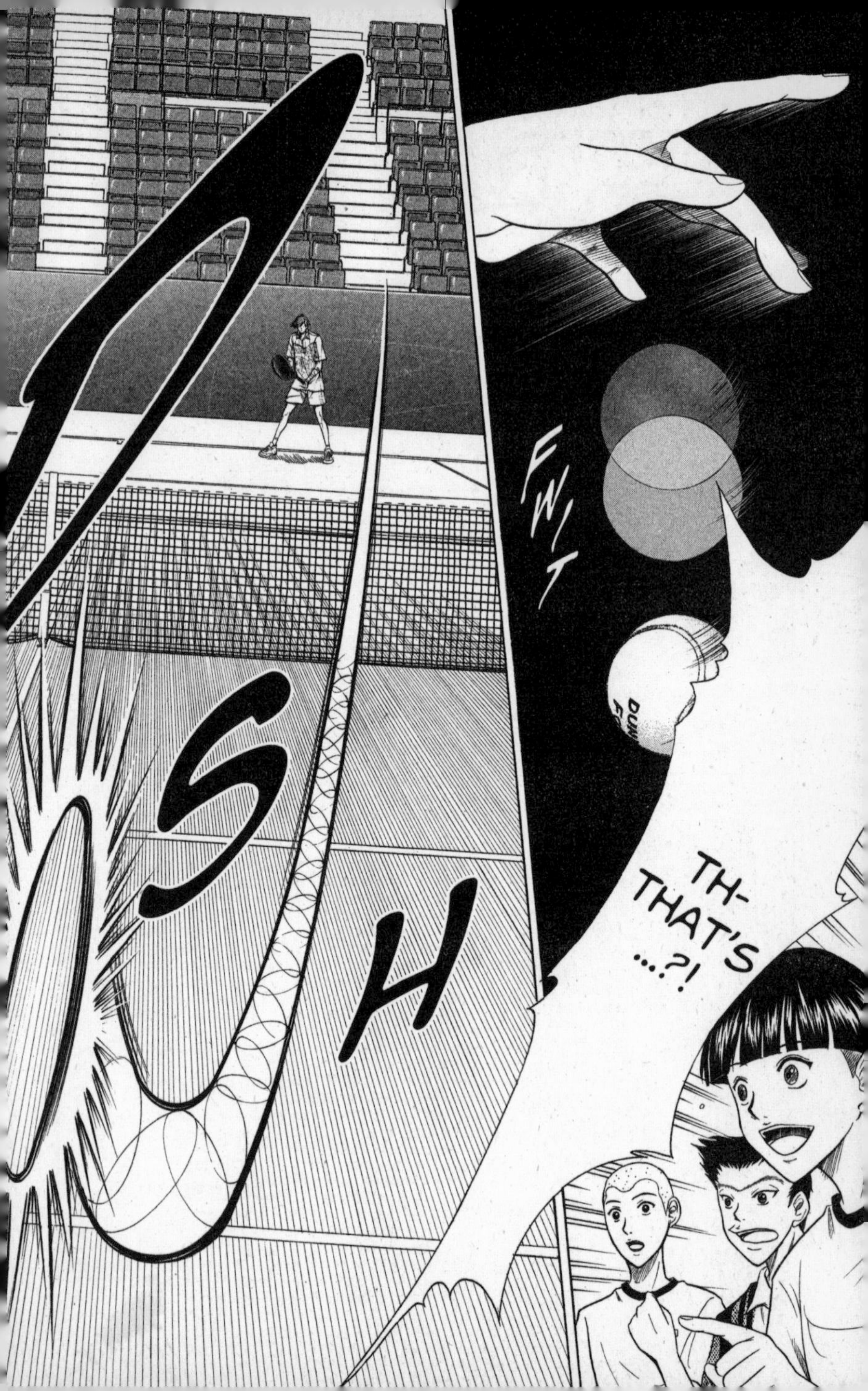
FWIT
TH-THAT'S ...?!

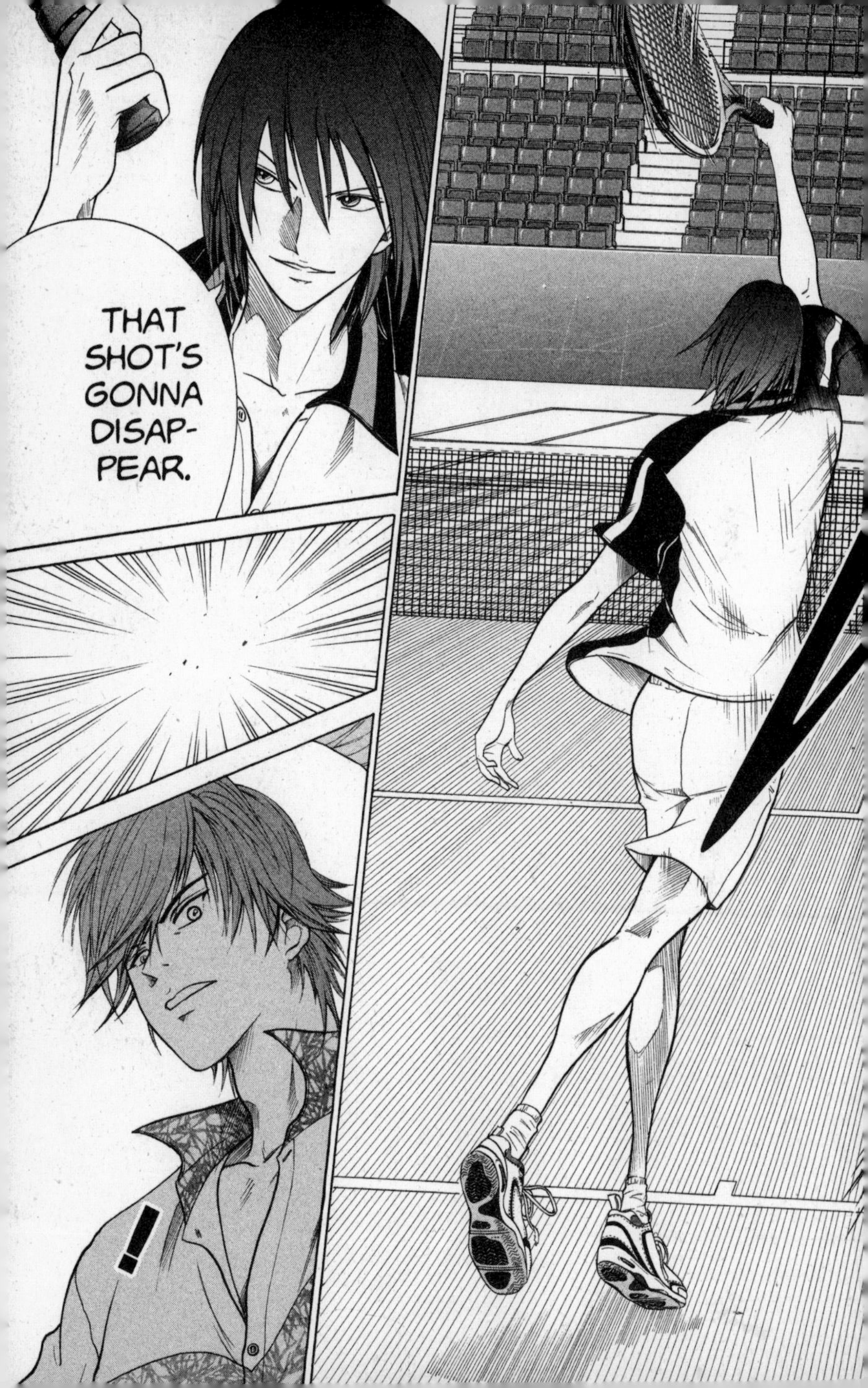
THAT SHOT'S GONNA DISAP- PEAR.
!

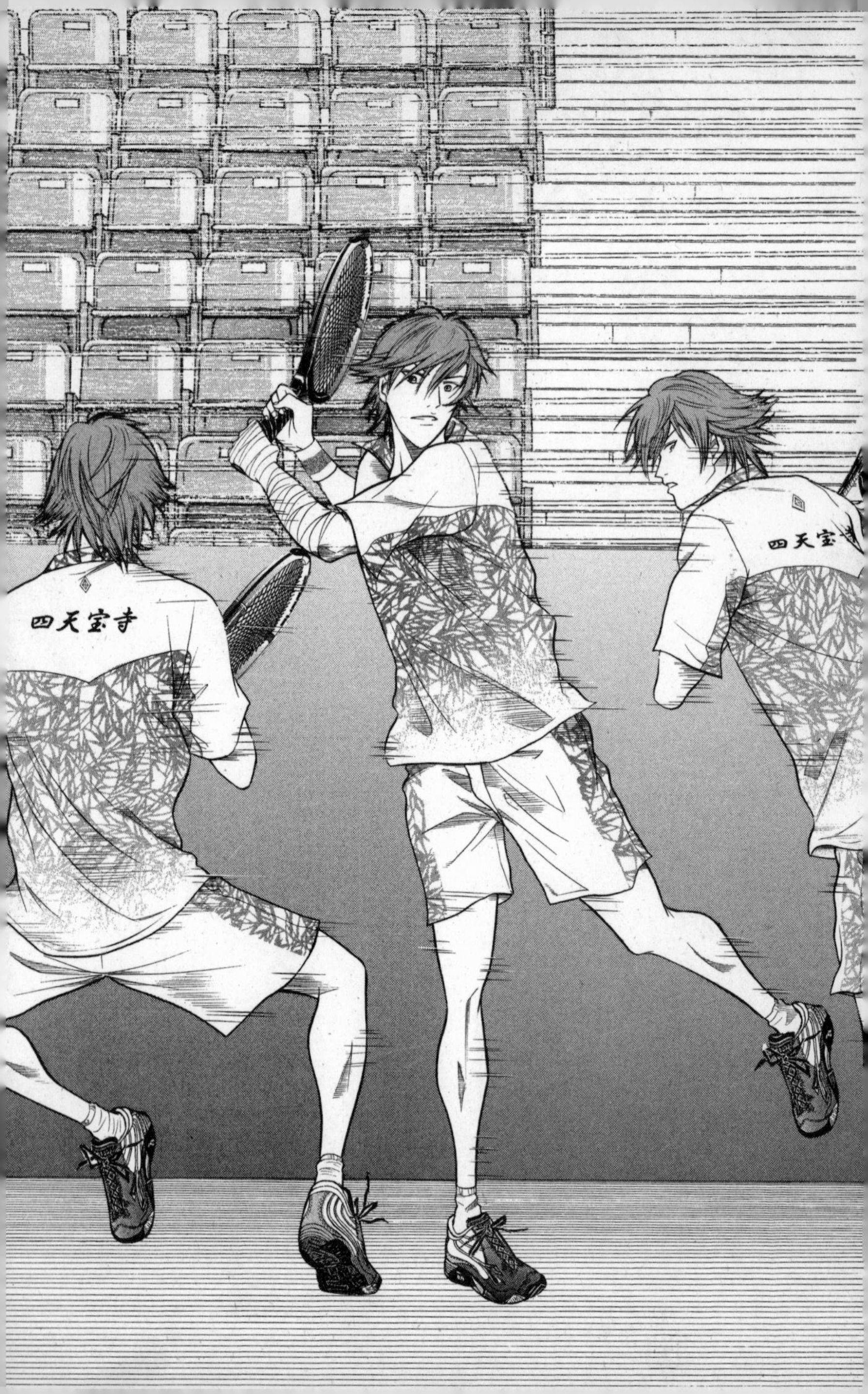
四天宝寺
四天宝寺

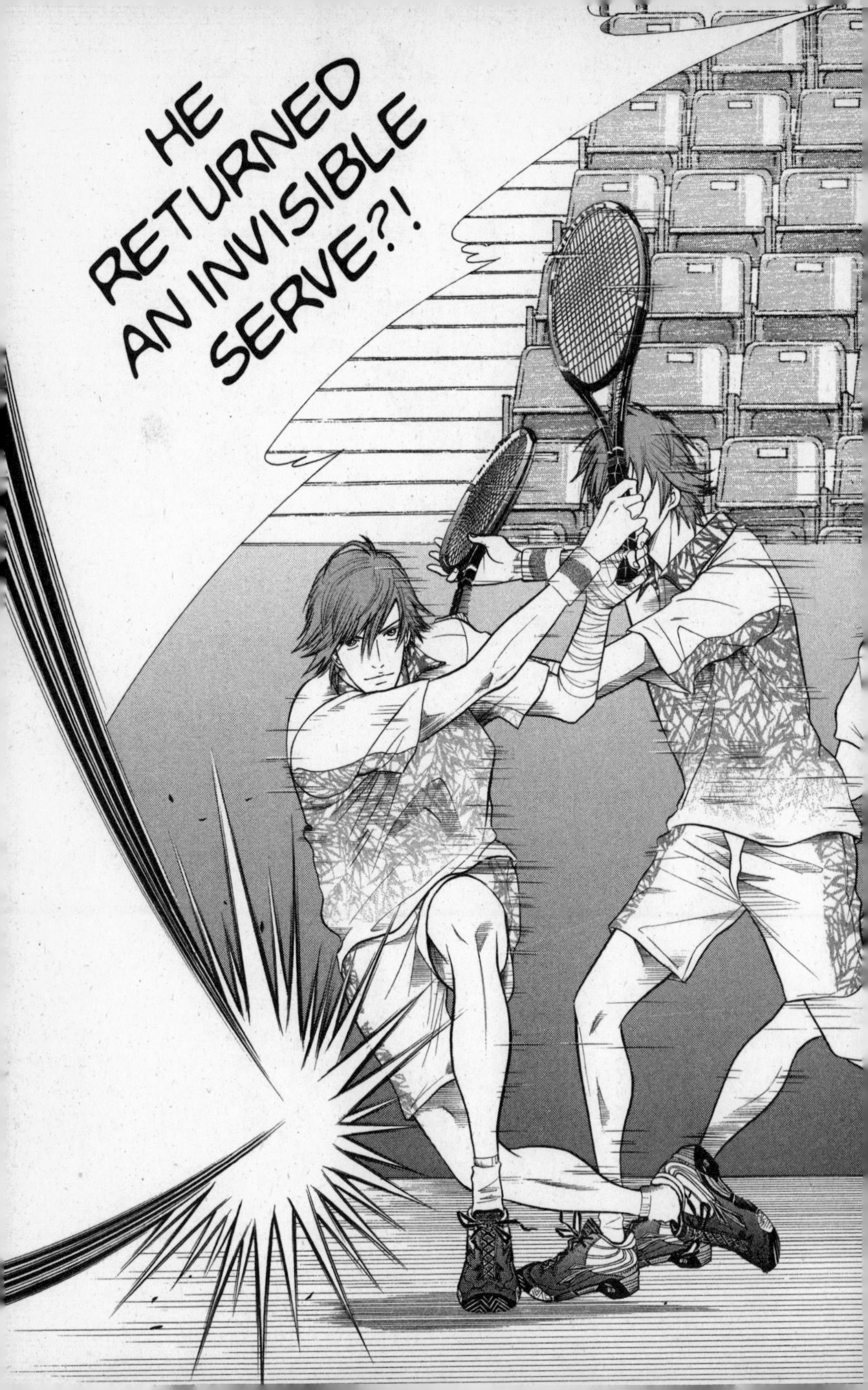
HE RETURNED AN INVISIBLE SERVE?!

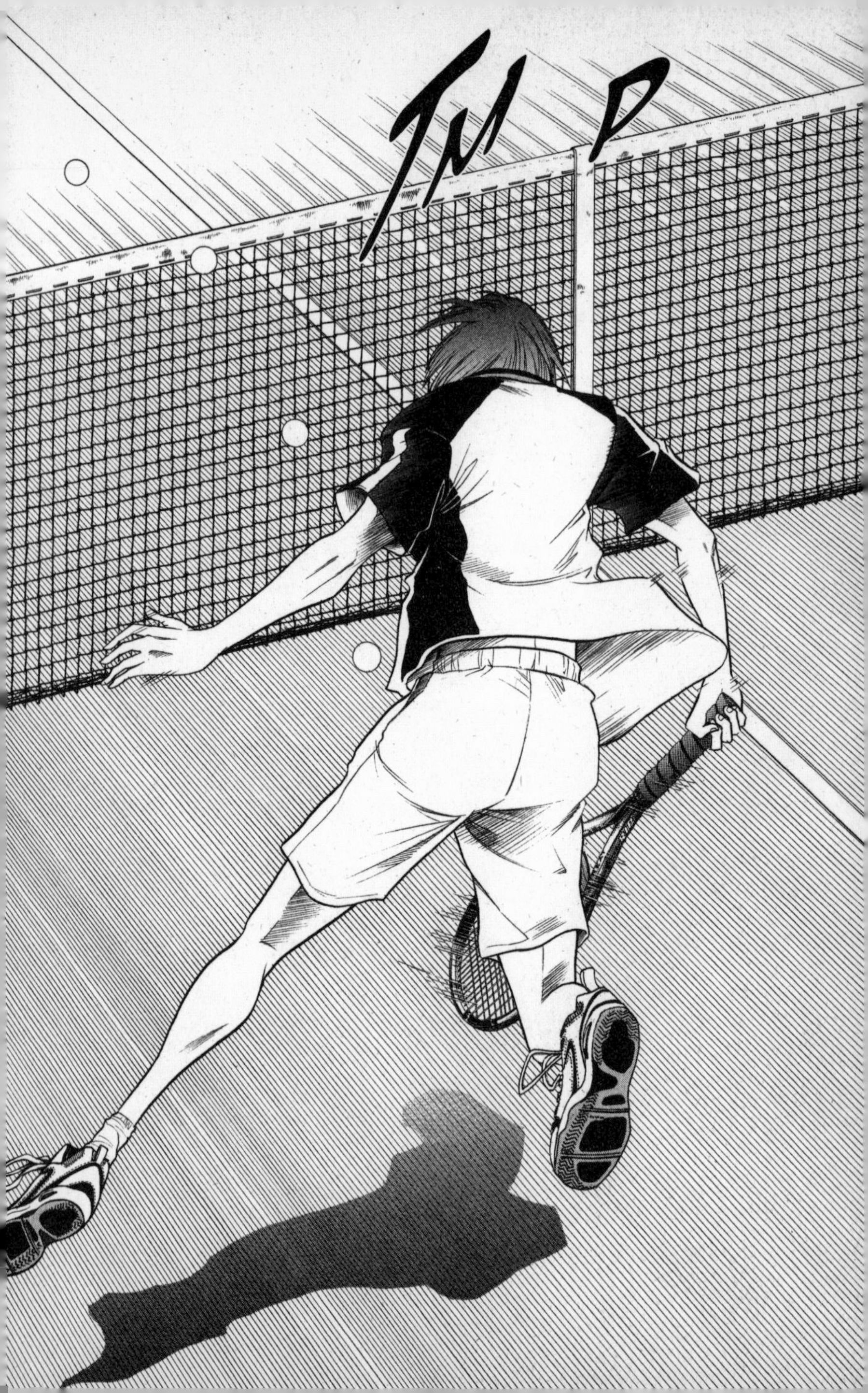
TAP

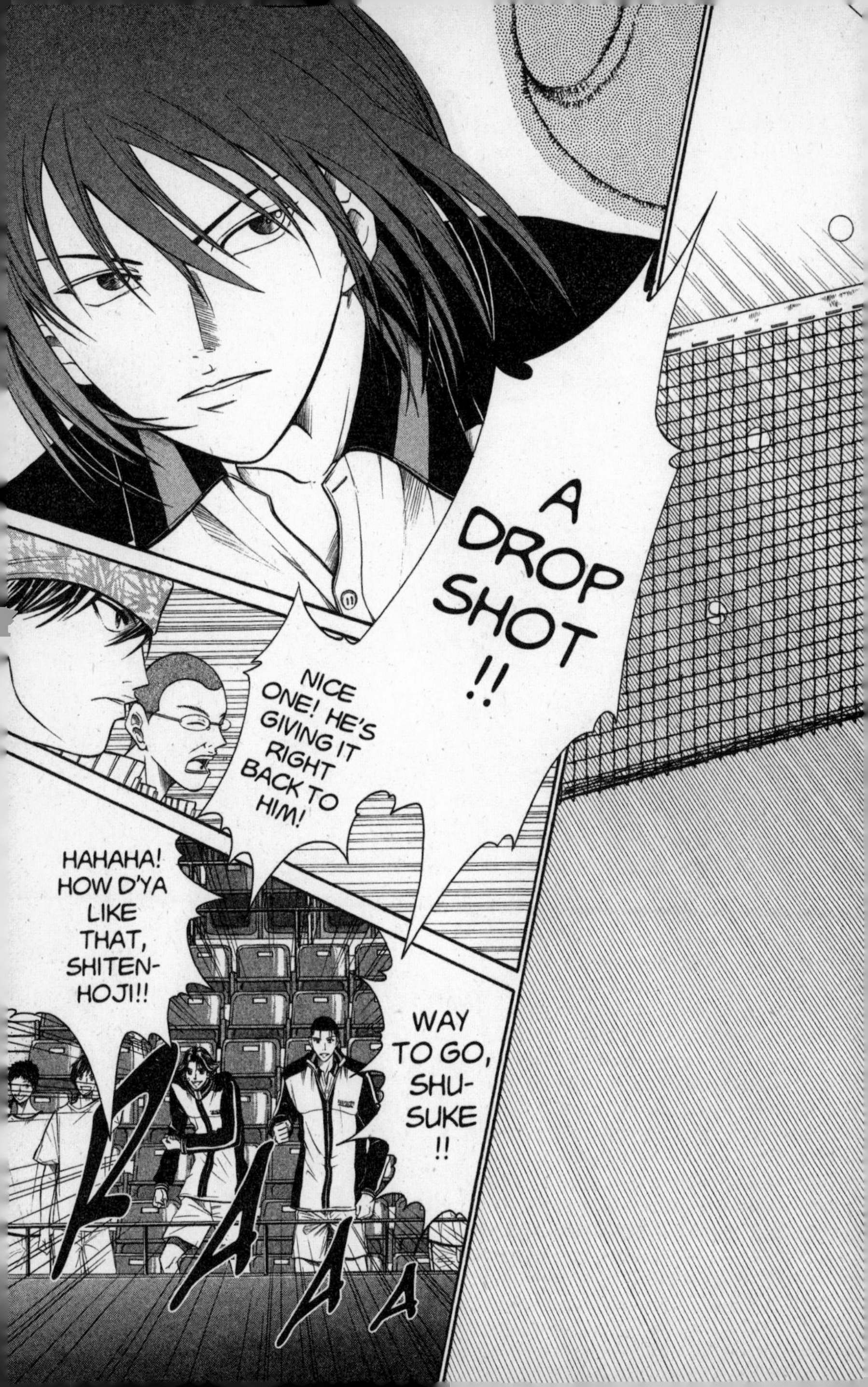
A DROP SHOT !!
NICE ONE! HE'S GIVING IT RIGHT BACK TO HIM!
WAY TO GO, SHUSUKE !!
HAHAHA! HOW D'YA LIKE THAT, SHITEN-HOJI!!

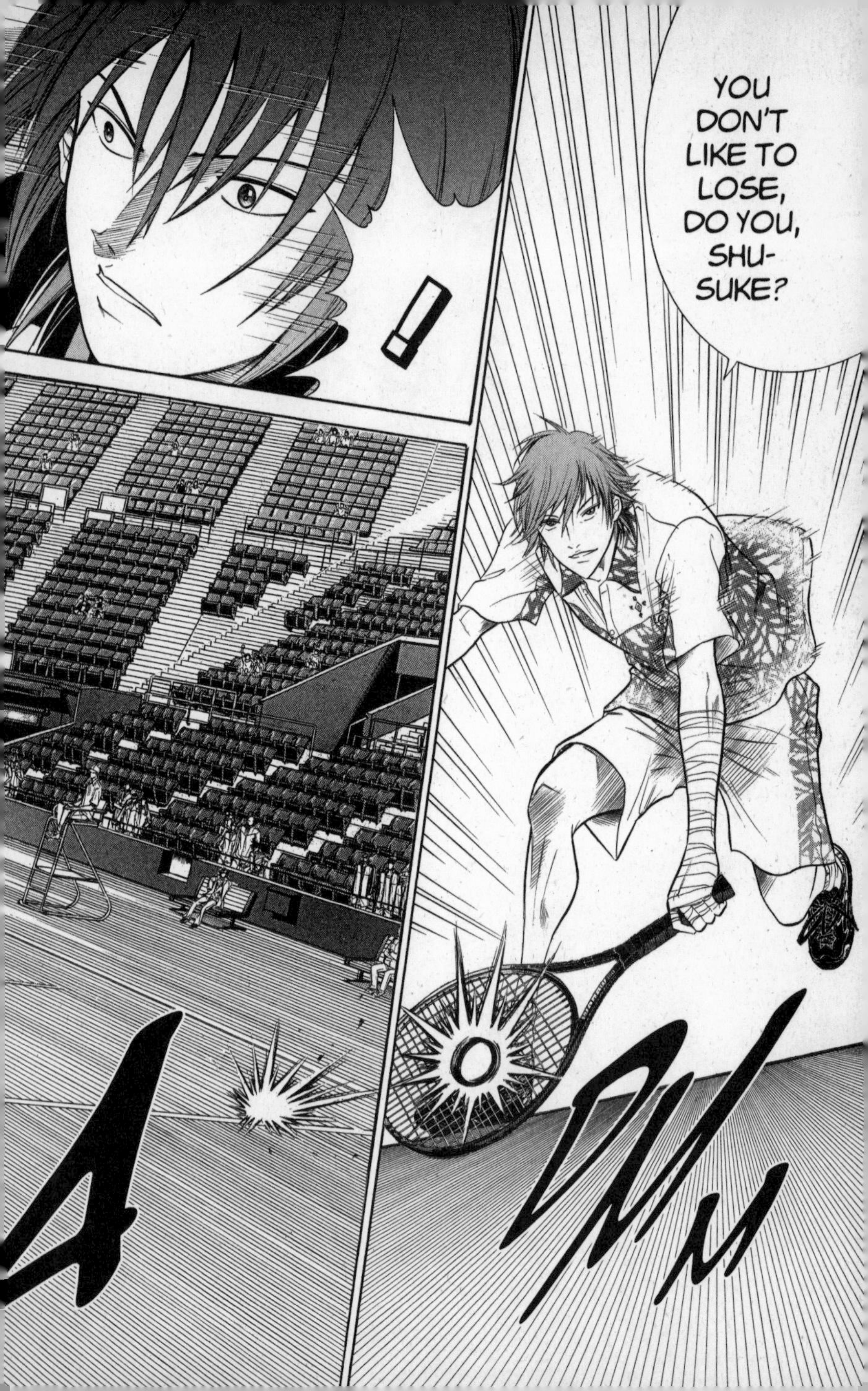
YOU DON'T LIKE TO LOSE, DO YOU, SHUSUKE?
!

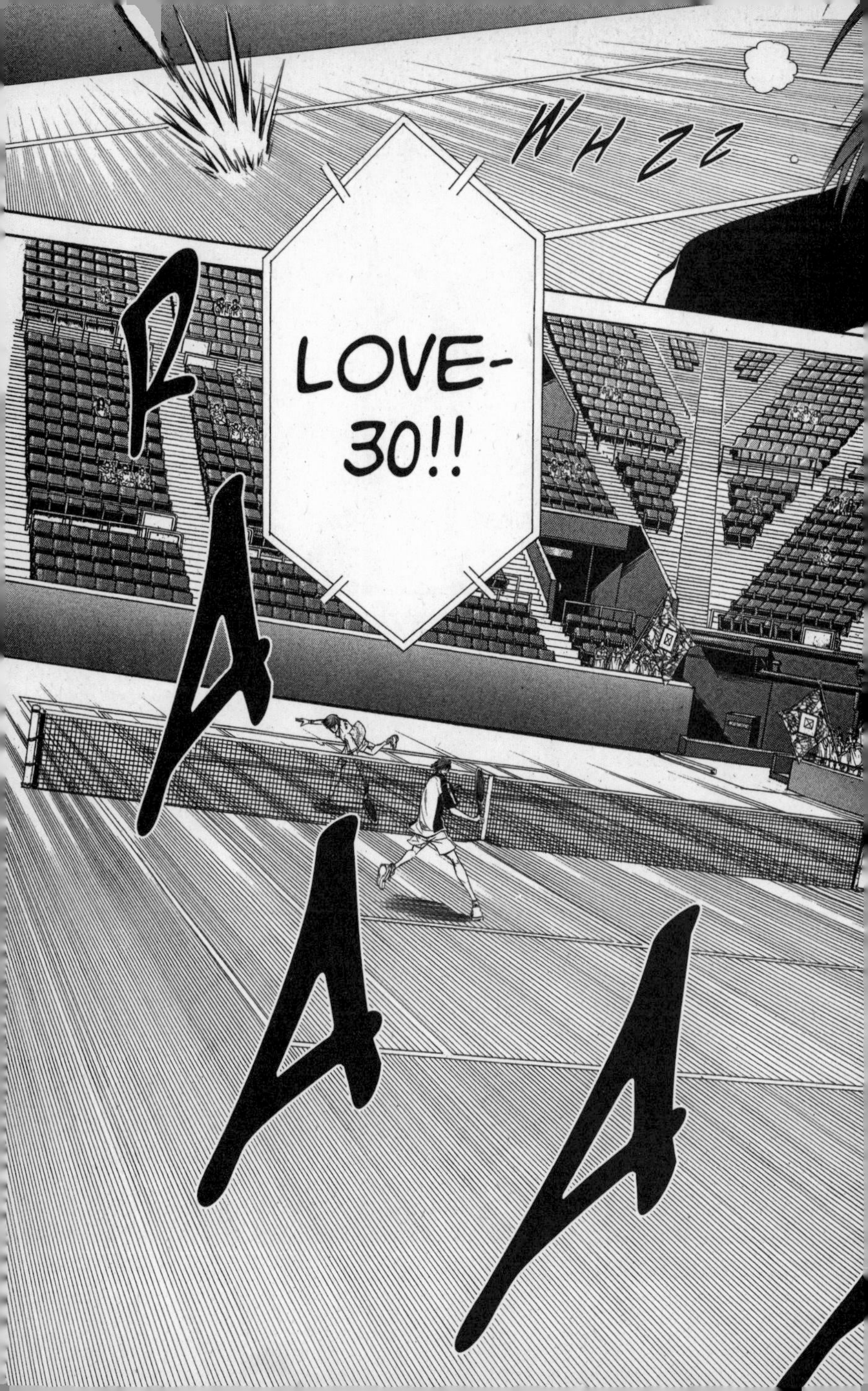
WHZZ
LOVE-30!!

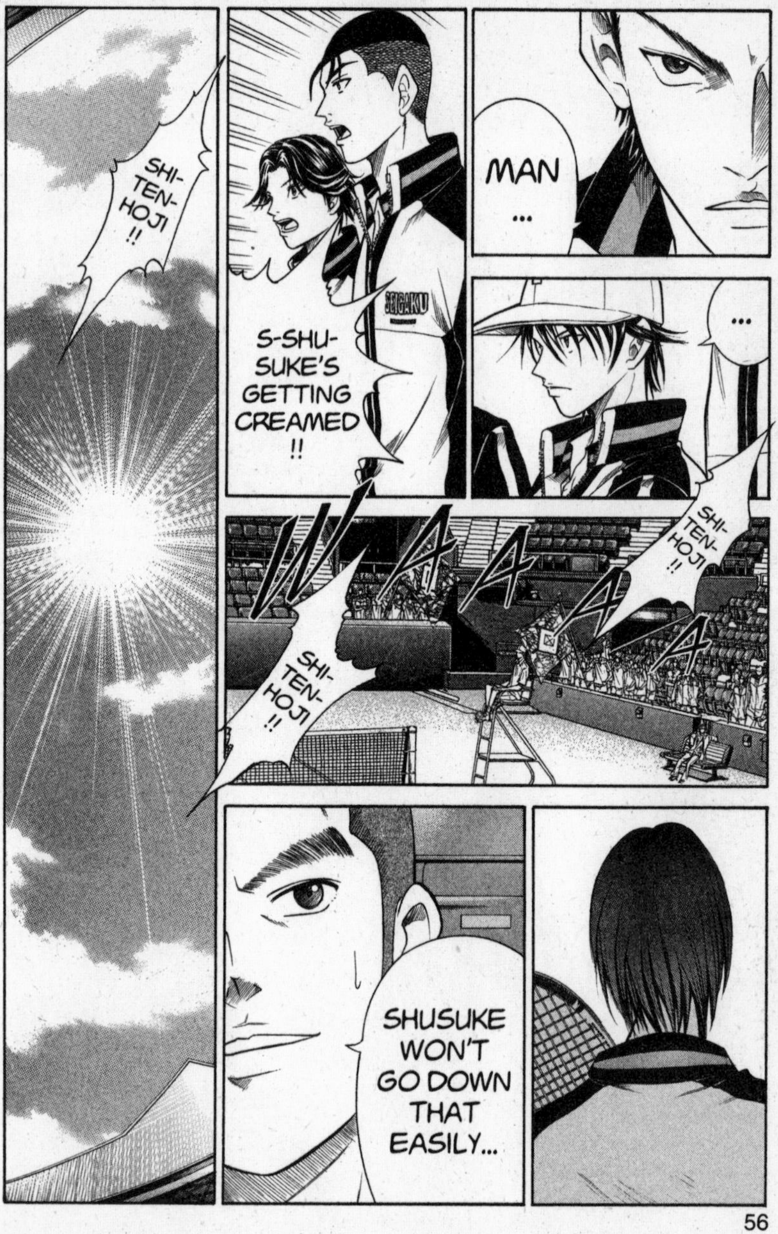
MAN ...
...
S-SHU-SUKE'S GETTING CREAMED!!
WAAAA
SHI-TEN-HOJI!!
SHI-TEN-HOJI!!
SHUSUKE WON'T GO DOWN THAT EASILY...
SHI-TEN-HOJI!!

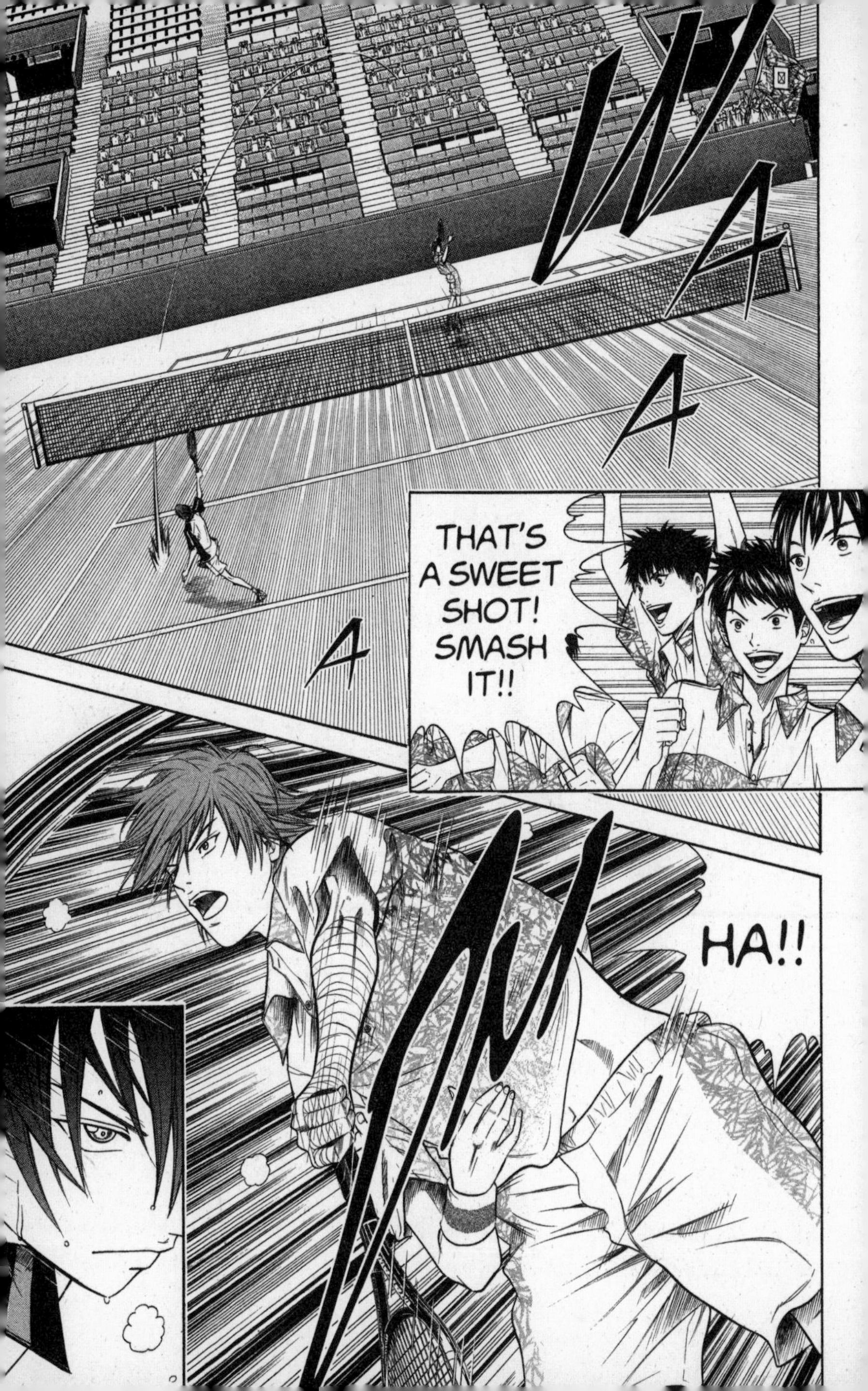
WAAA
THAT'S A SWEET SHOT! SMASH IT!!
HA!!

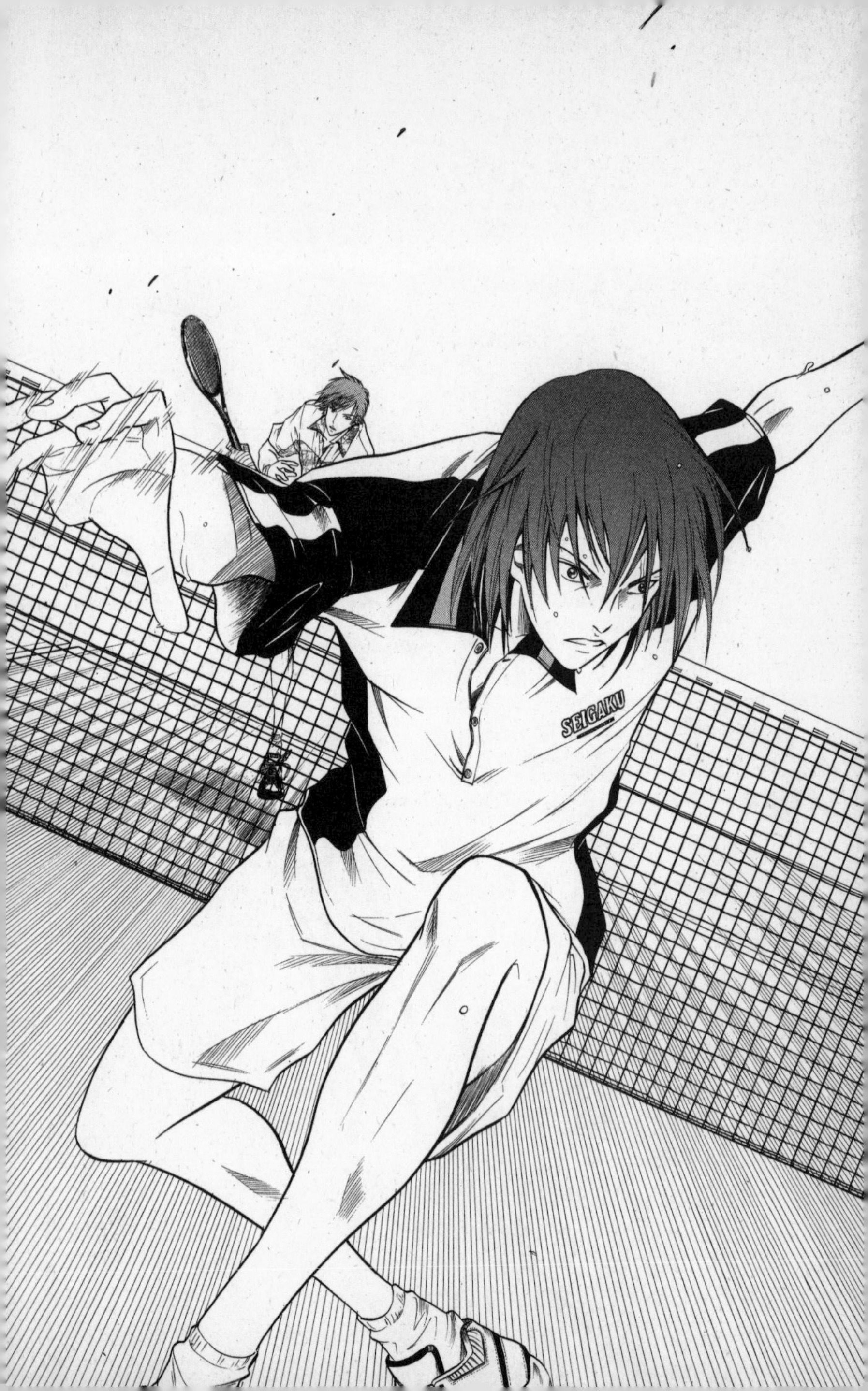
SEIGAKU

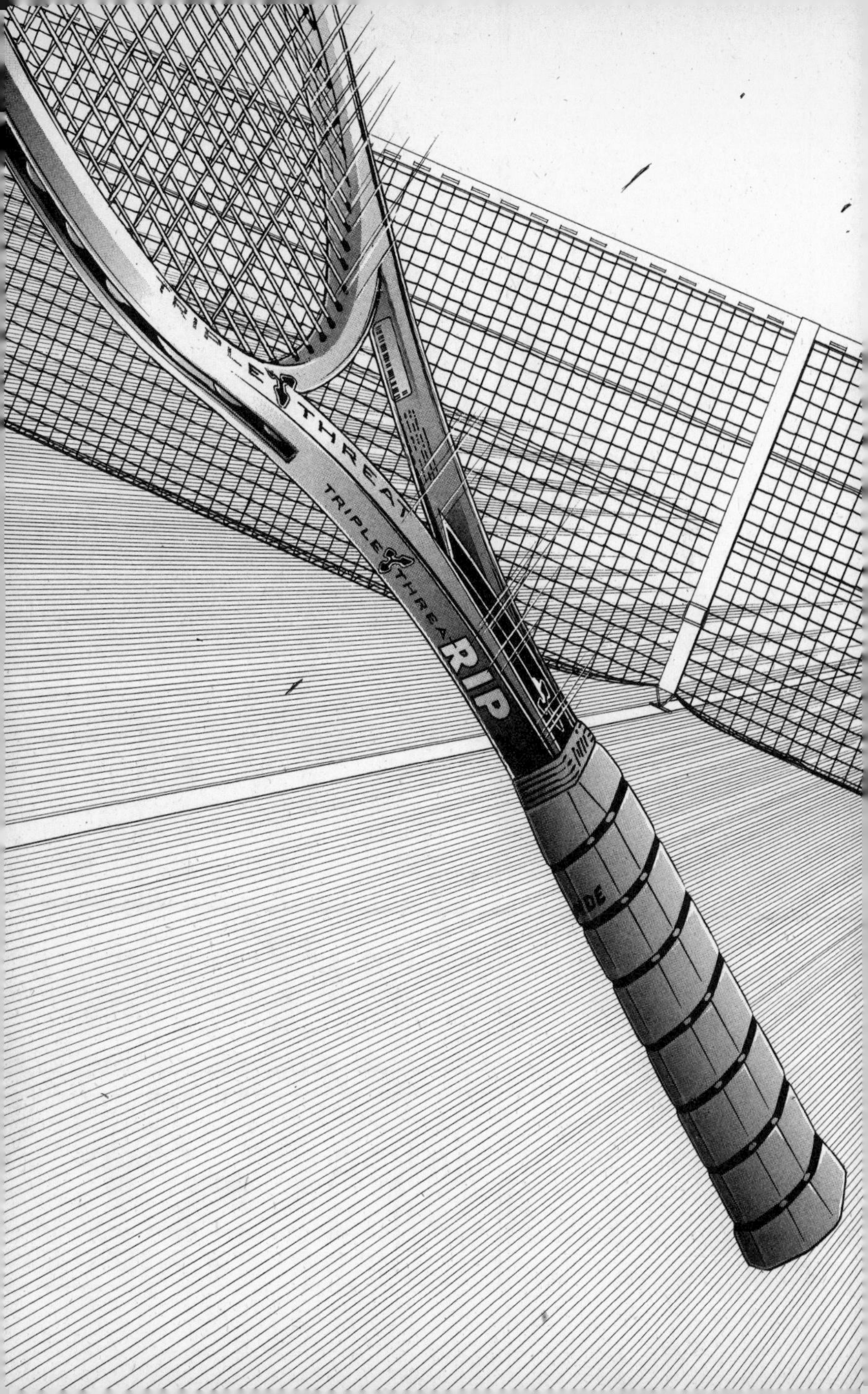
TRIPLE THREAT
TRIPLE THREAT
RIP

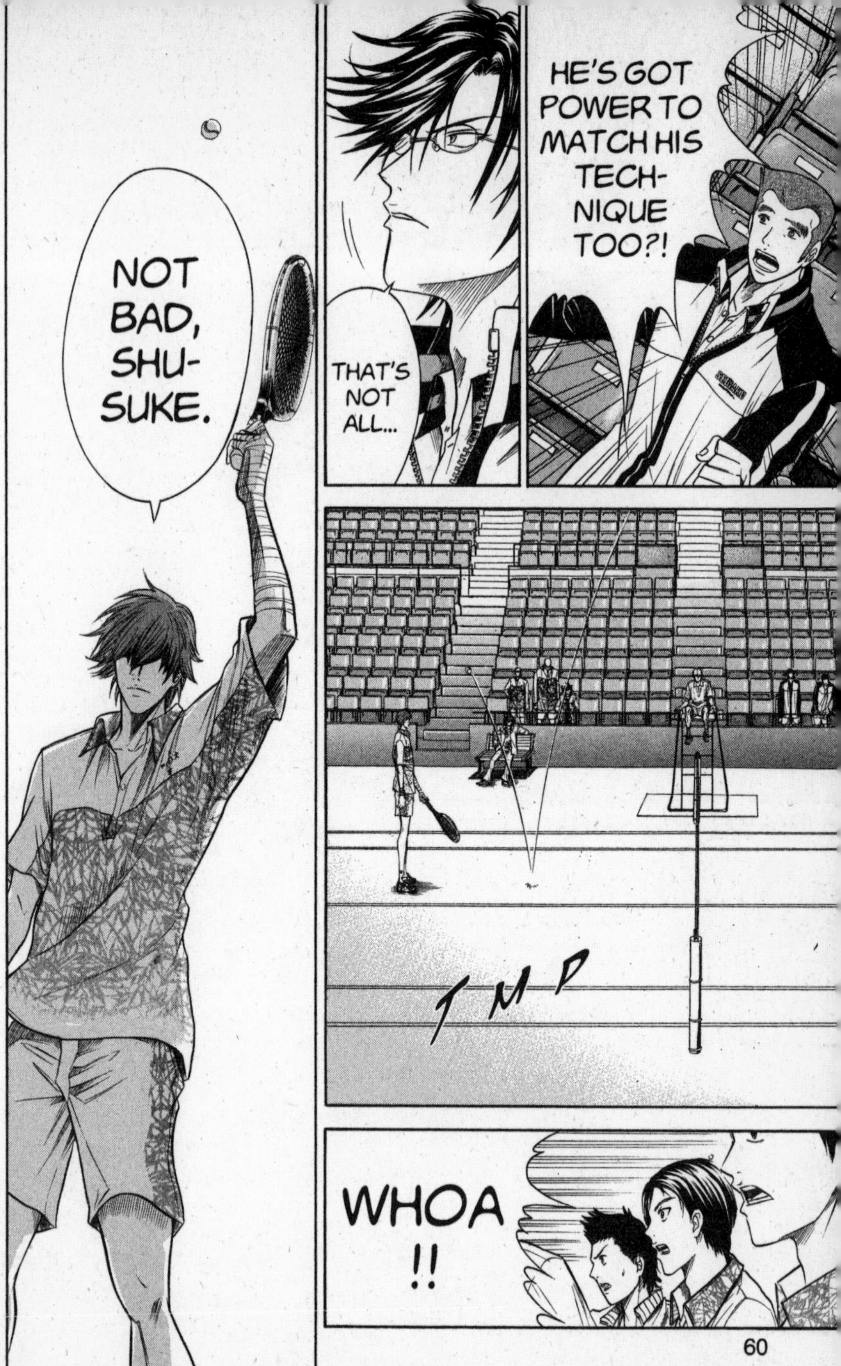
HE'S GOT POWER TO MATCH HIS TECHNIQUE TOO?!
THAT'S NOT ALL...
TMP
WHOA !!
NOT BAD, SHUSUKE.

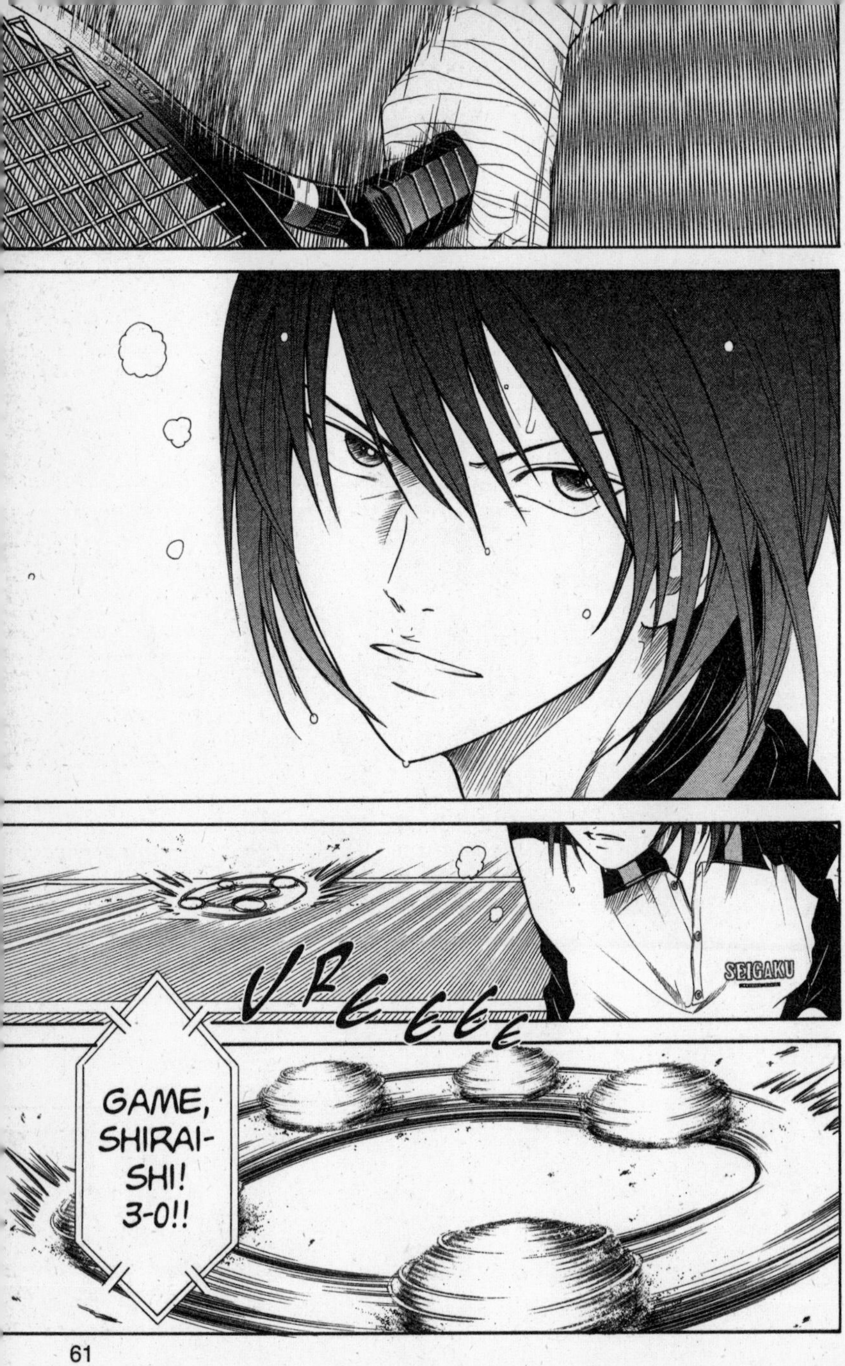

SEIGAKU
VREEEEE
GAME, SHIRAI-SHI! 3-0!!

テニスの王子様

THE PRINCE OF TENNIS

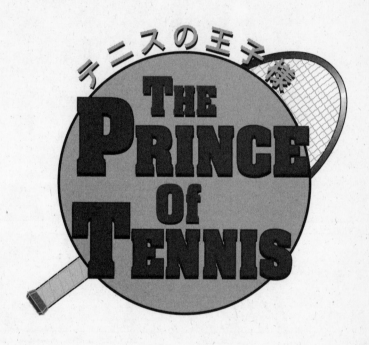

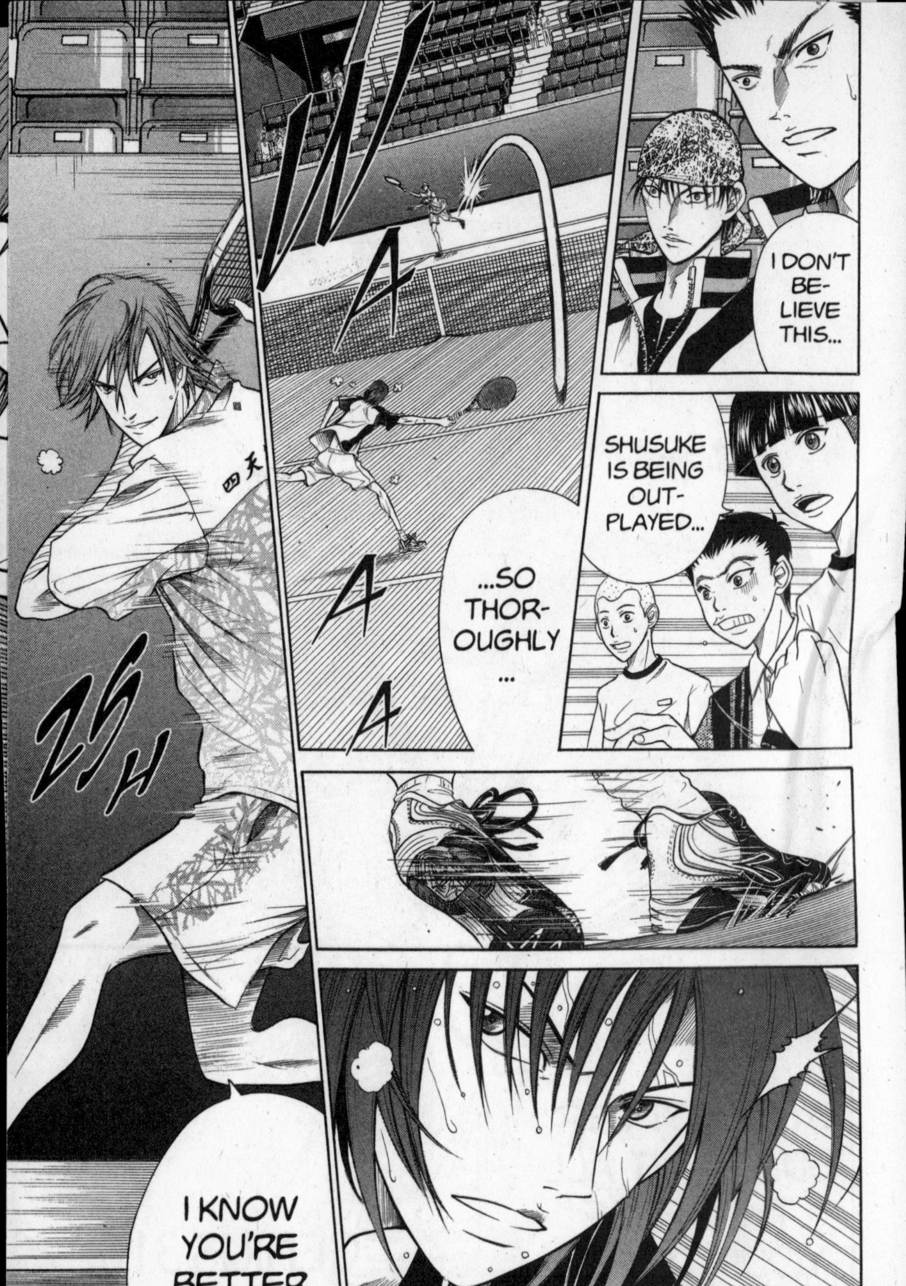
I DON'T BE-LIEVE THIS...
SHUSUKE IS BEING OUT-PLAYED...
...SO THOR-OUGHLY ...
WAAA
ZSH
I KNOW YOU'RE BETTER THAN THIS, SHUSUKE.

GENIUS 316: ONE RANK UP

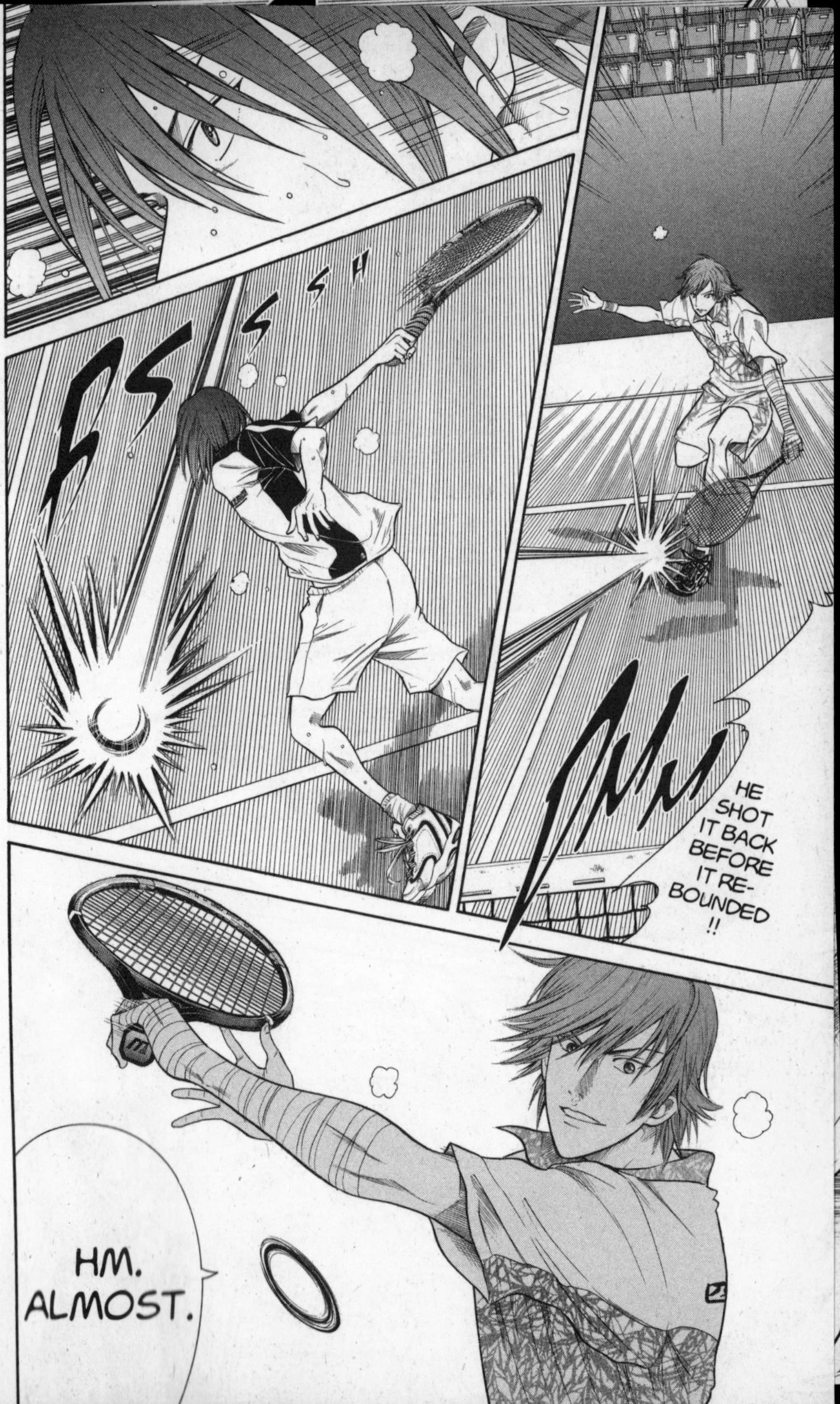
HE SHOT IT BACK BEFORE IT RE-BOUNDED!!
FSSSH
HM. ALMOST.

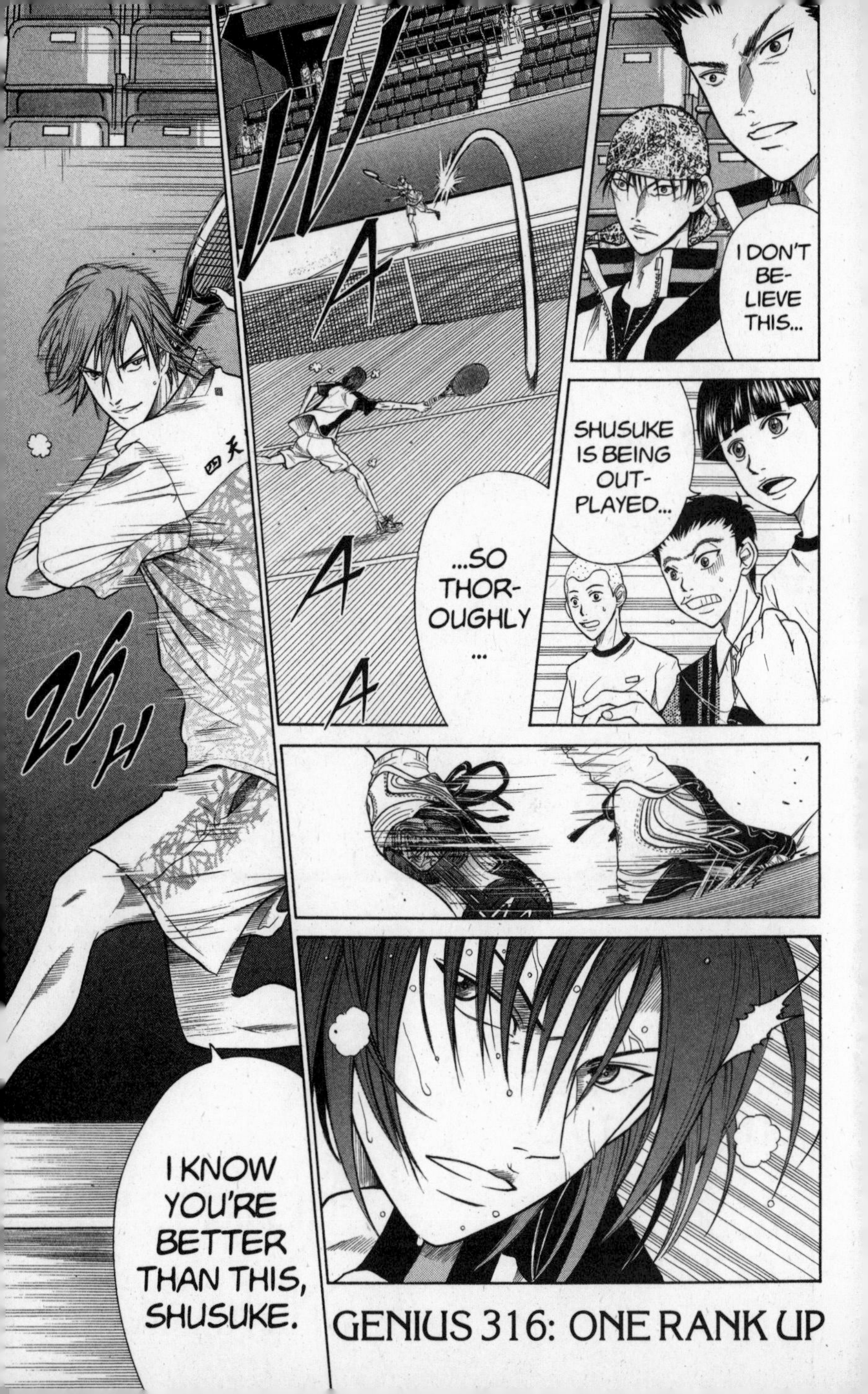
I DON'T BE-LIEVE THIS...
WAAA
SHUSUKE IS BEING OUT-PLAYED...
...SO THOR-OUGHLY...
ZSH
I KNOW YOU'RE BETTER THAN THIS, SHUSUKE.

GENIUS 316: ONE RANK UP

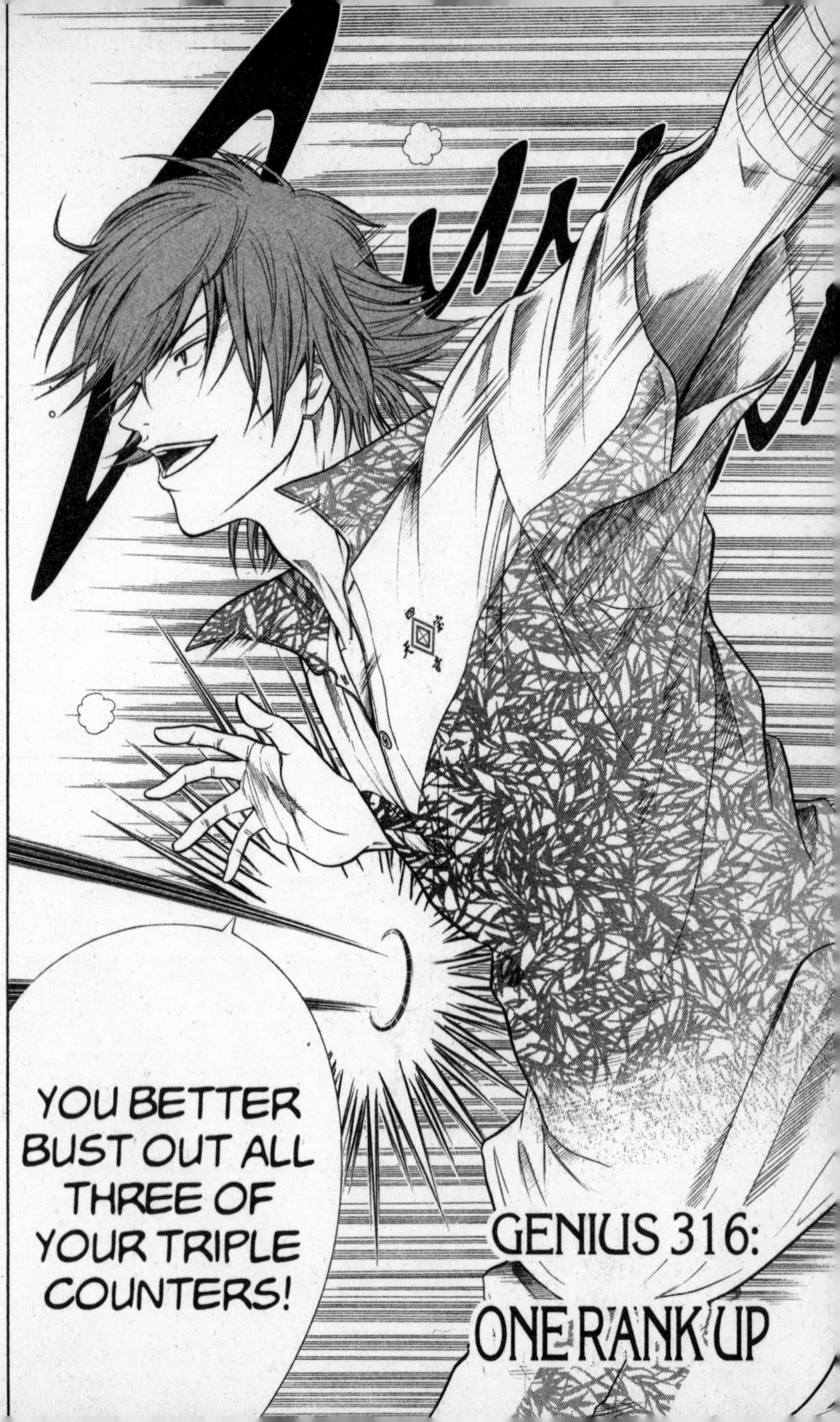
YOU BETTER BUST OUT ALL THREE OF YOUR TRIPLE COUNTERS!
GENIUS 316:
ONE RANK UP

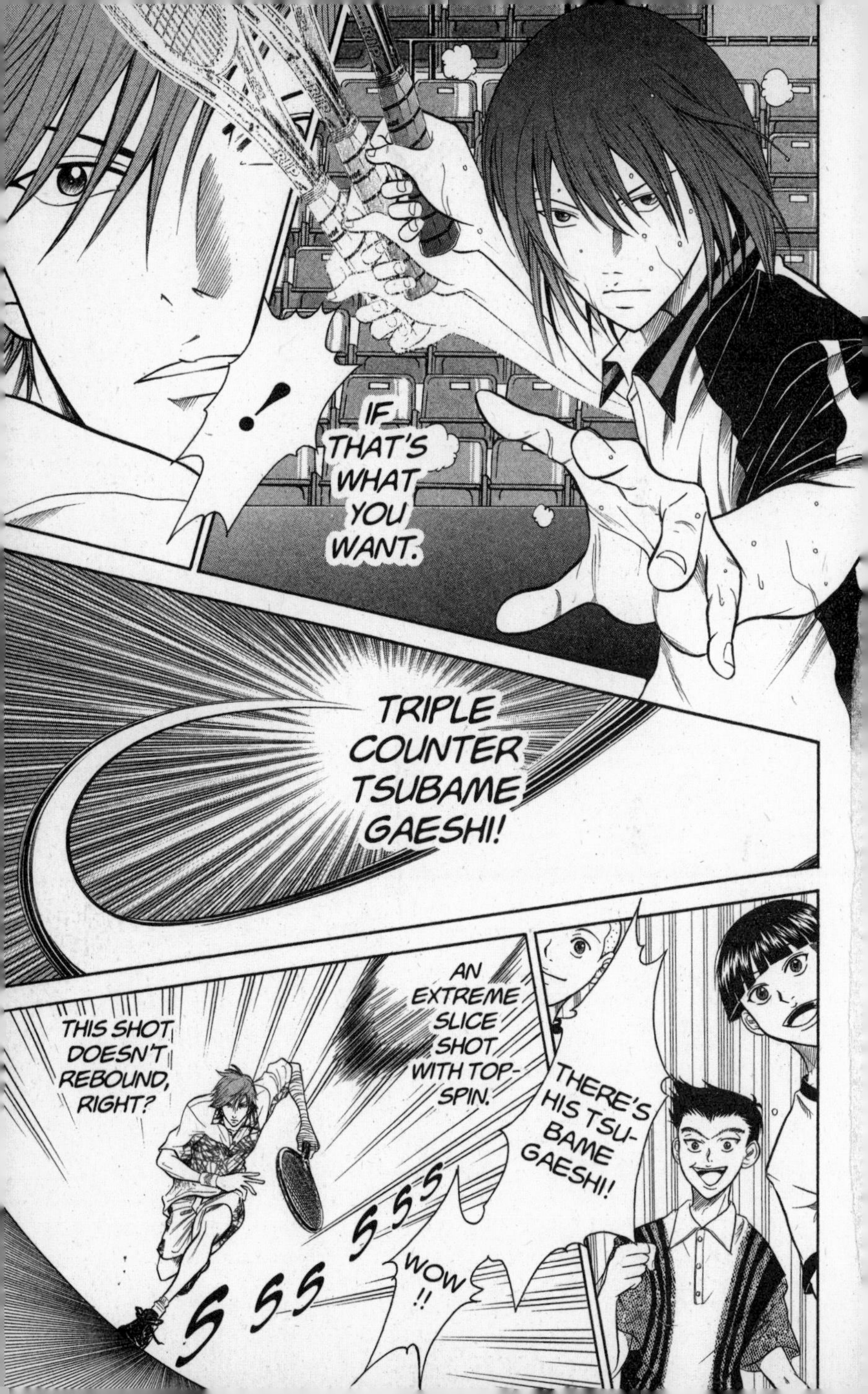
!
IF THAT'S WHAT YOU WANT.
TRIPLE COUNTER TSUBAME GAESHI!
THERE'S HIS TSU-BAME GAESHI!
AN EXTREME SLICE SHOT WITH TOP-SPIN.
THIS SHOT DOESN'T REBOUND, RIGHT?
WOW!!
SSS SSS SSS

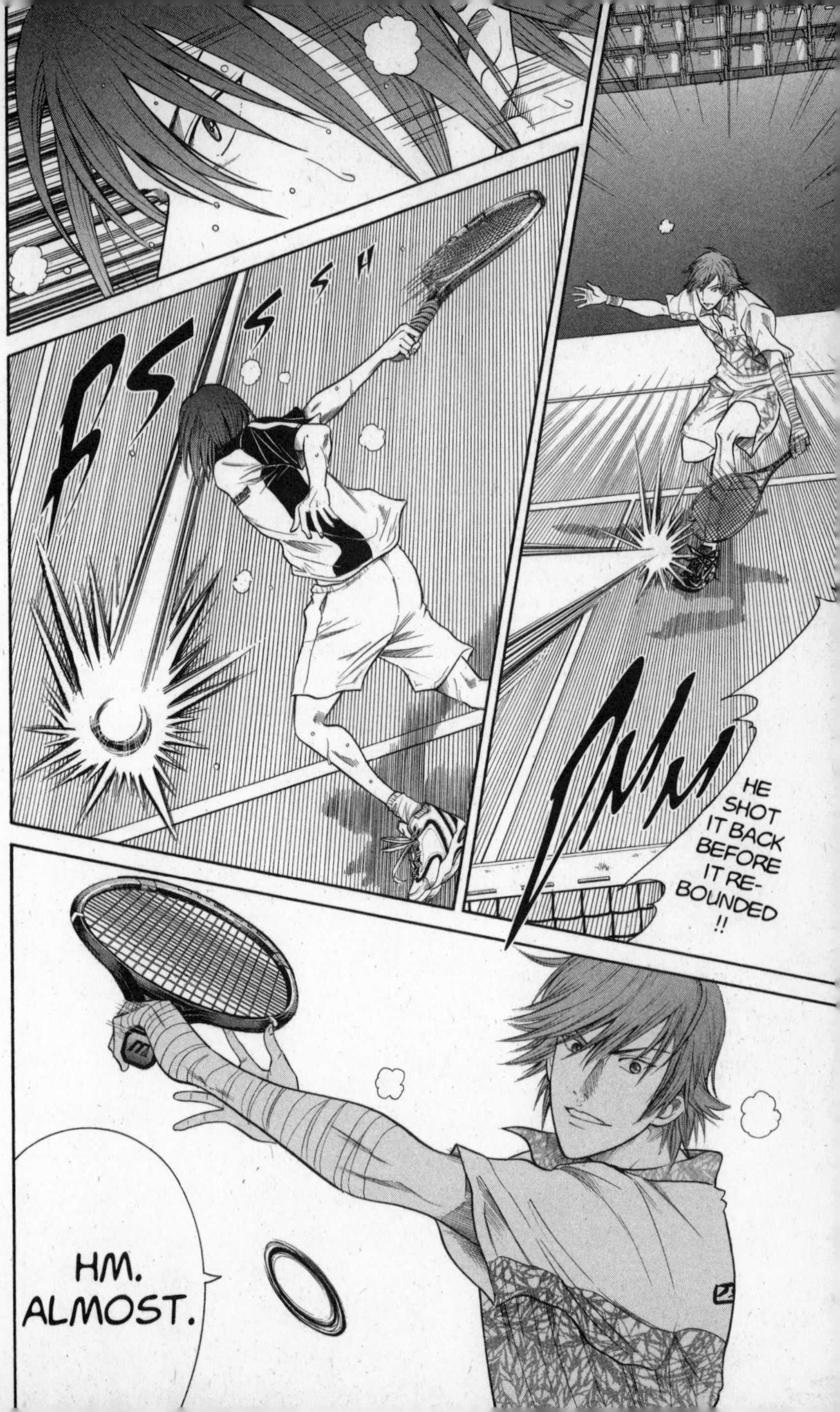
FSSSH
FS
HE SHOT IT BACK BEFORE IT REBOUNDED!!
HM. ALMOST.

テニスの王子様

THE PRINCE OF TENNIS

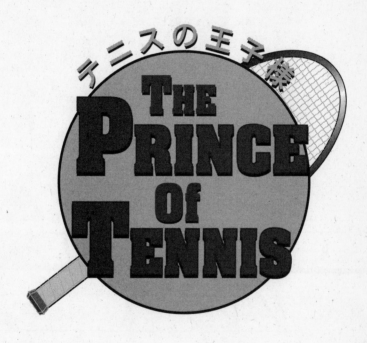

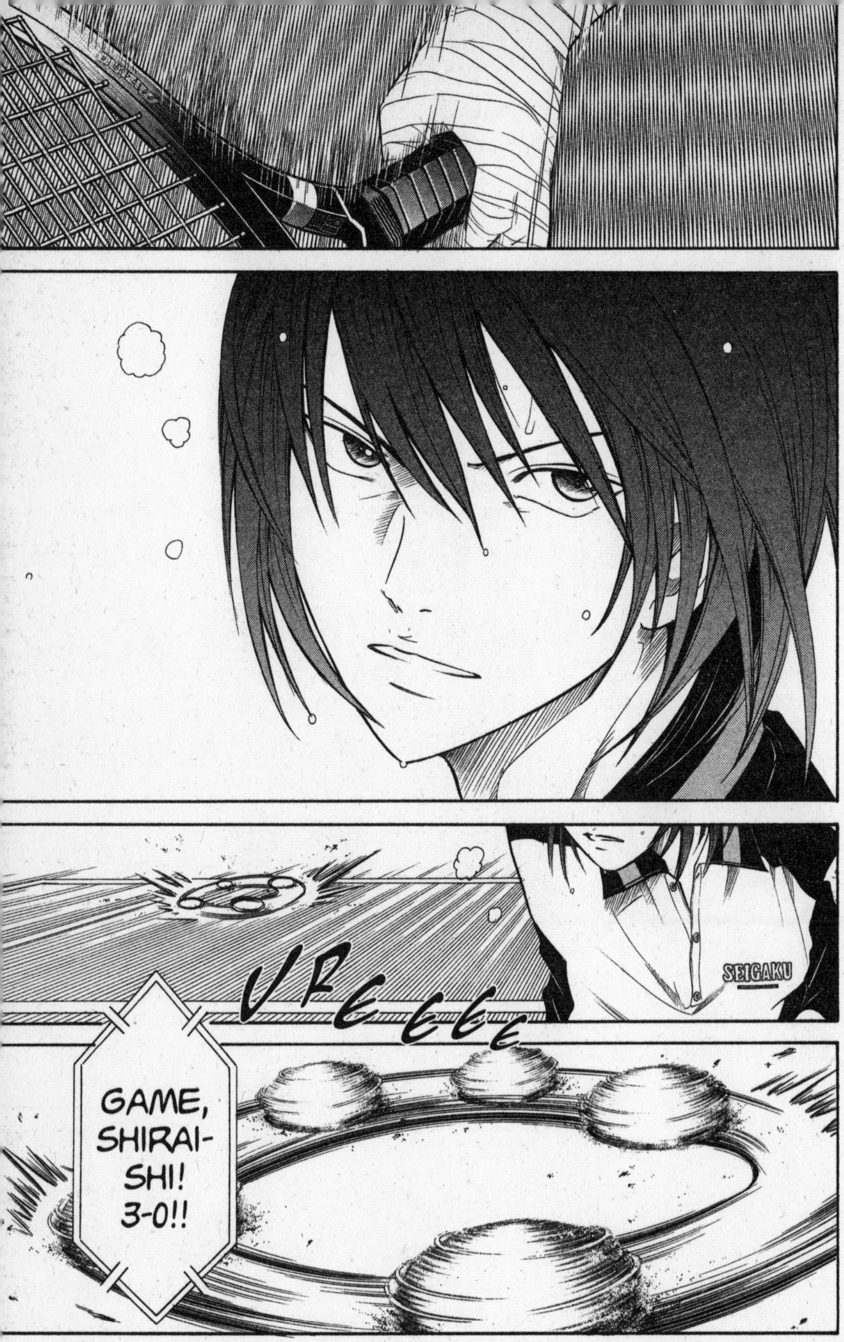
VREEEEE
GAME, SHIRAISHI! 3-0!!
SEIGAKU

テニスの王子様

THE PRINCE OF TENNIS

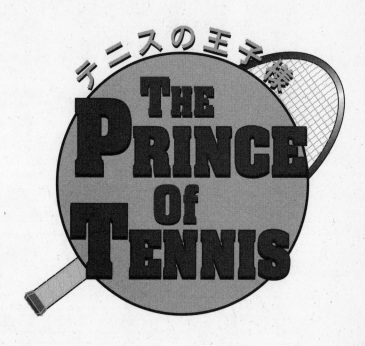

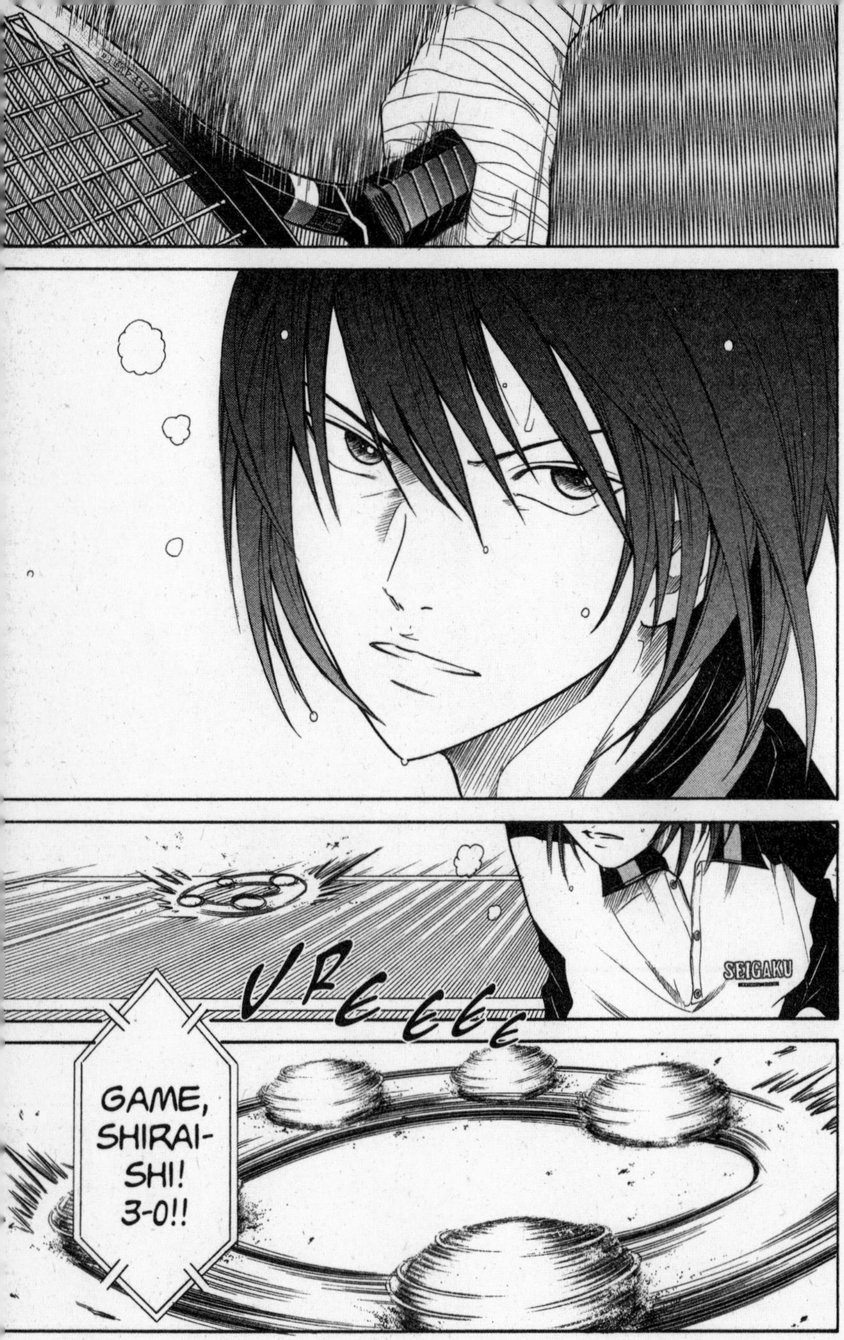
SEIGAKU
VREEEEE
GAME, SHIRAI-SHI! 3-0!!

テニスの王子様

THE PRINCE OF TENNIS

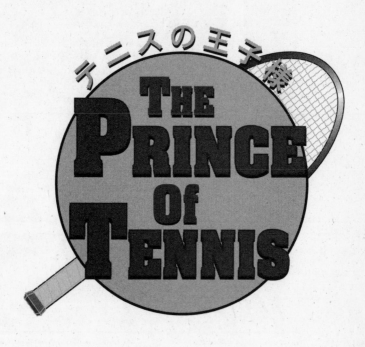

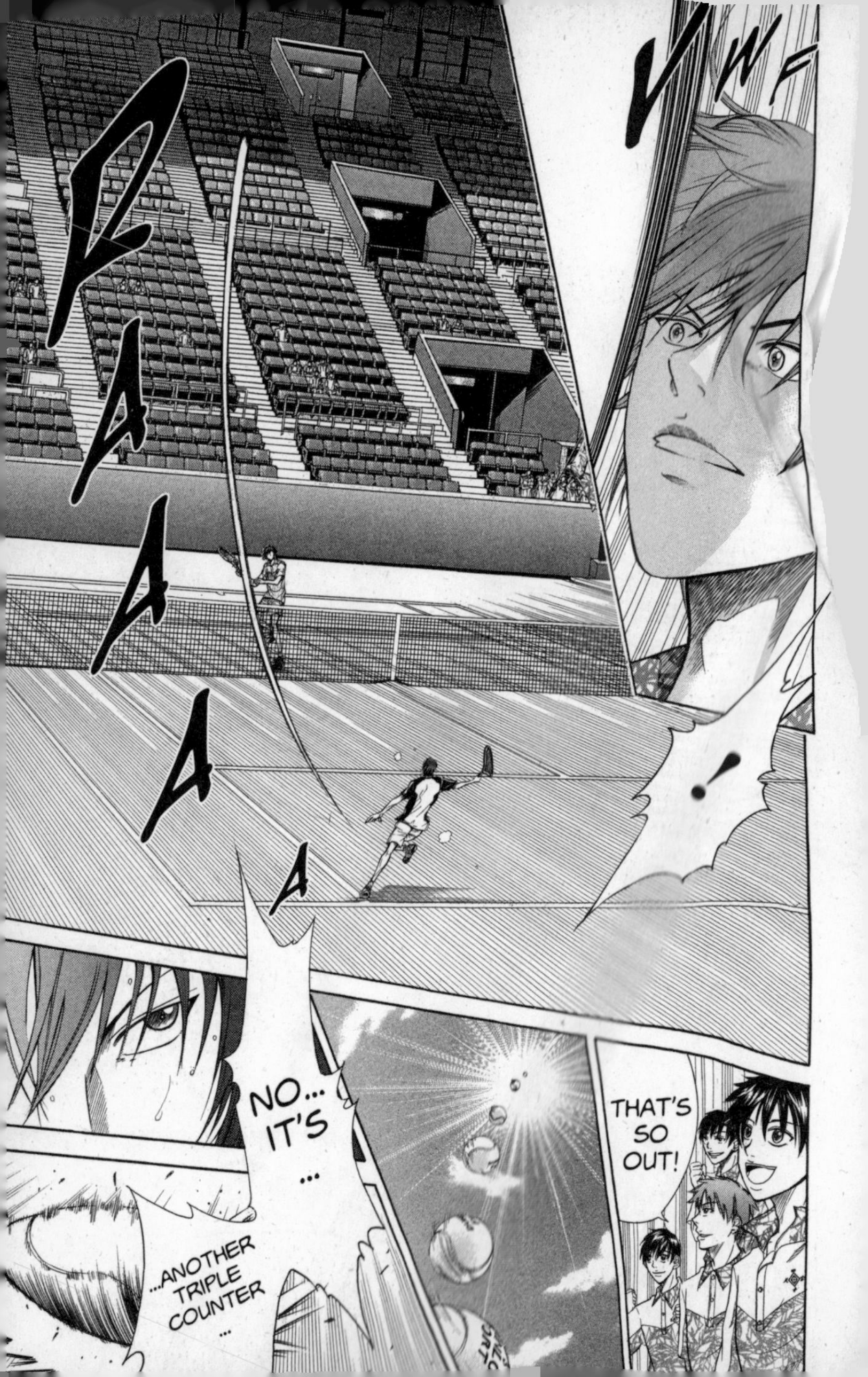
VWF
!
THAT'S SO OUT!
NO... IT'S ...
...ANOTHER TRIPLE COUNTER ...

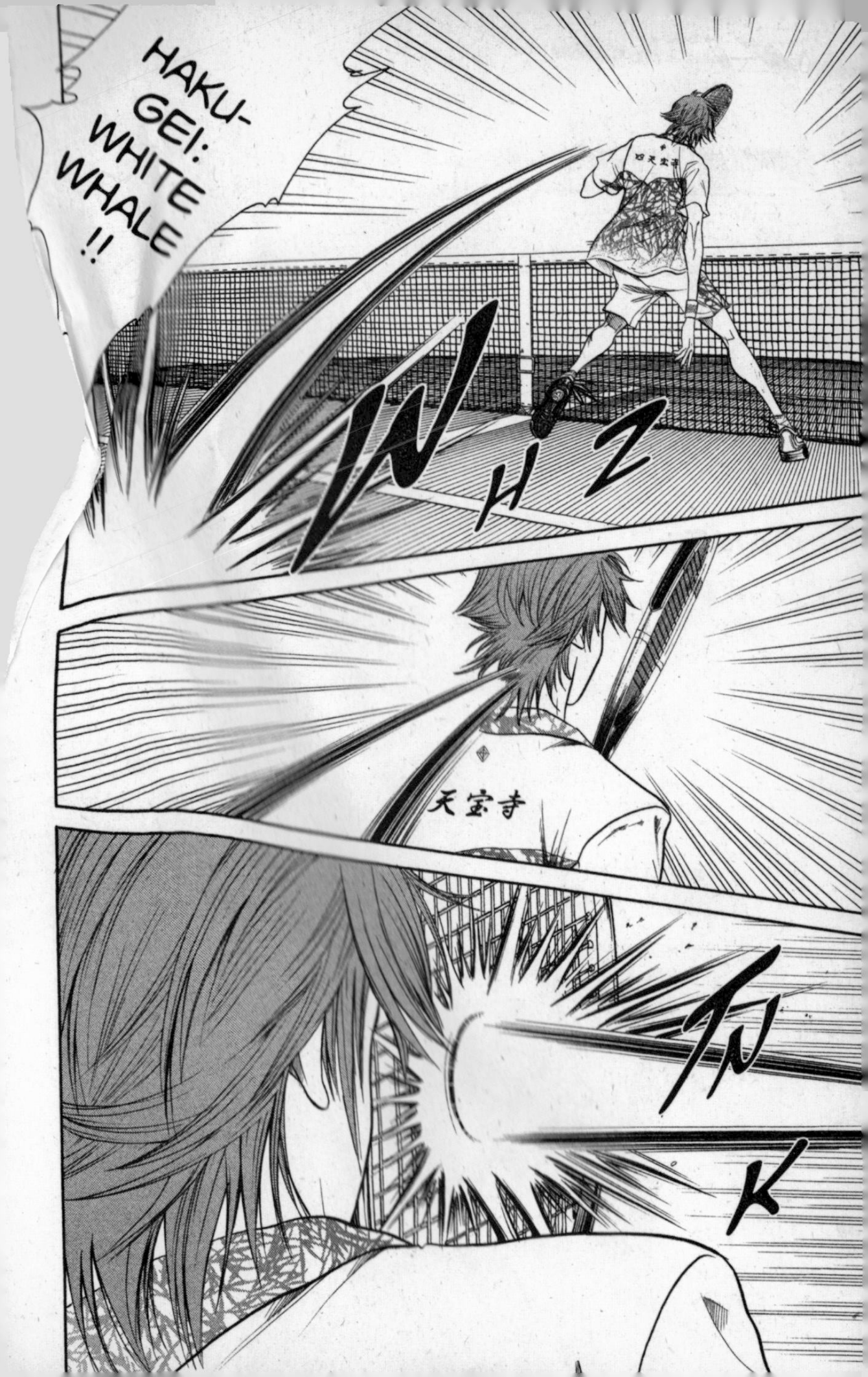
HAKU-GEI: WHITE WHALE!!
WHIZ
TNK

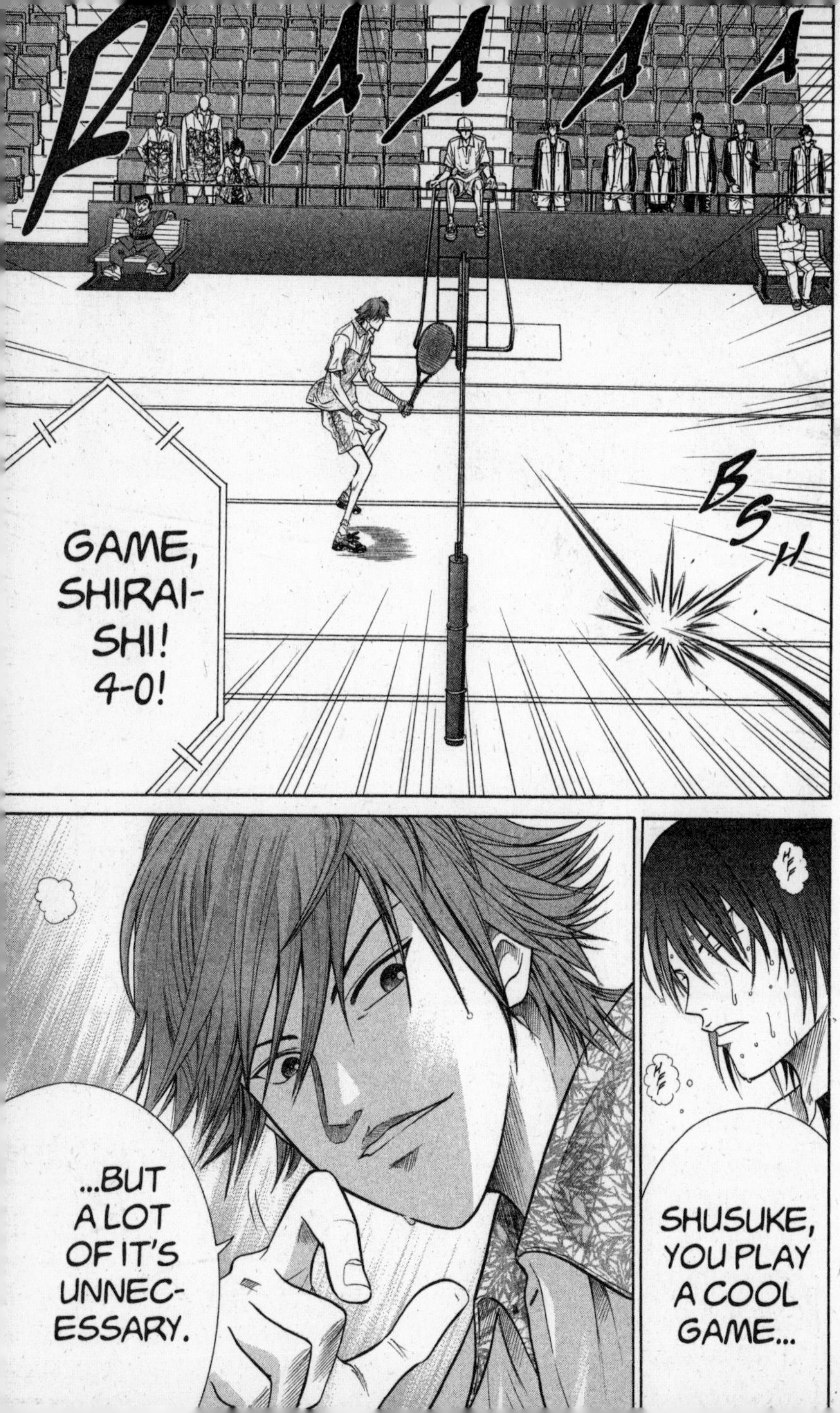
PAAAA
BSH
GAME, SHIRAI-SHI! 4-0!
HFF
HFF
SHUSUKE, YOU PLAY A COOL GAME...
...BUT A LOT OF IT'S UNNEC-ESSARY.

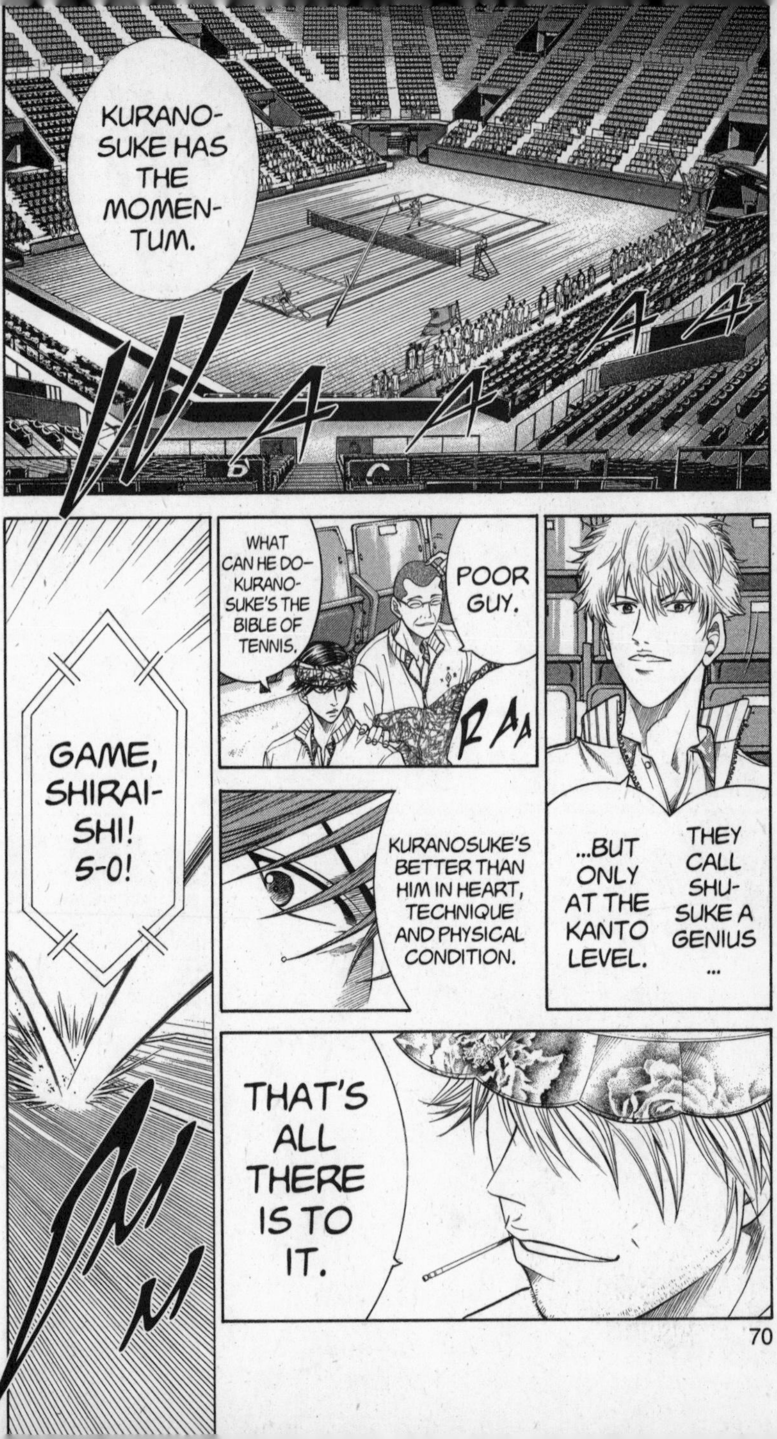

KURANOSUKE HAS THE MOMENTUM.
WAAAA
THEY CALL SHUSUKE A GENIUS...
...BUT ONLY AT THE KANTO LEVEL.
POOR GUY.
WHAT CAN HE DO— KURANOSUKE'S THE BIBLE OF TENNIS.
RAA
KURANOSUKE'S BETTER THAN HIM IN HEART, TECHNIQUE AND PHYSICAL CONDITION.
GAME, SHIRAISHI! 5-0!
THAT'S ALL THERE IS TO IT.

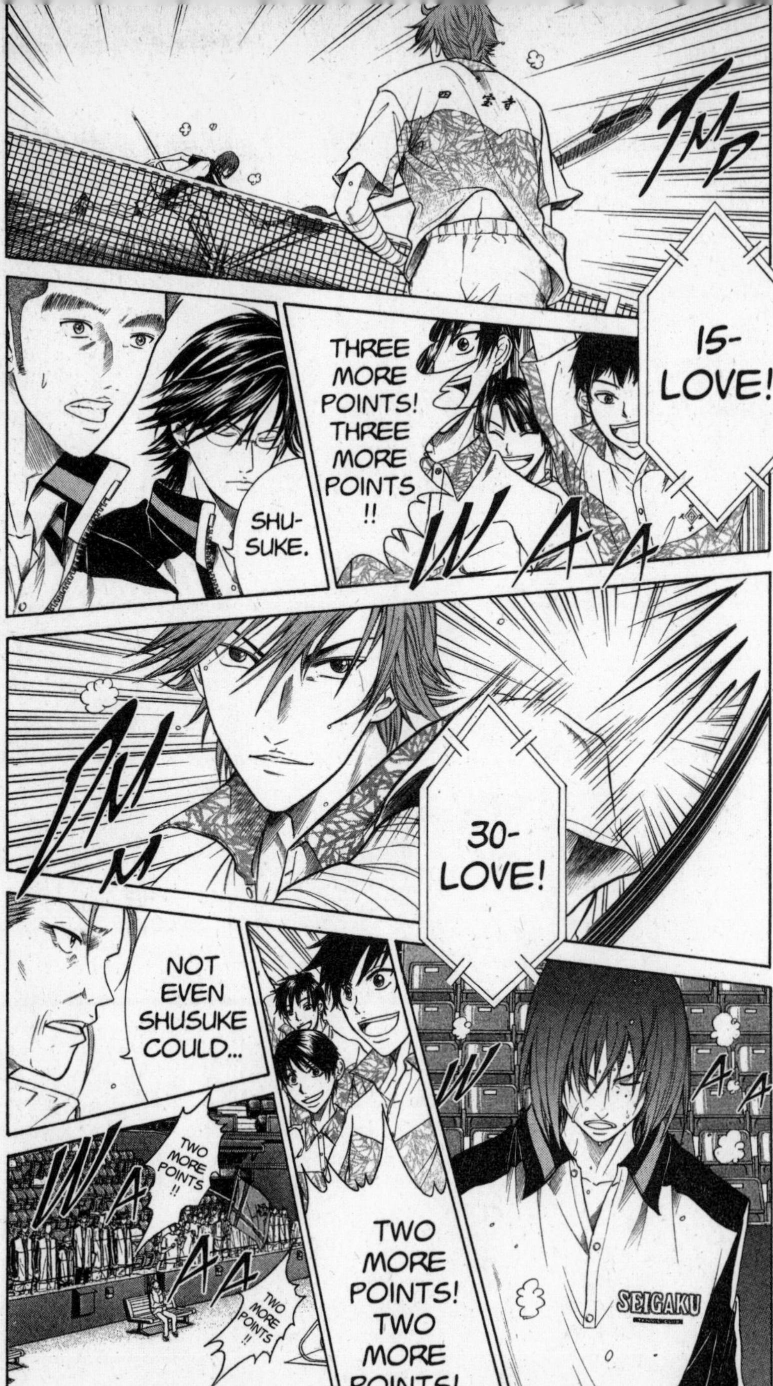
TMP
15-LOVE!
THREE MORE POINTS! THREE MORE POINTS!!
WAA
SHU-SUKE.
30-LOVE!
TMM
WAA
SEIGAKU
TWO MORE POINTS! TWO MORE POINTS!
NOT EVEN SHUSUKE COULD...
WAA
TWO MORE POINTS!!
TWO MORE POINTS!!

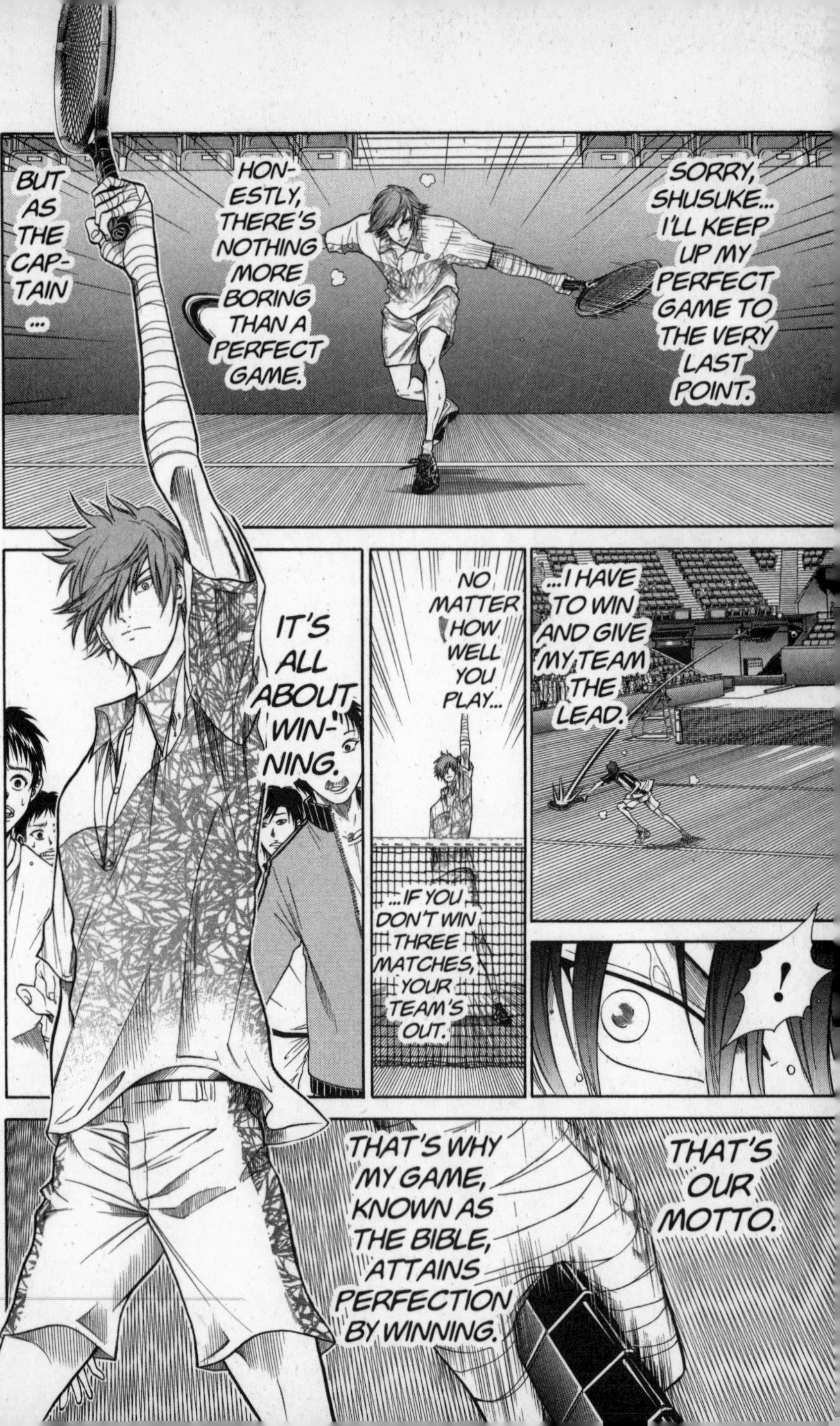
SORRY, SHUSUKE... I'LL KEEP UP MY PERFECT GAME TO THE VERY LAST POINT.
HON-ESTLY, THERE'S NOTHING MORE BORING THAN A PERFECT GAME.
BUT AS THE CAP-TAIN...
...I HAVE TO WIN AND GIVE MY TEAM THE LEAD.
!
NO MATTER HOW WELL YOU PLAY...
...IF YOU DON'T WIN THREE MATCHES, YOUR TEAM'S OUT.
IT'S ALL ABOUT WIN-NING.
THAT'S OUR MOTTO.
THAT'S WHY MY GAME, KNOWN AS THE BIBLE, ATTAINS PERFECTION BY WINNING.

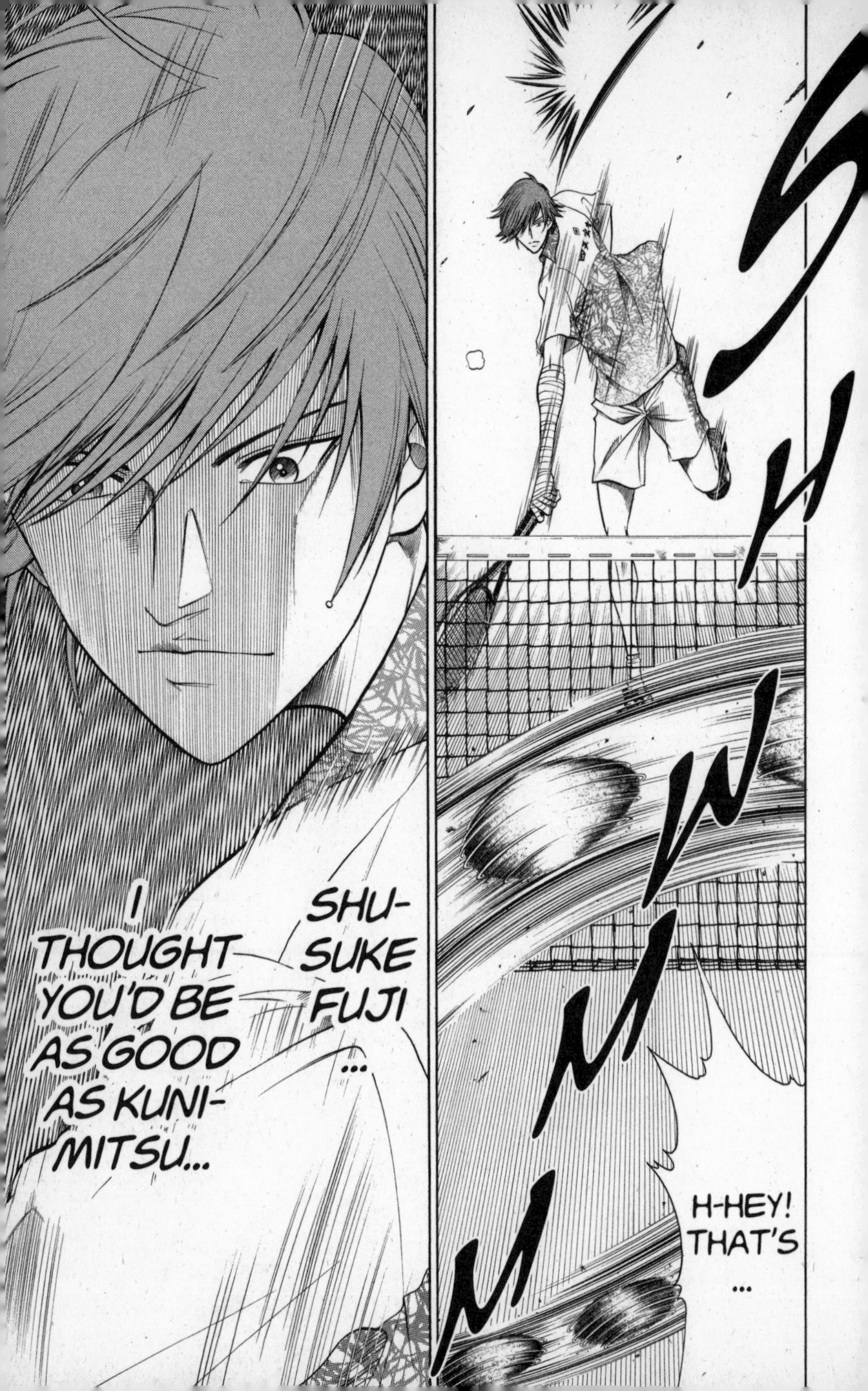
SHWMMM
H-HEY! THAT'S ...
SHUSUKE FUJI ...
I THOUGHT YOU'D BE AS GOOD AS KUNIMITSU...

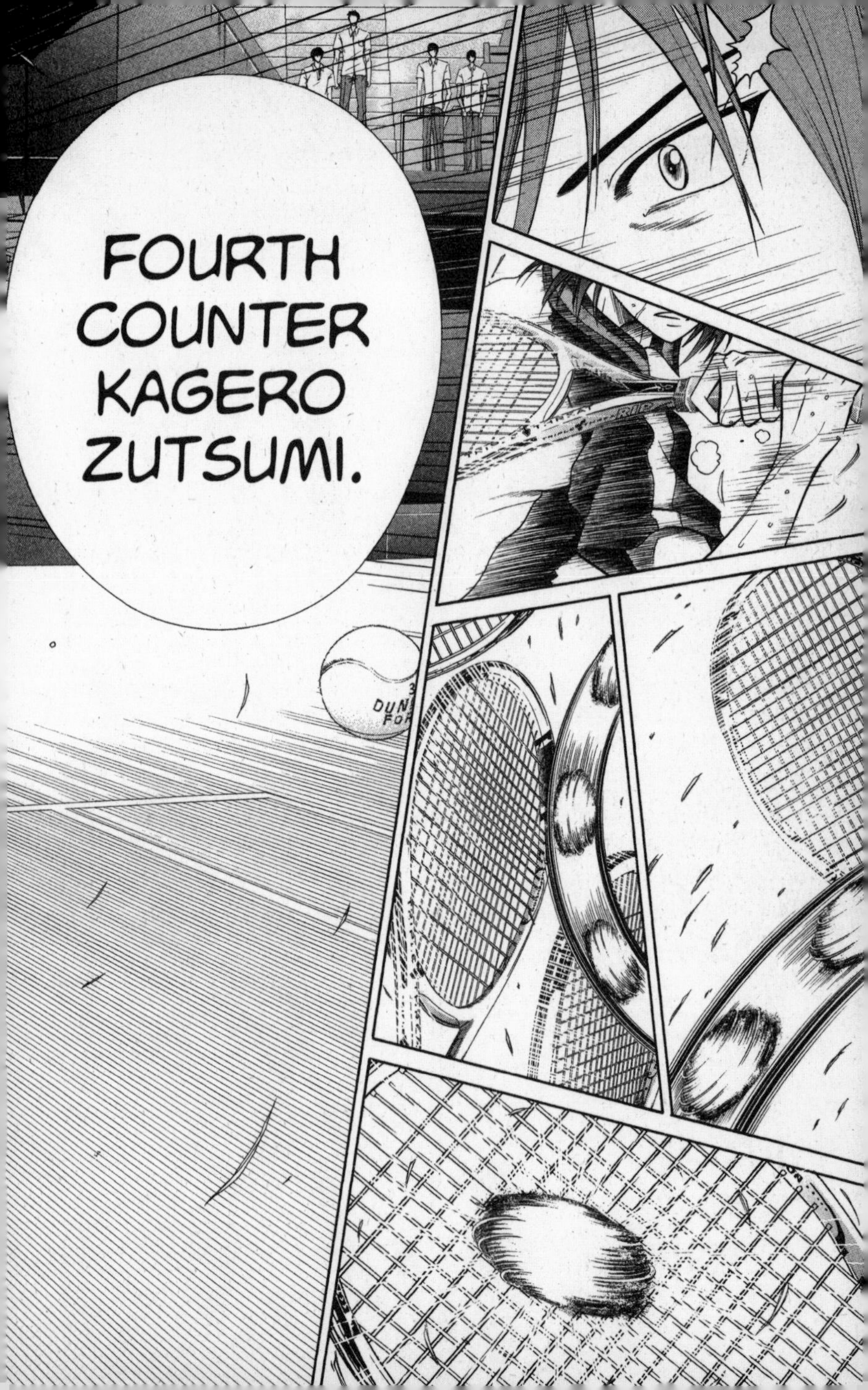
FOURTH COUNTER KAGERO ZUTSUMI.

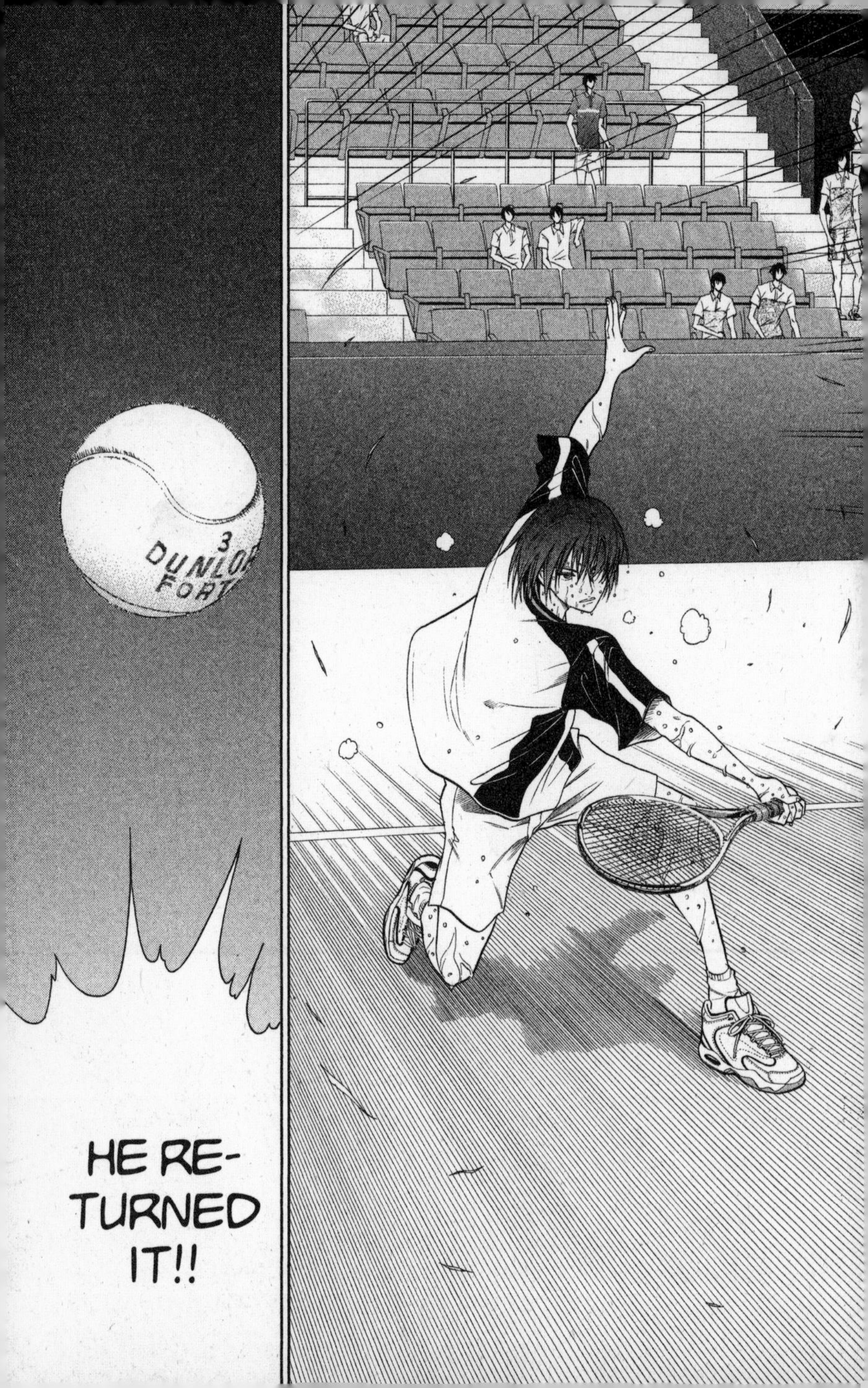
HE RE-TURNED IT!!

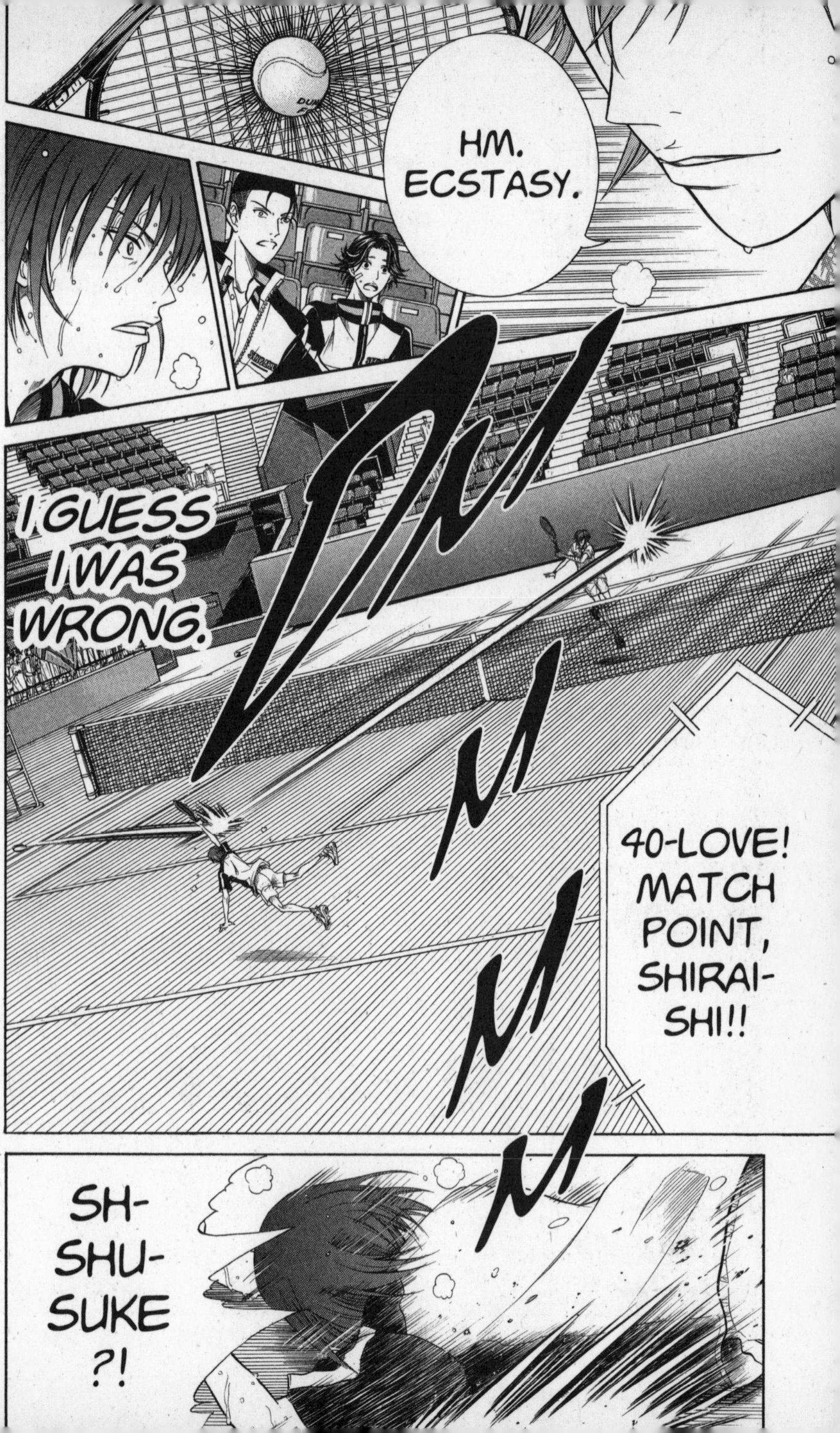
HM. ECSTASY.
I GUESS I WAS WRONG.
40-LOVE! MATCH POINT, SHIRAI-SHI!!
SH-SHU-SUKE ?!

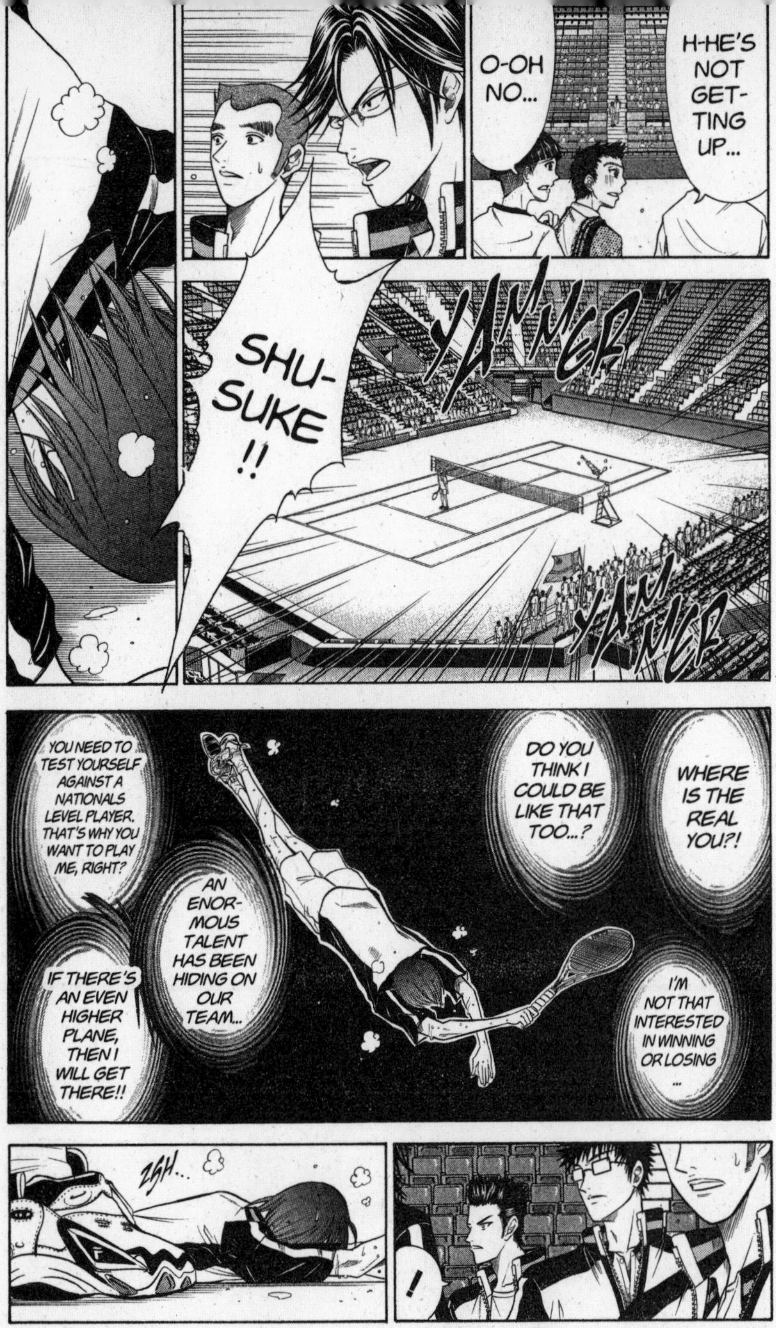
H-HE'S NOT GET-TING UP...
O-OH NO...
SHU-SUKE!!
YAMMER
YAMMER
WHERE IS THE REAL YOU?!
DO YOU THINK I COULD BE LIKE THAT TOO...?
I'M NOT THAT INTERESTED IN WINNING OR LOSING...
YOU NEED TO TEST YOURSELF AGAINST A NATIONALS LEVEL PLAYER. THAT'S WHY YOU WANT TO PLAY ME, RIGHT?
AN ENOR-MOUS TALENT HAS BEEN HIDING ON OUR TEAM...
IF THERE'S AN EVEN HIGHER PLANE, THEN I WILL GET THERE!!
!
ZSH...

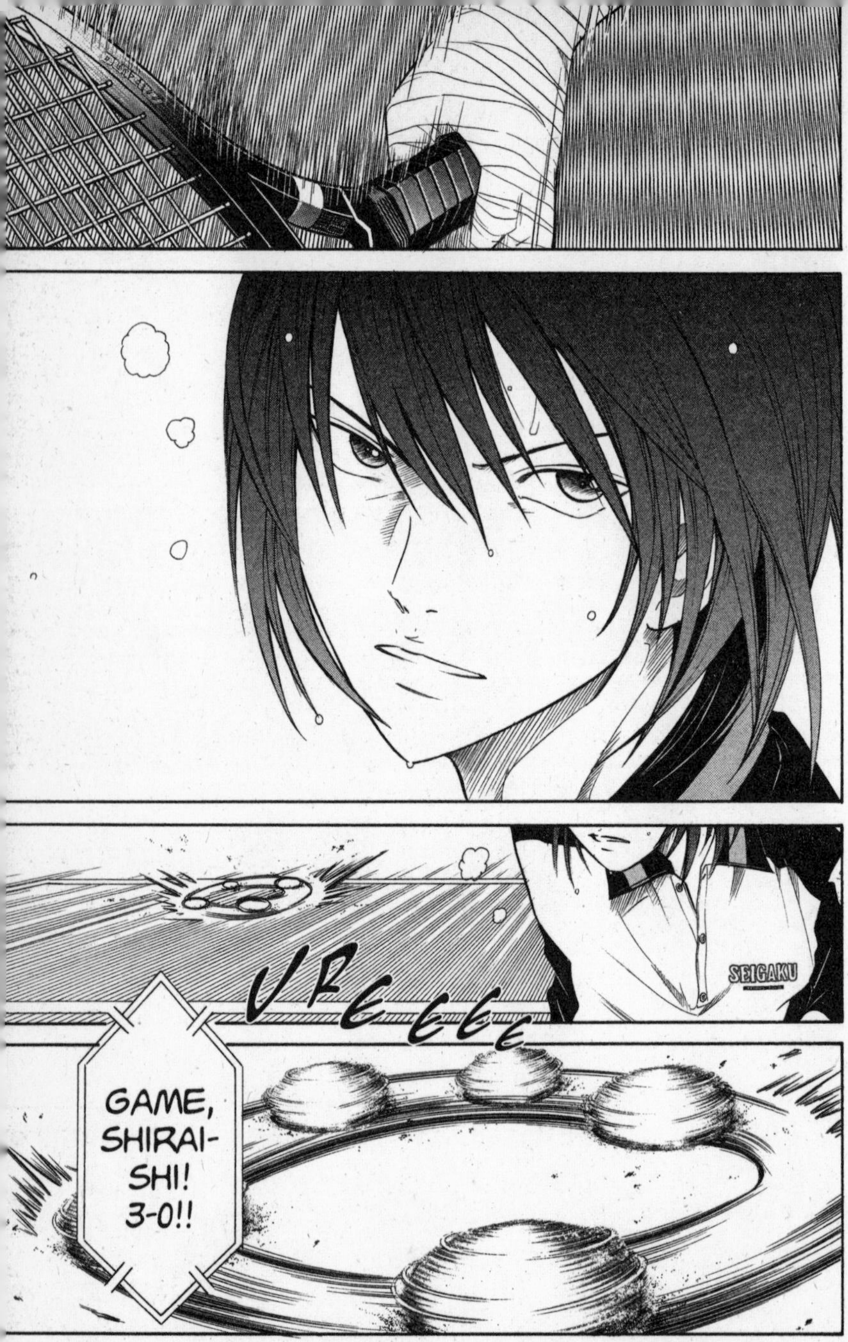
SEIGAKU
VREEEEE
GAME, SHIRAI-SHI! 3-0!!

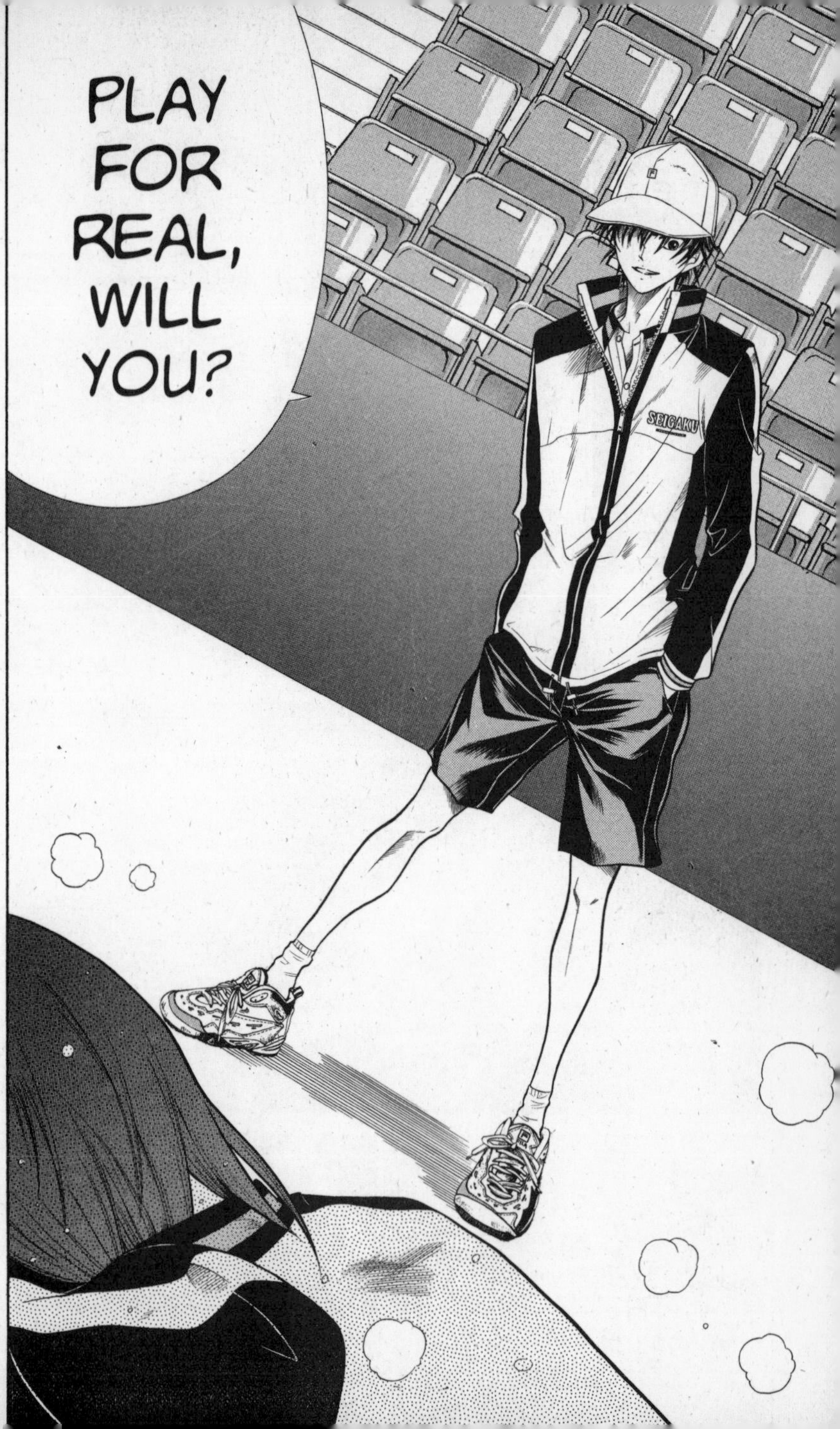
PLAY FOR REAL, WILL YOU?
SEIGAKU

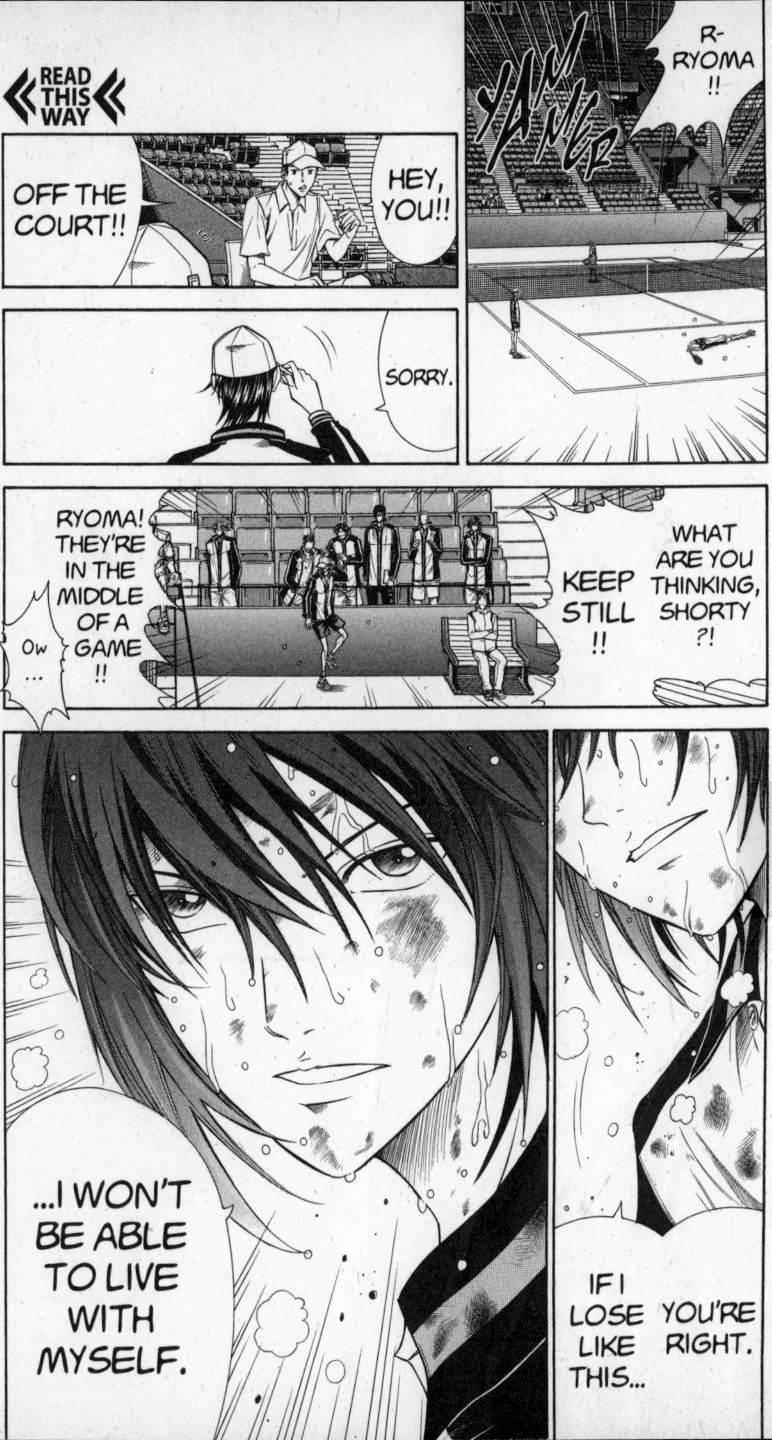
READ THIS WAY
R-RYOMA!!
YAMMER
HEY, YOU!!
OFF THE COURT!!
SORRY.
WHAT ARE YOU THINKING, SHORTY?!
KEEP STILL!!
RYOMA! THEY'RE IN THE MIDDLE OF A GAME!!
Ow...
YOU'RE RIGHT.
IF I LOSE LIKE THIS...
...I WON'T BE ABLE TO LIVE WITH MYSELF.

テニスの王子様

THE PRINCE OF TENNIS

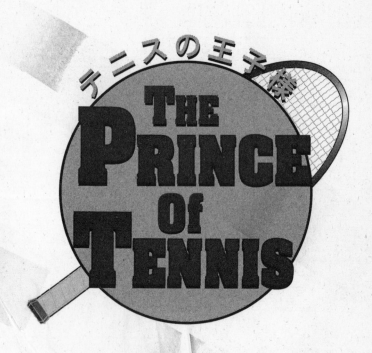

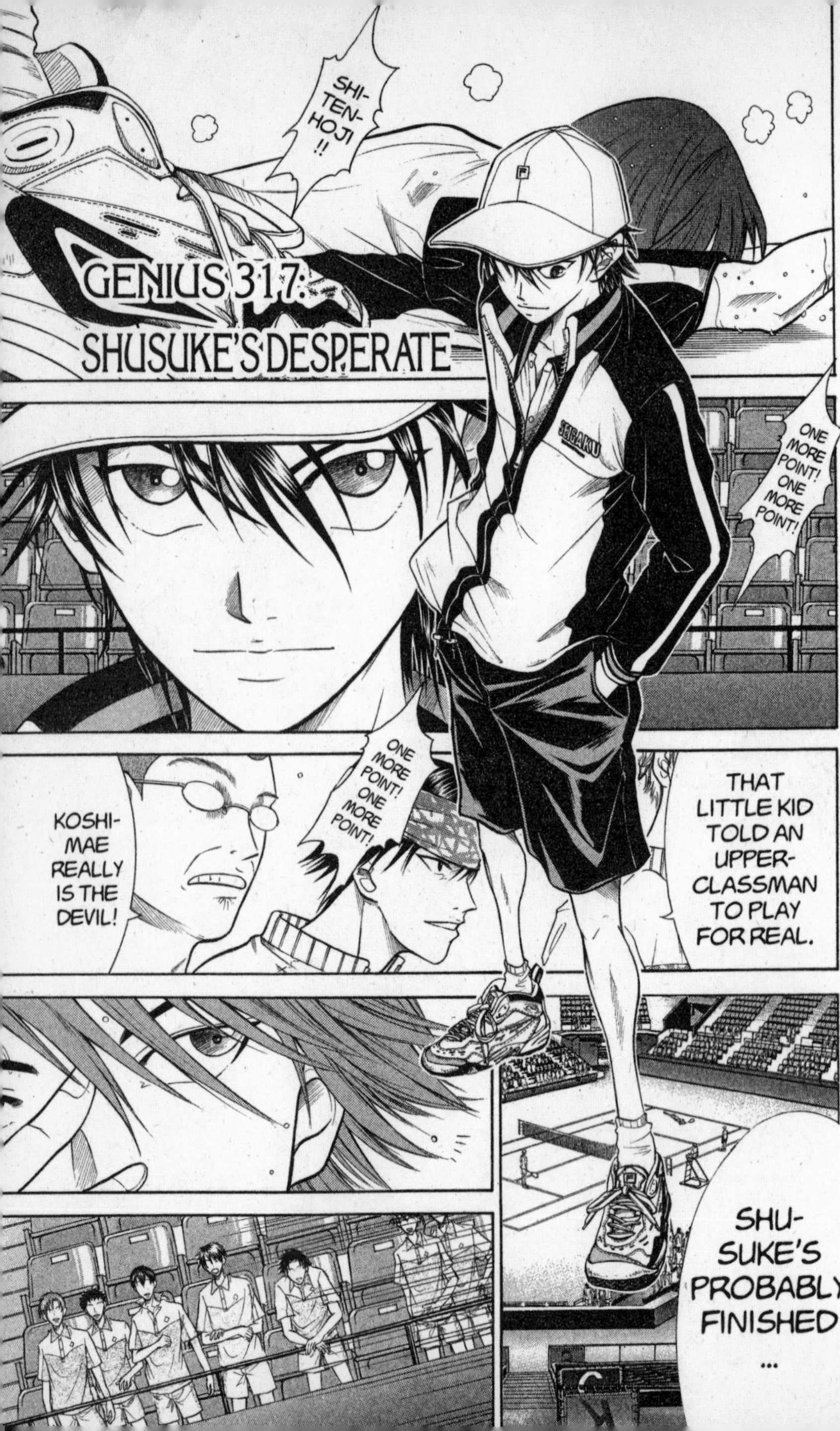
SHI-TEN-HOJI!!
GENIUS 317: SHUSUKE'S DESPERATE
ONE MORE POINT! ONE MORE POINT!
THAT LITTLE KID TOLD AN UPPER-CLASSMAN TO PLAY FOR REAL.
ONE MORE POINT! ONE MORE POINT!
KOSHI-MAE REALLY IS THE DEVIL!
SHU-SUKE'S PROBABLY FINISHED ...

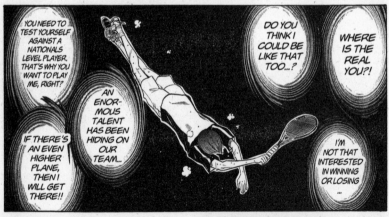

77

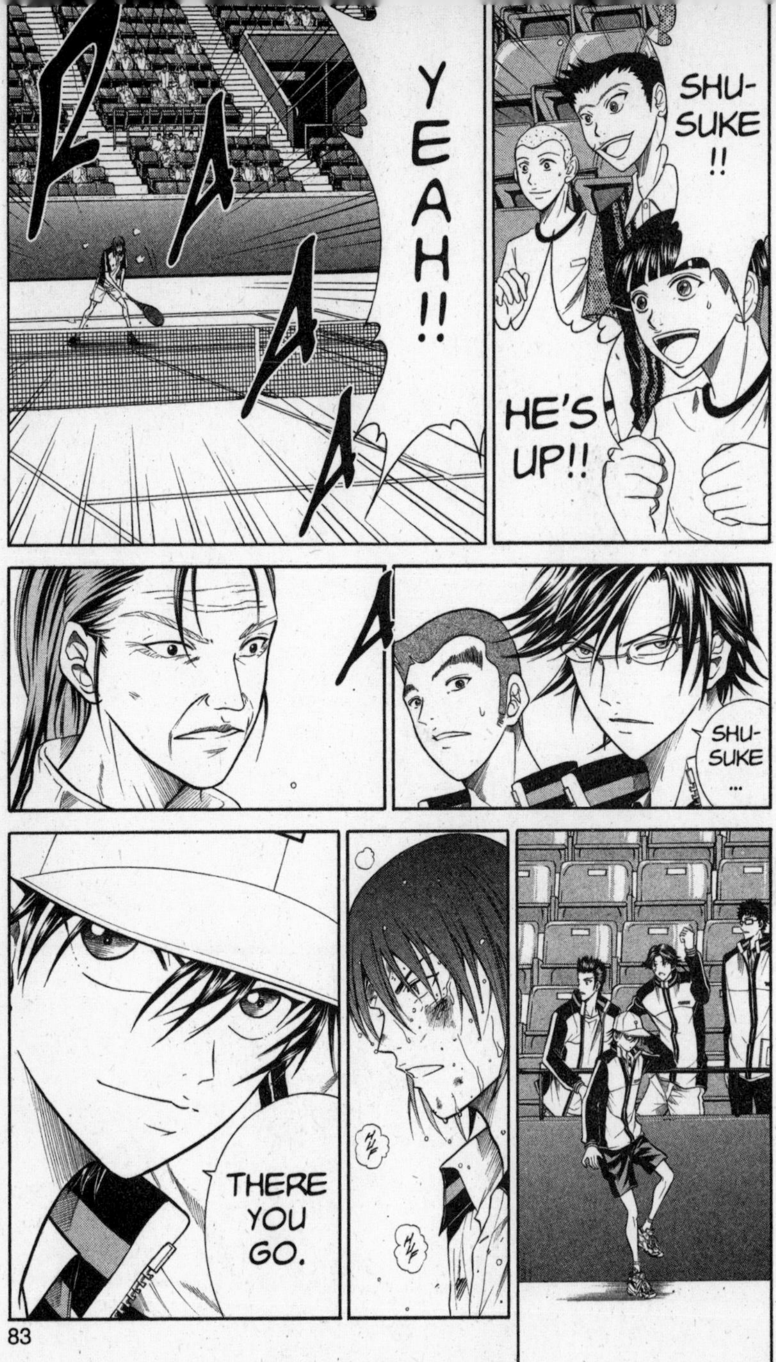
SHU-SUKE!!
HE'S UP!!
YEAH!!
SHU-SUKE...
THERE YOU GO.

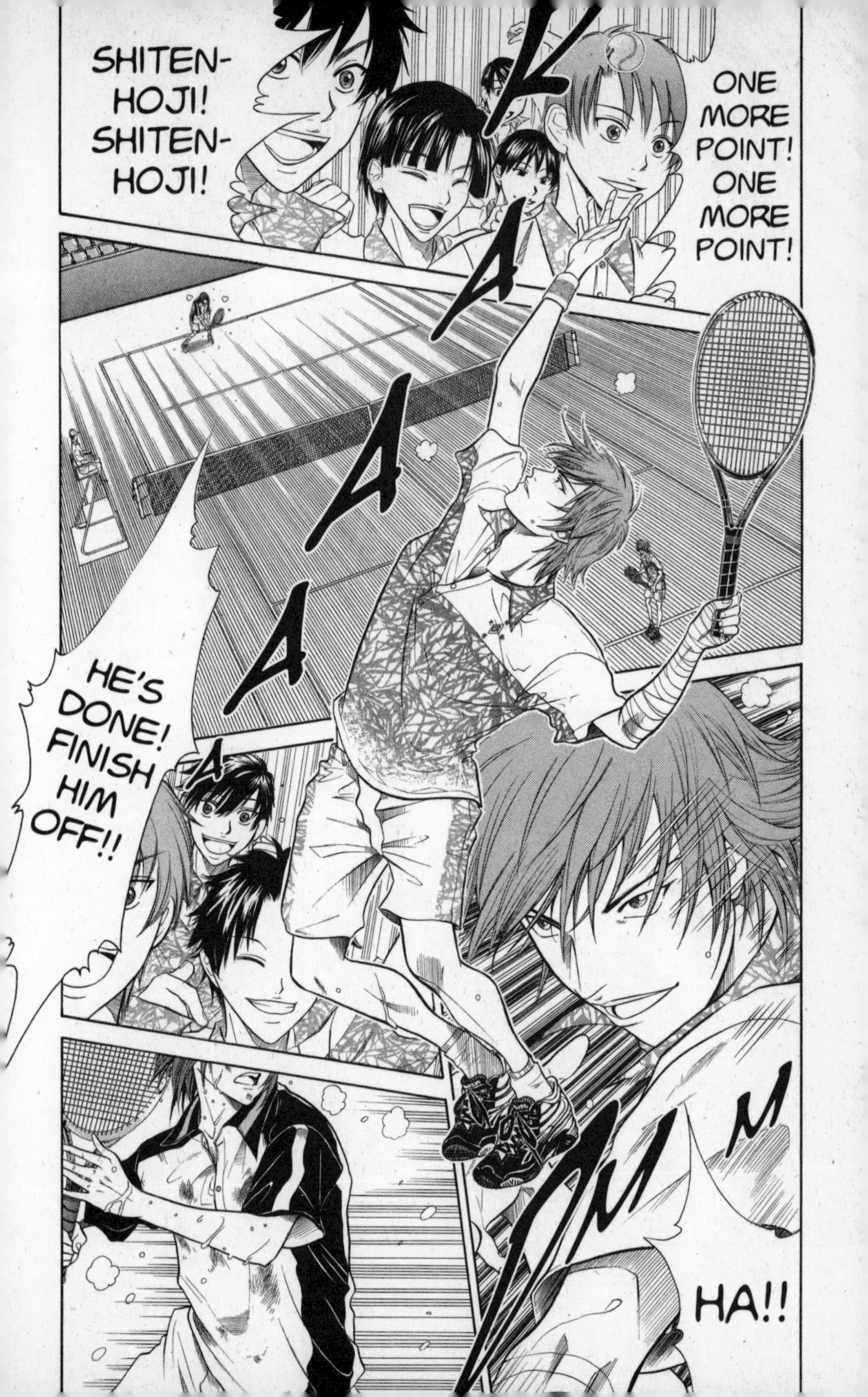
ONE MORE POINT! ONE MORE POINT!
SHITEN-HOJI! SHITEN-HOJI!
KAAAAAA
HE'S DONE! FINISH HIM OFF!!
MMM
HA!!

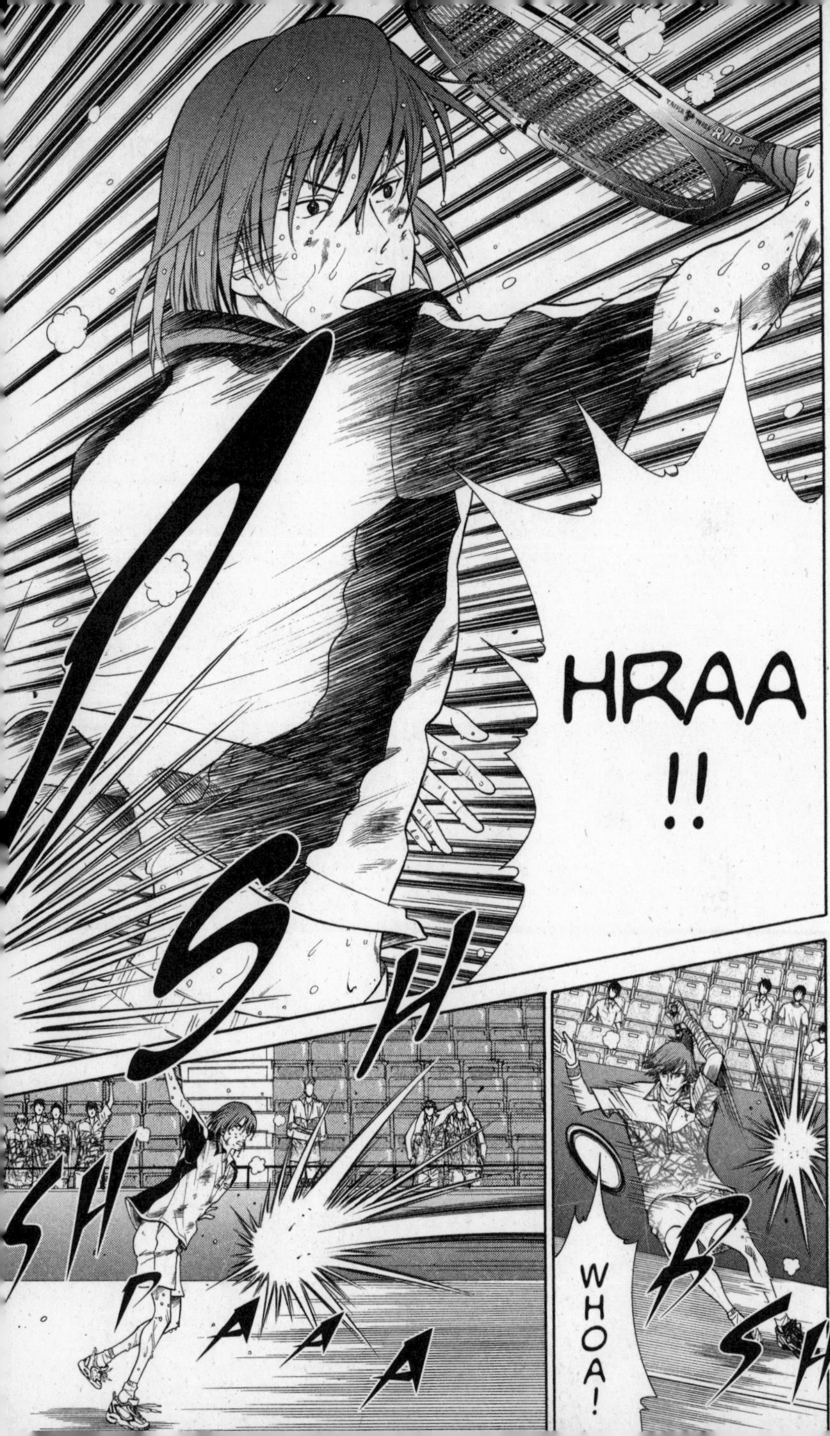
HRAA !!
WHOA!

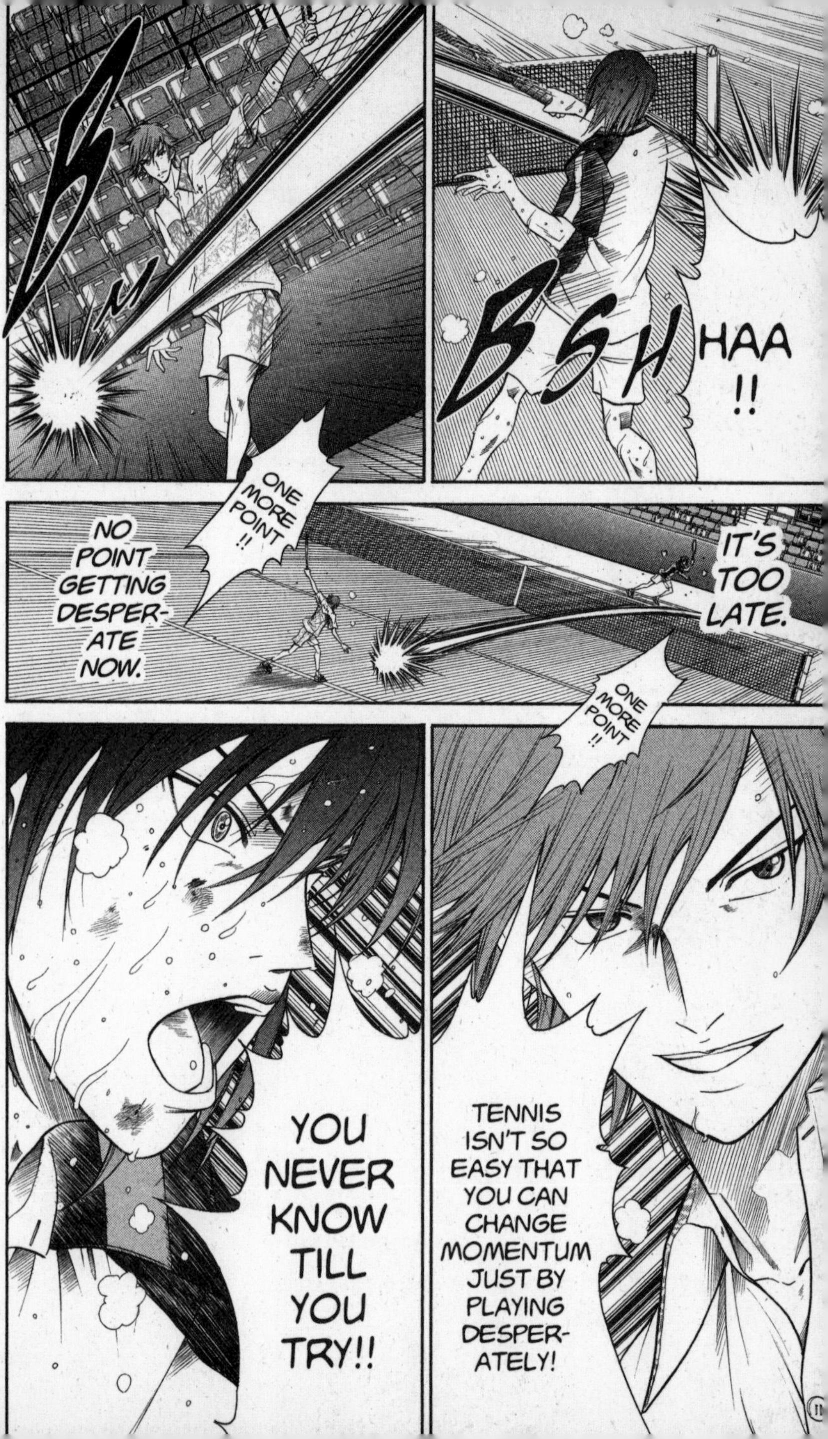
BSH
HAA!!
Bu
IT'S TOO LATE.
ONE MORE POINT!!
NO POINT GETTING DESPER-ATE NOW.
ONE MORE POINT!!
TENNIS ISN'T SO EASY THAT YOU CAN CHANGE MOMENTUM JUST BY PLAYING DESPER-ATELY!
YOU NEVER KNOW TILL YOU TRY!!

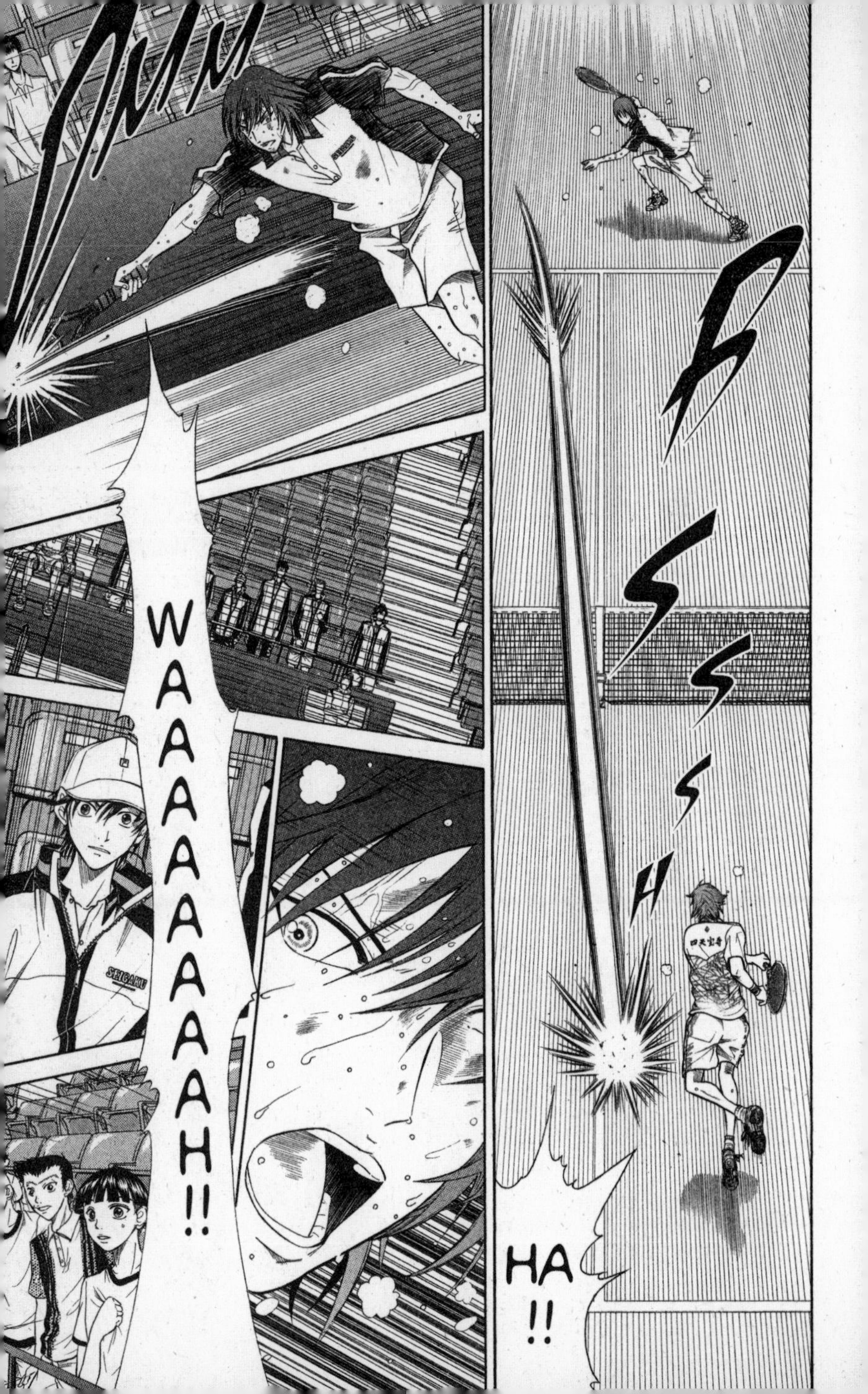
KSSSSH
HA!!
FWUM
WAAAAAAAAAH!!

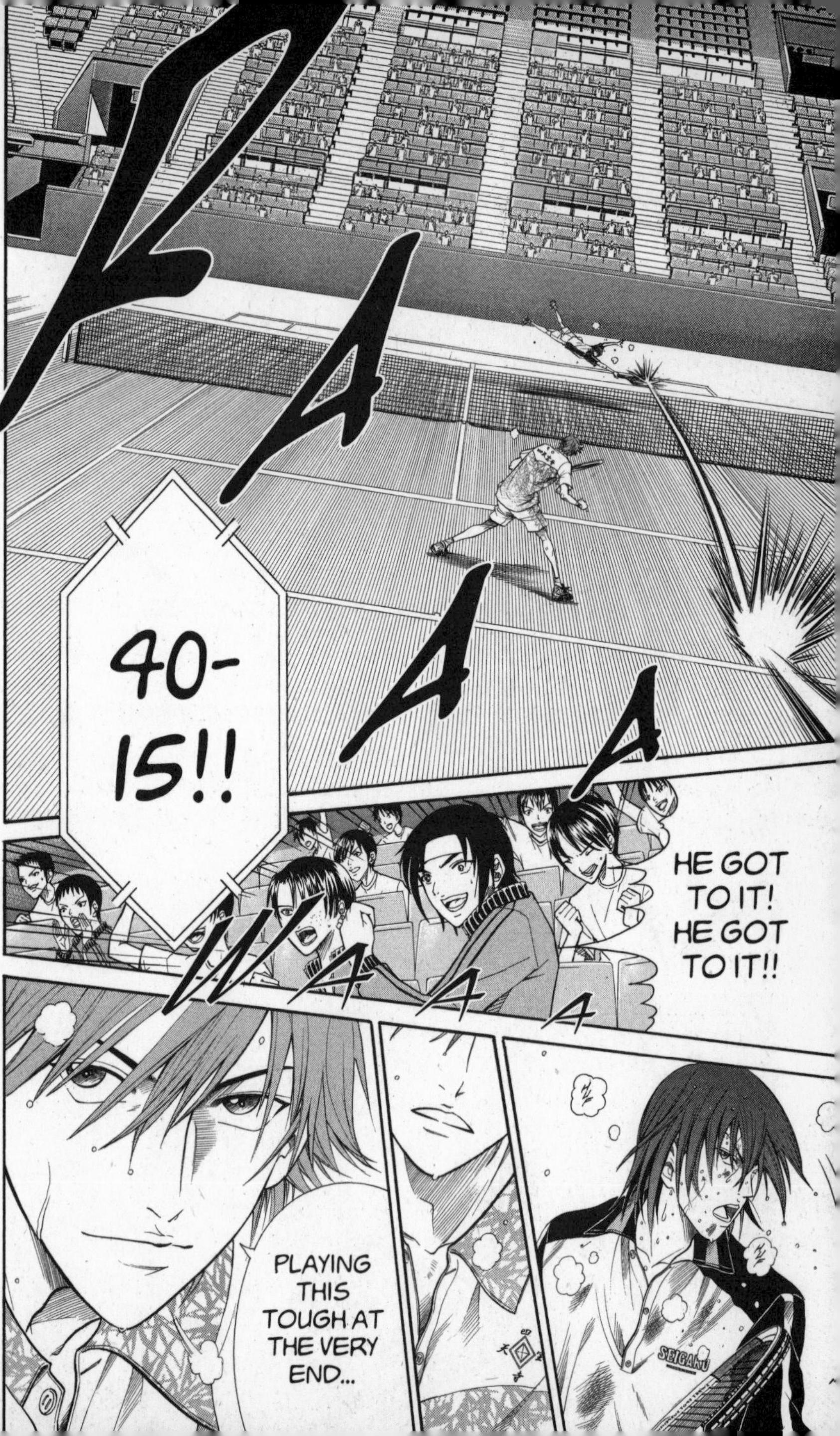
40-15!!
WAAA
HE GOT TO IT! HE GOT TO IT!!
PLAYING THIS TOUGH AT THE VERY END...
SEIGAKU

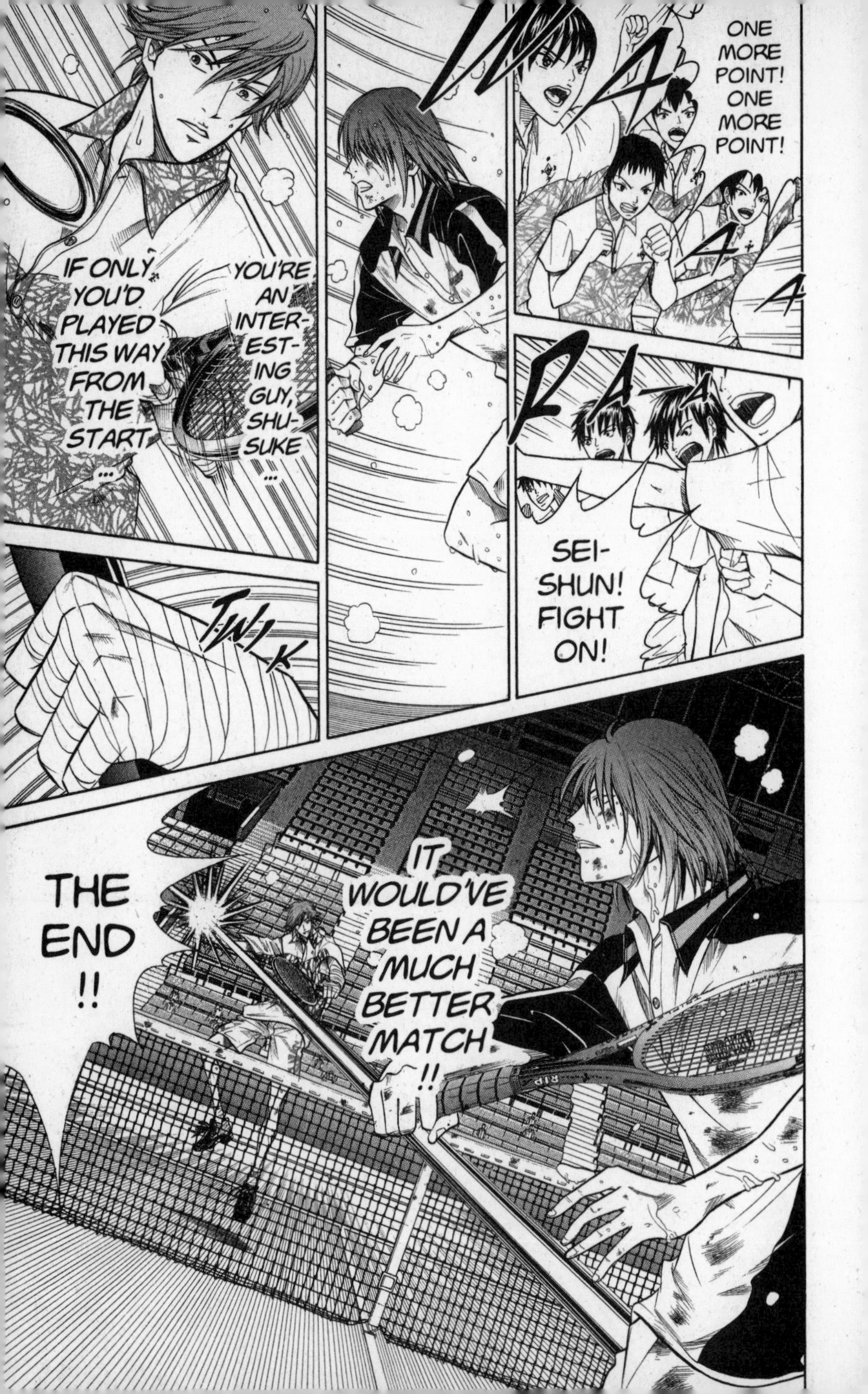

ONE MORE POINT! ONE MORE POINT!
SEI-SHUN! FIGHT ON!
YOU'RE AN INTER-EST-ING GUY, SHUSUKE...
IF ONLY YOU'D PLAYED THIS WAY FROM THE START...
TWIK
IT WOULD'VE BEEN A MUCH BETTER MATCH!!
THE END!!

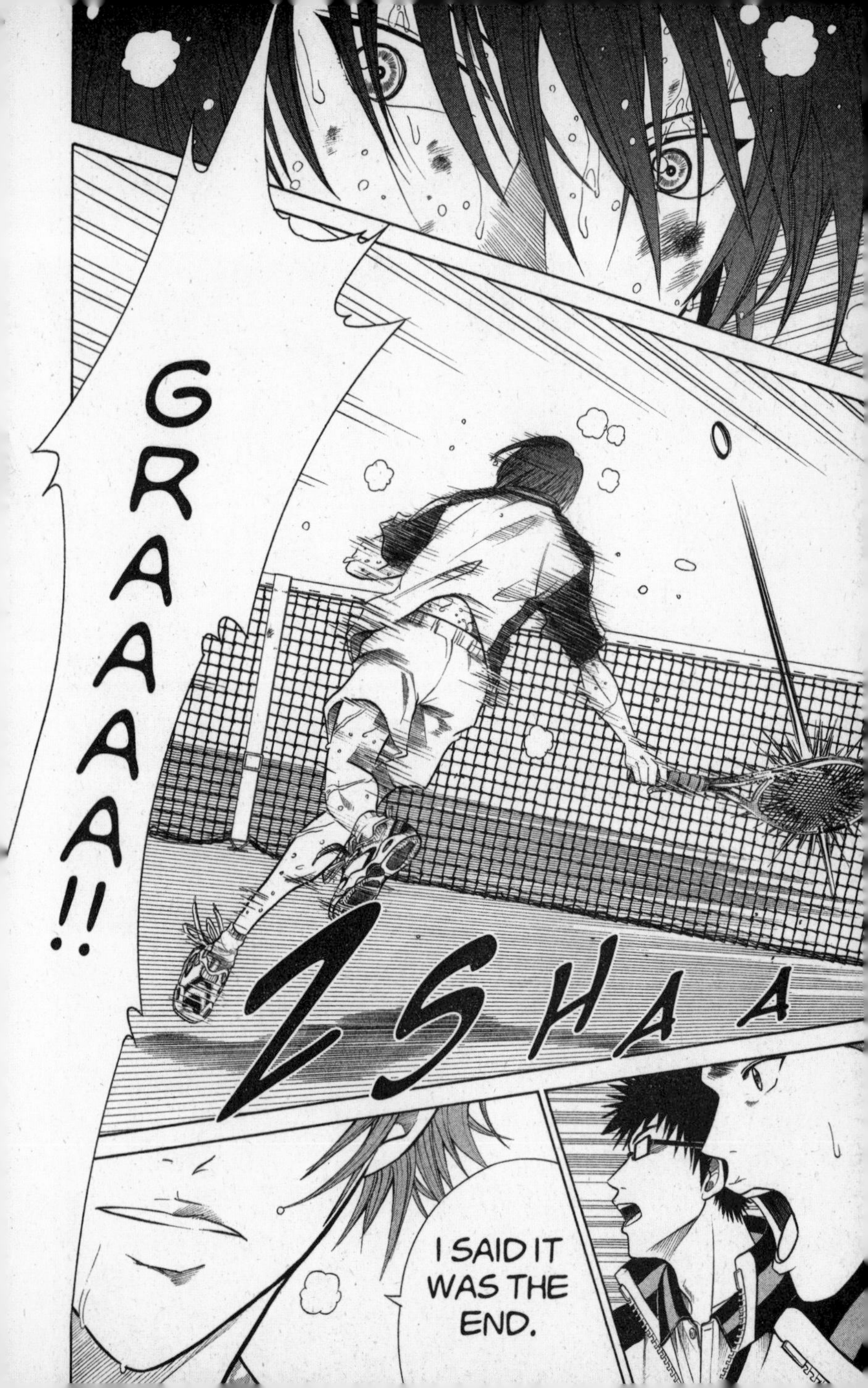
GRAAAA!!
ZSHAA
I SAID IT WAS THE END.

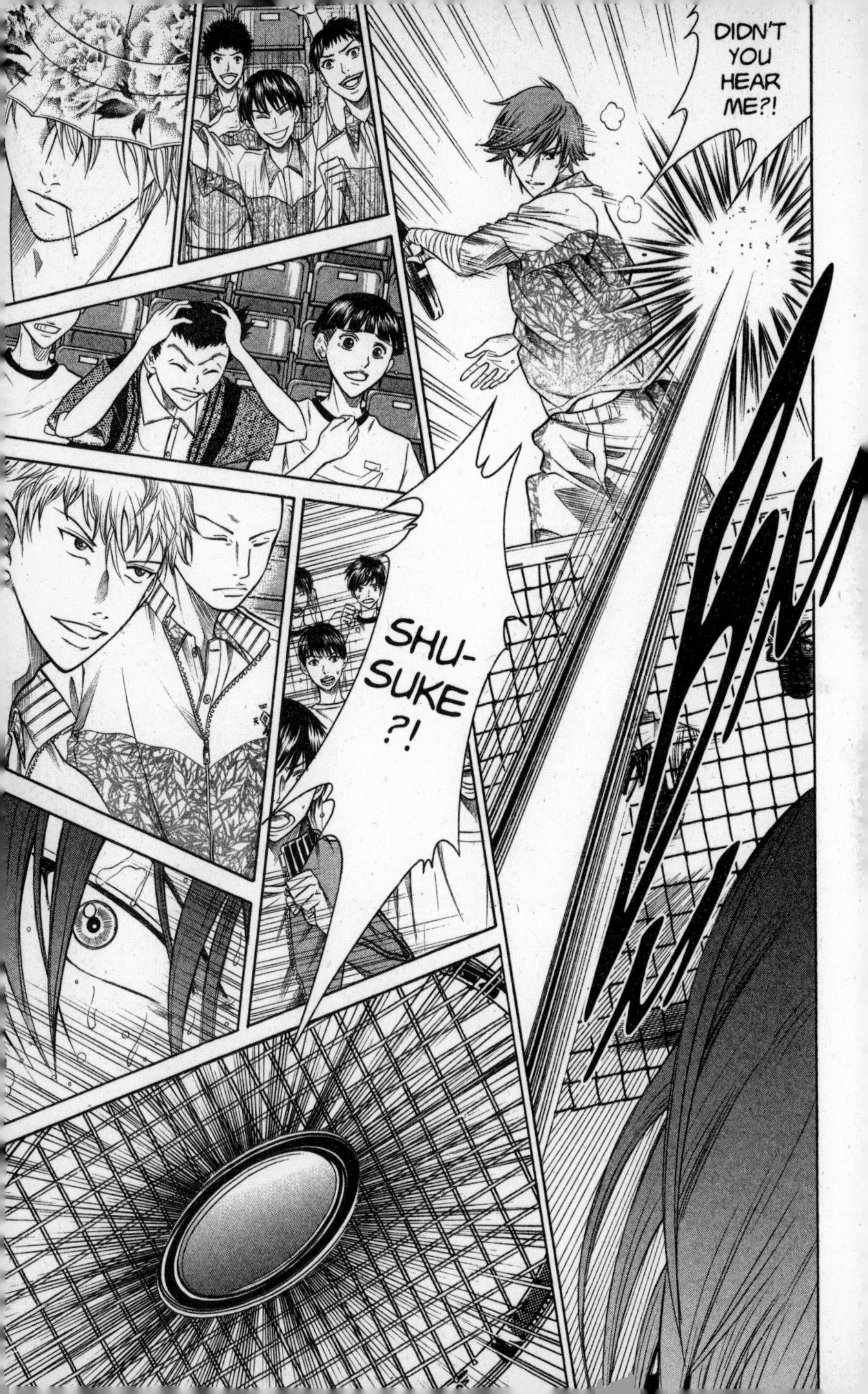
DIDN'T YOU HEAR ME?!
SHU-SUKE ?!

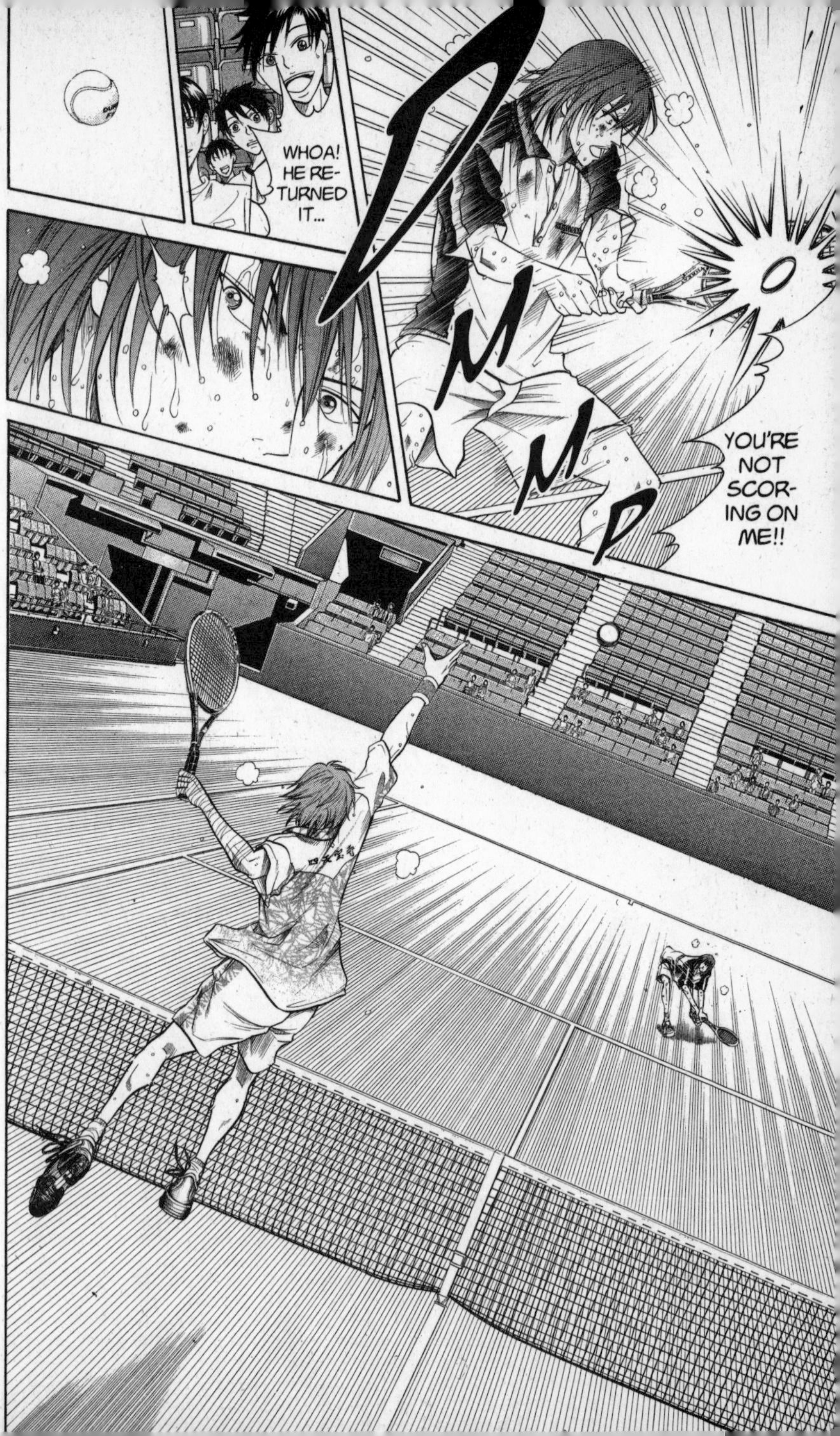
WHUMP
YOU'RE NOT SCOR-ING ON ME!!
WHOA! HE RE-TURNED IT...

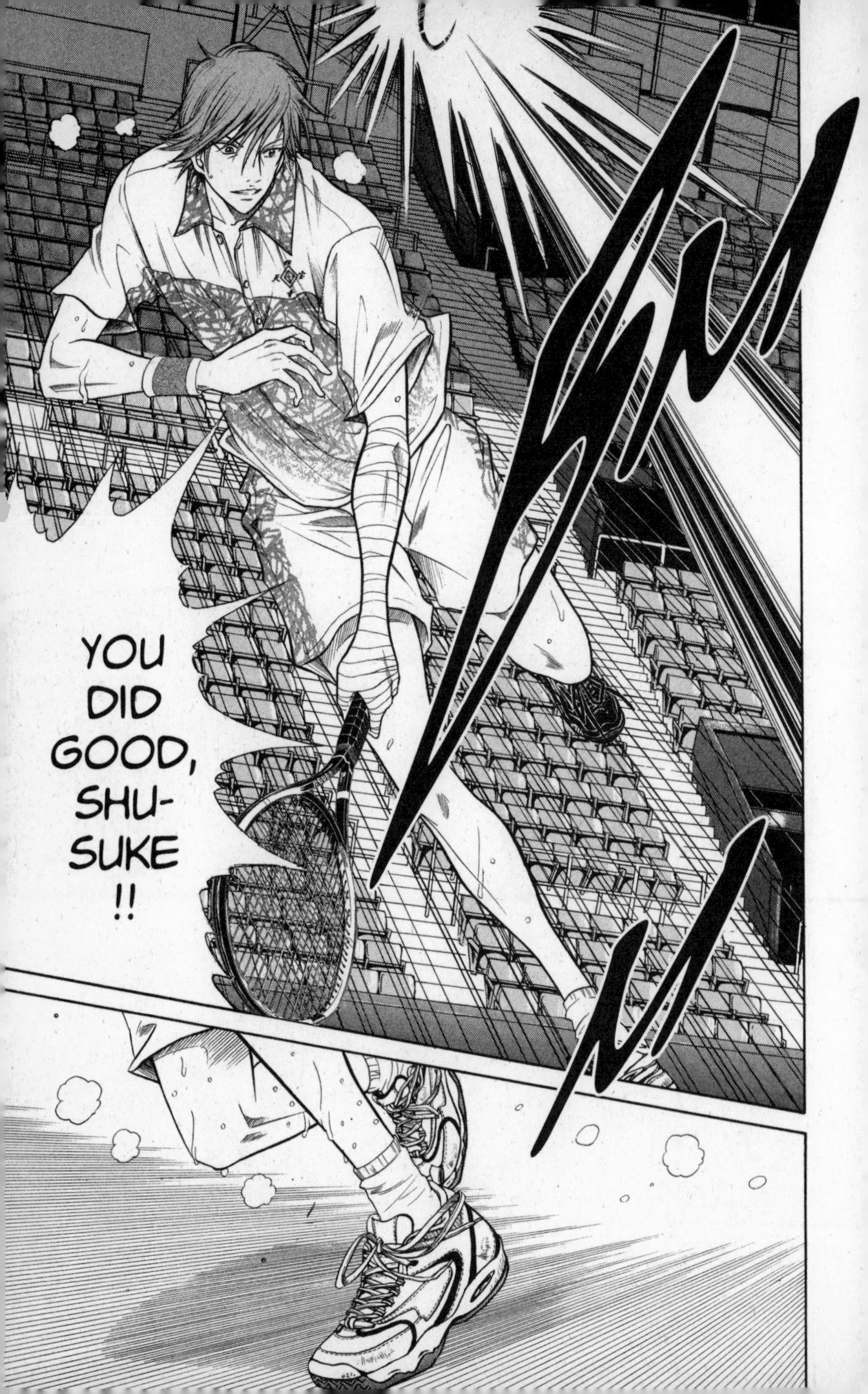
YOU DID GOOD, SHU-SUKE !!

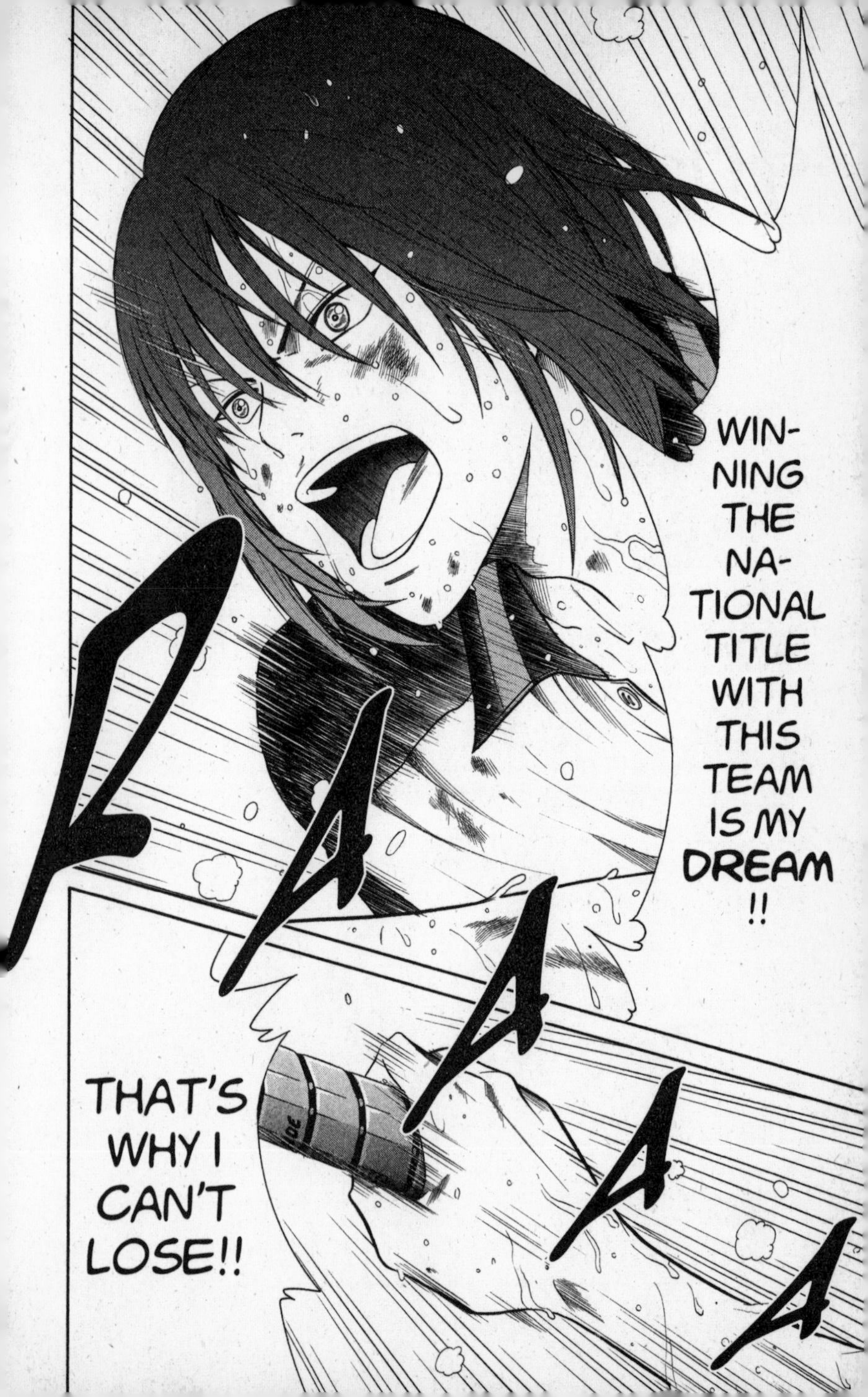
WIN-
NING
THE
NA-
TIONAL
TITLE
WITH
THIS
TEAM
IS MY
DREAM
!!
THAT'S
WHY I
CAN'T
LOSE!!

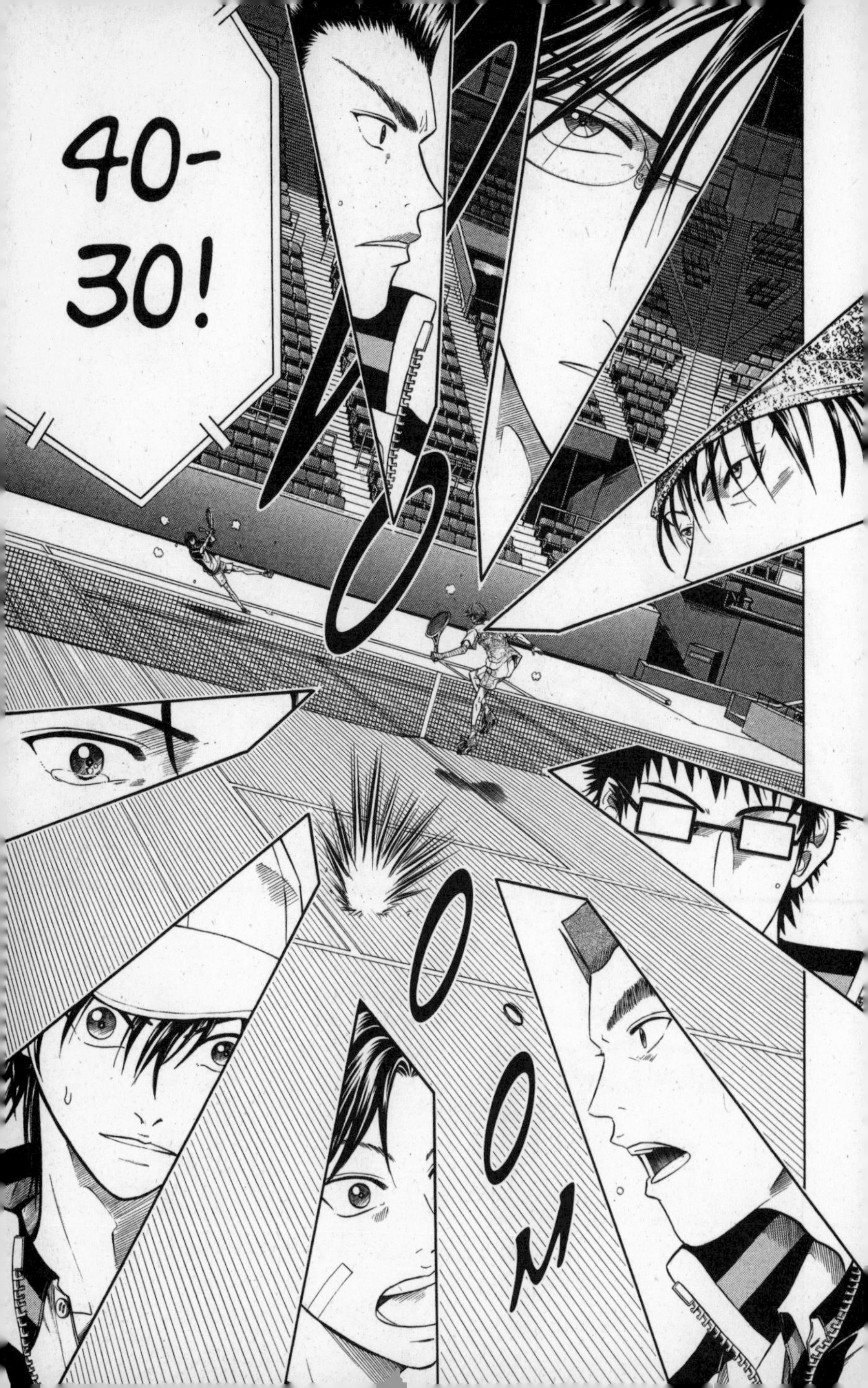
40-30!
VOOOOOM

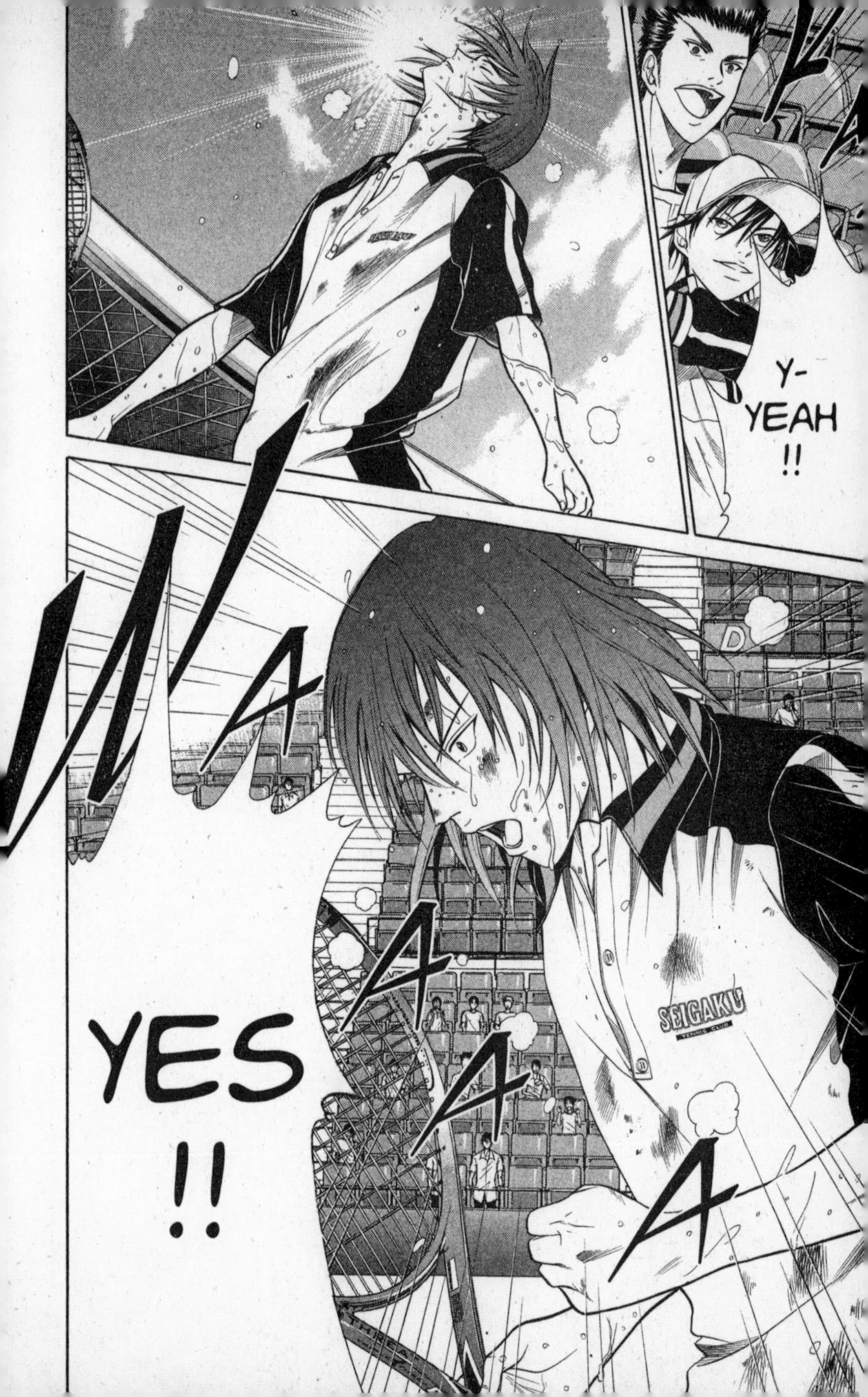
Y-YEAH!!
WAAAAA
YES!!
SEIGAKU

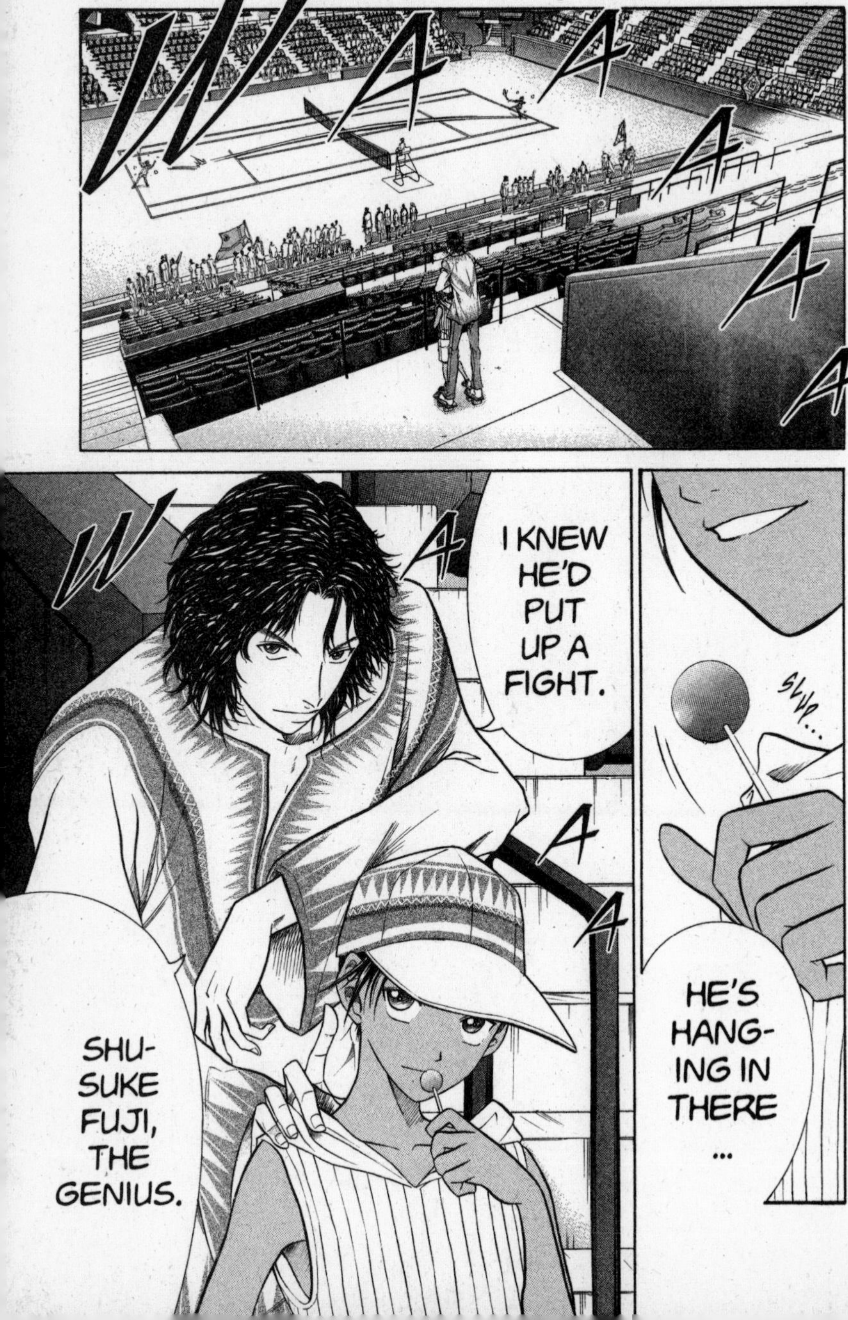
WAAAAAA
SLUP...
HE'S HANGING IN THERE ...
WAAA
I KNEW HE'D PUT UP A FIGHT.
SHUSUKE FUJI, THE GENIUS.

テニスの王子様

THE PRINCE OF TENNIS

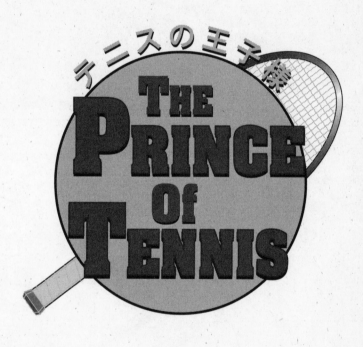

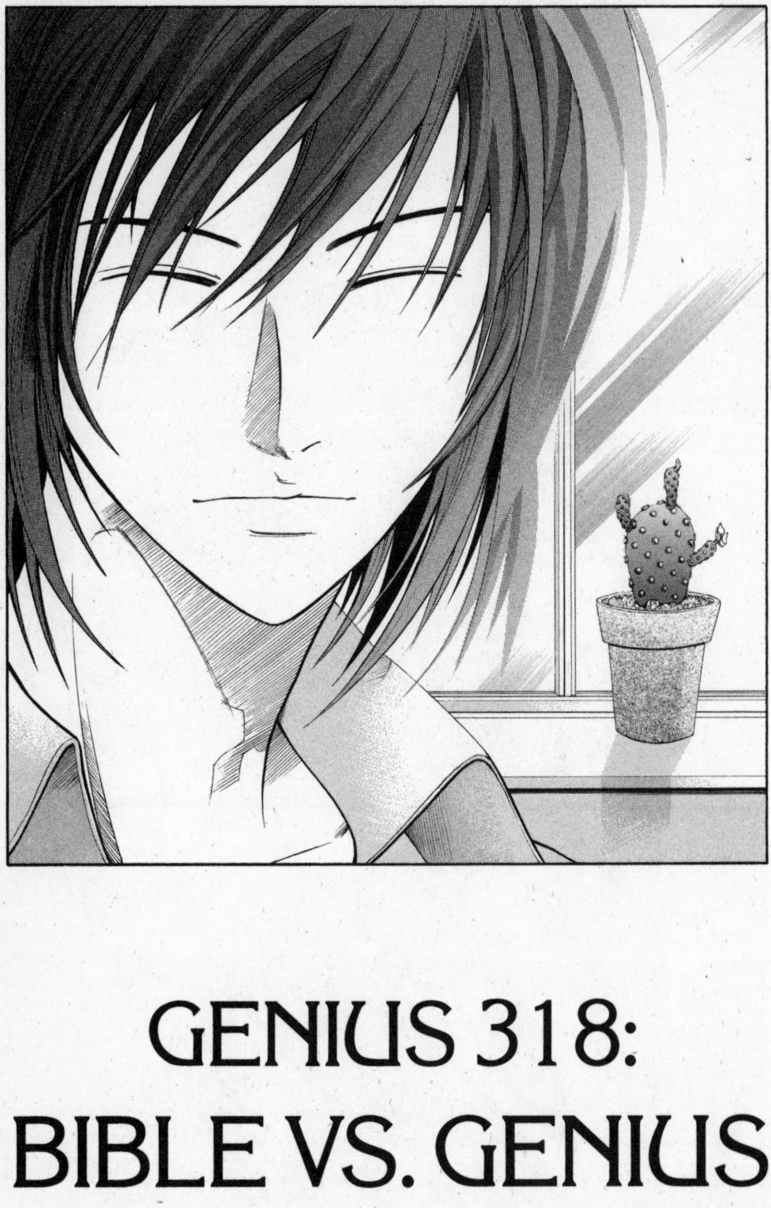

GENIUS 318: BIBLE VS. GENIUS

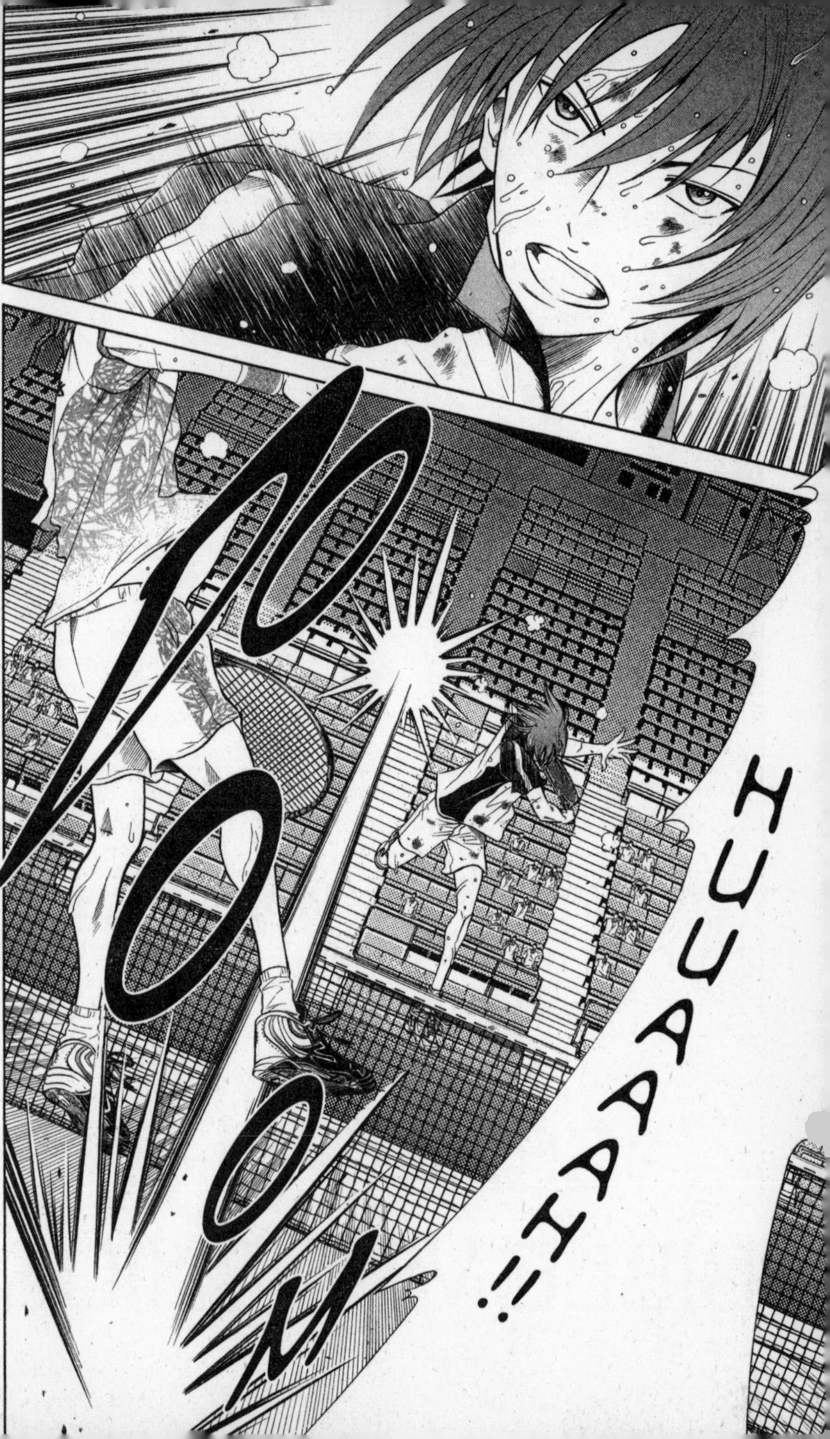
HUUAAAAH!!!
VROOM

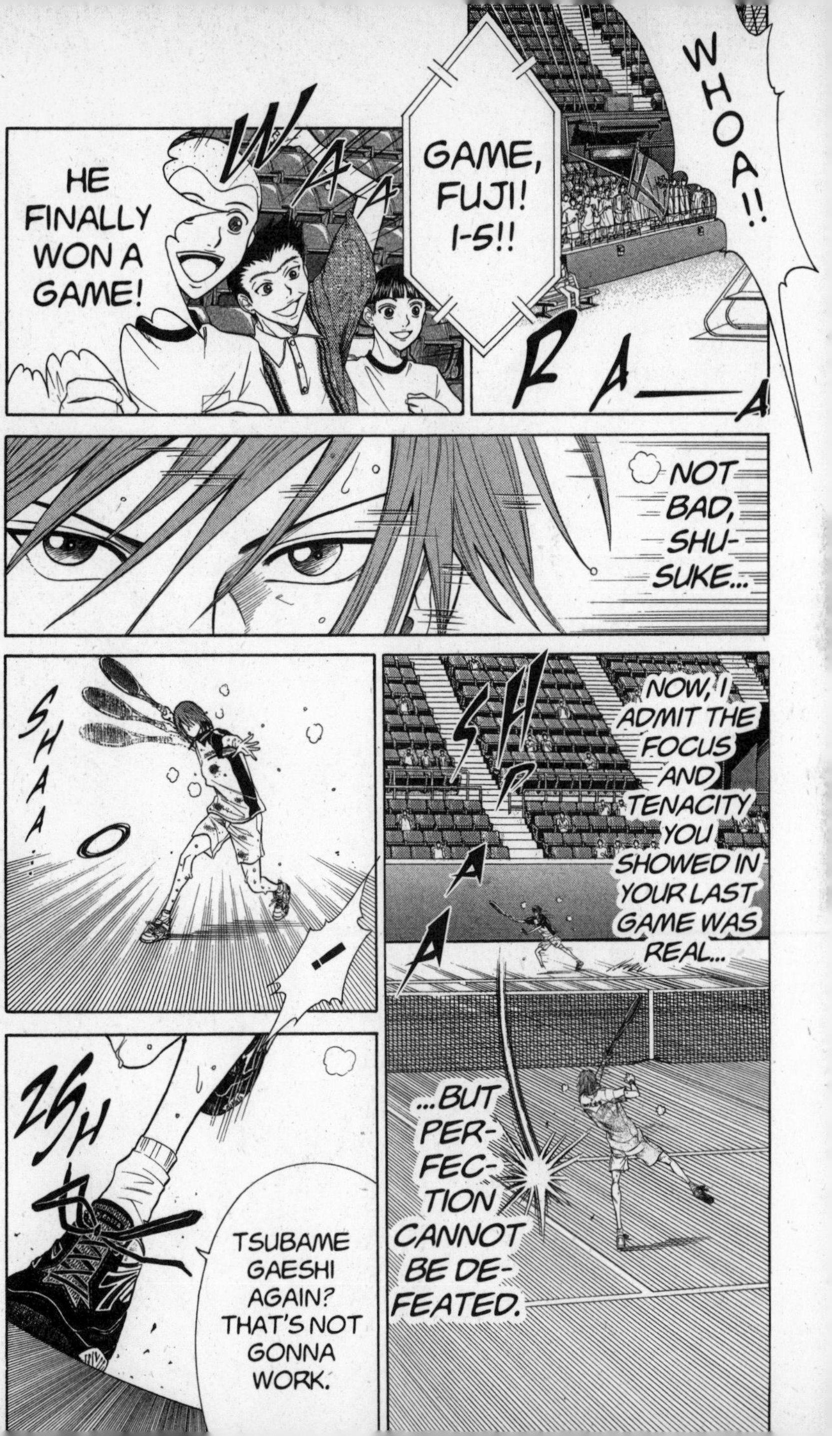
WHOA!!
GAME, FUJI! 1-5!!
RA—A
WAA
HE FINALLY WON A GAME!
NOT BAD, SHU-SUKE...
SHAA
NOW, I ADMIT THE FOCUS AND TENACITY YOU SHOWED IN YOUR LAST GAME WAS REAL...
...BUT PER-FEC-TION CANNOT BE DE-FEATED.
SHAAO
!
ZSH
TSUBAME GAESHI AGAIN? THAT'S NOT GONNA WORK.

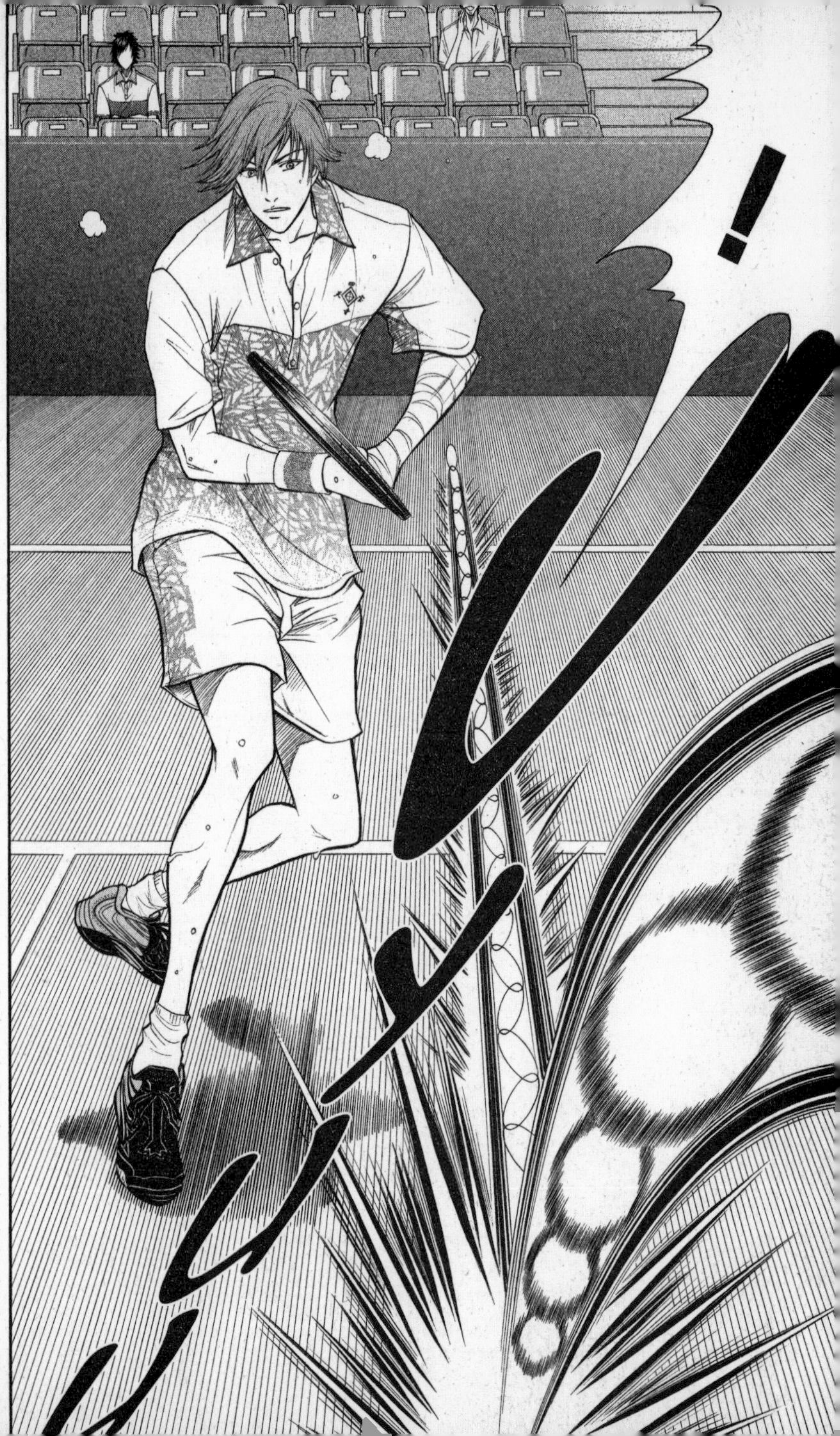

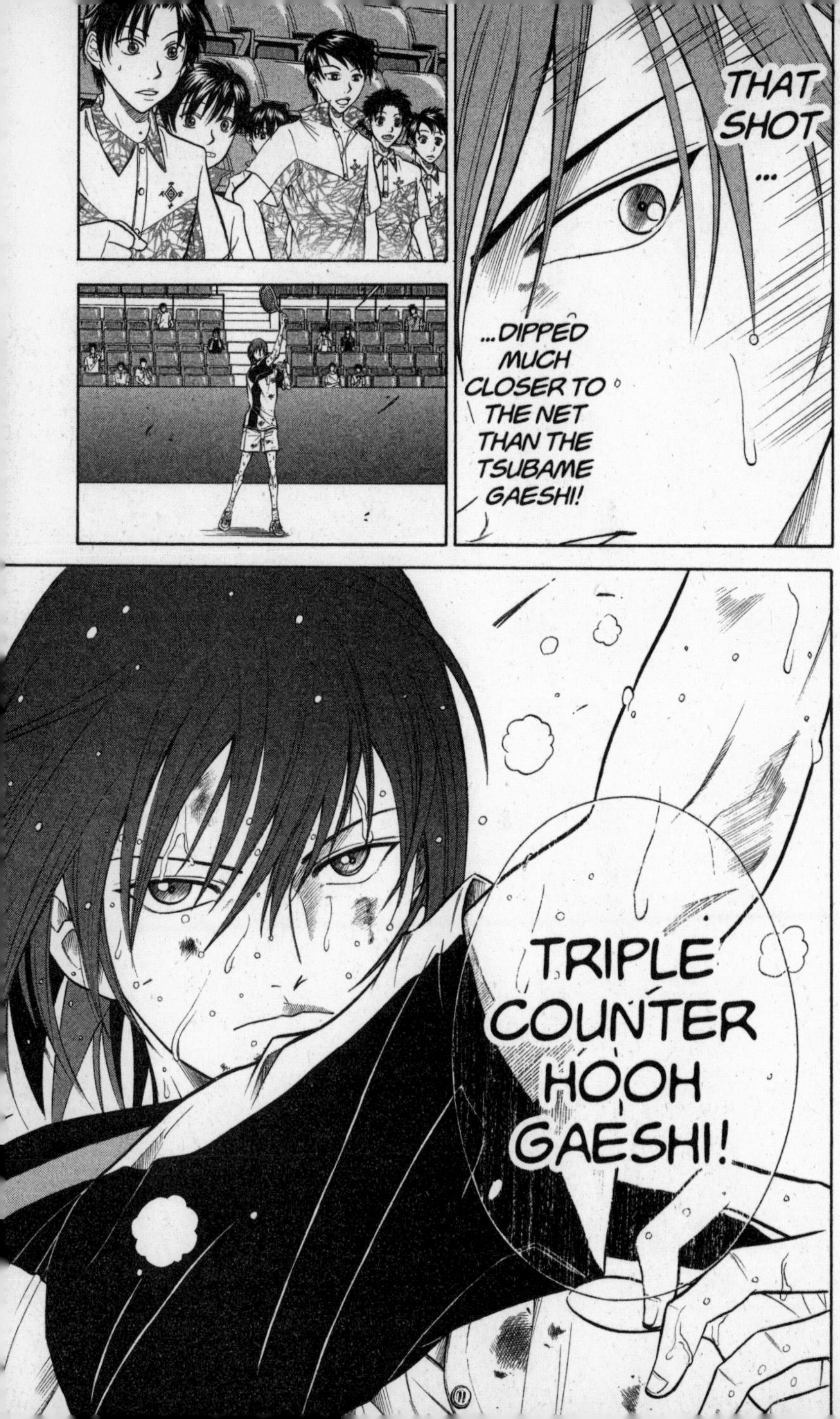
THAT SHOT ...
...DIPPED MUCH CLOSER TO THE NET THAN THE TSUBAME GAESHI!
TRIPLE COUNTER HOOH GAESHI!

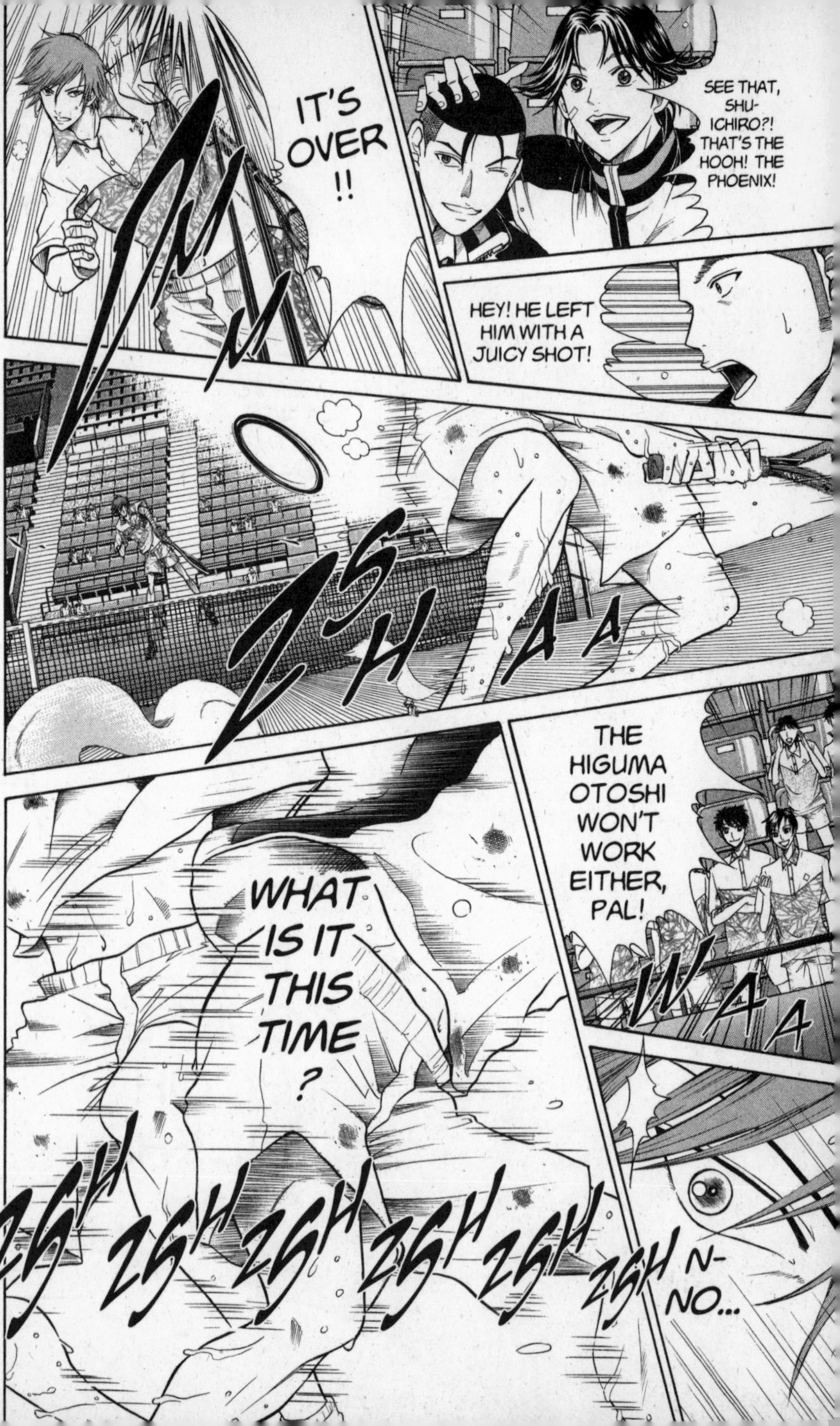
SEE THAT, SHUICHIRO?! THAT'S THE HOOH! THE PHOENIX!
HEY! HE LEFT HIM WITH A JUICY SHOT!
IT'S OVER !!
ZMM
ZSHAA
THE HIGUMA OTOSHI WON'T WORK EITHER, PAL!
WAA
N-NO...
WHAT IS IT THIS TIME?
ZSH ZSH ZSH ZSH ZSH ZSH

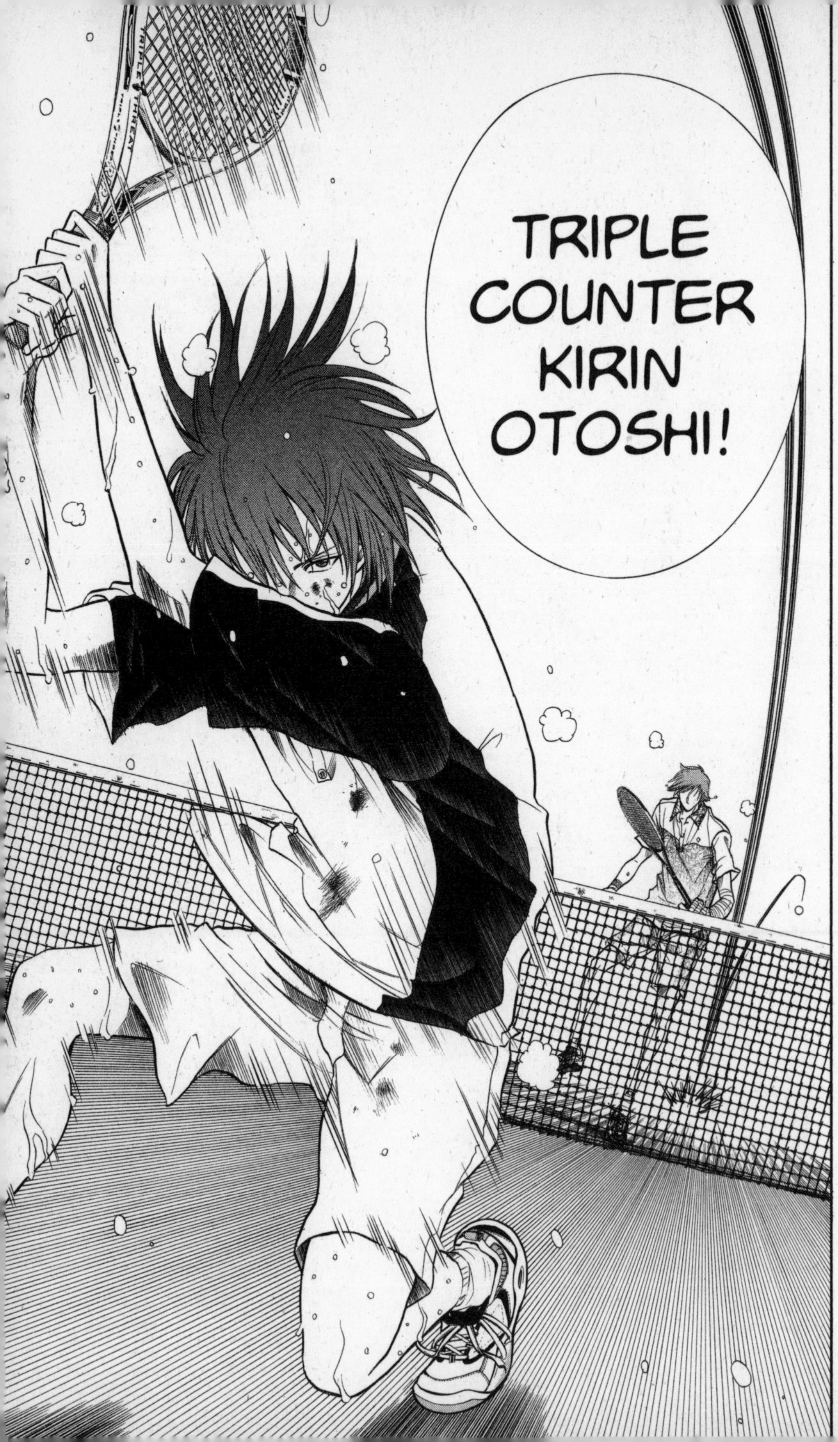
TRIPLE COUNTER KIRIN OTOSHI!

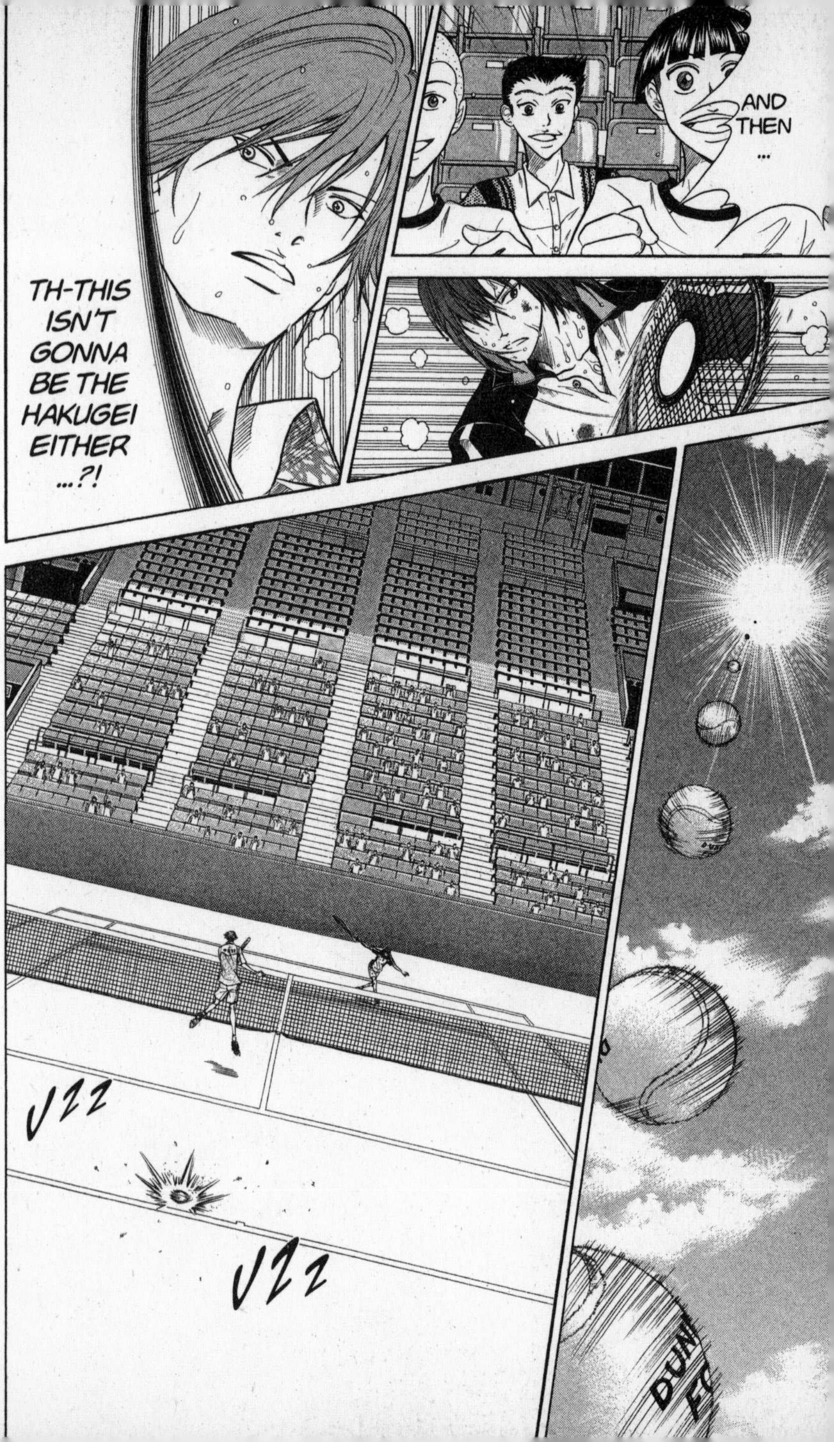
AND THEN ...
TH-THIS ISN'T GONNA BE THE HAKUGEI EITHER ...?!
VZZ
VZZ

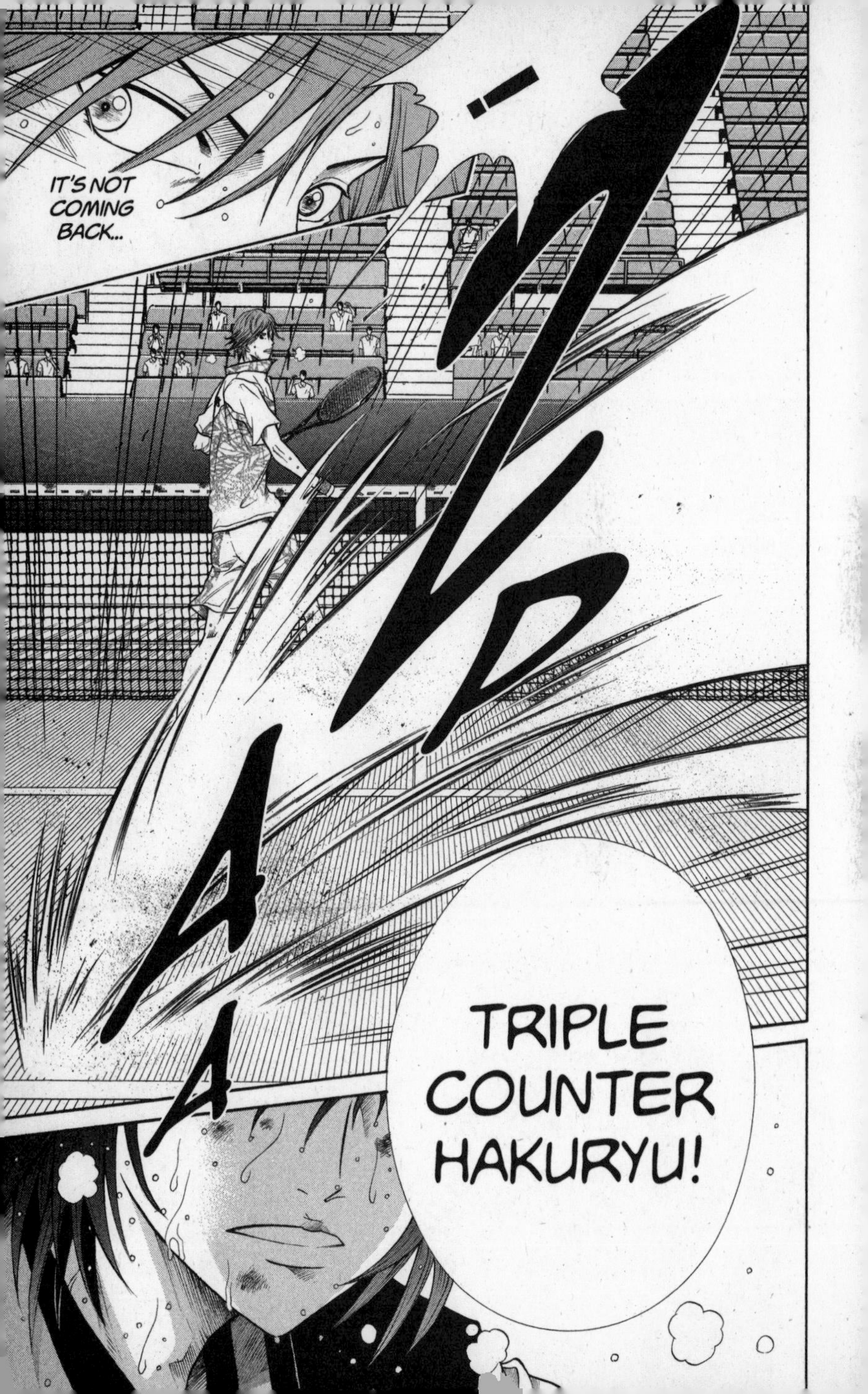
IT'S NOT COMING BACK...
TRIPLE COUNTER HAKURYU!

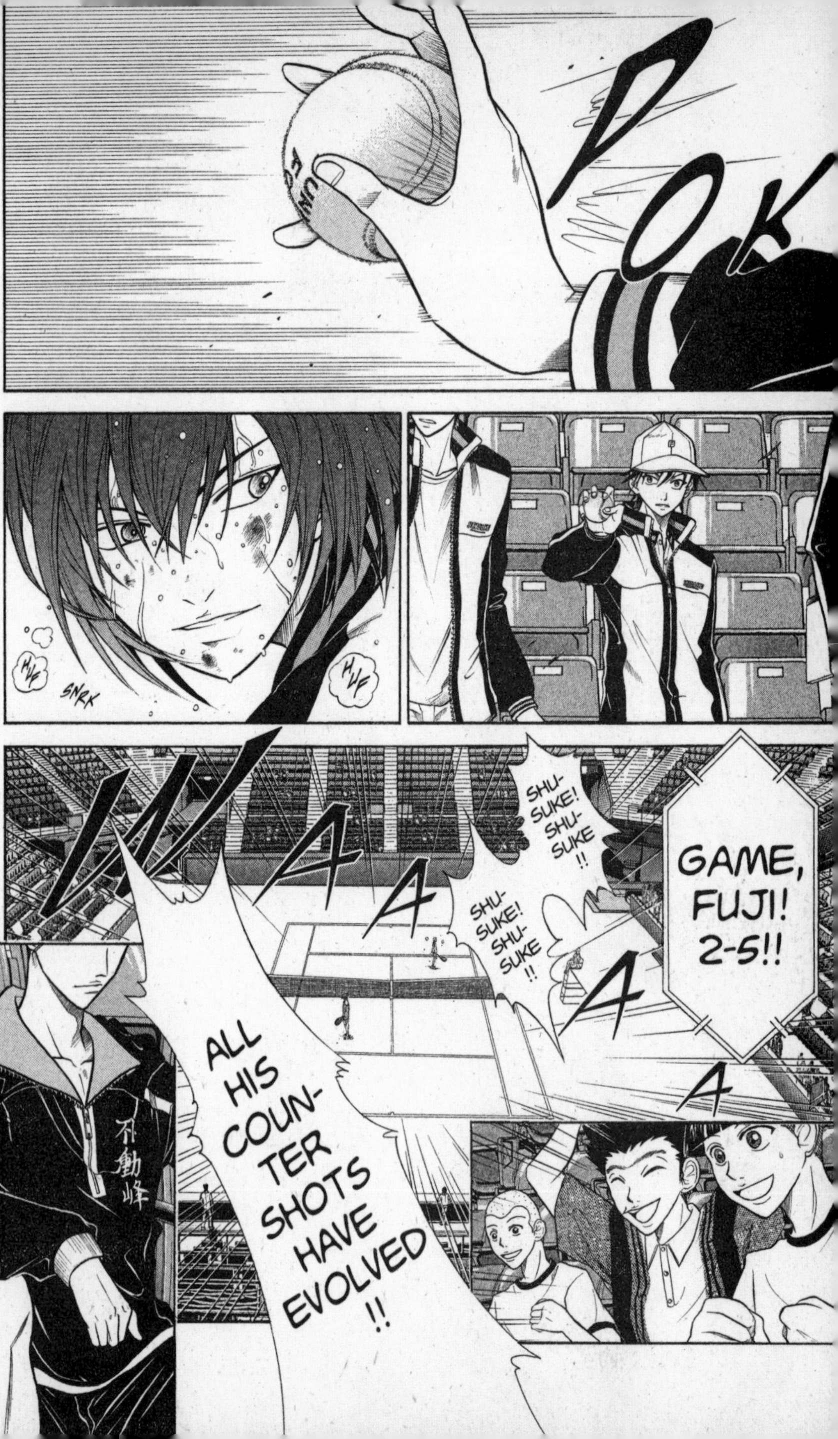
POK
HUF
SNRK
HUF
GAME, FUJI! 2-5!!
SHU-SUKE! SHU-SUKE!!
SHU-SUKE! SHU-SUKE!!
WAAAAA
ALL HIS COUNTER-SHOTS HAVE EVOLVED!!
不動峰

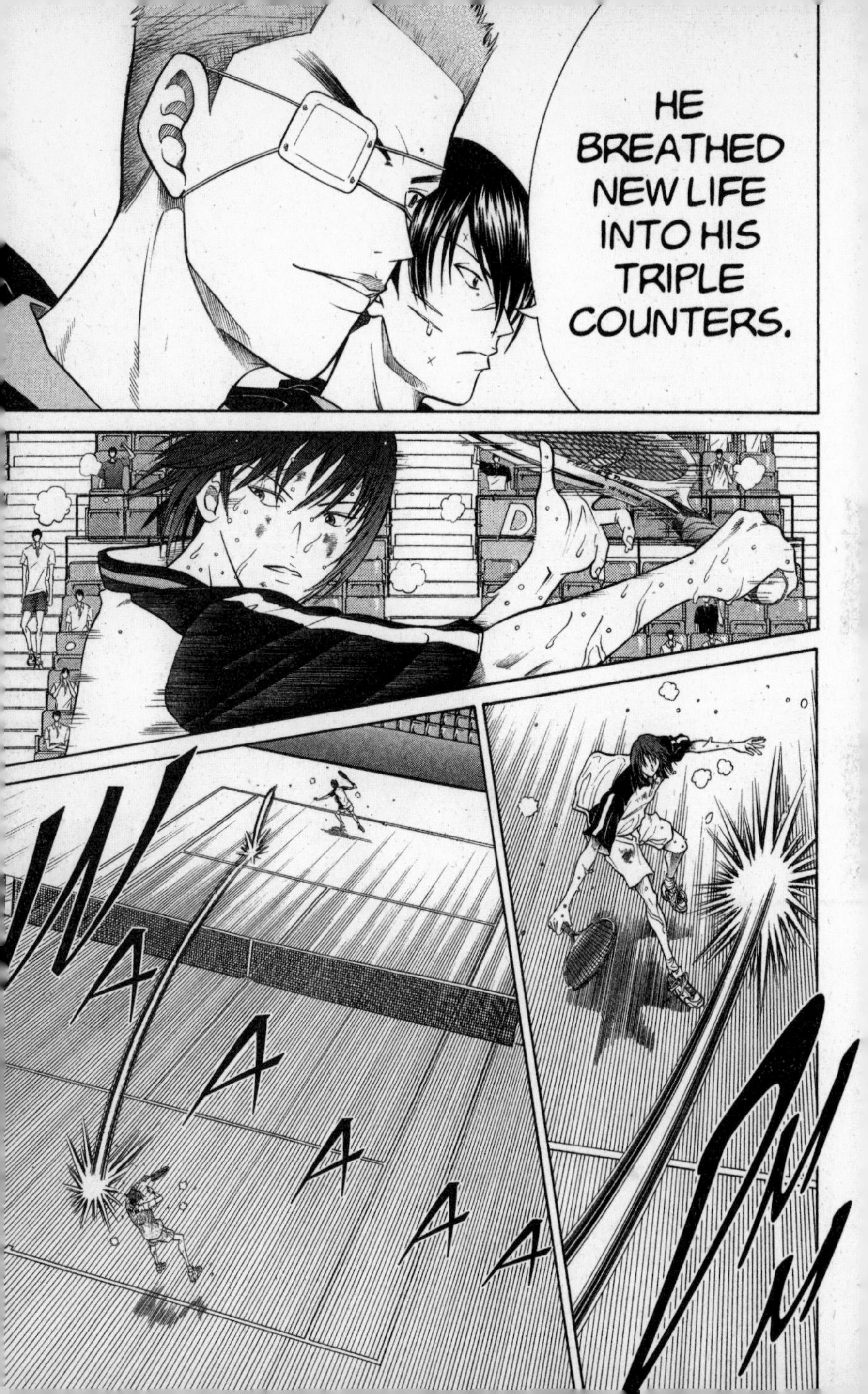
HE BREATHED NEW LIFE INTO HIS TRIPLE COUNTERS.
WAAAAA

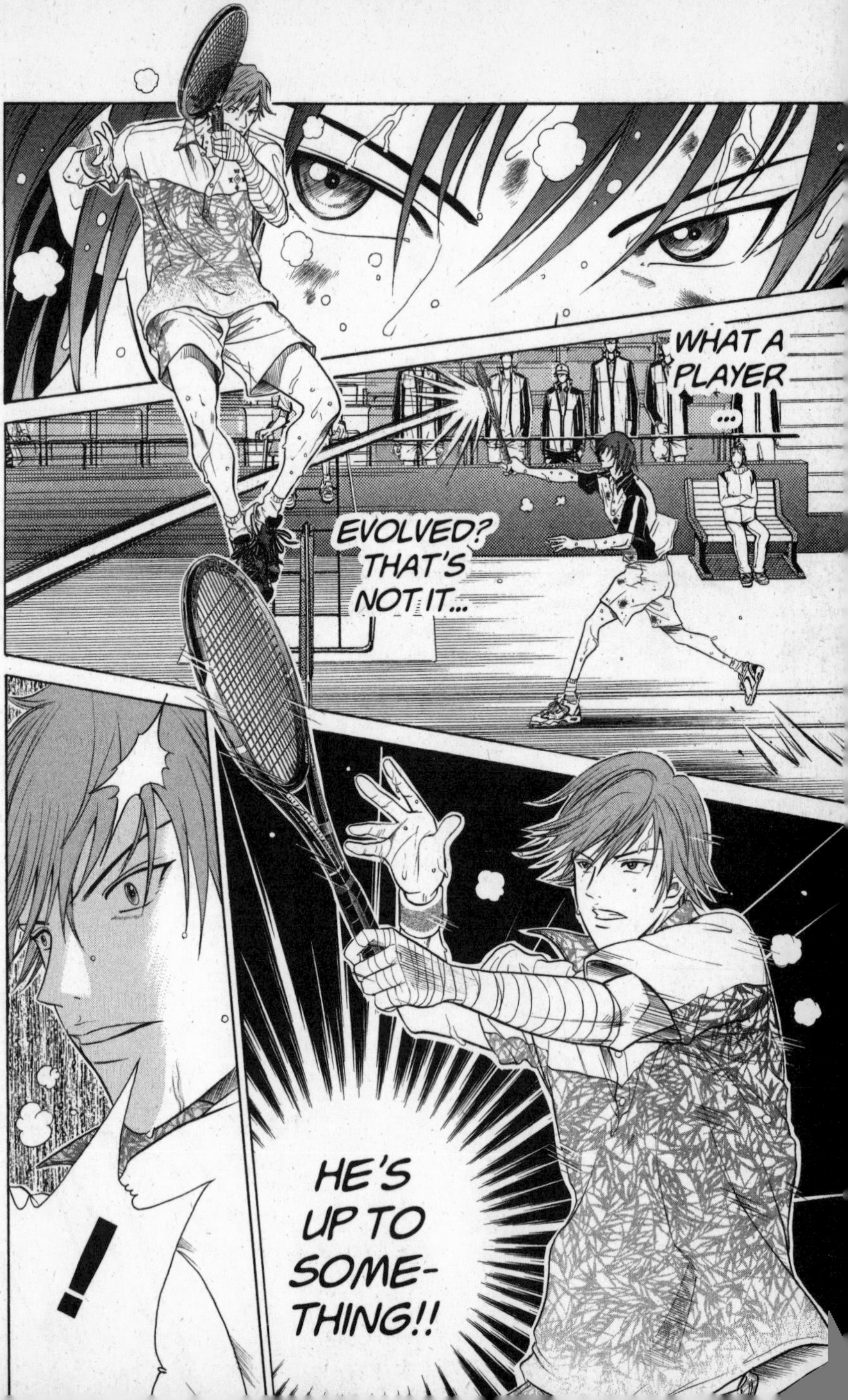
WHAT A PLAYER ...
EVOLVED? THAT'S NOT IT...
HE'S UP TO SOME-THING!!
!

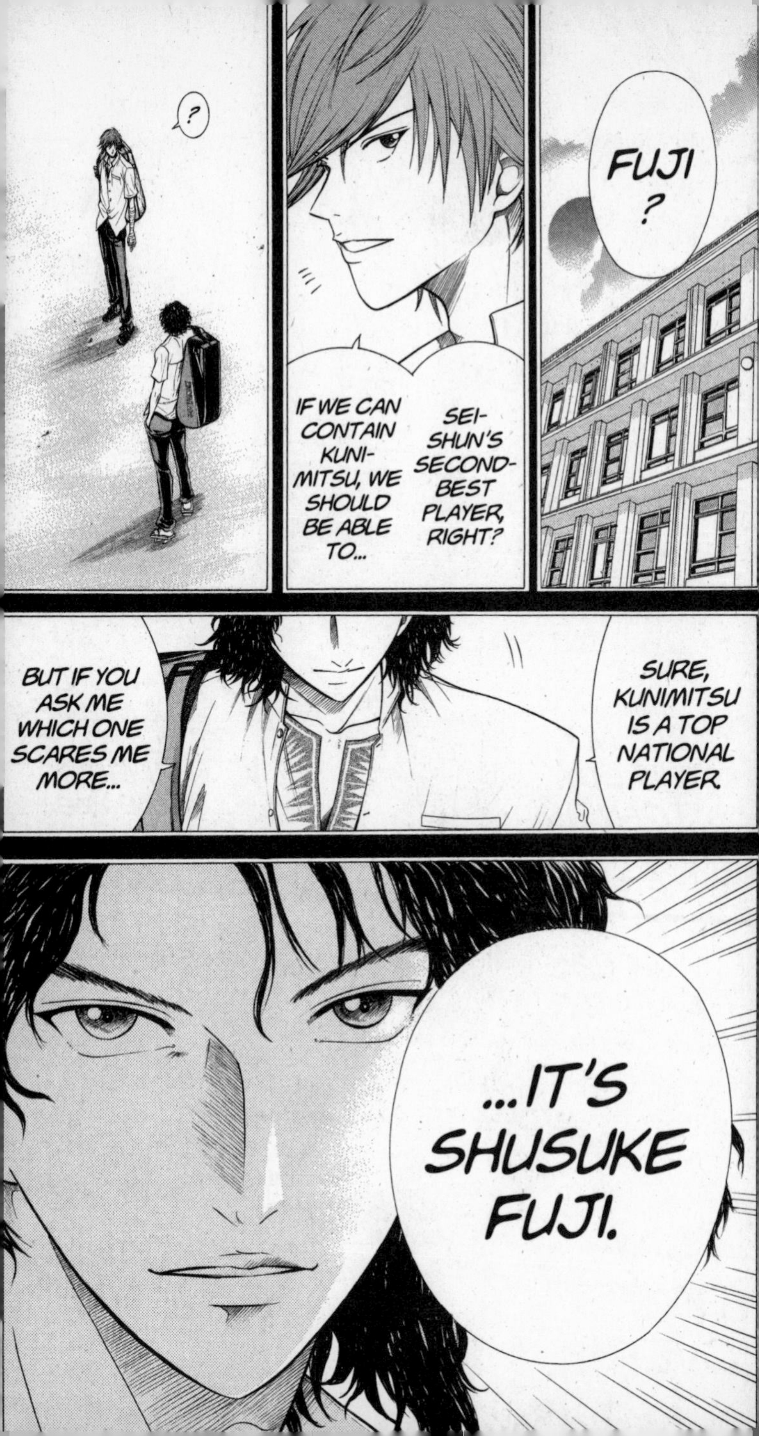
FUJI ?
SEI-SHUN'S SECOND-BEST PLAYER, RIGHT?
IF WE CAN CONTAIN KUNIMITSU, WE SHOULD BE ABLE TO...
?
SURE, KUNIMITSU IS A TOP NATIONAL PLAYER.
BUT IF YOU ASK ME WHICH ONE SCARES ME MORE...
...IT'S SHUSUKE FUJI.

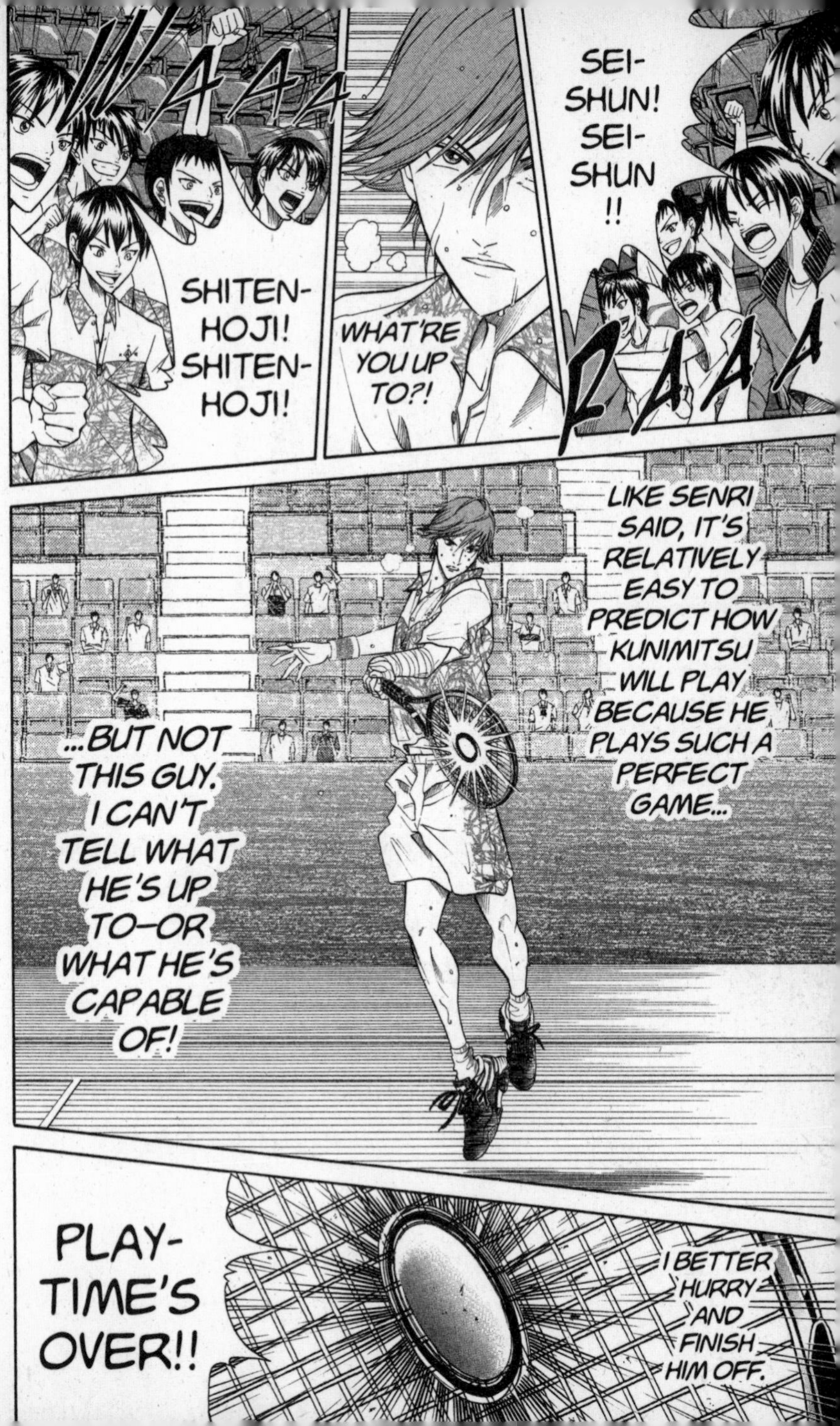
SEI-SHUN! SEI-SHUN!!
RAAA
WHAT'RE YOU UP TO?!
WAAA
SHITEN-HOJI! SHITEN-HOJI!
LIKE SENRI SAID, IT'S RELATIVELY EASY TO PREDICT HOW KUNIMITSU WILL PLAY BECAUSE HE PLAYS SUCH A PERFECT GAME...
...BUT NOT THIS GUY. I CAN'T TELL WHAT HE'S UP TO—OR WHAT HE'S CAPABLE OF!
I BETTER HURRY AND FINISH HIM OFF.
PLAY-TIME'S OVER!!

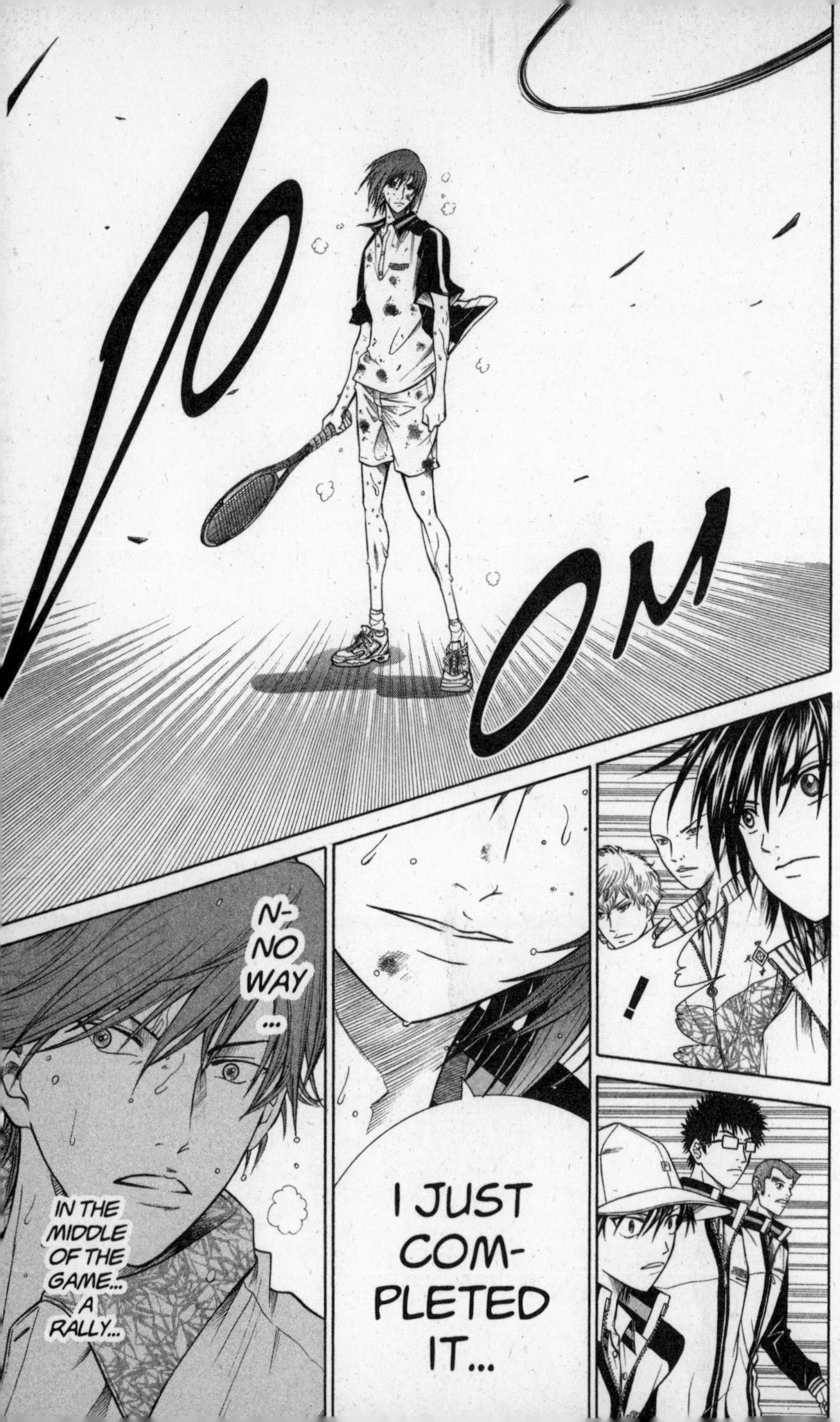
DOOM
!
I JUST COMPLETED IT...
N-NO WAY...
IN THE MIDDLE OF THE GAME... A RALLY...

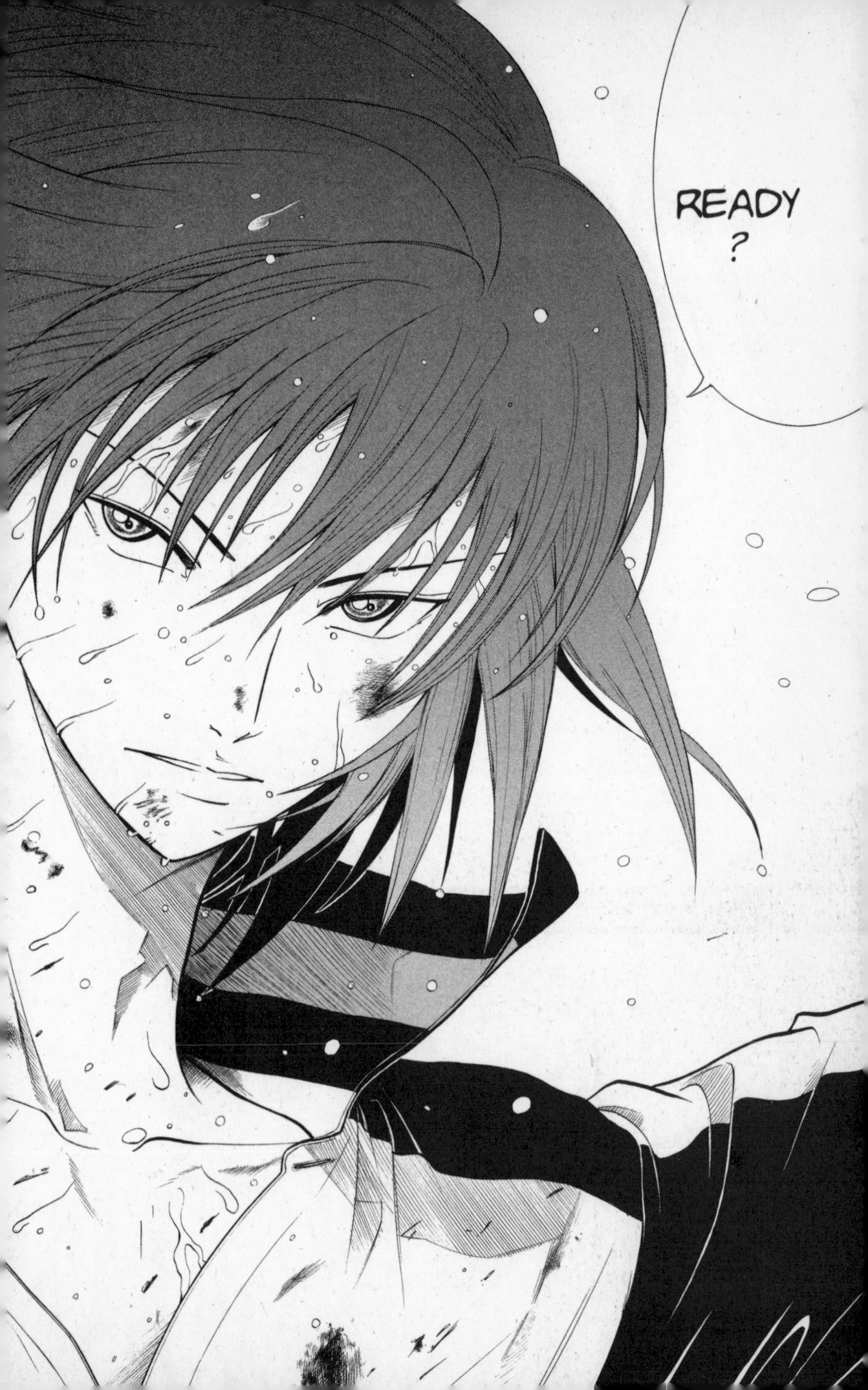
READY
?

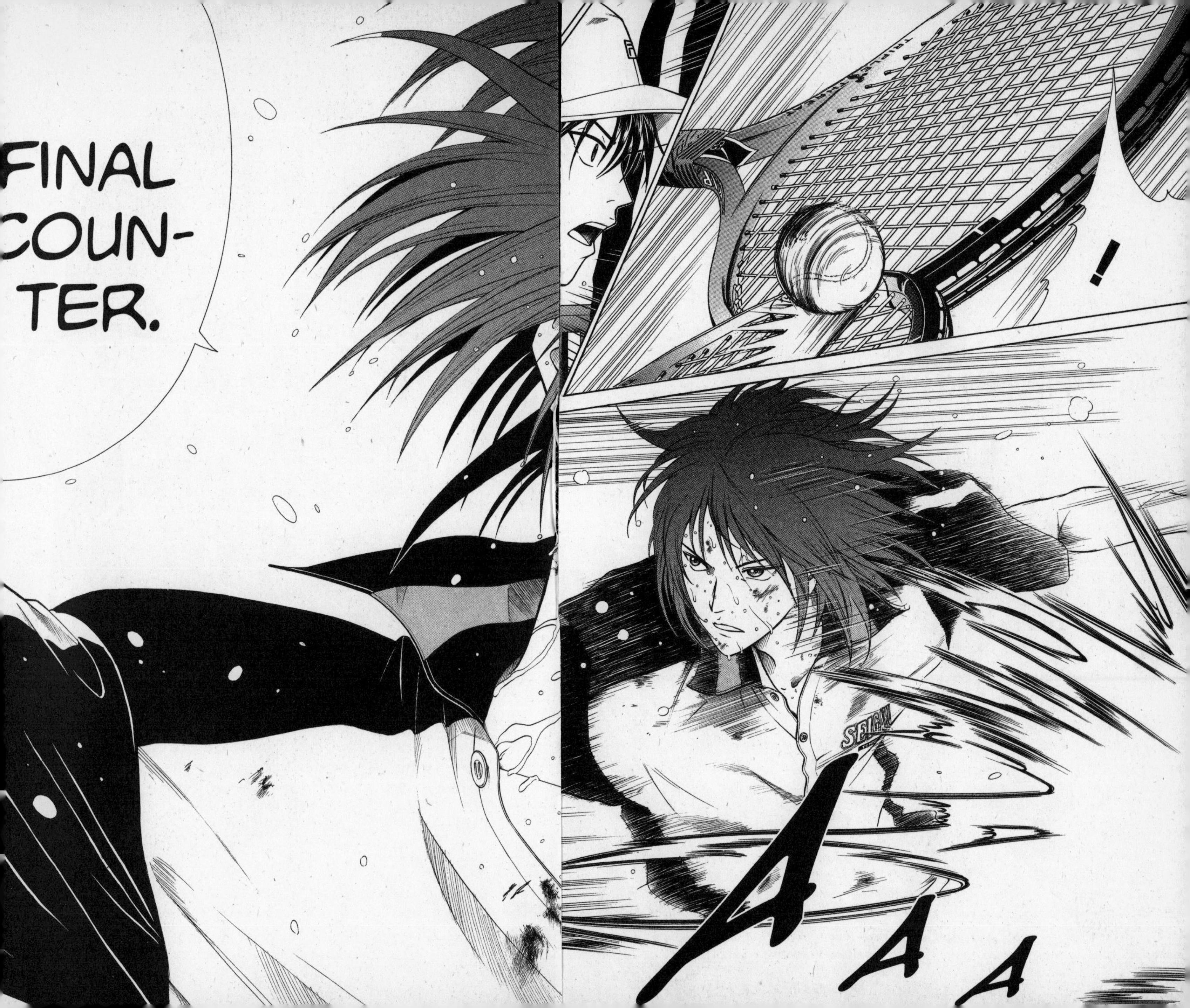
!
AAA
FINAL COUNTER.

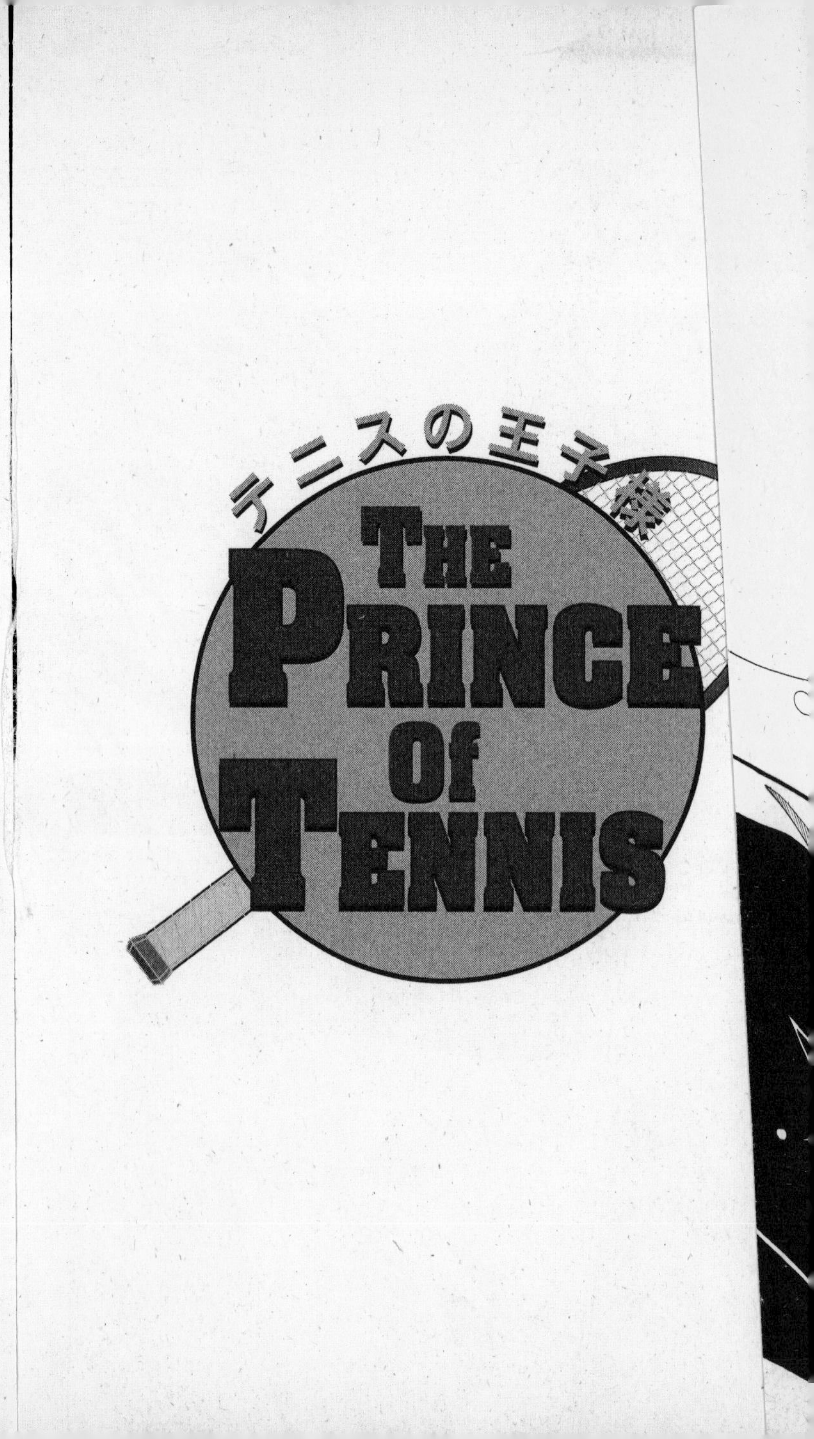
テニスの王子様
THE PRINCE OF TENNIS

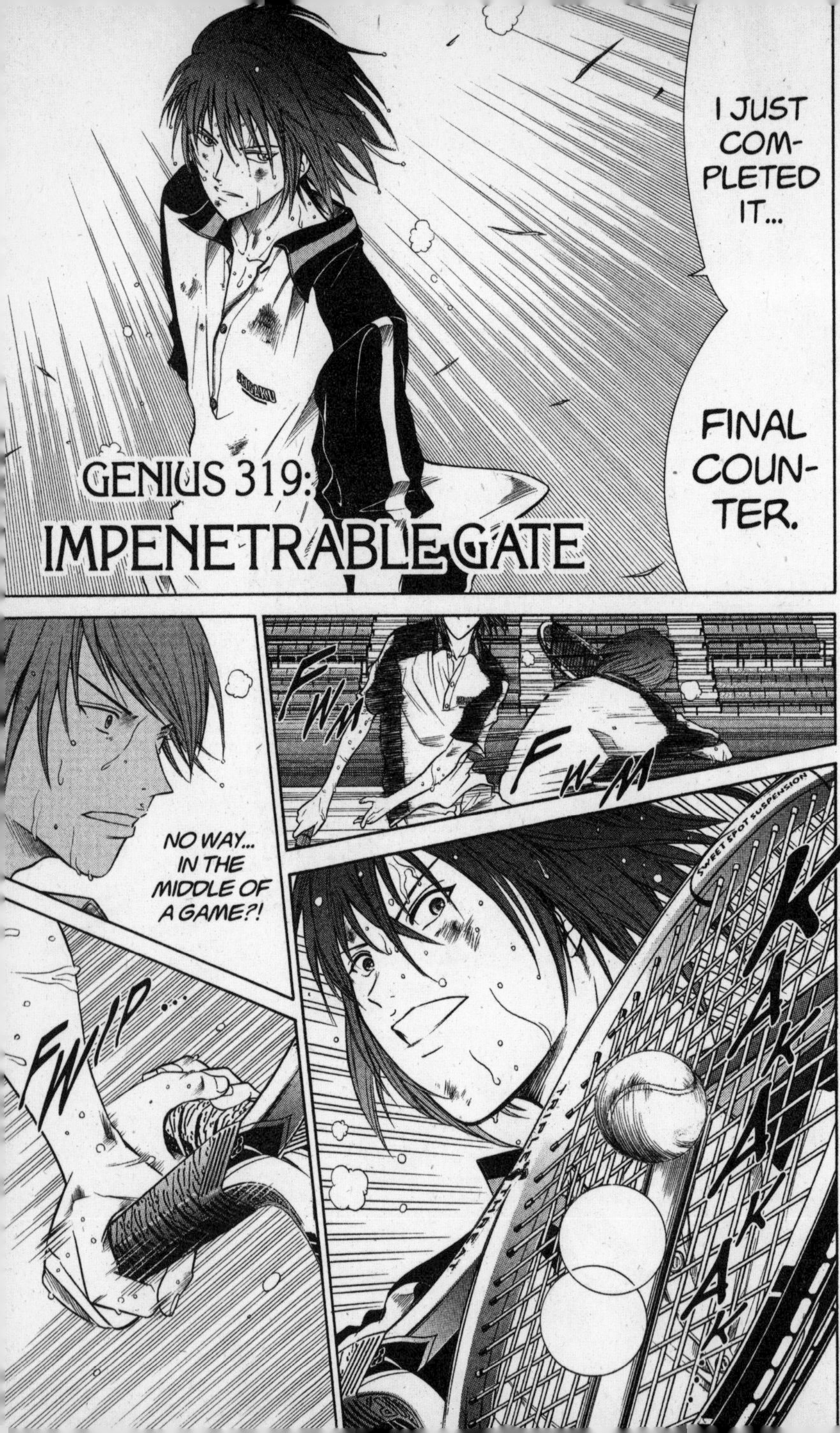
I JUST COMPLETED IT...
FINAL COUNTER.
GENIUS 319: IMPENETRABLE GATE
FWM
FWM
KAKAKAK
NO WAY... IN THE MIDDLE OF A GAME?!
FWIP...

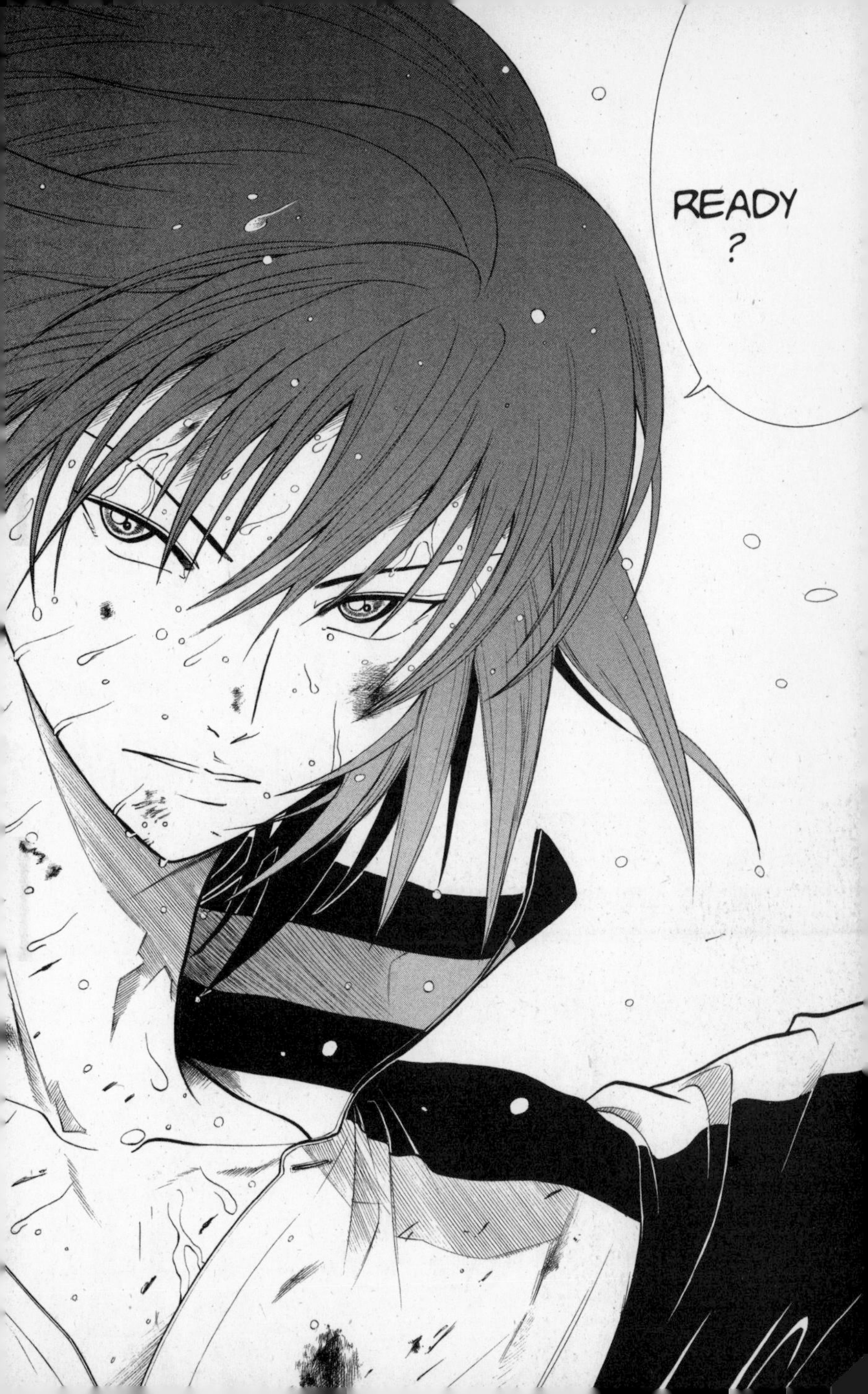
READY?

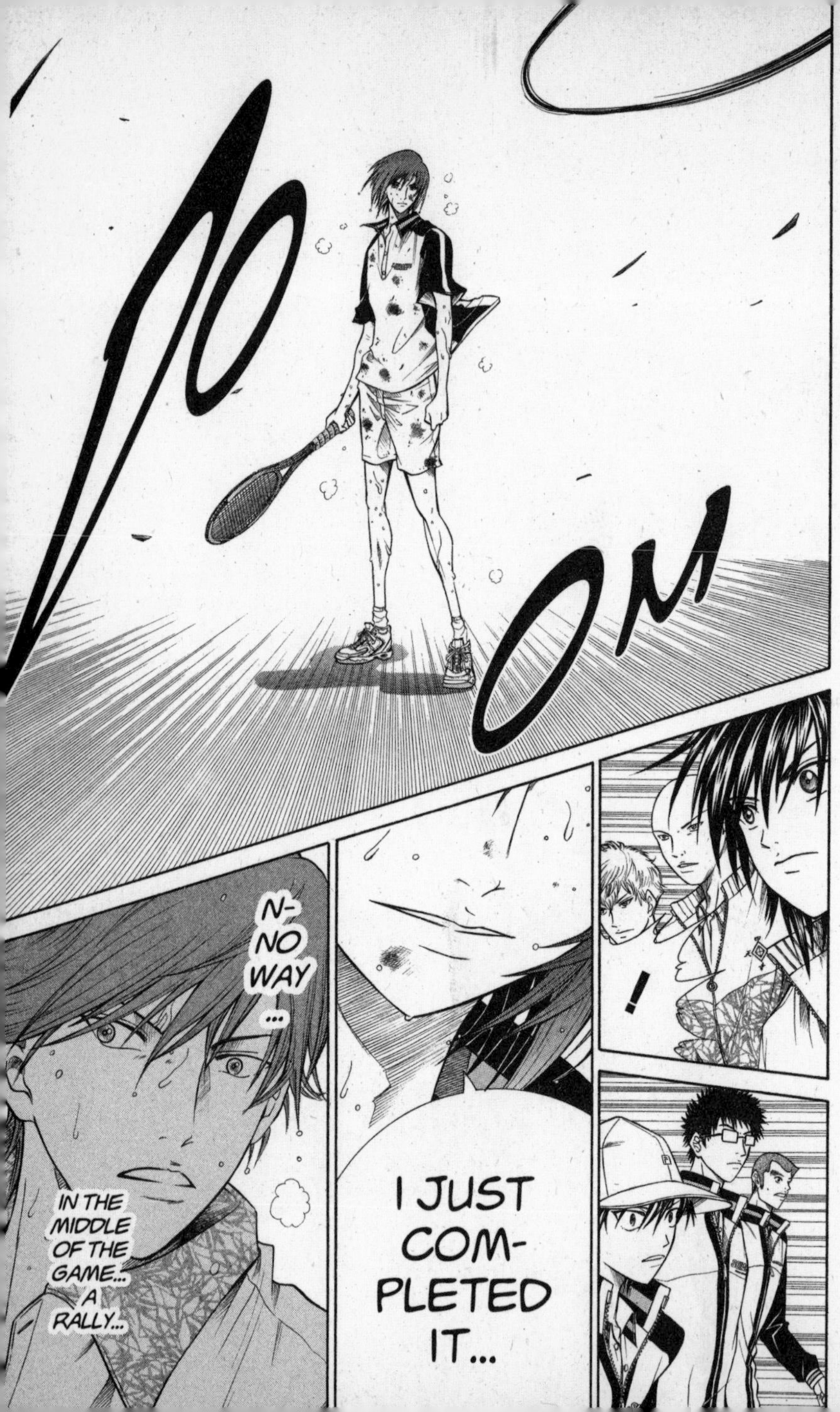
!
I JUST COM-PLETED IT...
N-NO WAY...
IN THE MIDDLE OF THE GAME... A RALLY...

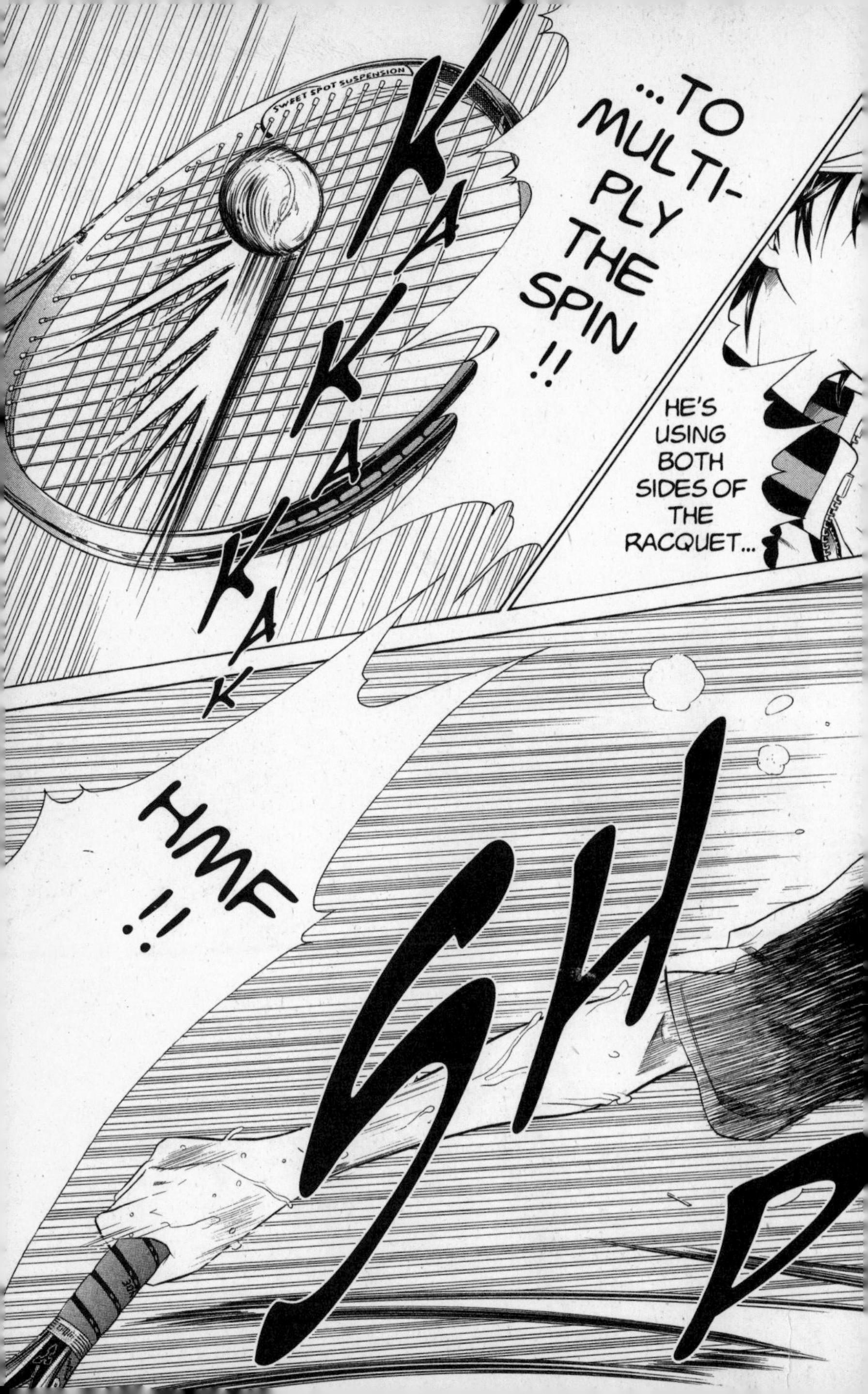
HE'S USING BOTH SIDES OF THE RACQUET...
...TO MULTI-PLY THE SPIN!!
SWEET SPOT SUSPENSION
KAKAKAK
HMF!!
SHP

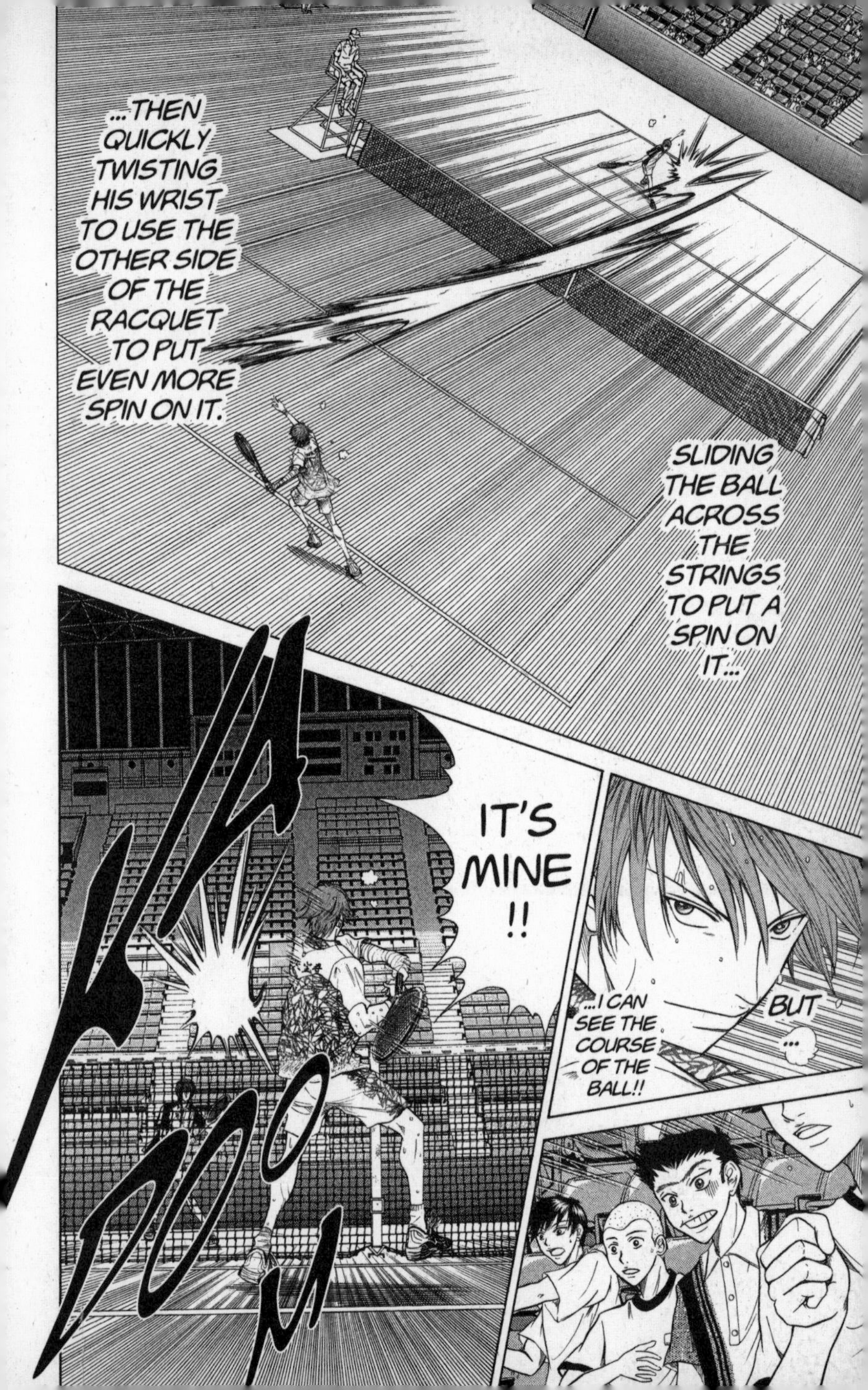
SLIDING THE BALL ACROSS THE STRINGS TO PUT A SPIN ON IT...
...THEN QUICKLY TWISTING HIS WRIST TO USE THE OTHER SIDE OF THE RACQUET TO PUT EVEN MORE SPIN ON IT.
BUT...
...I CAN SEE THE COURSE OF THE BALL!!
IT'S MINE!!

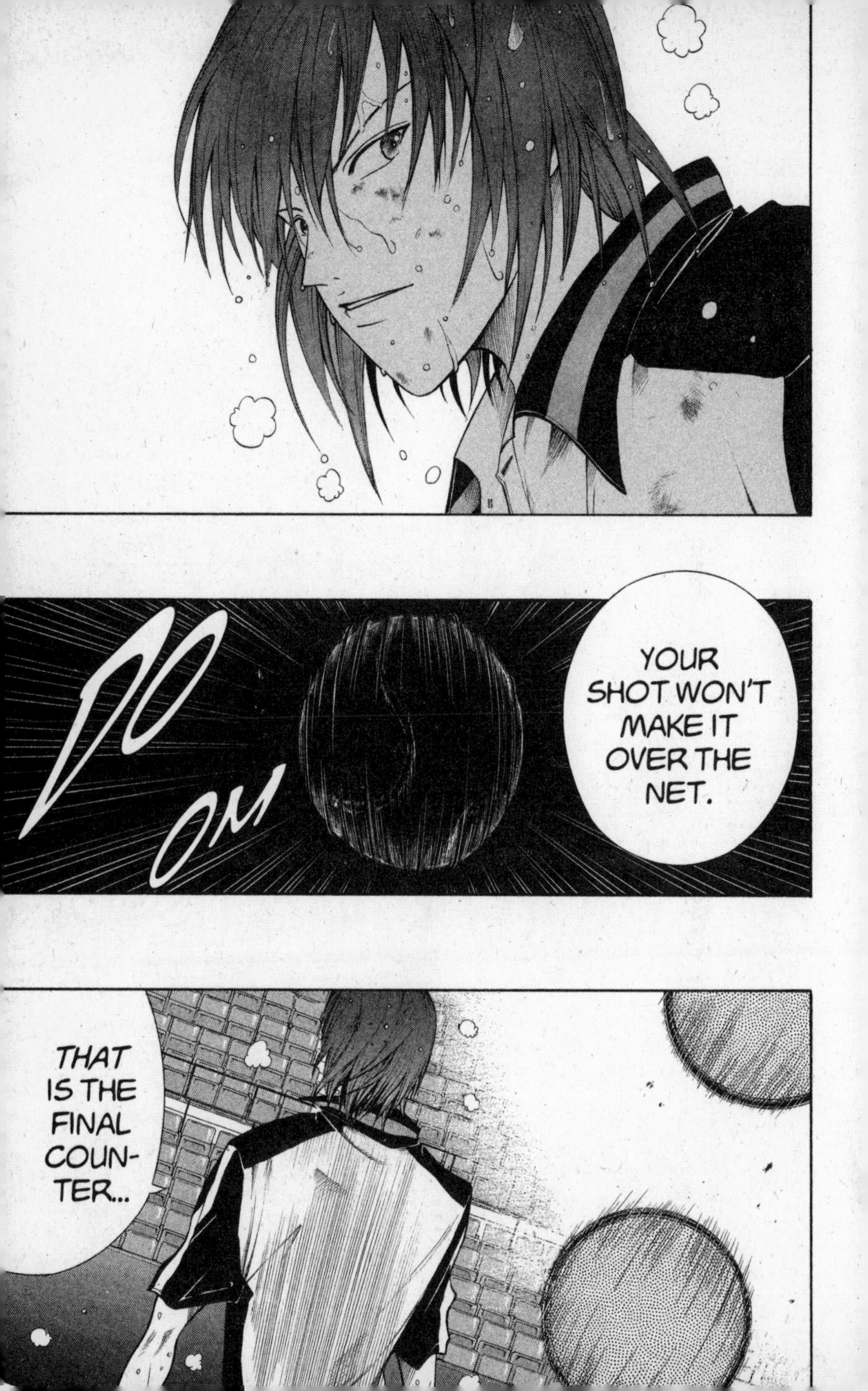
YOUR SHOT WON'T MAKE IT OVER THE NET.
THAT IS THE FINAL COUN-TER...

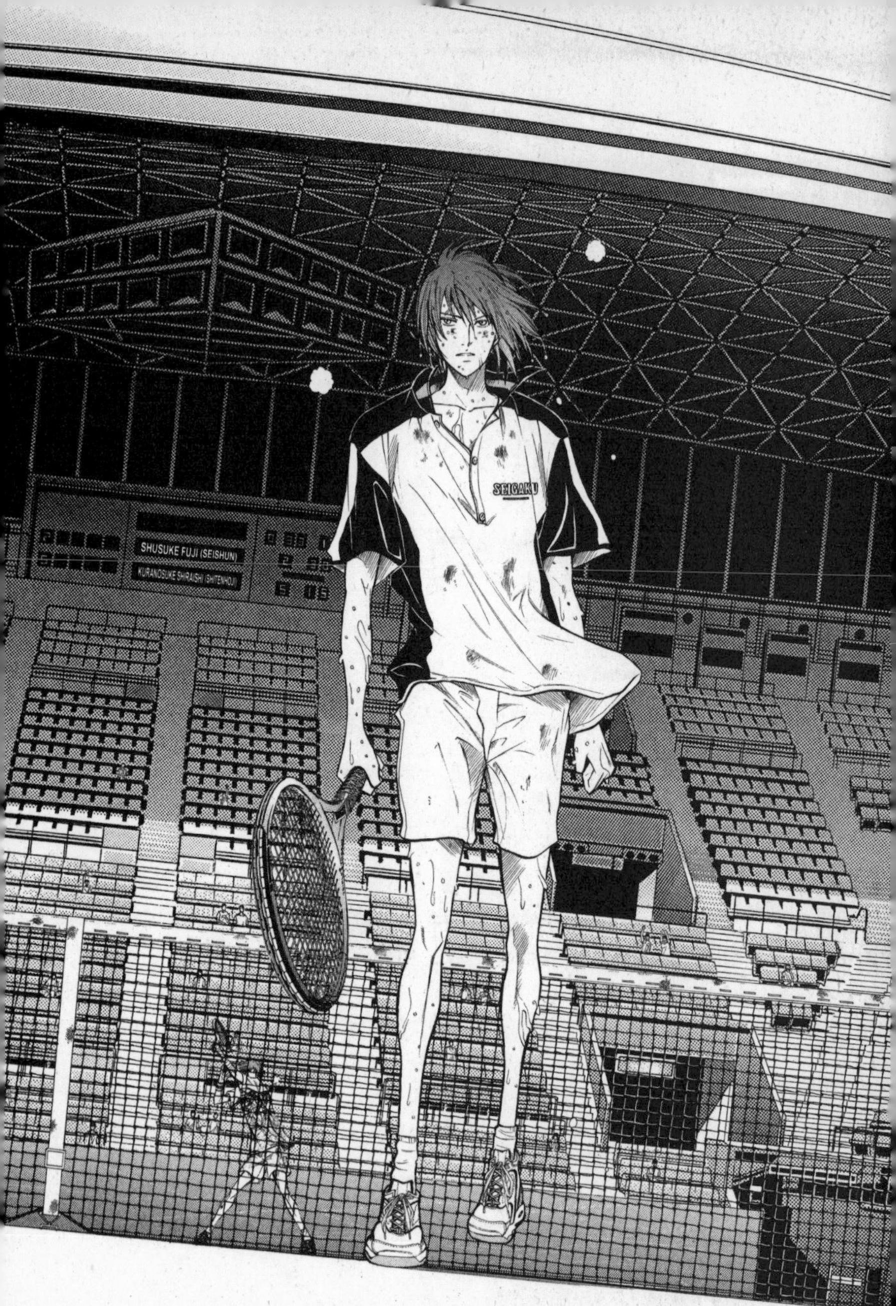
SHUSUKE FUJI (SEISHUN)
KURANOSUKE SHIRAISHI (SHITENHOJI)
SEIGAKU

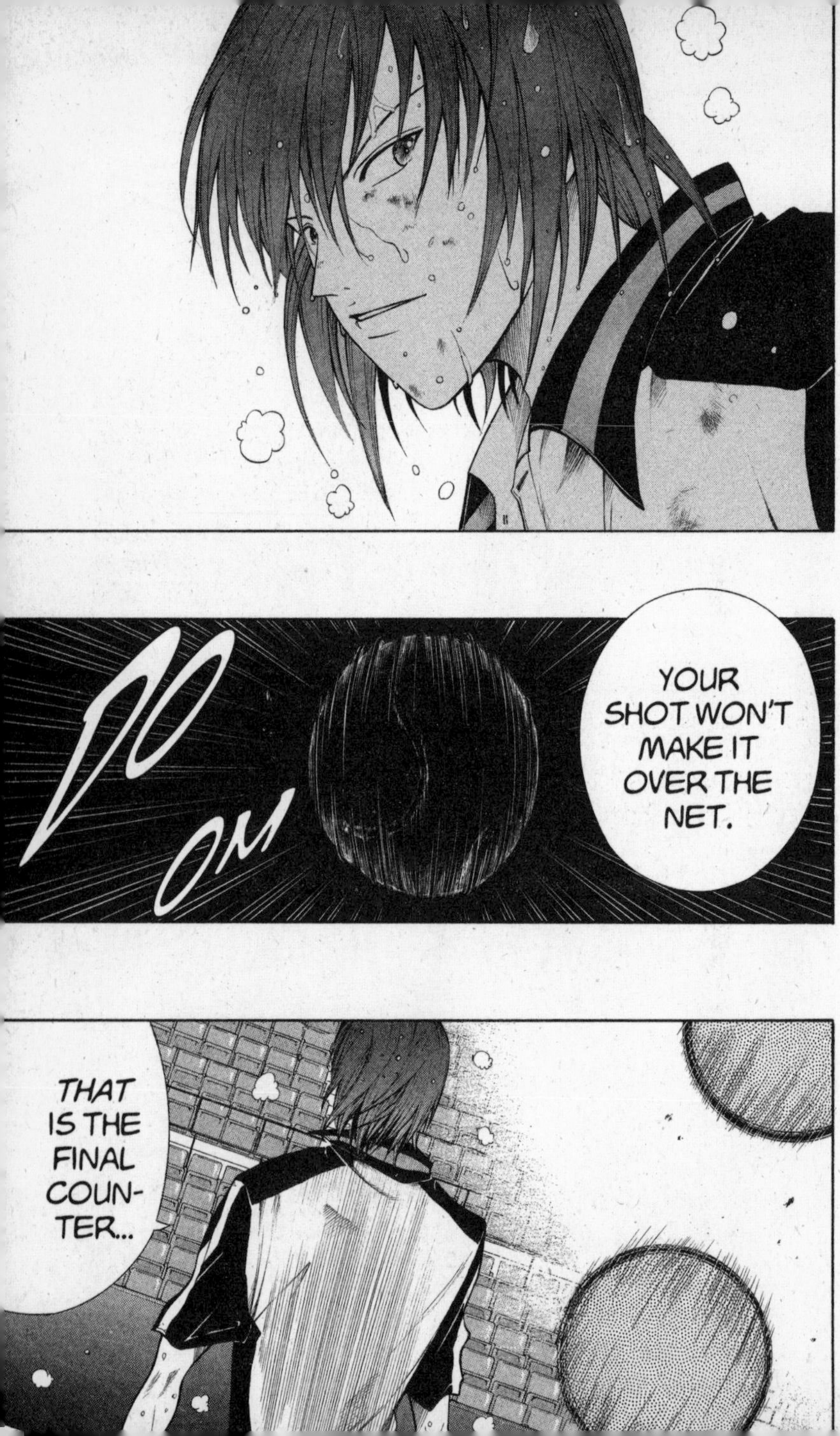
YOUR SHOT WON'T MAKE IT OVER THE NET.
DOOM
THAT IS THE FINAL COUN-TER...

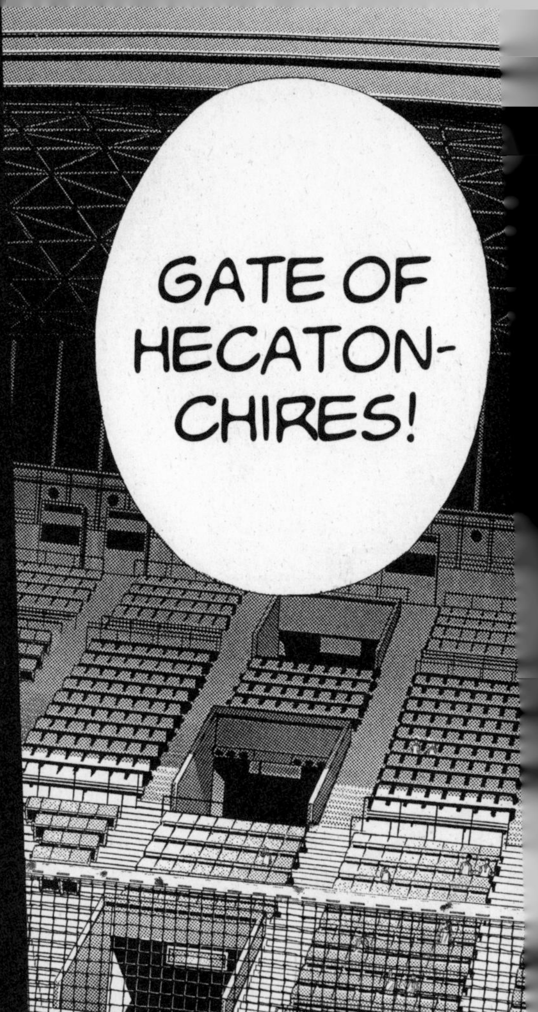
GATE OF HECATON-CHIRES!

GENIUS 319: IMPENETRABLE GATE

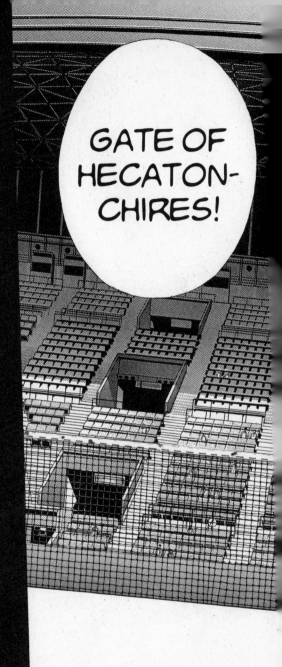

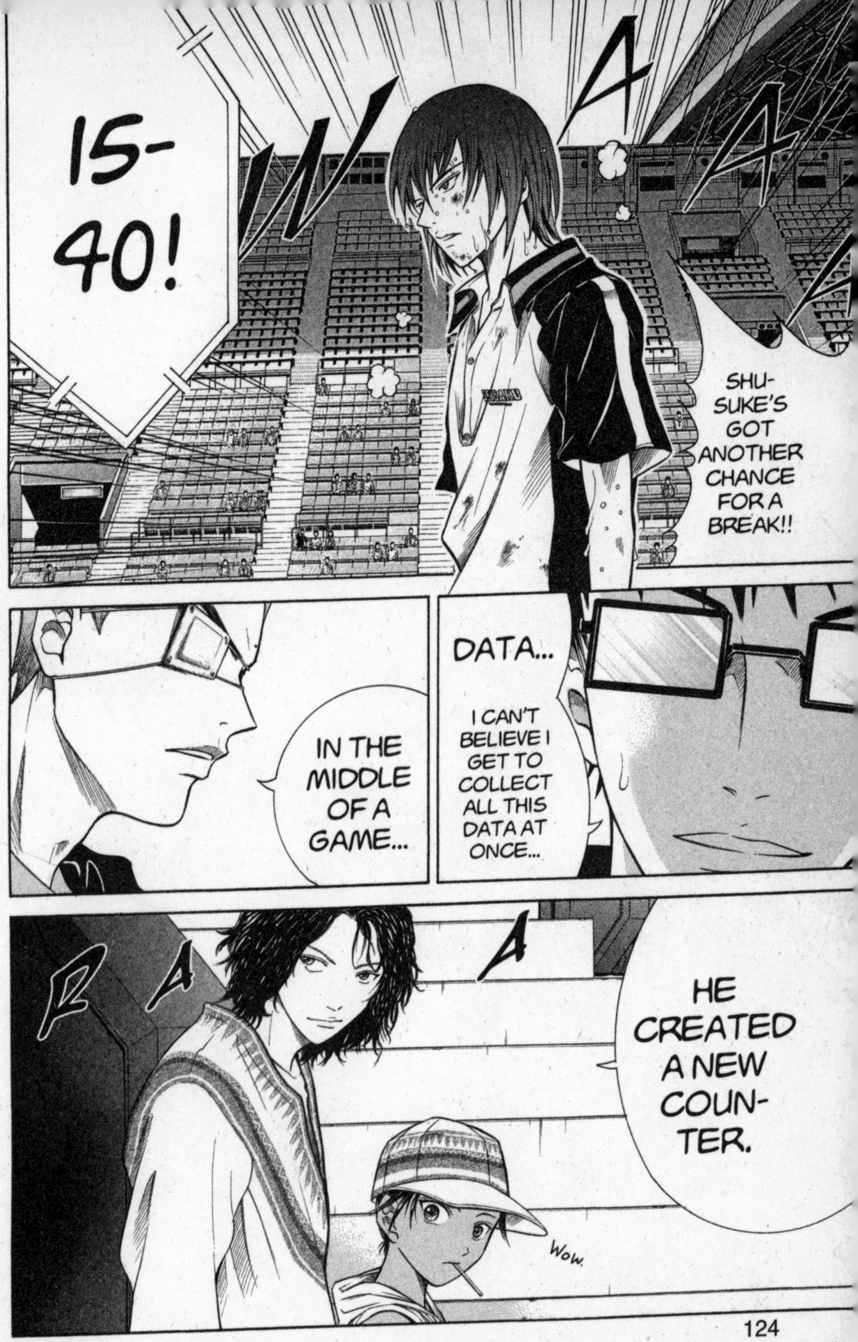
WAAA
15-40!
SHUSUKE'S GOT ANOTHER CHANCE FOR A BREAK!!
DATA...
I CAN'T BELIEVE I GET TO COLLECT ALL THIS DATA AT ONCE...
IN THE MIDDLE OF A GAME...
RAA
HE CREATED A NEW COUNTER.
Wow.

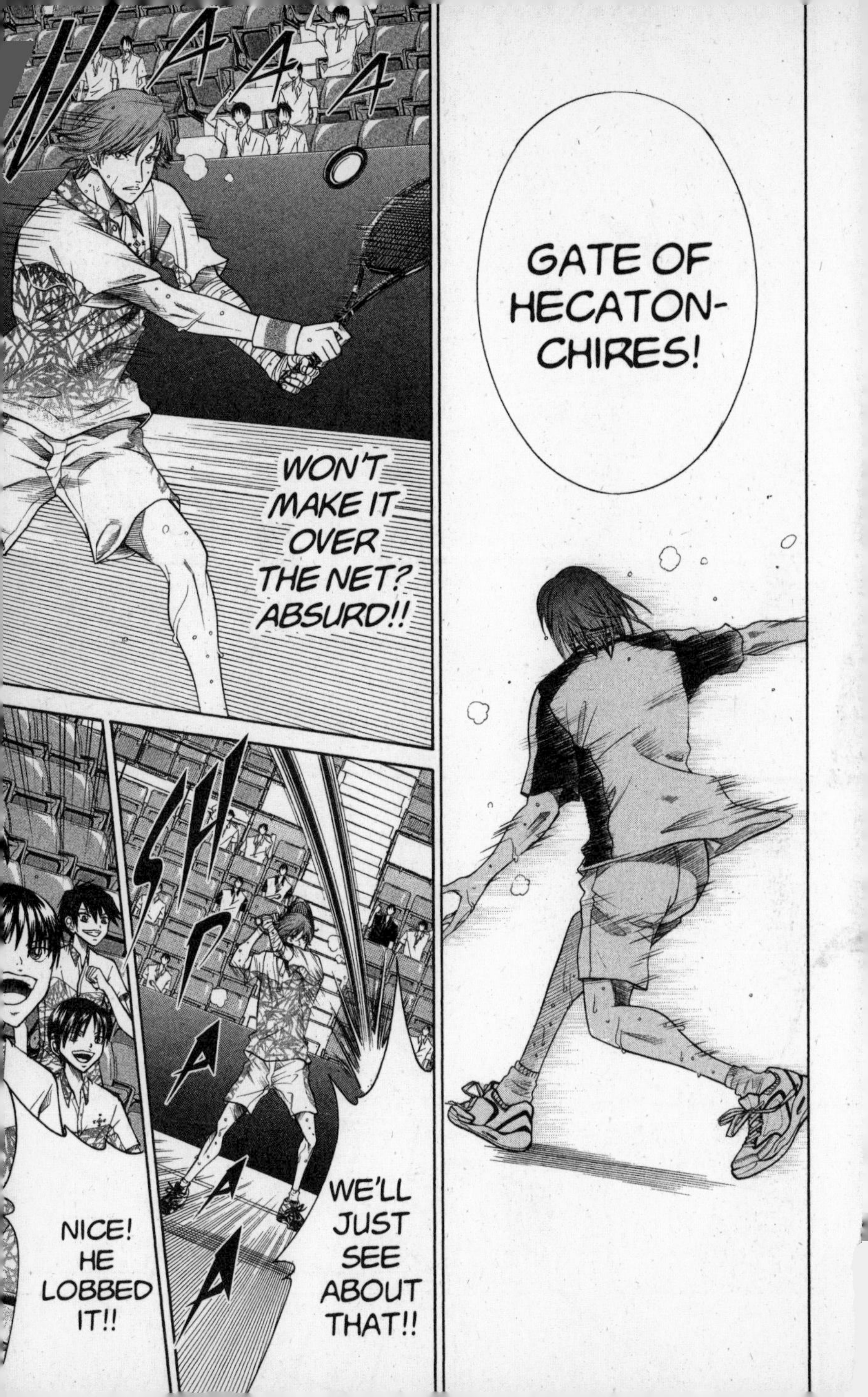
GATE OF HECATON-CHIRES!
WON'T MAKE IT OVER THE NET? ABSURD!!
WE'LL JUST SEE ABOUT THAT!!
NICE! HE LOBBED IT!!

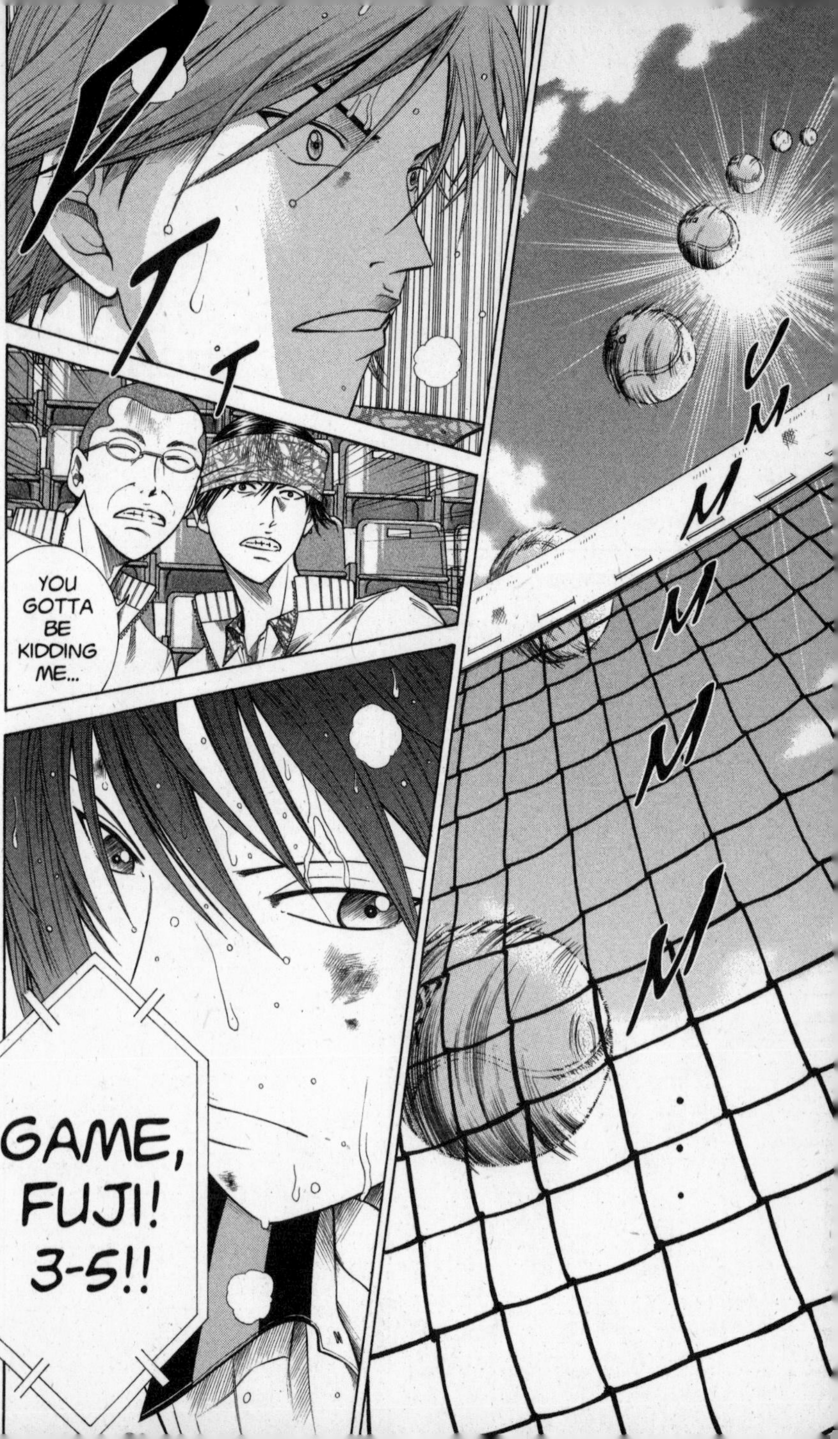
YOU GOTTA BE KIDDING ME...
GAME, FUJI! 3-5!!

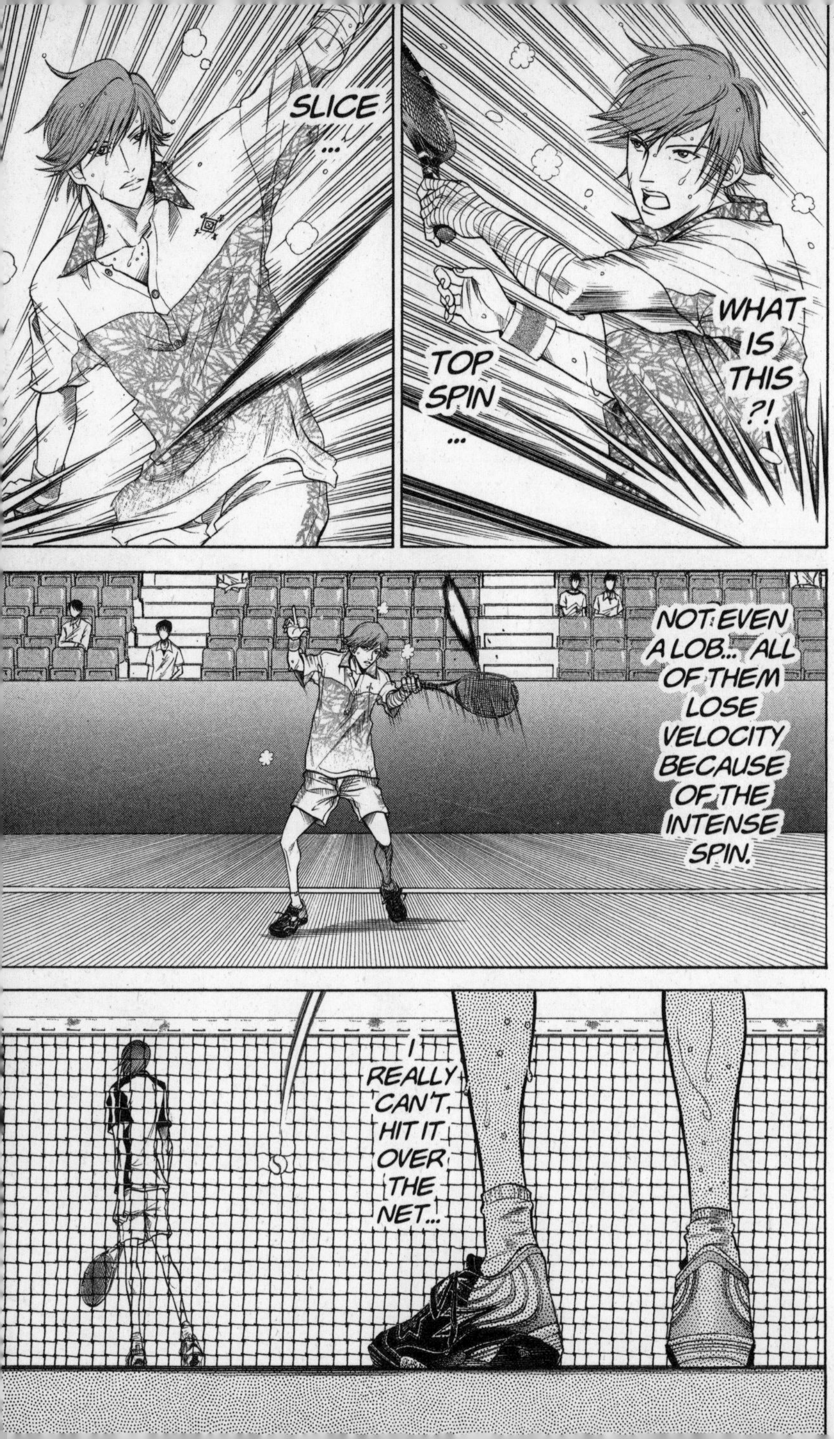
WHAT IS THIS ?!
TOP SPIN ...
SLICE ...
NOT EVEN A LOB... ALL OF THEM LOSE VELOCITY BECAUSE OF THE INTENSE SPIN.
I REALLY CAN'T HIT IT OVER THE NET...

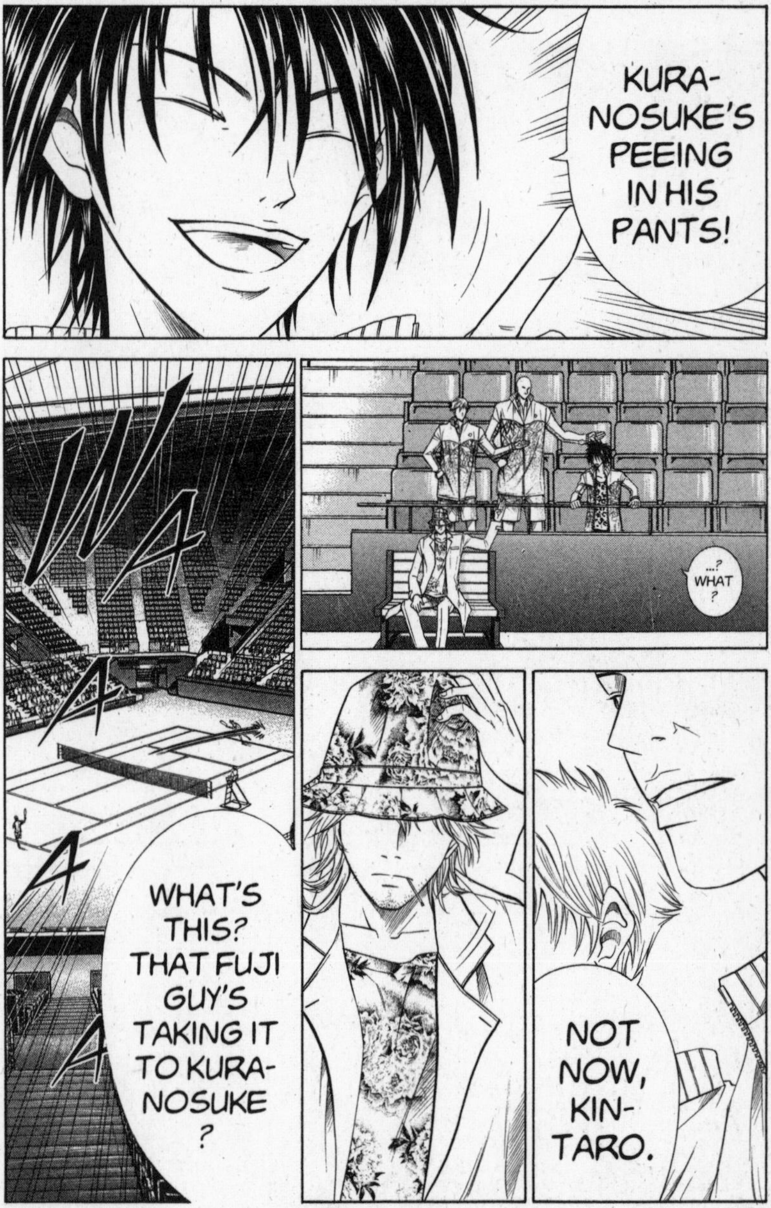
KURA-NOSUKE'S PEEING IN HIS PANTS!
...? WHAT ?
NOT NOW, KIN-TARO.
WAAAA
WHAT'S THIS? THAT FUJI GUY'S TAKING IT TO KURA-NOSUKE ?

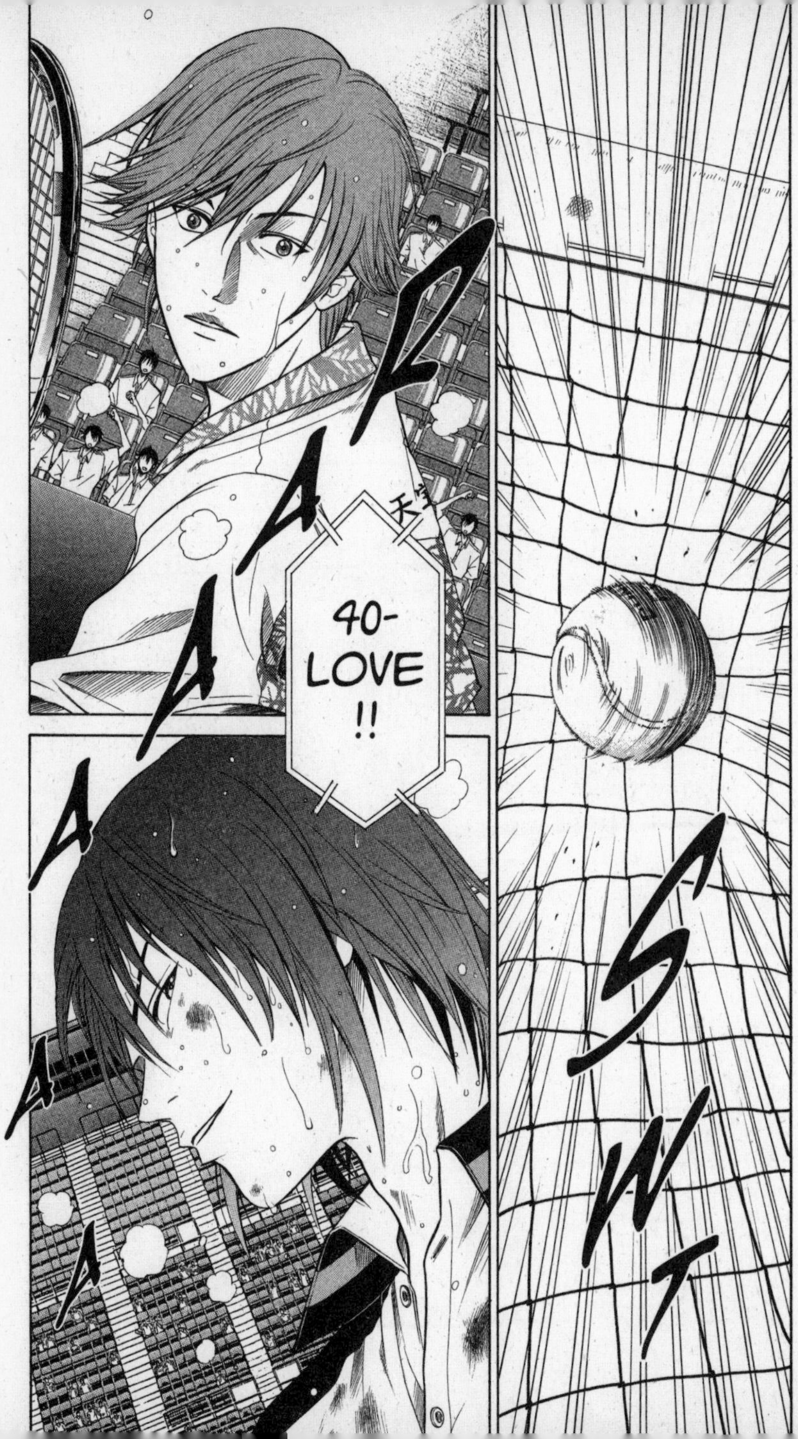
40-
LOVE
!!

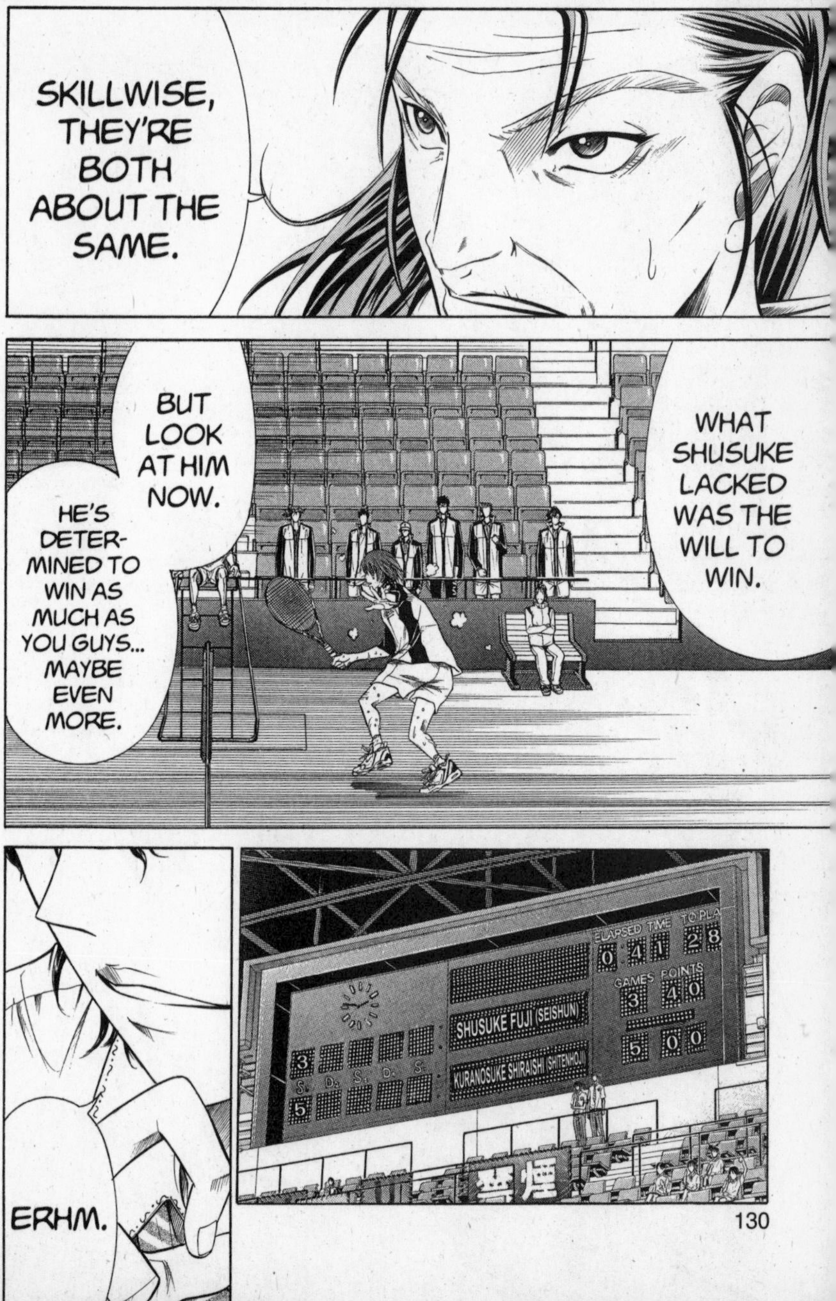
SKILLWISE, THEY'RE BOTH ABOUT THE SAME.
WHAT SHUSUKE LACKED WAS THE WILL TO WIN.
BUT LOOK AT HIM NOW.
HE'S DETERMINED TO WIN AS MUCH AS YOU GUYS... MAYBE EVEN MORE.
ELAPSED TIME
0 41 28
GAMES POINTS
3 40
SHUSUKE FUJI (SEISHUN)
KURANOSUKE SHIRAISHI (SHITENHOJI)
5 00
禁煙
ERHM.

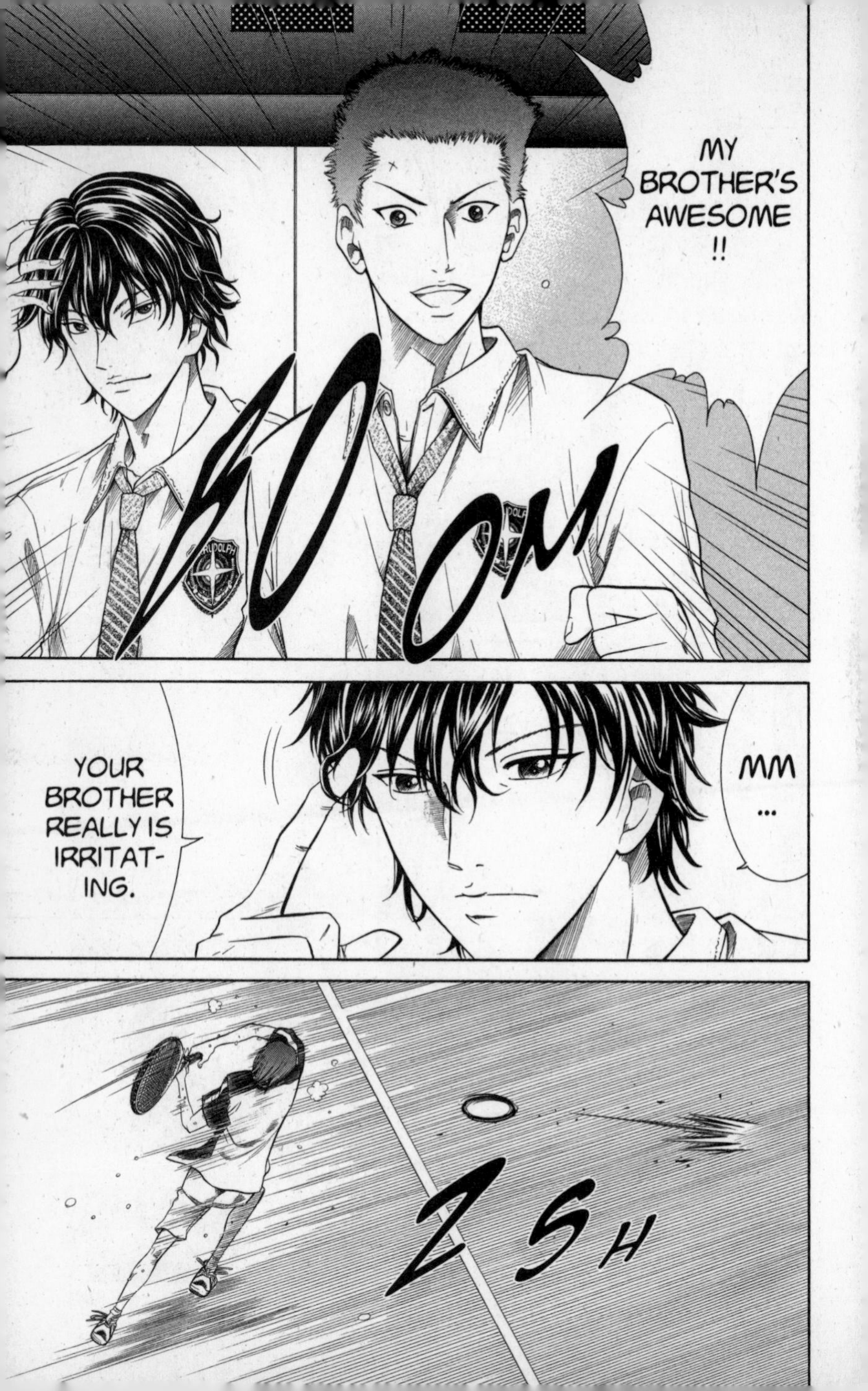
MY BROTHER'S AWESOME !!
BOOM
MM ...
YOUR BROTHER REALLY IS IRRITAT-ING.
ZSH

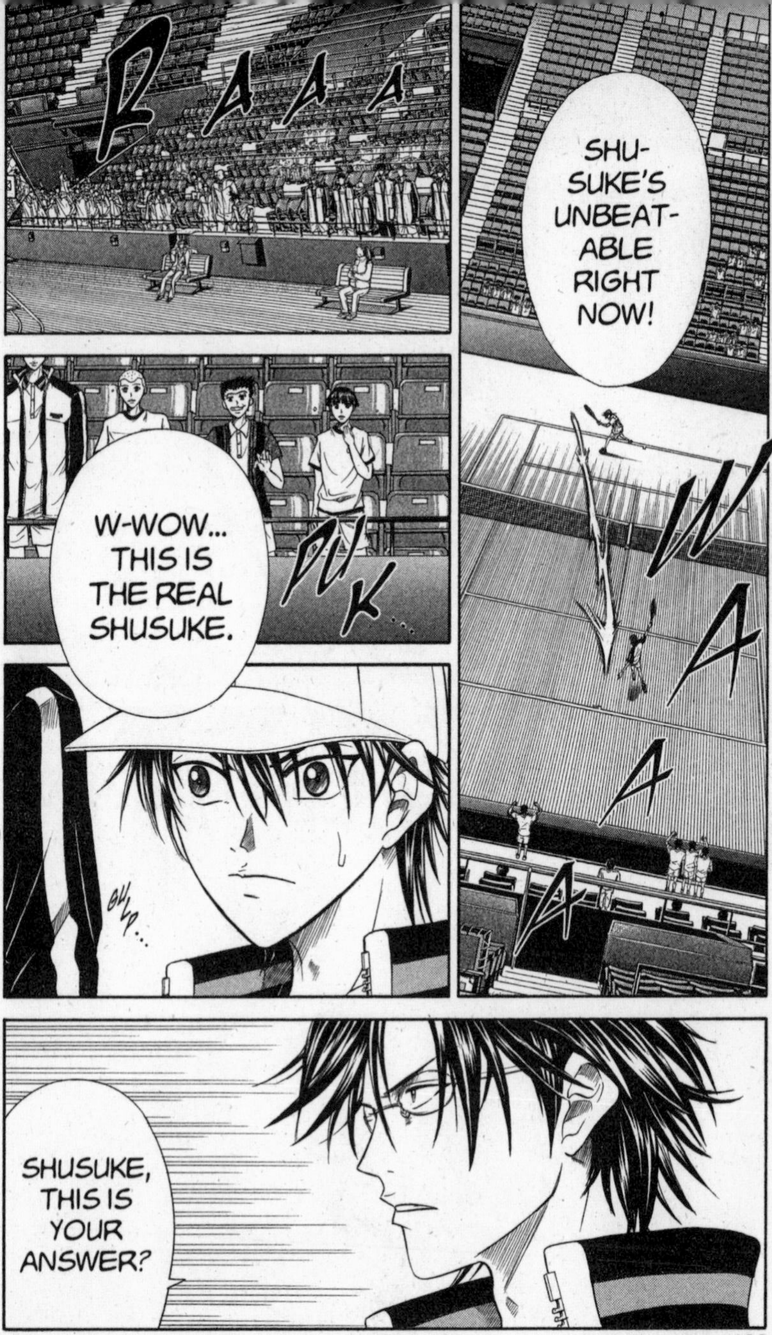
SHUSUKE'S UNBEATABLE RIGHT NOW!
WAAAA
RAAAA
W-WOW... THIS IS THE REAL SHUSUKE.
DUK...
GULP...
SHUSUKE, THIS IS YOUR ANSWER?

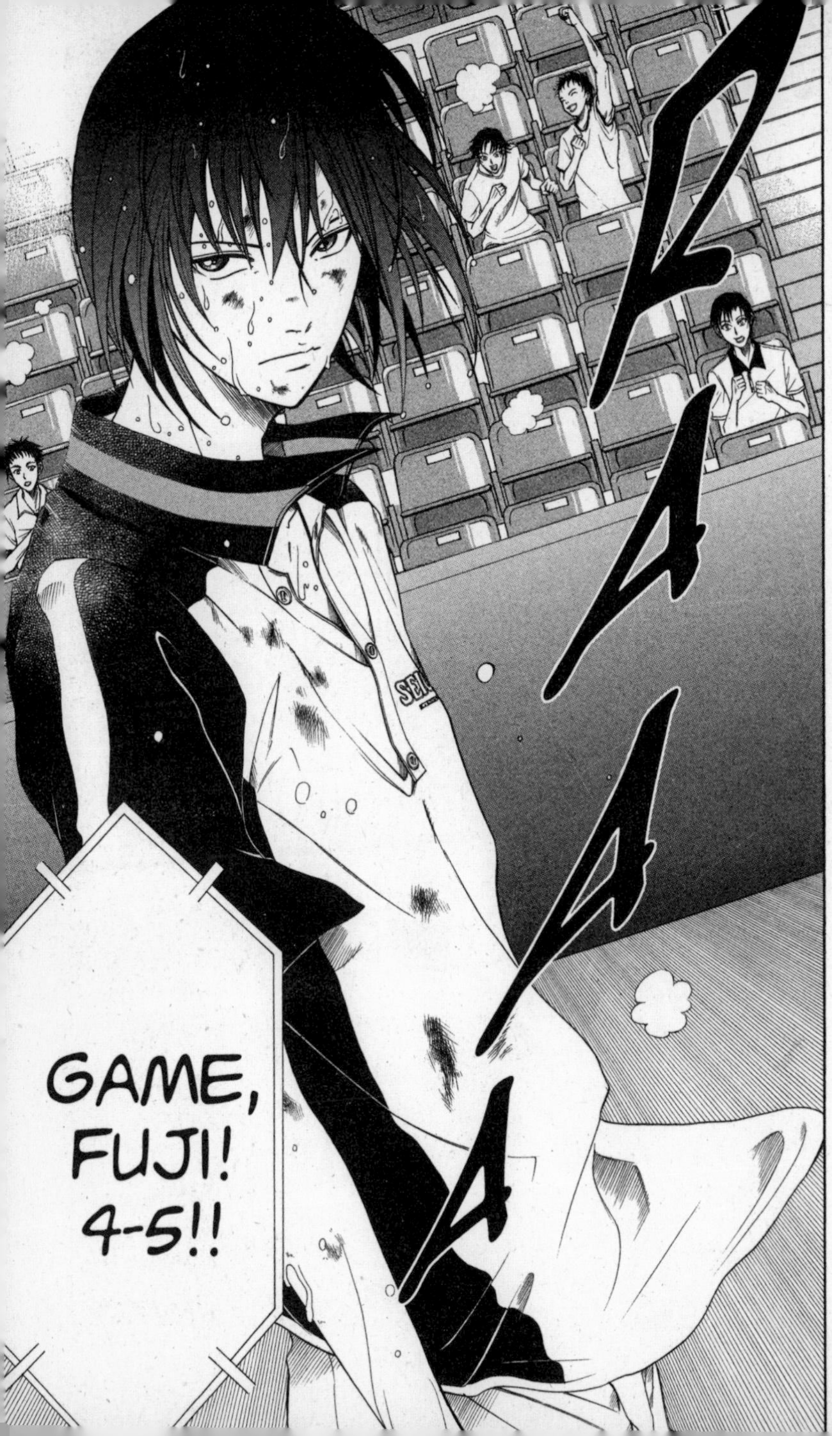
GAME, FUJI! 4-5!!

テニスの王子様

THE PRINCE OF TENNIS

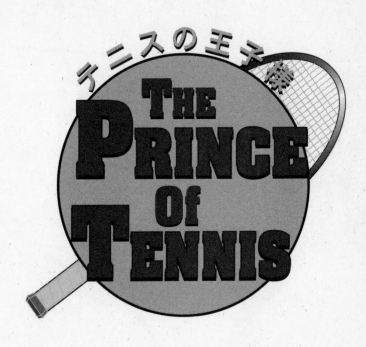

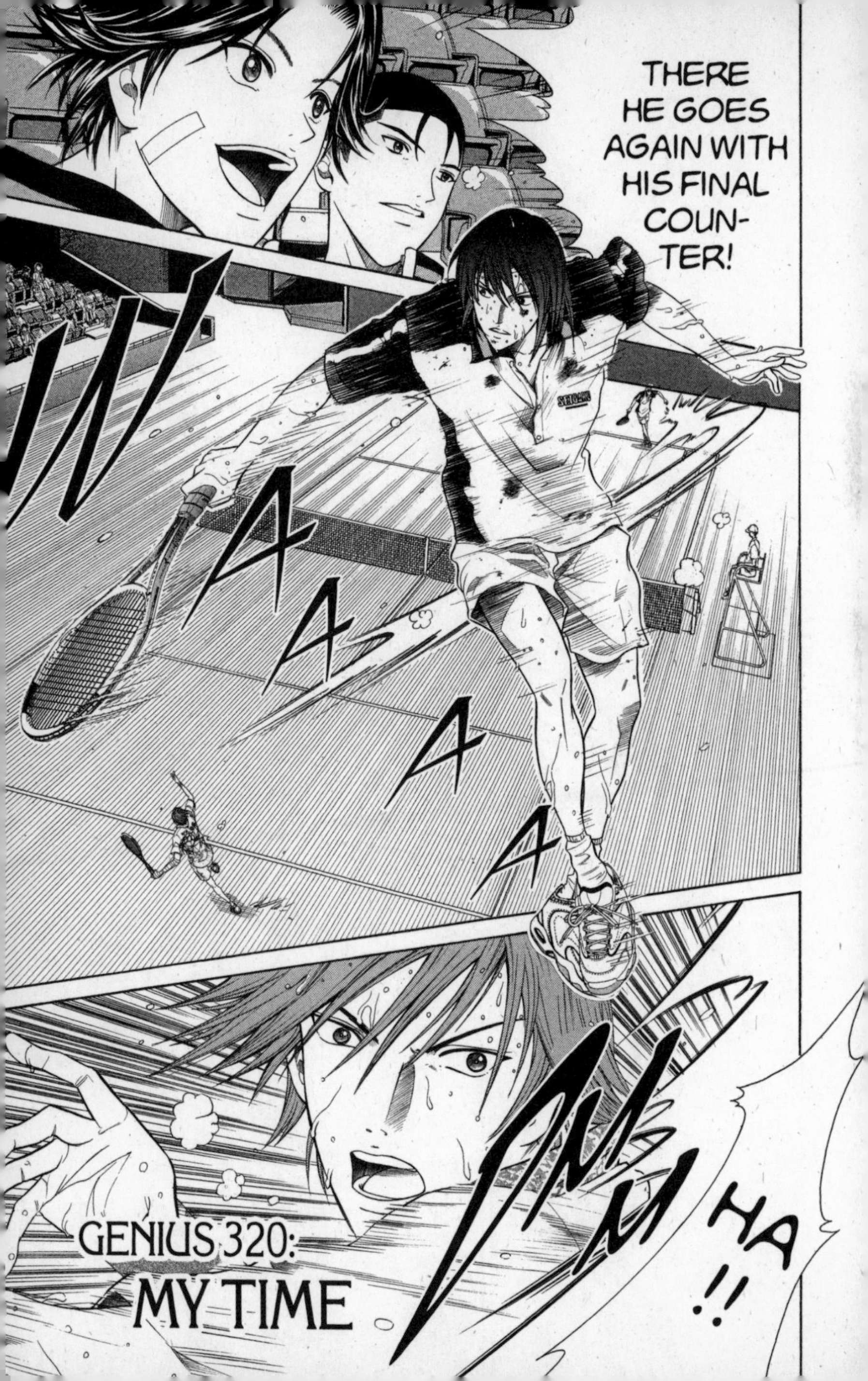
THERE HE GOES AGAIN WITH HIS FINAL COUN-TER!
WAAAAA
MM
HA!!

GENIUS 320: MY TIME

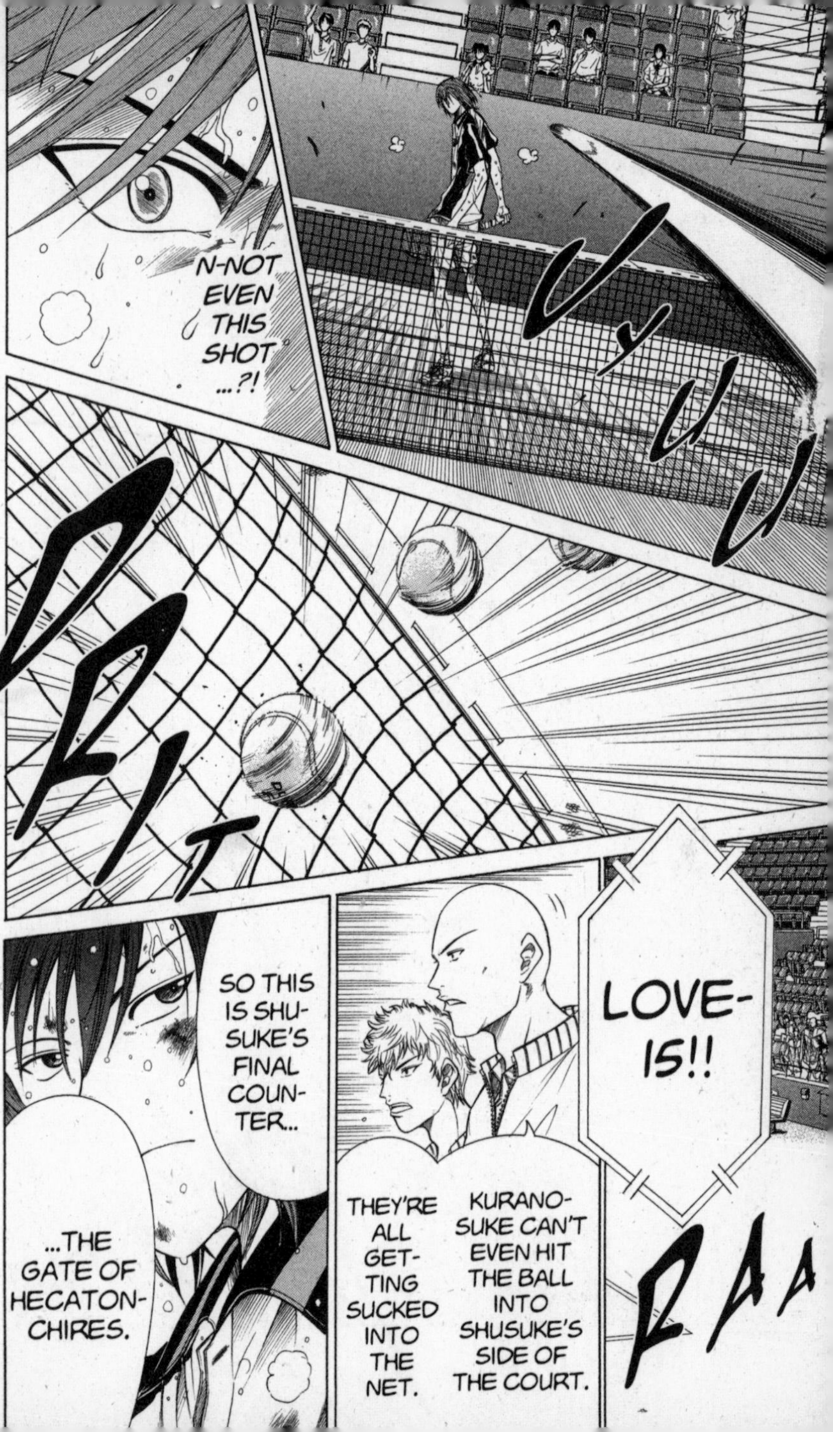
N-NOT EVEN THIS SHOT ...?!
LOVE-15!!
RAA
KURANOSUKE CAN'T EVEN HIT THE BALL INTO SHUSUKE'S SIDE OF THE COURT.
THEY'RE ALL GETTING SUCKED INTO THE NET.
SO THIS IS SHUSUKE'S FINAL COUNTER...
...THE GATE OF HECATONCHIRES.

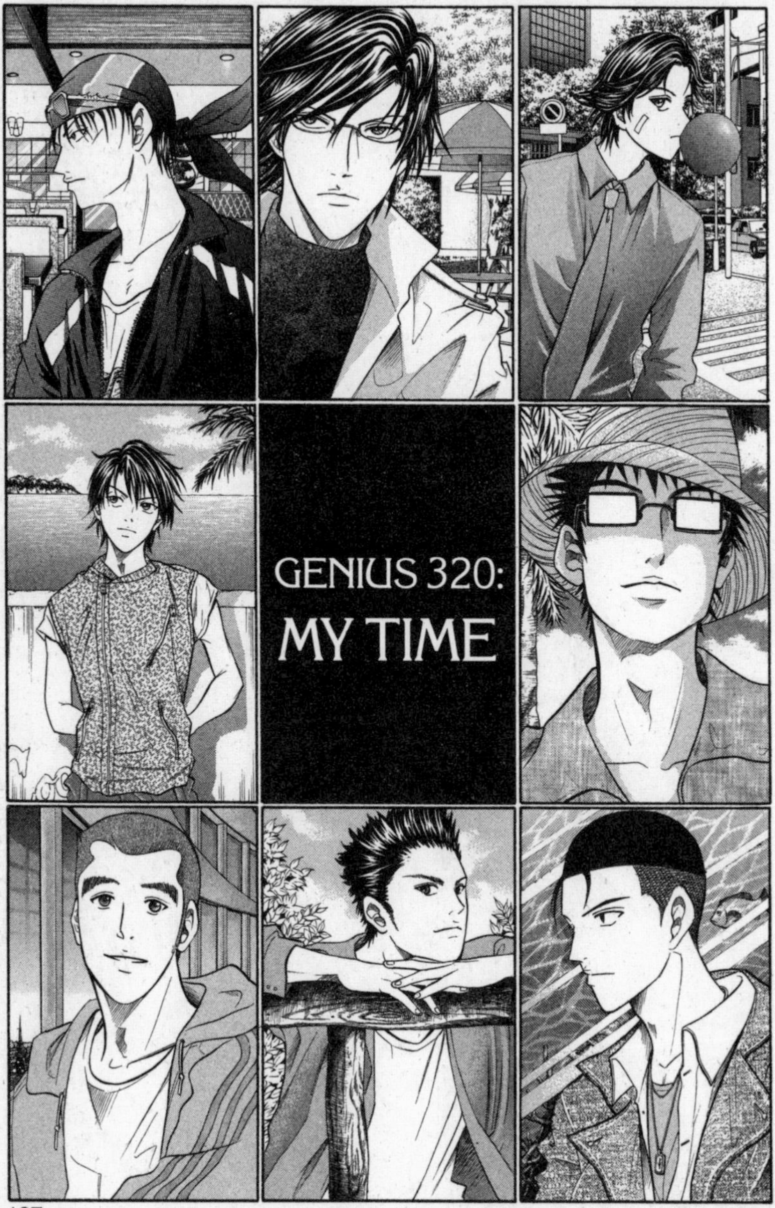
GENIUS 320:
MY TIME

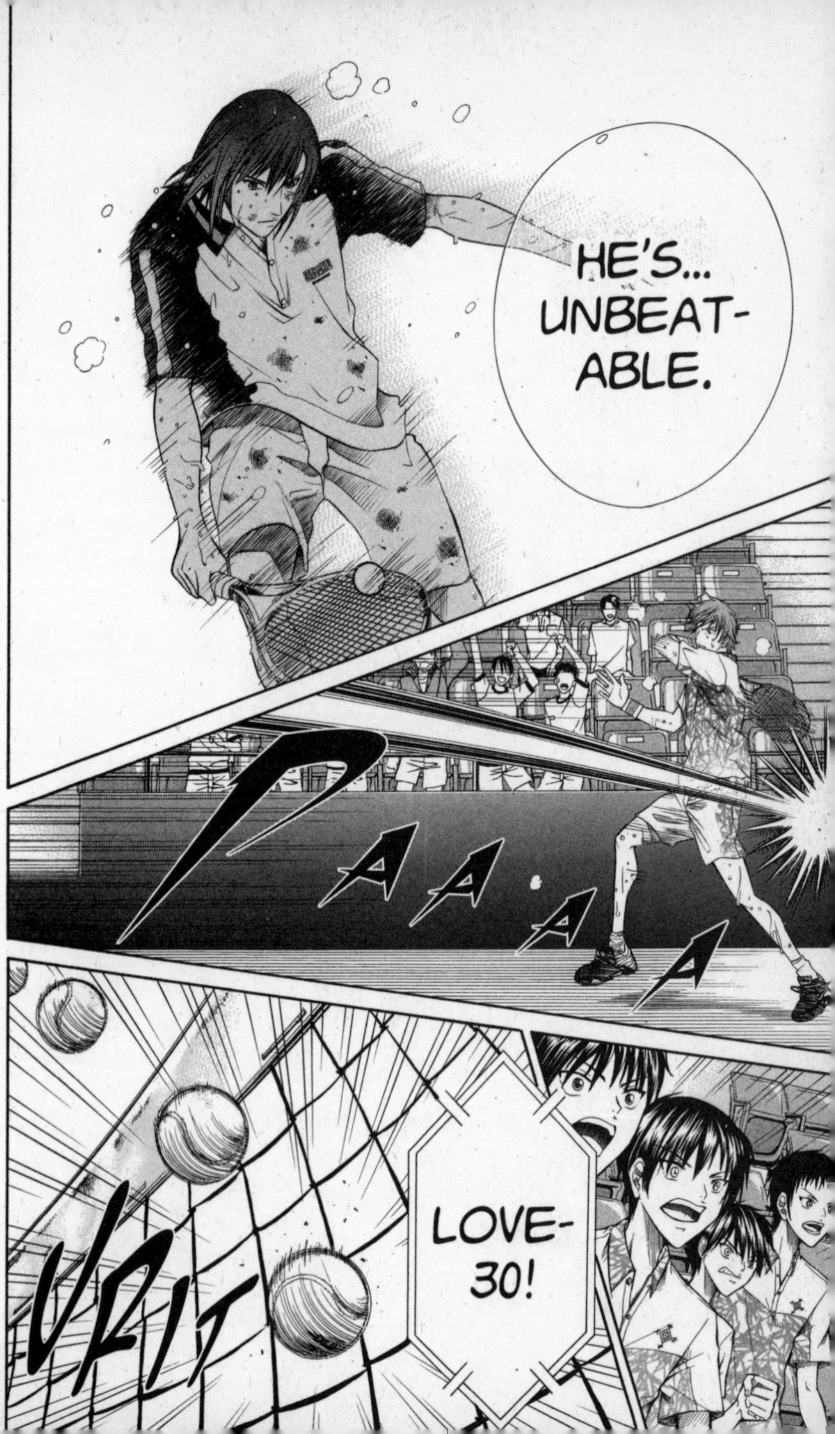
HE'S... UNBEAT-ABLE.
PAAAA
VRIT
LOVE-30!

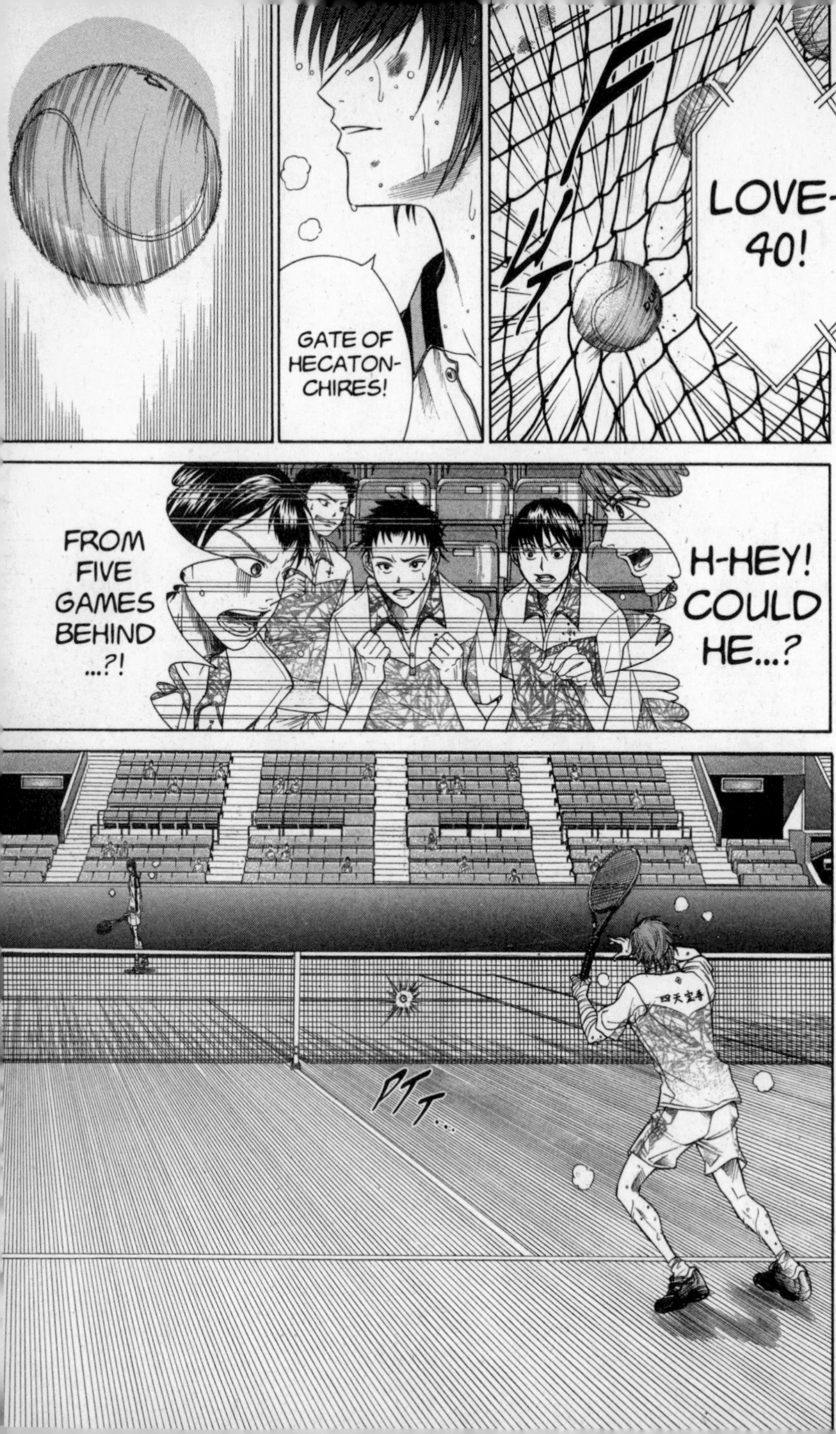
LOVE-40!
GATE OF HECATON-CHIRES!
H-HEY! COULD HE...?
FROM FIVE GAMES BEHIND ...?!

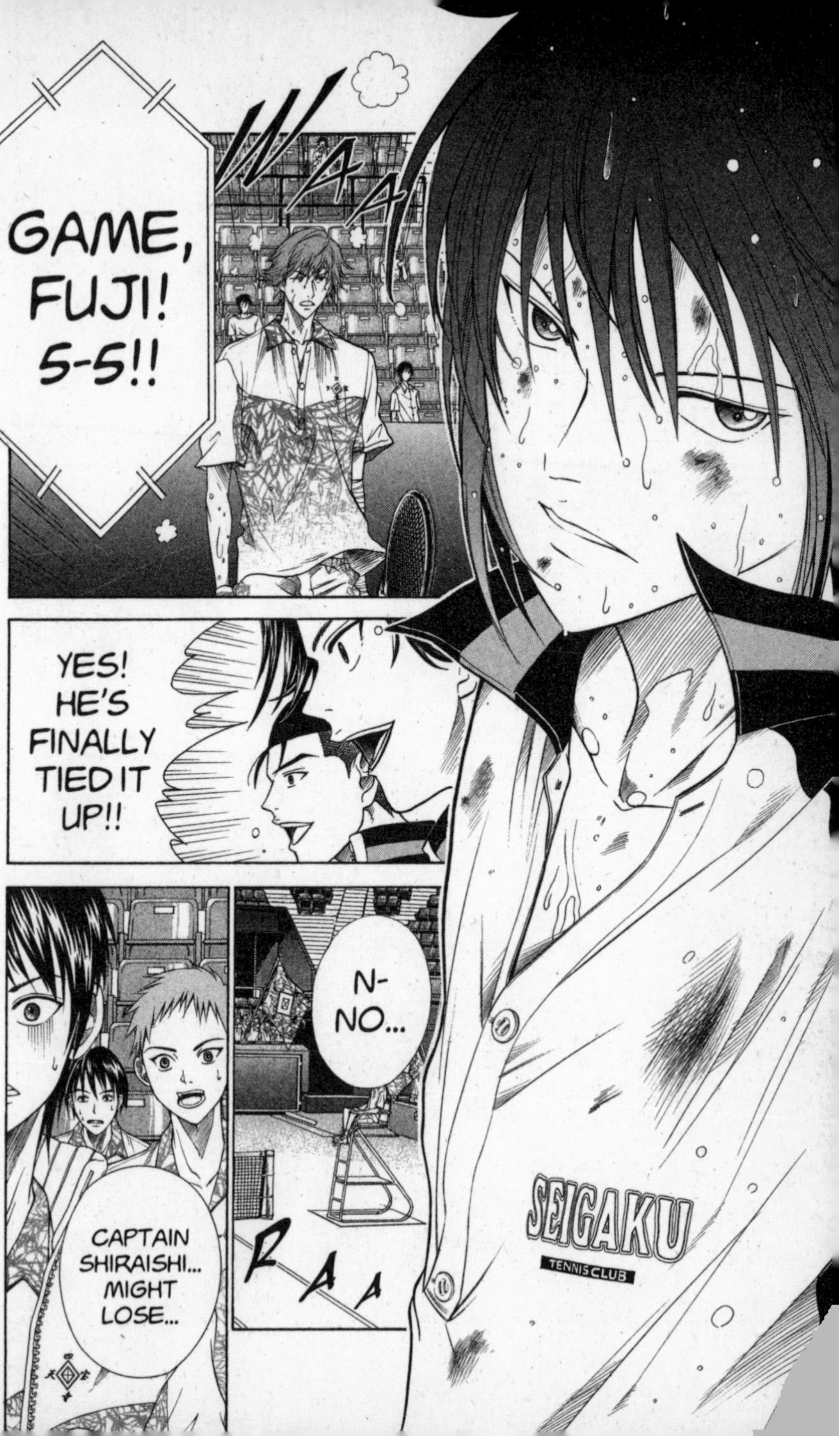
SEIGAKU
TENNIS CLUB
WAAA
GAME, FUJI! 5-5!!
YES! HE'S FINALLY TIED IT UP!!
N-NO...
RAA
CAPTAIN SHIRAISHI... MIGHT LOSE...

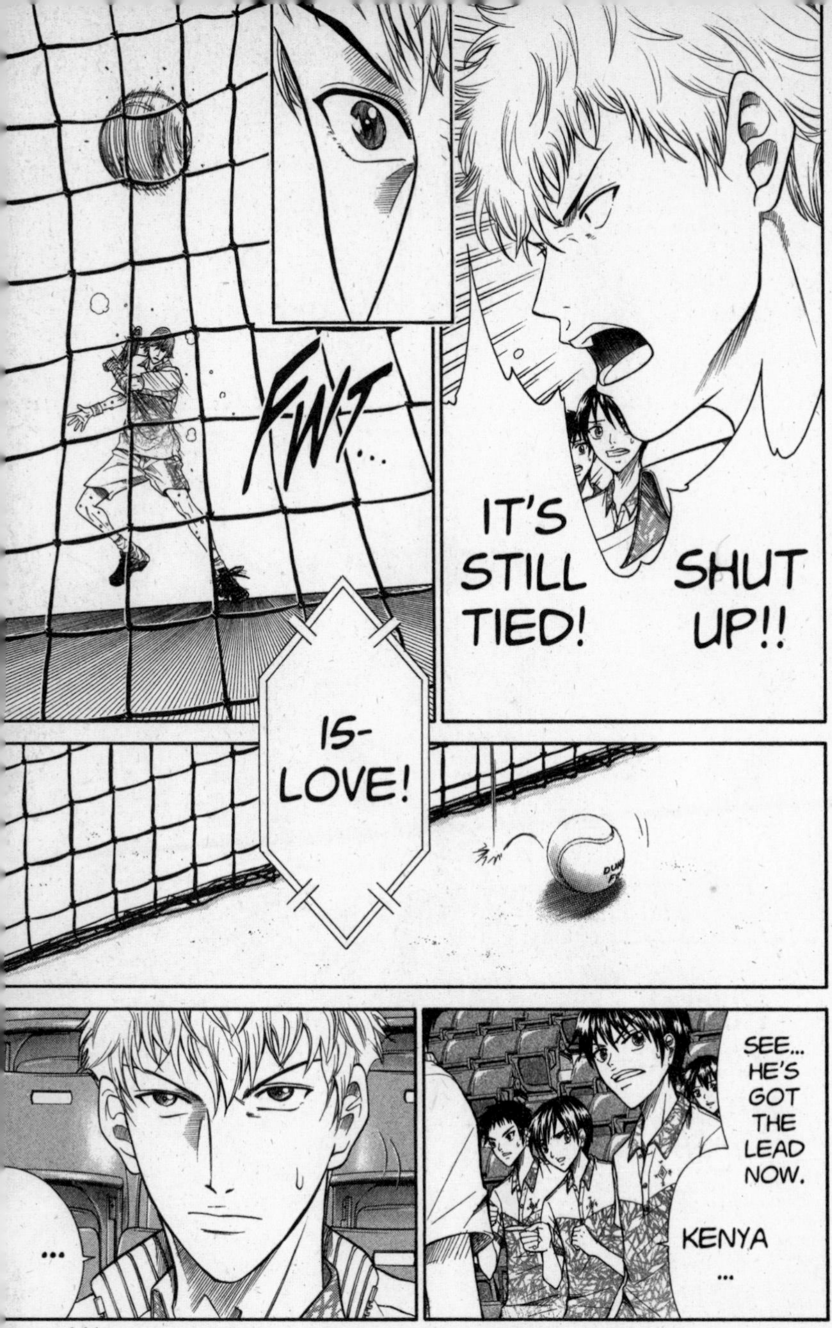
IT'S STILL TIED!
SHUT UP!!
F-WT...
15-LOVE!
SEE... HE'S GOT THE LEAD NOW.
KENYA ...
...

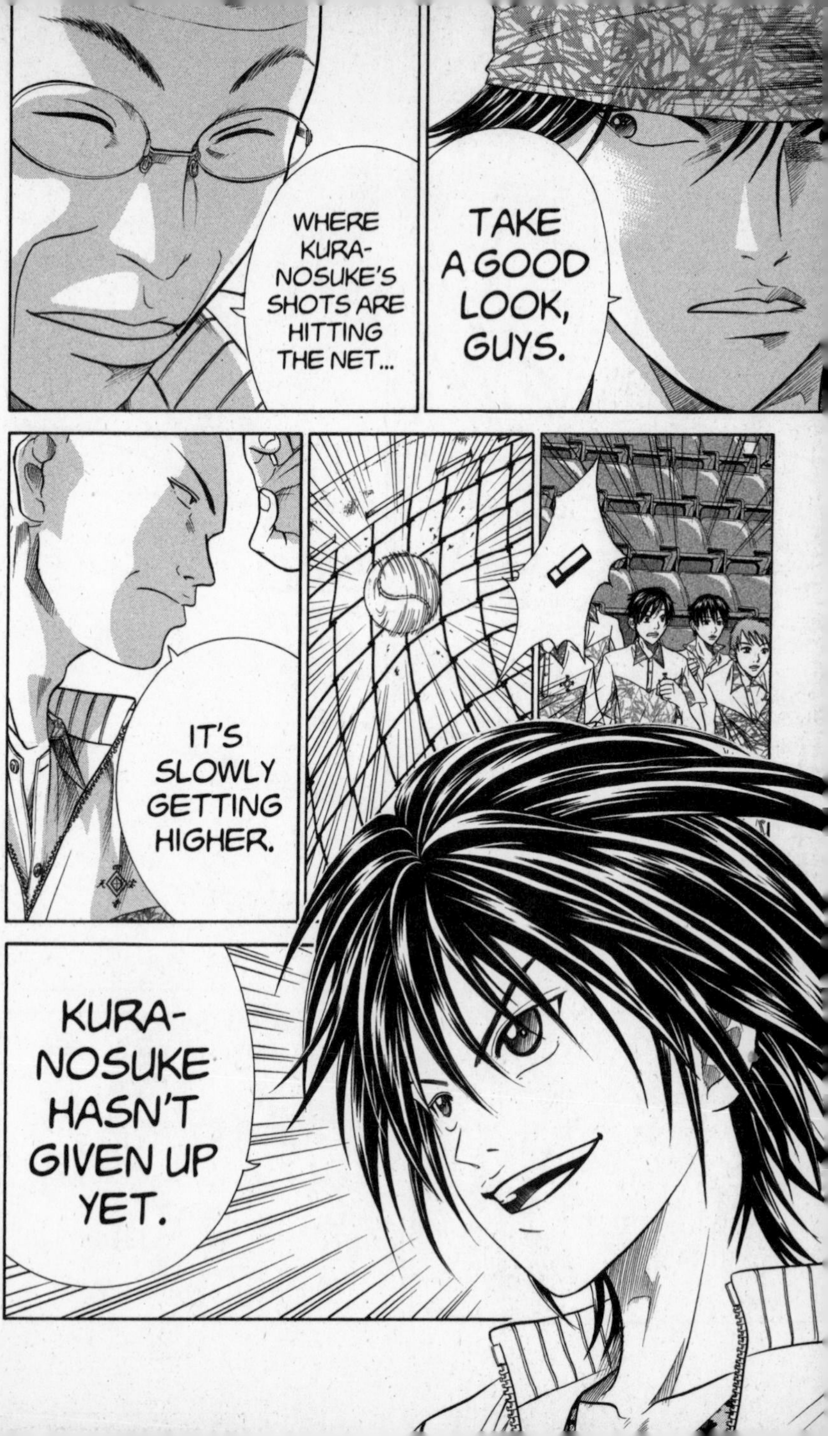
TAKE A GOOD LOOK, GUYS.
WHERE KURA-NOSUKE'S SHOTS ARE HITTING THE NET...
IT'S SLOWLY GETTING HIGHER.
KURA-NOSUKE HASN'T GIVEN UP YET.

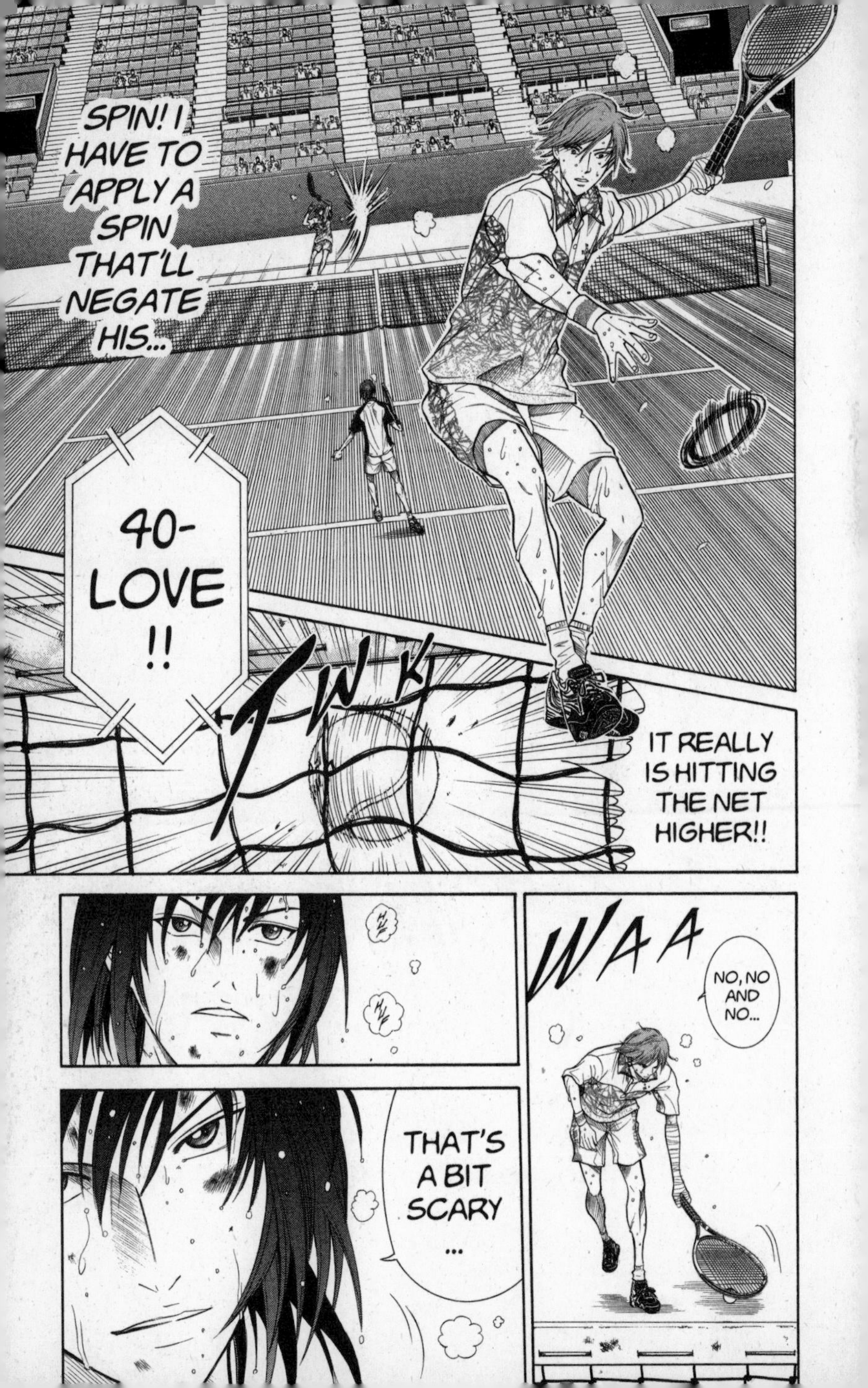
SPIN! I HAVE TO APPLY A SPIN THAT'LL NEGATE HIS...
40-LOVE!!
IT REALLY IS HITTING THE NET HIGHER!!
TWK
WAA
NO, NO AND NO...
THAT'S A BIT SCARY...

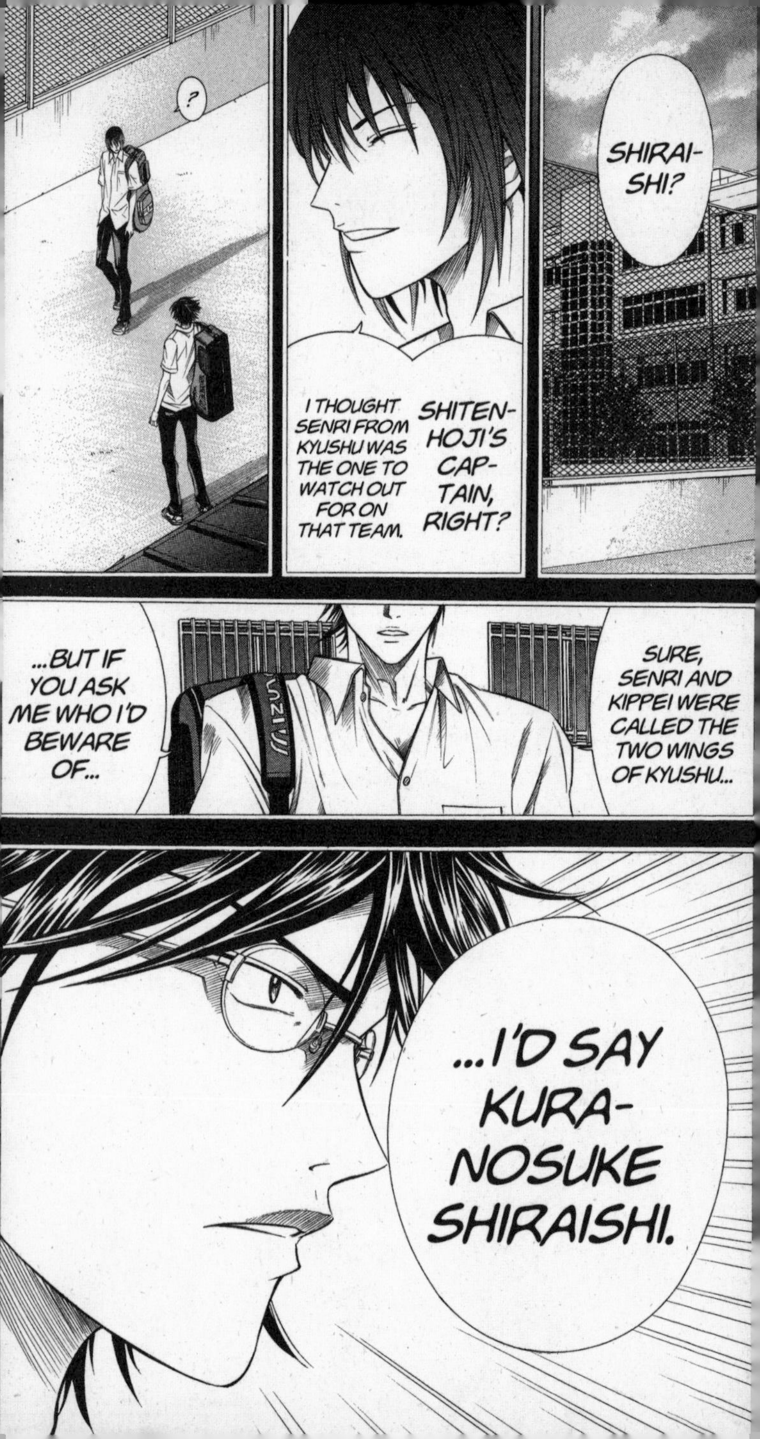
SHIRAI-SHI?
SHITEN-HOJI'S CAP-TAIN, RIGHT?
I THOUGHT SENRI FROM KYUSHU WAS THE ONE TO WATCH OUT FOR ON THAT TEAM.
?
SURE, SENRI AND KIPPEI WERE CALLED THE TWO WINGS OF KYUSHU...
...BUT IF YOU ASK ME WHO I'D BEWARE OF...
...I'D SAY KURA-NOSUKE SHIRAISHI.

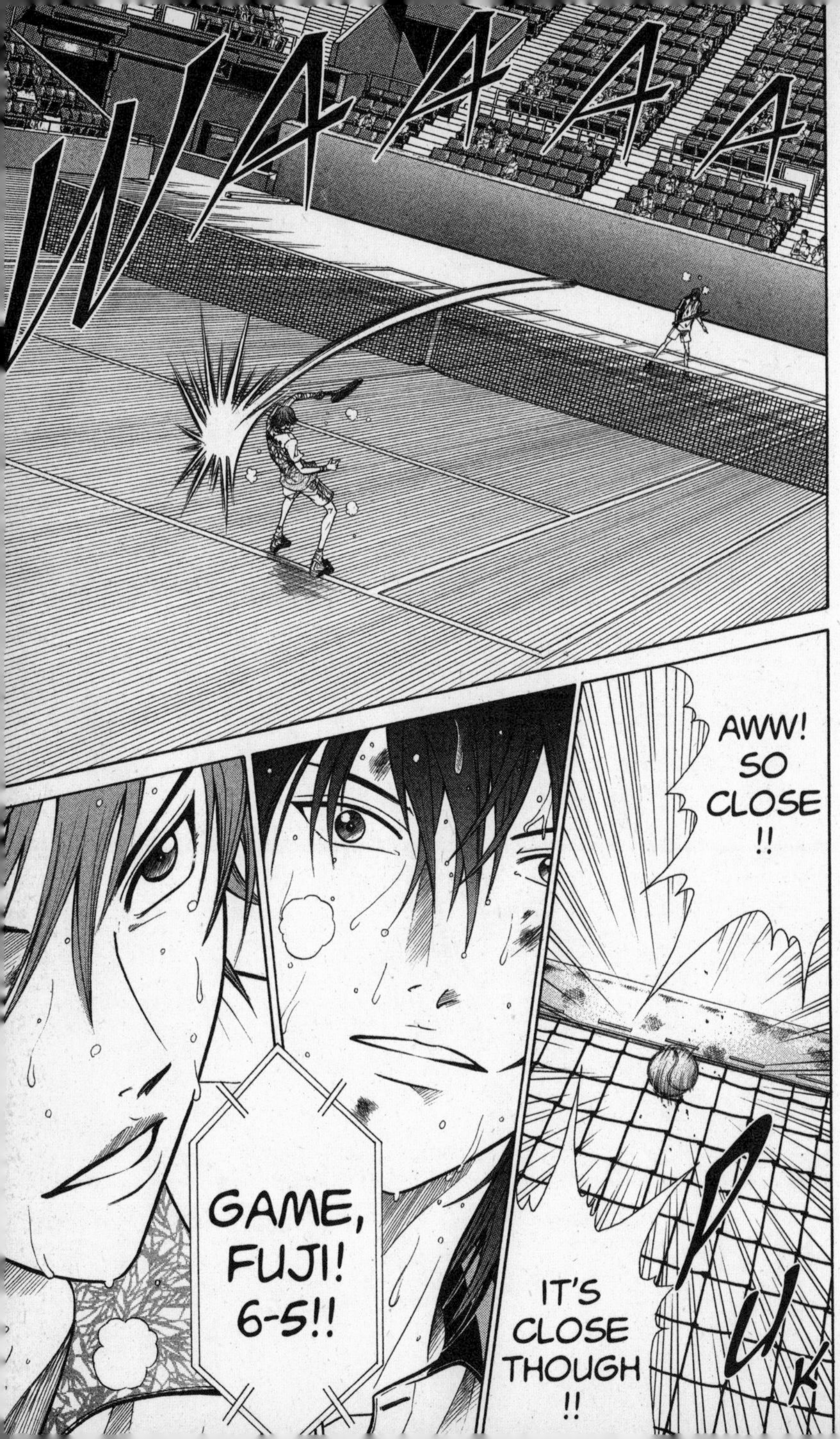
WAAAA
AWW! SO CLOSE !!
IT'S CLOSE THOUGH !!
GAME, FUJI! 6-5!!

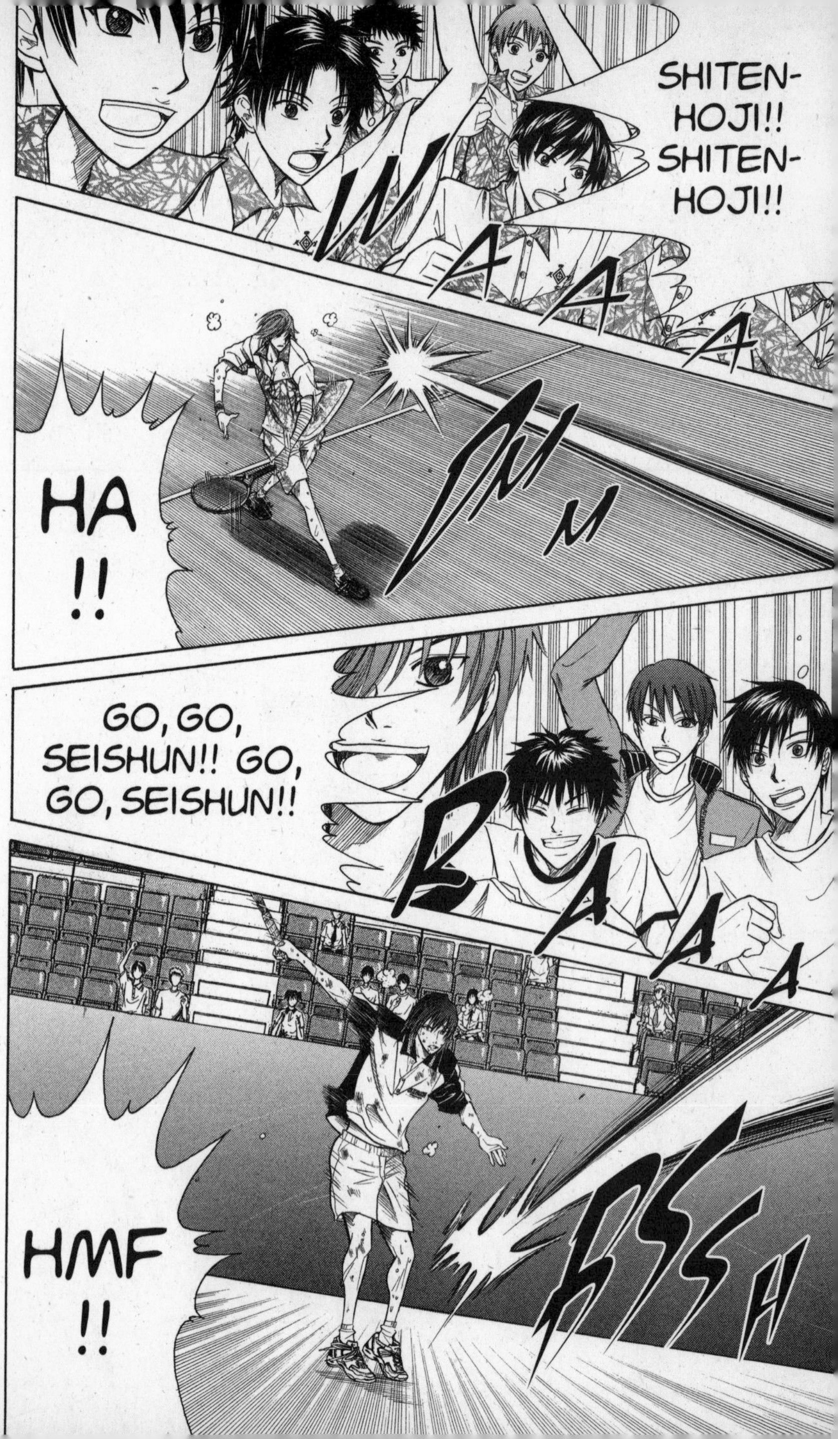
SHITEN-HOJI!! SHITEN-HOJI!!
WAAAA
MMM
HA!!
BAAAA
GO, GO, SEISHUN!! GO, GO, SEISHUN!!
KSSH
HMF!!

READ THIS WAY

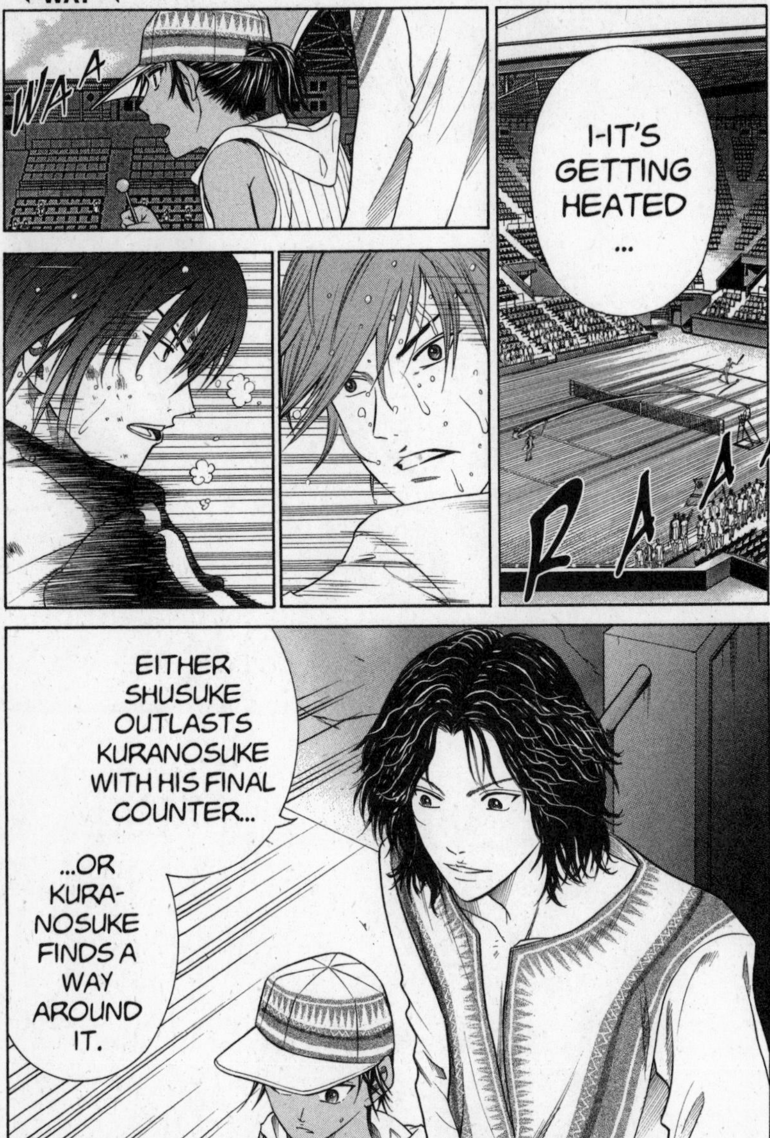
I-IT'S GETTING HEATED ...
RAAA
WAA
EITHER SHUSUKE OUTLASTS KURANOSUKE WITH HIS FINAL COUNTER...
...OR KURA-NOSUKE FINDS A WAY AROUND IT.

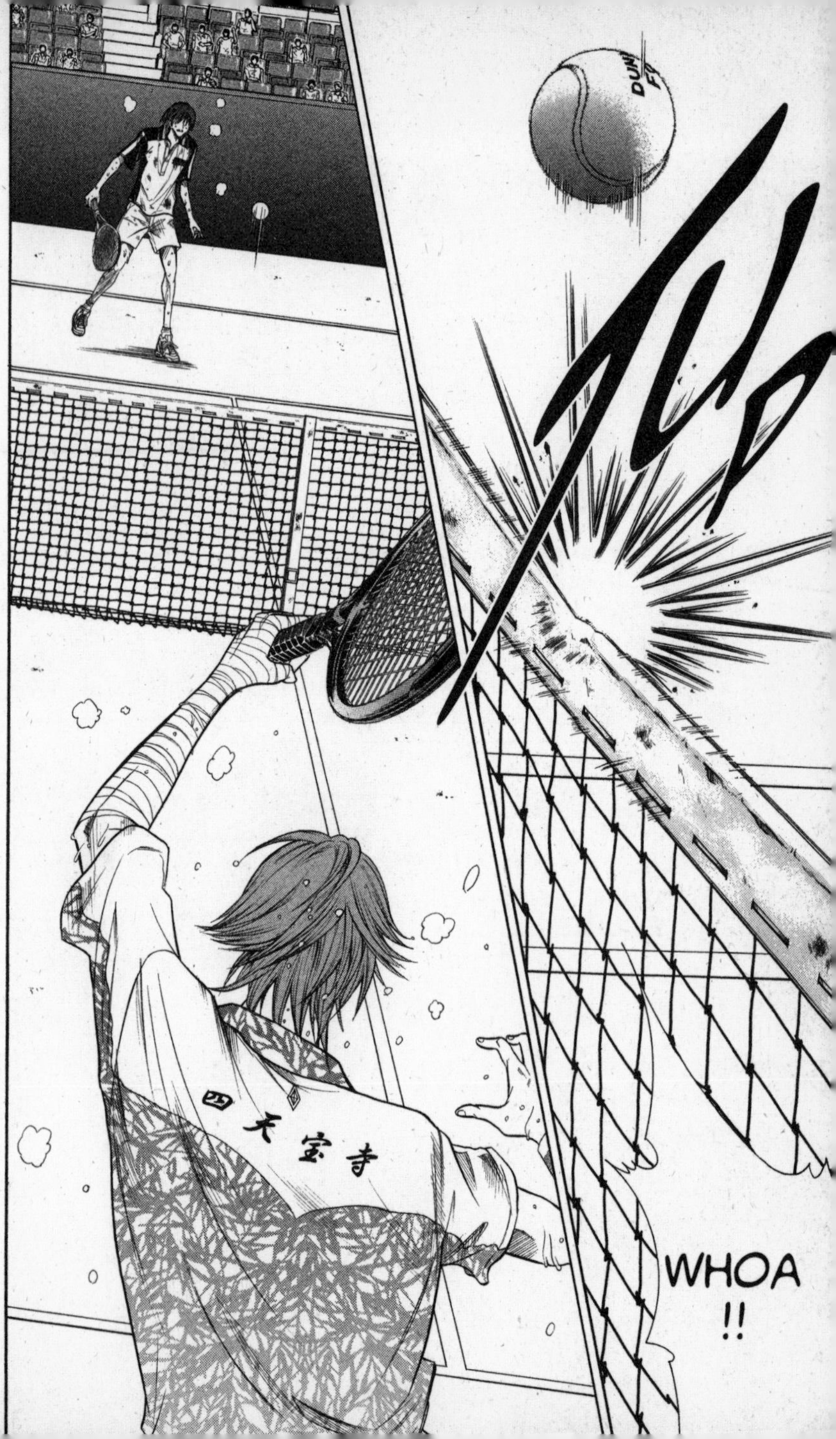
四天宝寺
WHOA
!!

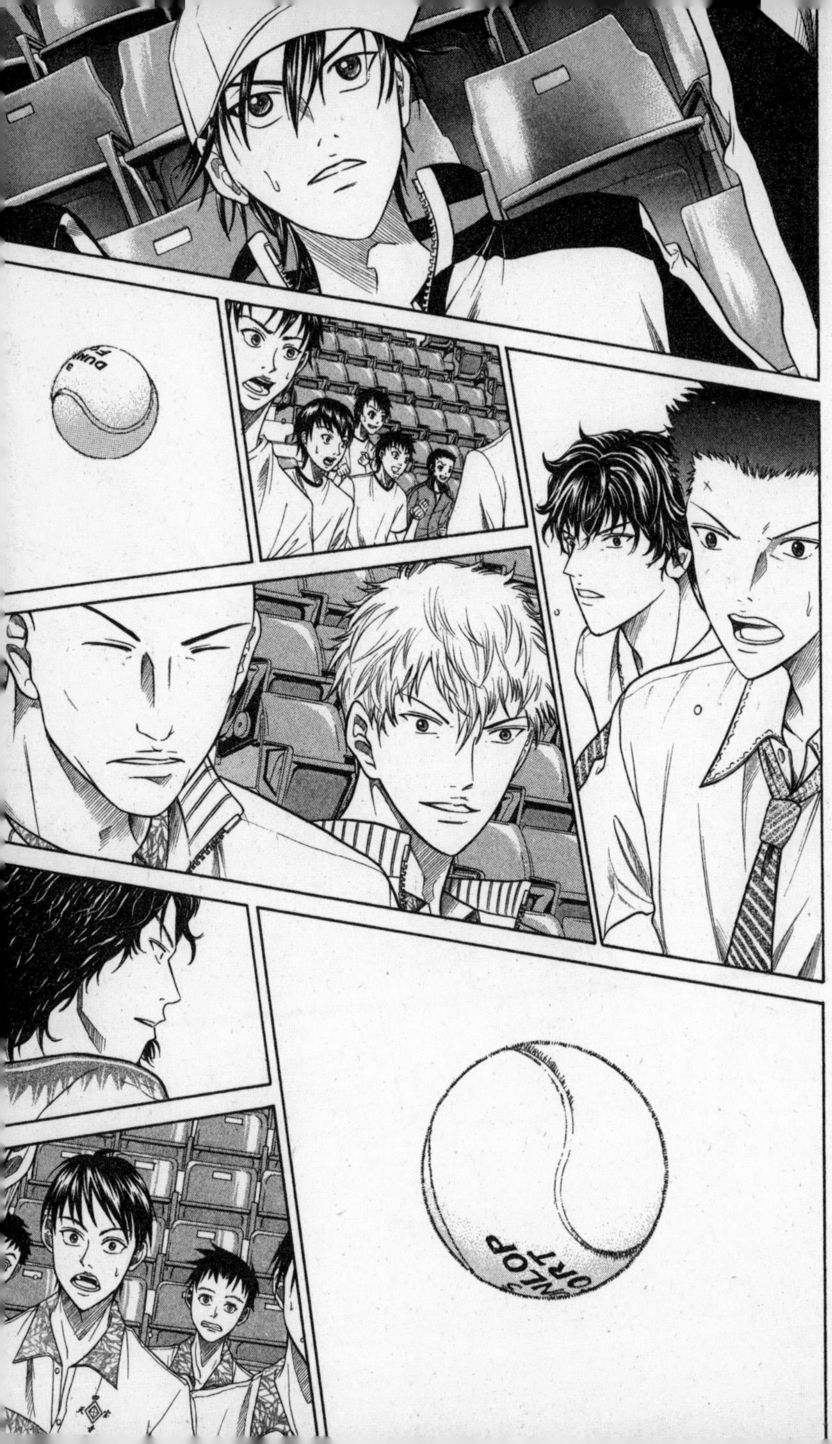

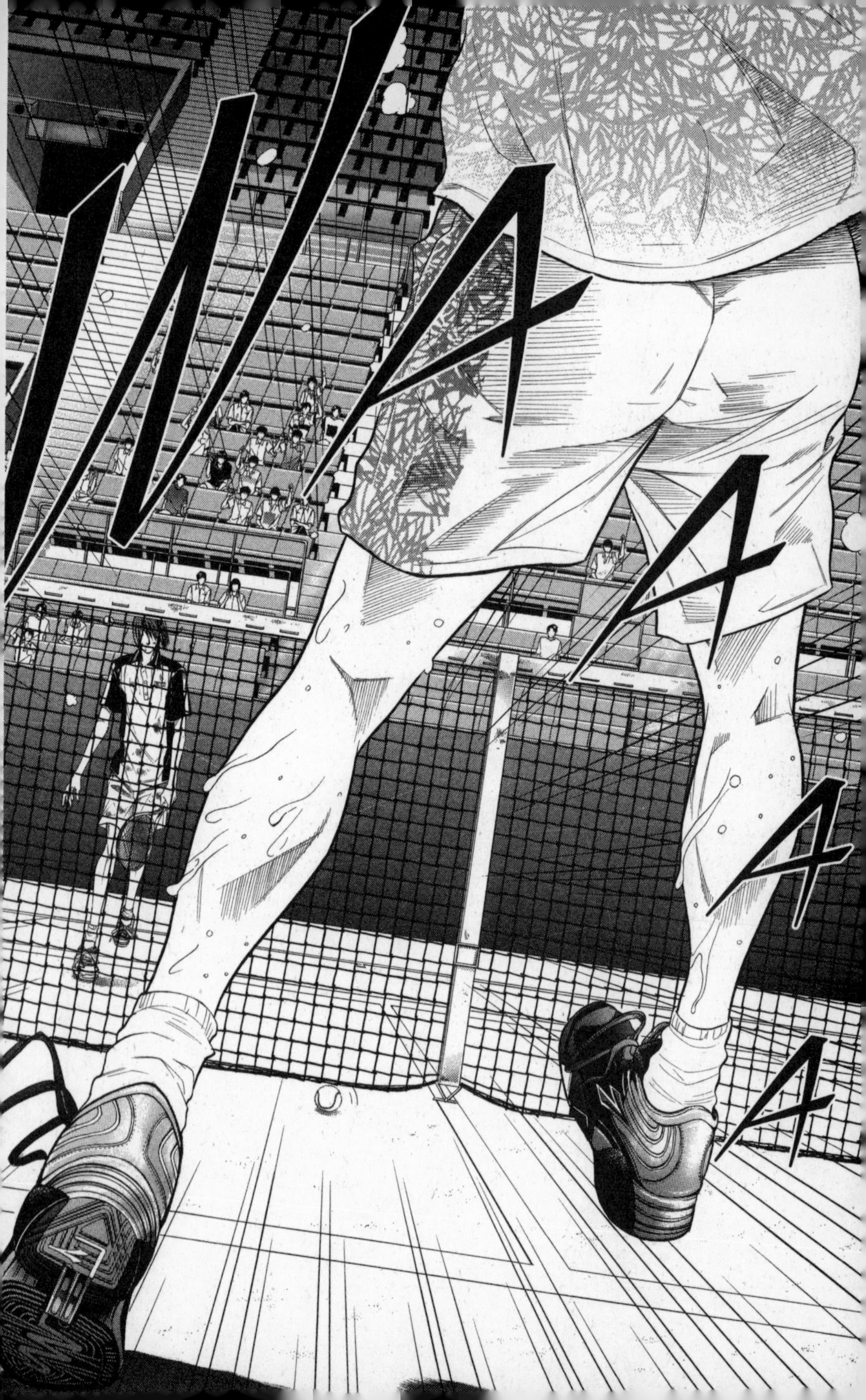
WAAAAA

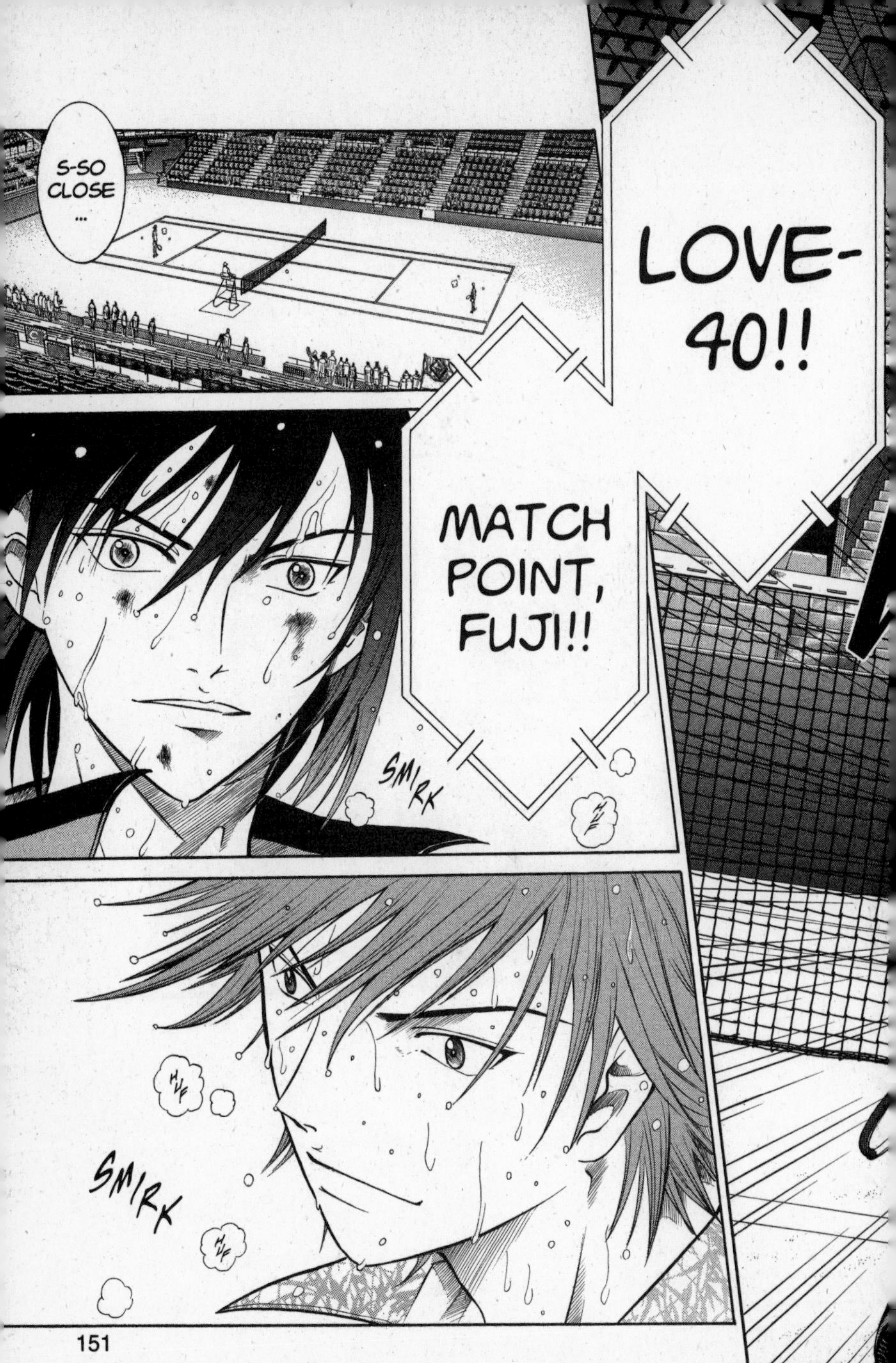
LOVE-40!!
S-SO CLOSE ...
MATCH POINT, FUJI!!
HUF
SMIRK
HUF
SMIRK
HUF

テニスの王子様

THE PRINCE OF TENNIS

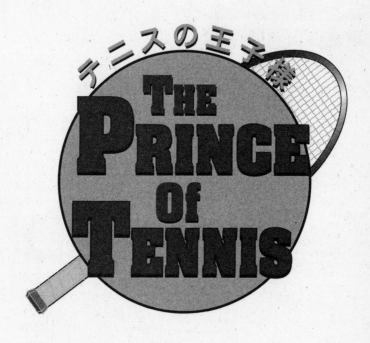

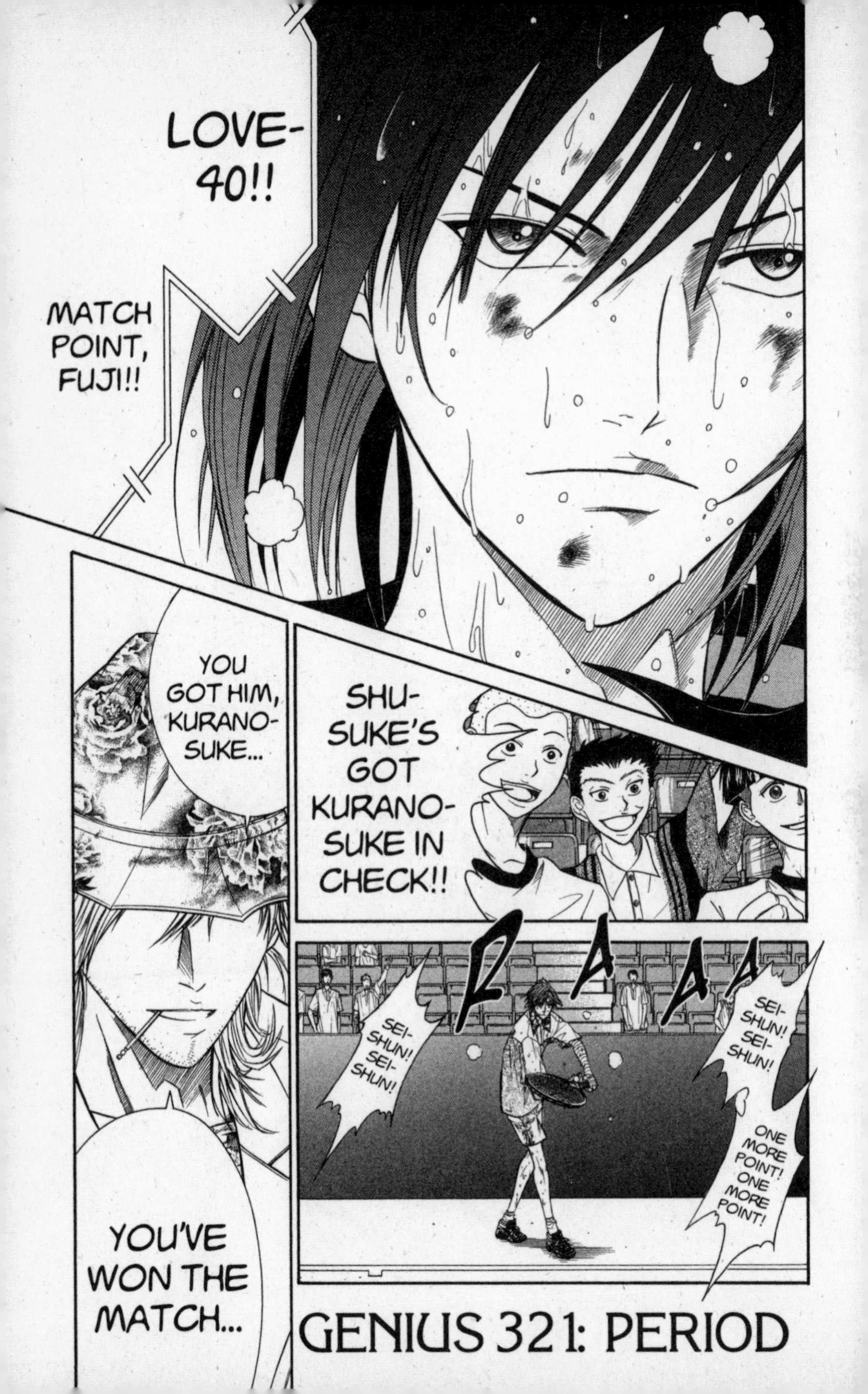
LOVE-40!!
MATCH POINT, FUJI!!
SHU-SUKE'S GOT KURANO-SUKE IN CHECK!!
RAAA
SEI-SHUN! SEI-SHUN!
ONE MORE POINT! ONE MORE POINT!
SEI-SHUN! SEI-SHUN!
YOU GOT HIM, KURANO-SUKE...
YOU'VE WON THE MATCH...

GENIUS 321: PERIOD

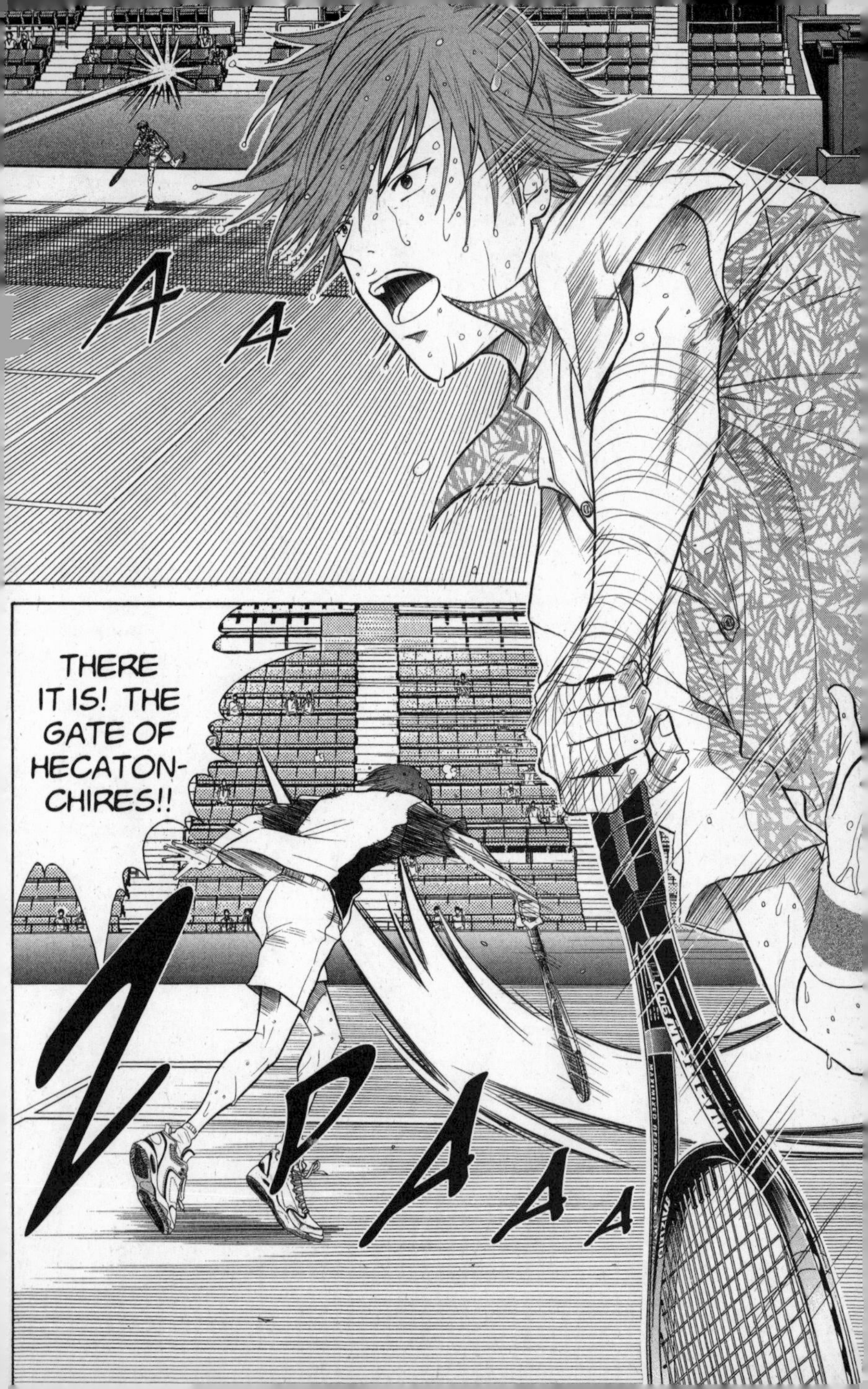
AA
THERE IT IS! THE GATE OF HECATONCHIRES!!
ZDAAAA

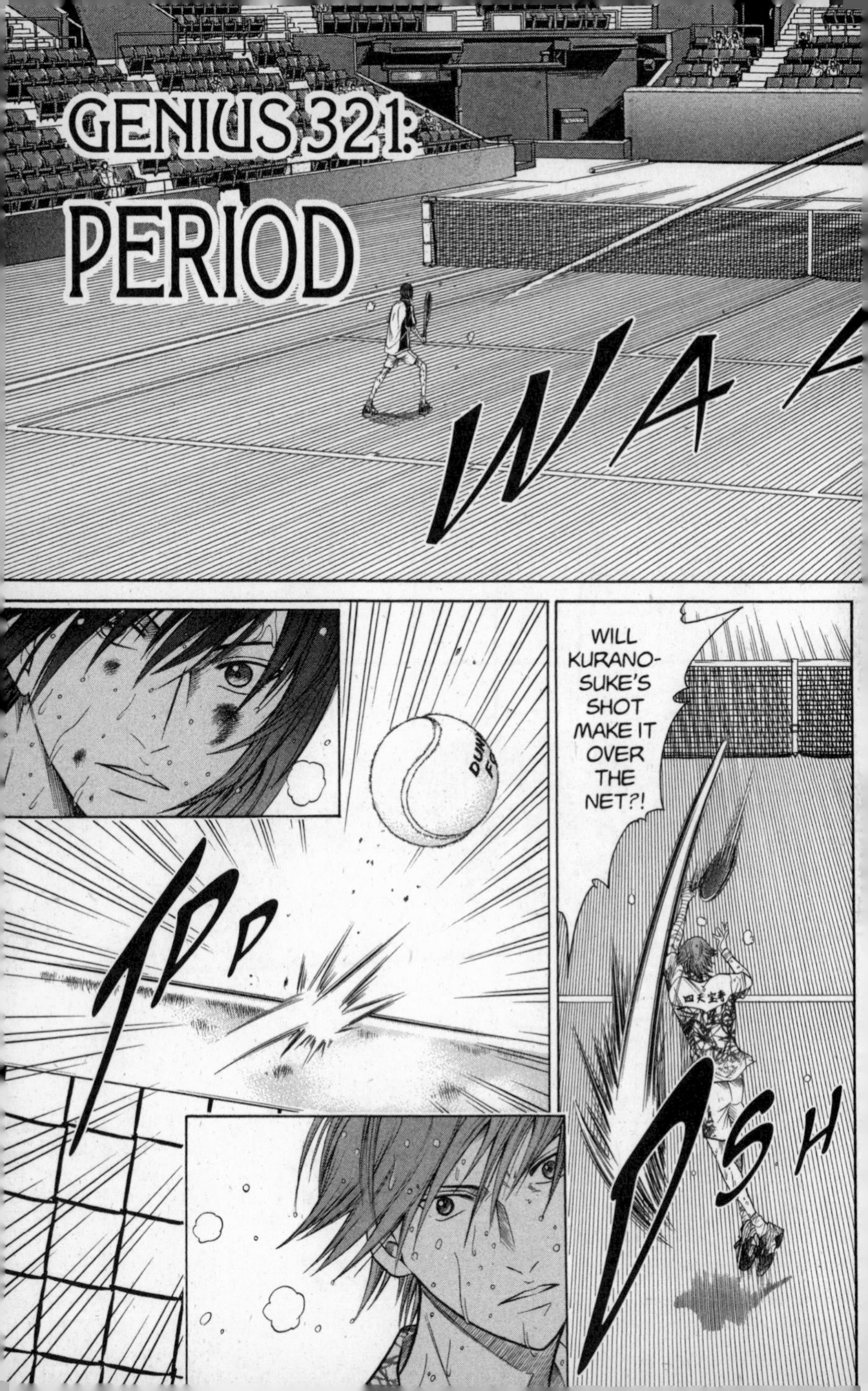
GENIUS 321:
PERIOD
WA
WILL KURANO-SUKE'S SHOT MAKE IT OVER THE NET?!

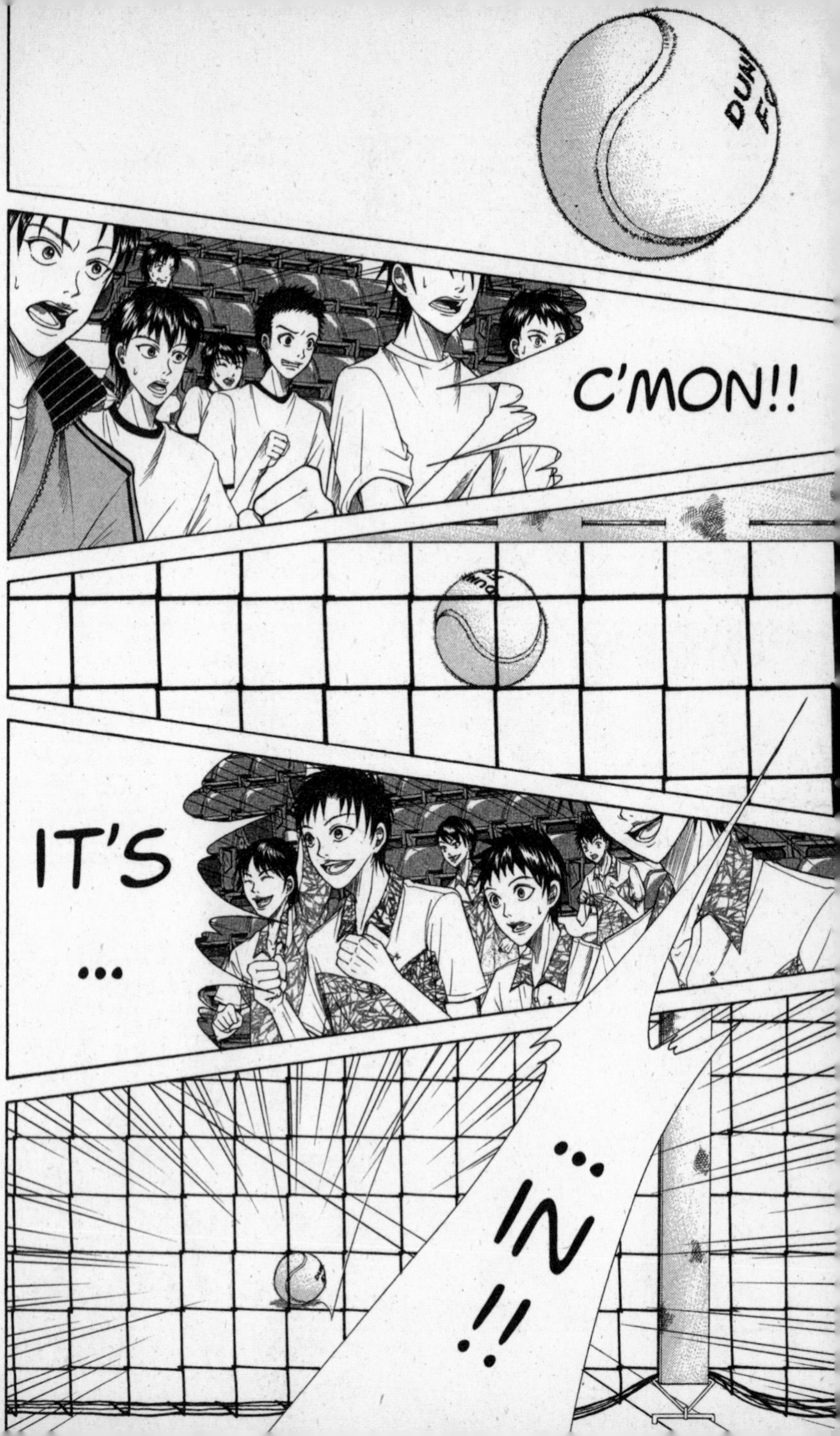
C'MON!!
IT'S
...
...IN!!

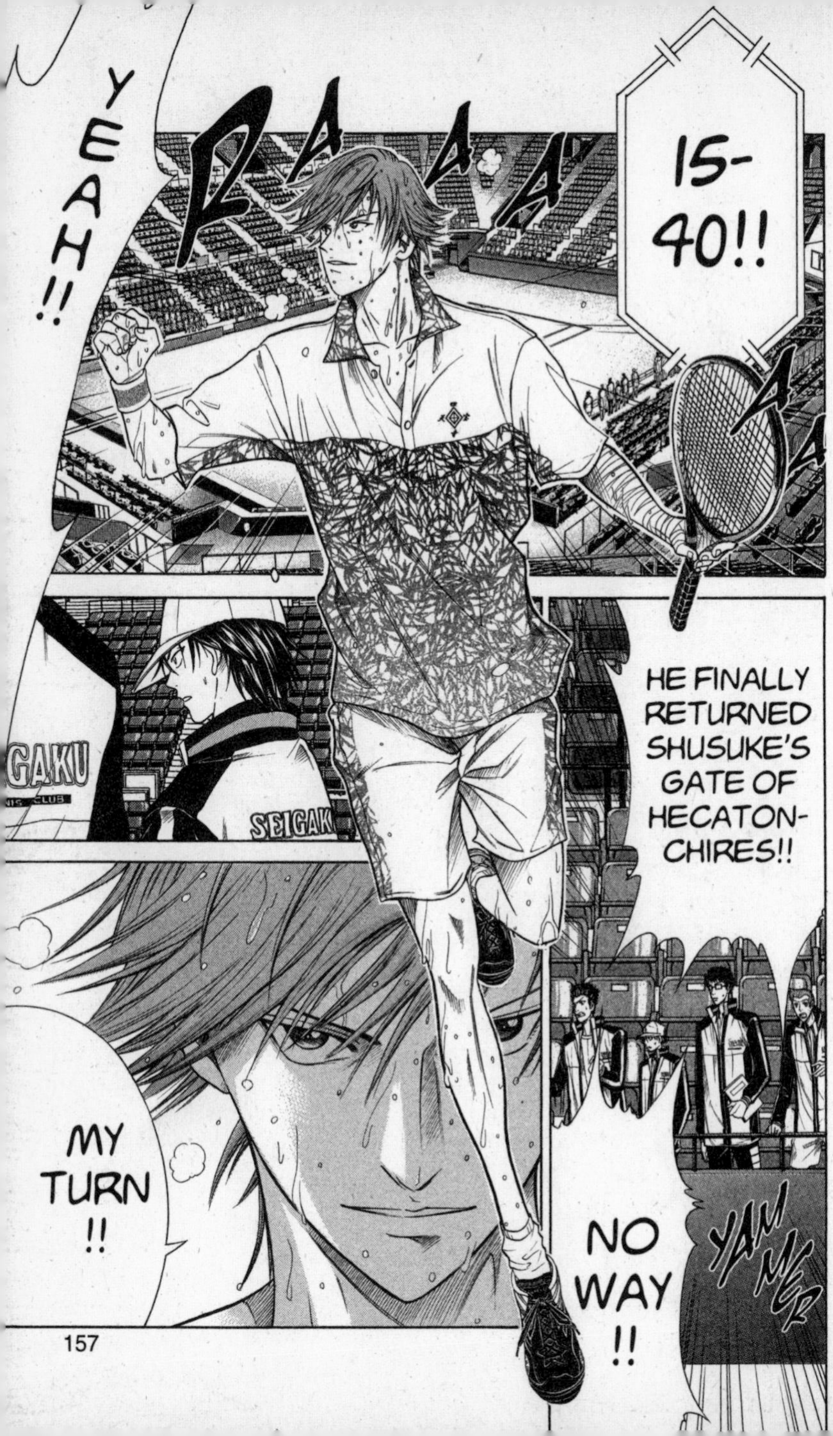
15-40!!
YEAH!!
HE FINALLY RETURNED SHUSUKE'S GATE OF HECATON-CHIRES!!
GAKU
SEIGAK
NO WAY!!
MY TURN!!

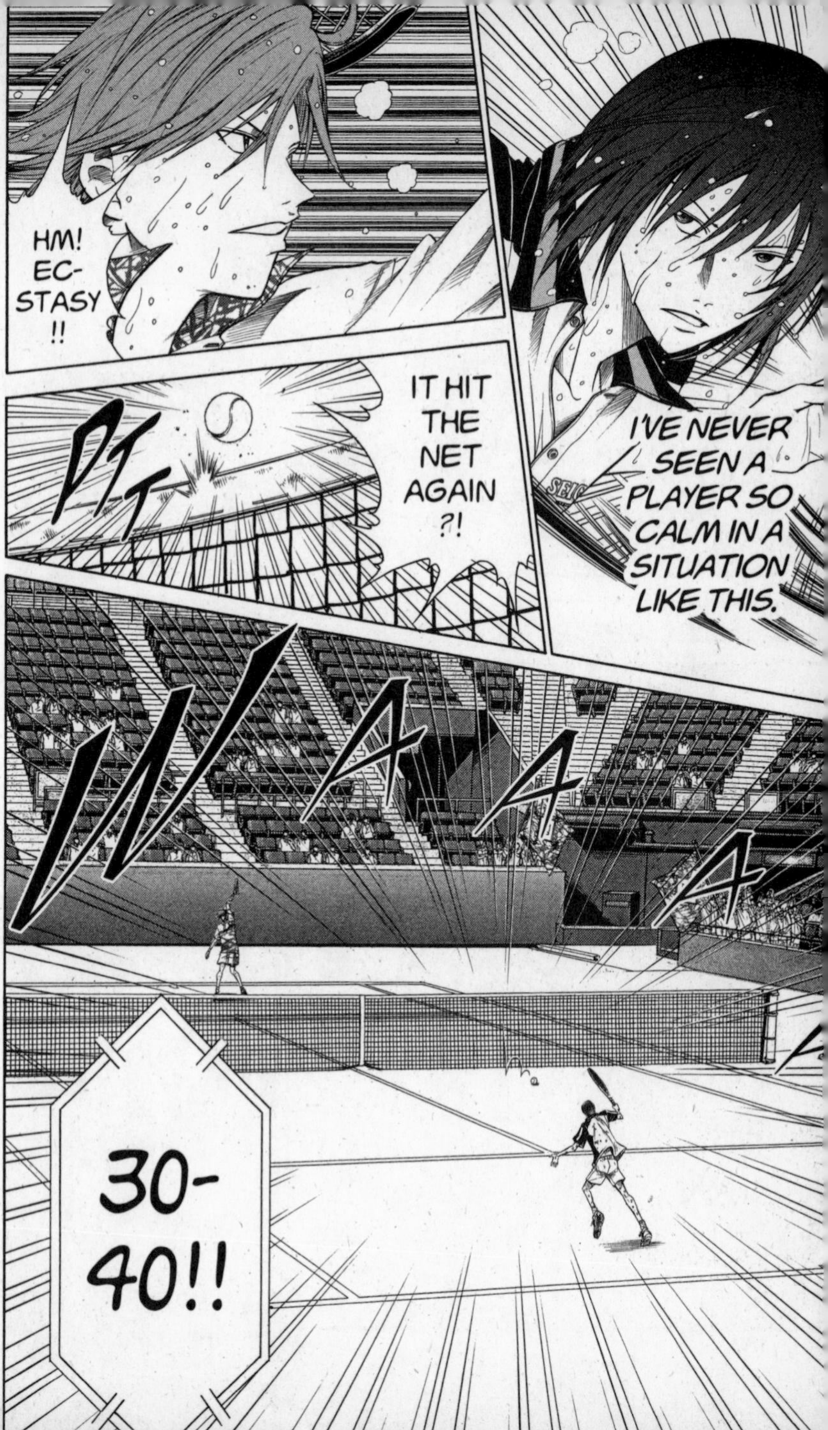
I'VE NEVER SEEN A PLAYER SO CALM IN A SITUATION LIKE THIS.
HM! EC-STASY !!
IT HIT THE NET AGAIN ?!
WAAAA
30-40!!

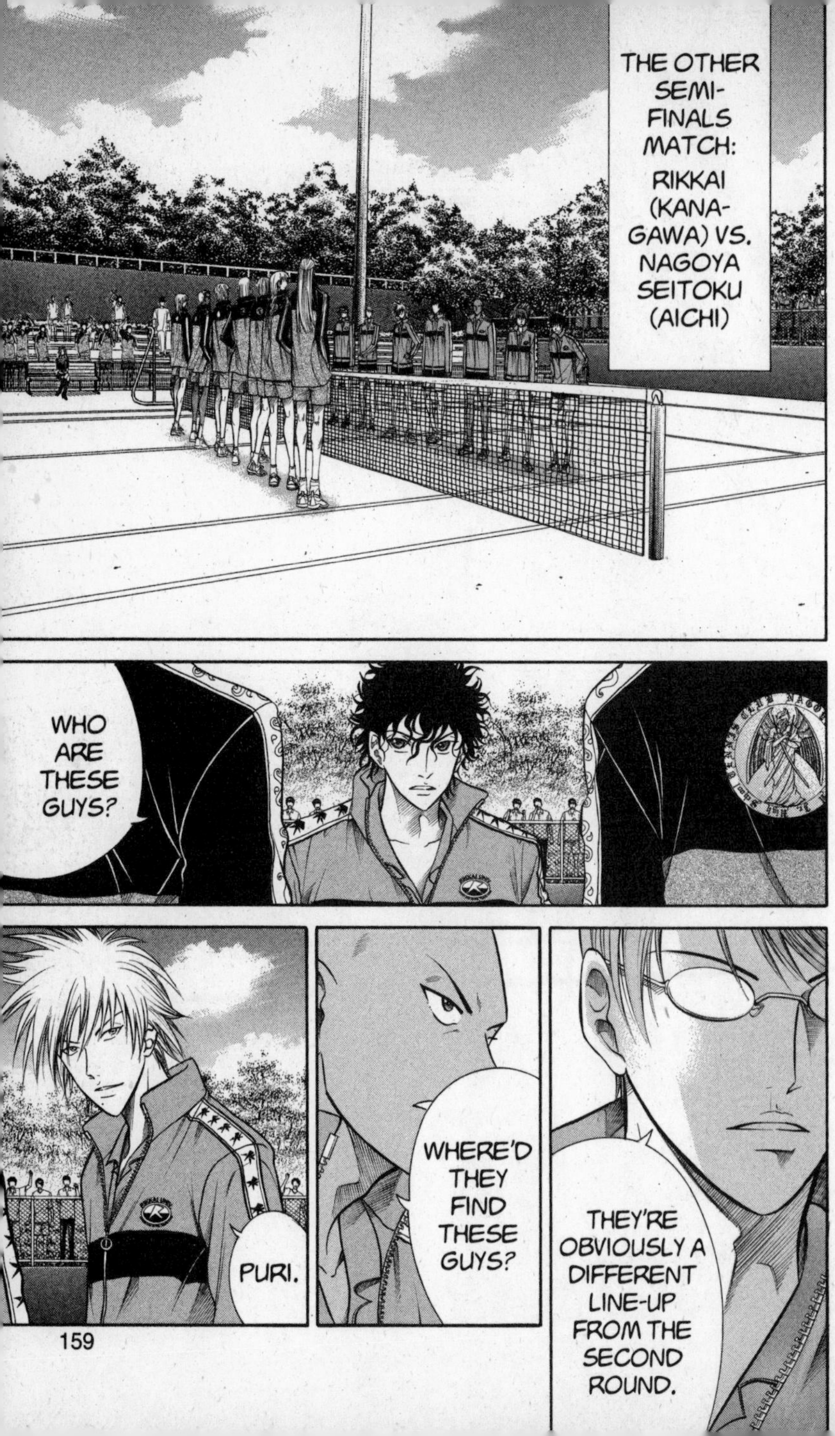
THE OTHER SEMI-FINALS MATCH: RIKKAI (KANAGAWA) VS. NAGOYA SEITOKU (AICHI)
WHO ARE THESE GUYS?
THEY'RE OBVIOUSLY A DIFFERENT LINE-UP FROM THE SECOND ROUND.
WHERE'D THEY FIND THESE GUYS?
PURI.

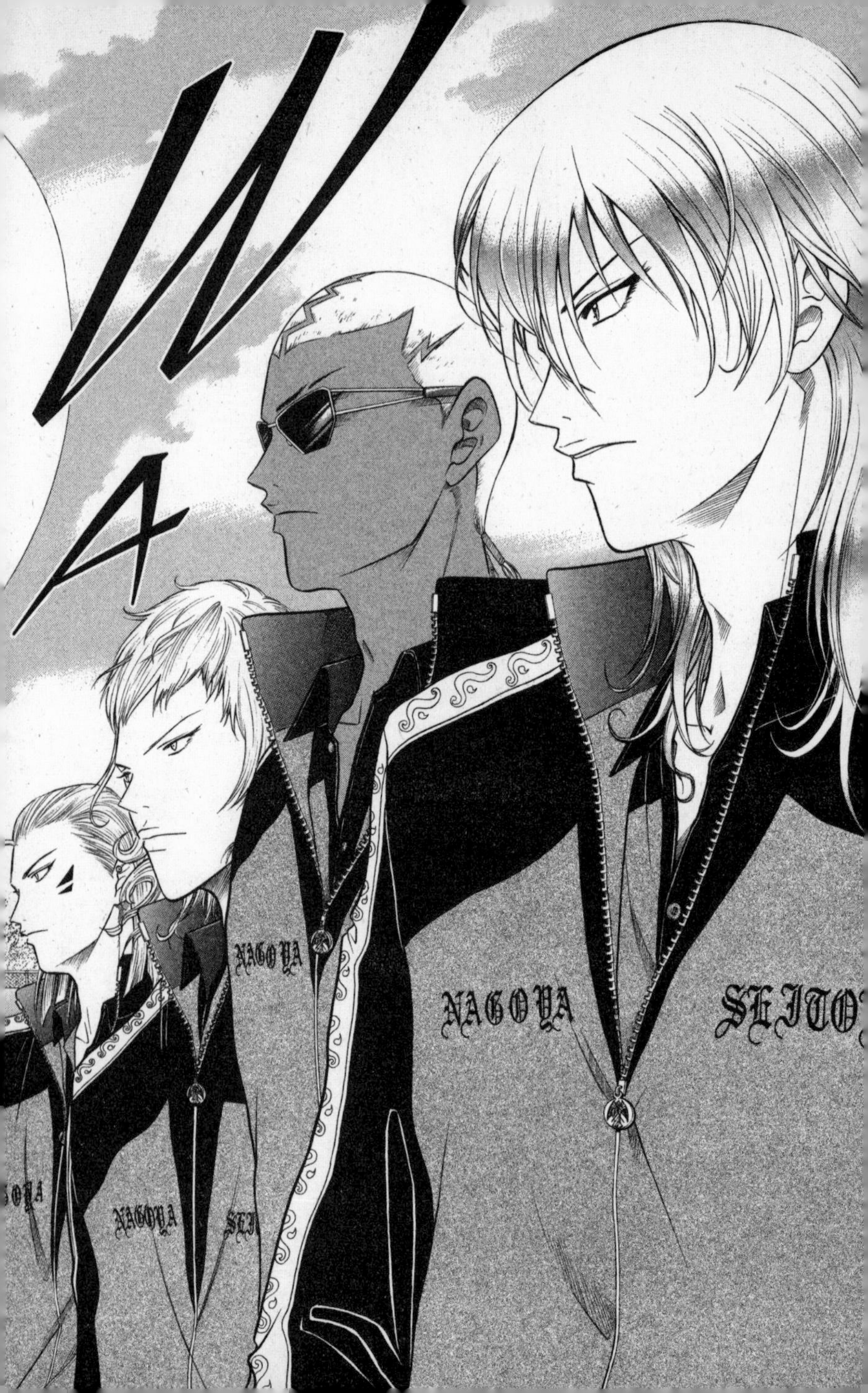
NAGOYA
NAGOYA
NAGOYA

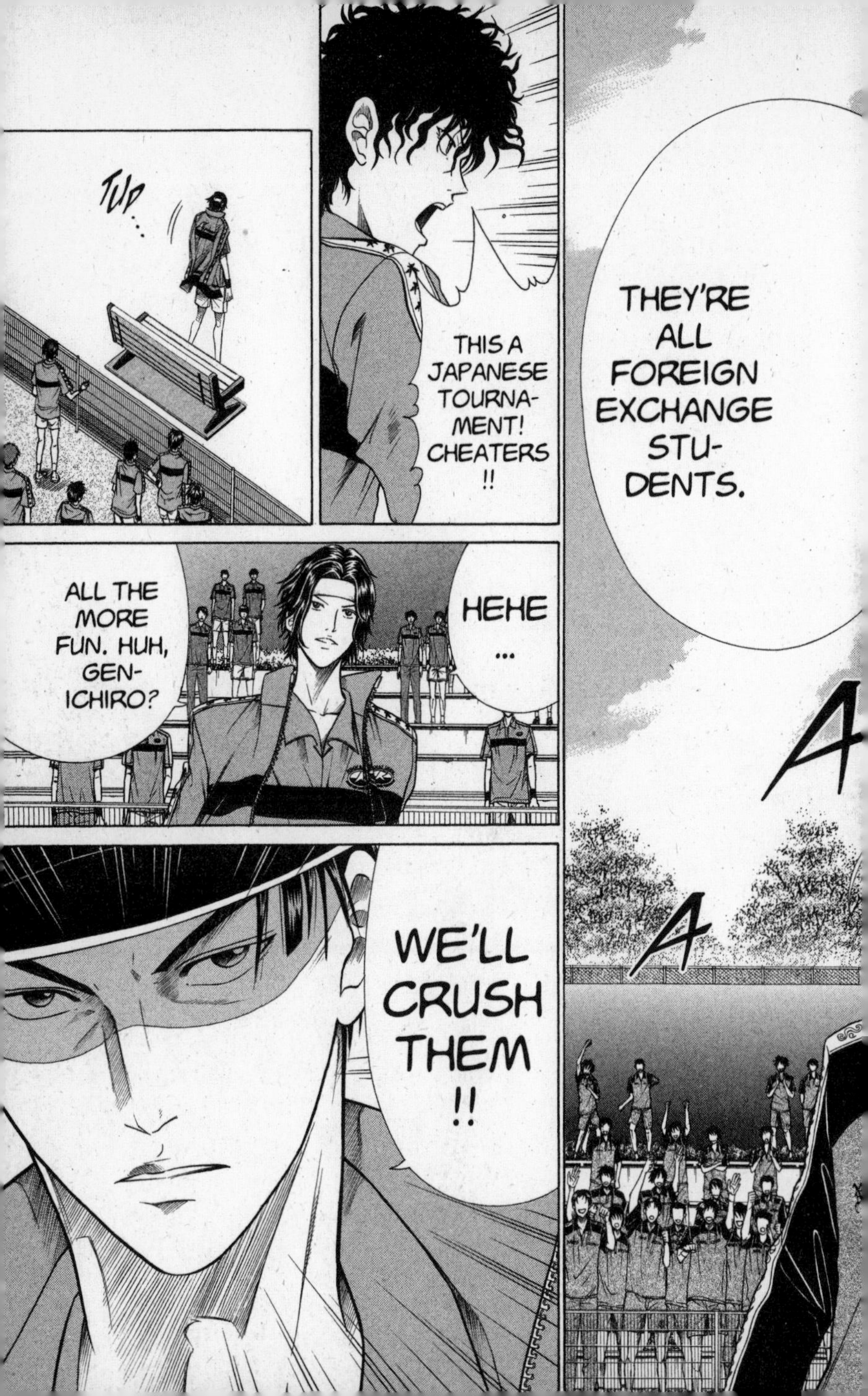
THEY'RE ALL FOREIGN EXCHANGE STU- DENTS.
A
A
THIS A JAPANESE TOURNA- MENT! CHEATERS !!
TUP...
HEHE ...
ALL THE MORE FUN. HUH, GEN- ICHIRO?
WE'LL CRUSH THEM !!

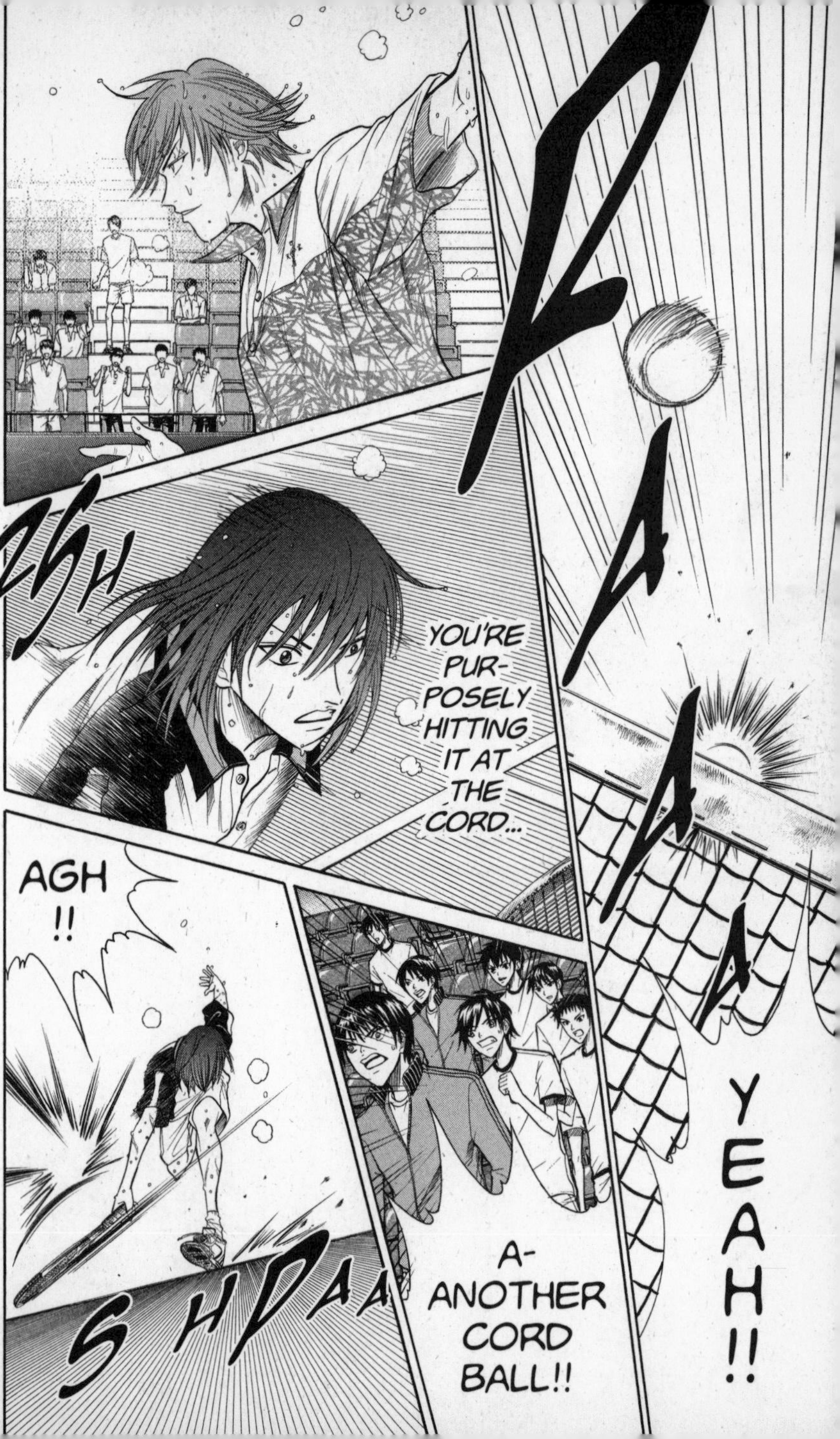
YOU'RE PUR-POSELY HITTING IT AT THE CORD...
YEAH!!
A-ANOTHER CORD BALL!!
AGH!!
SHPAA

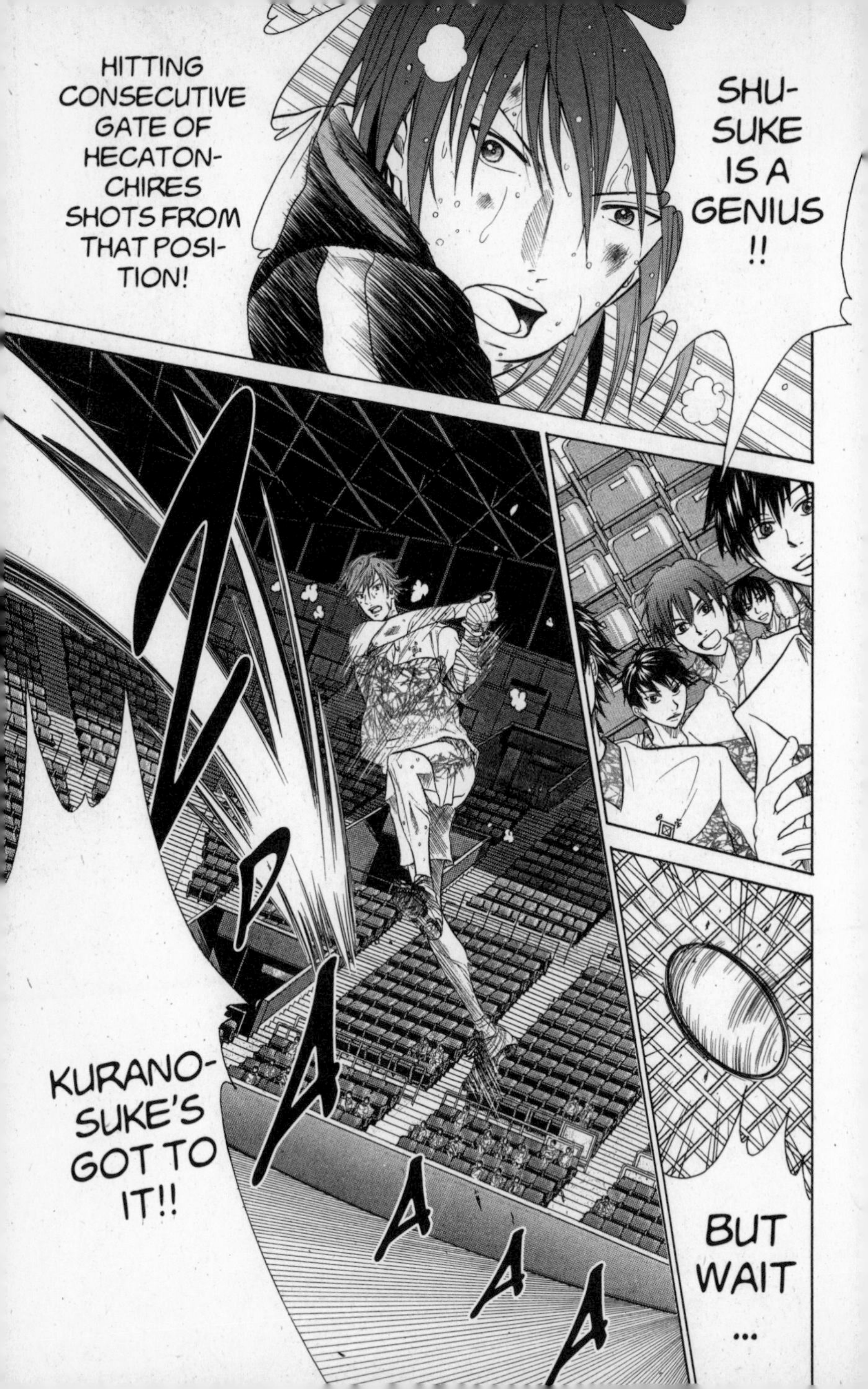
SHUSUKE IS A GENIUS!!
HITTING CONSECUTIVE GATE OF HECATONCHIRES SHOTS FROM THAT POSITION!
BUT WAIT...
KURANOSUKE'S GOT TO IT!!

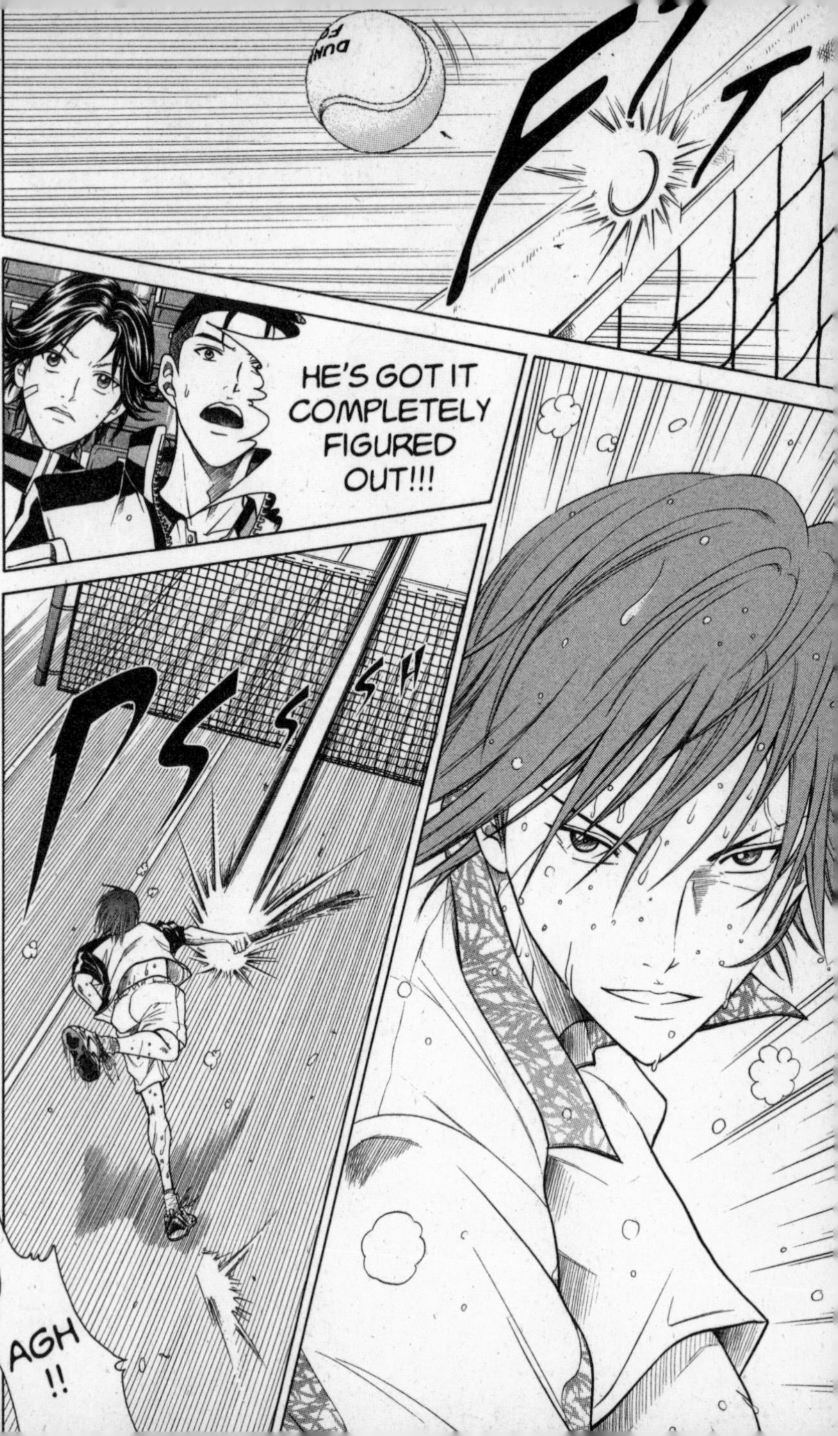
FWT
HE'S GOT IT COMPLETELY FIGURED OUT!!!
WSSSH
AGH !!

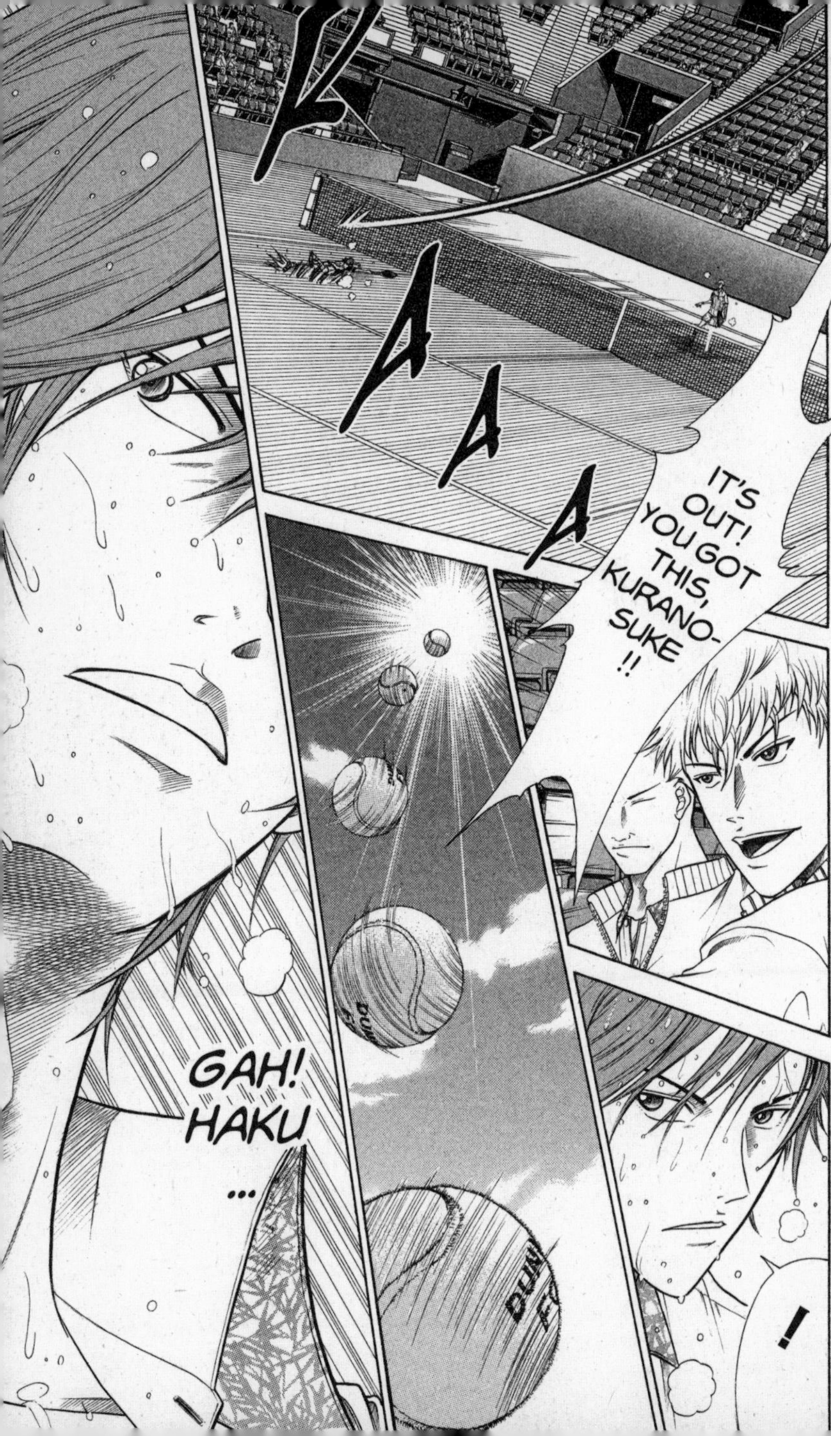
IT'S OUT! YOU GOT THIS, KURANOSUKE!!
!
GAH! HAKU...

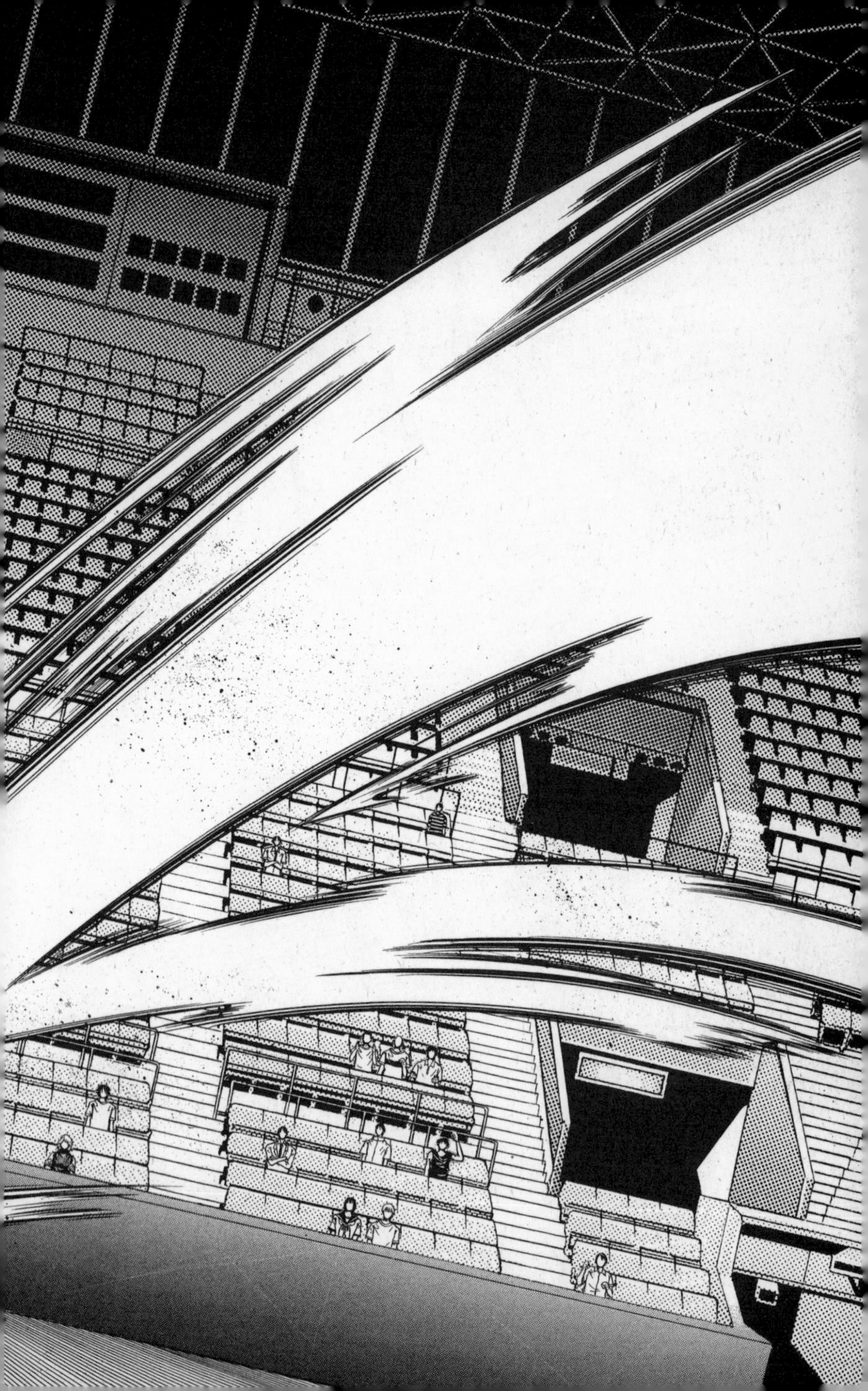

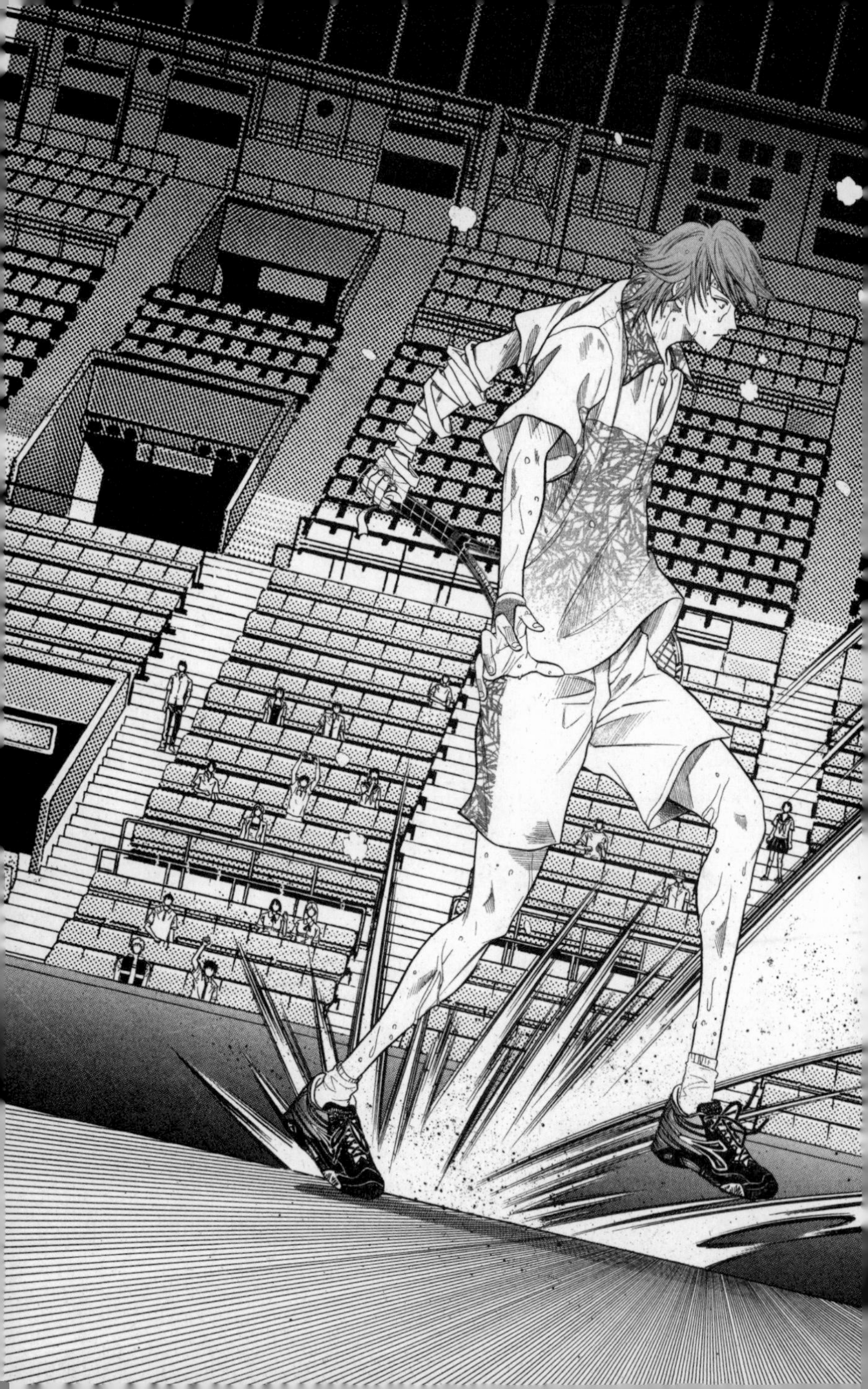

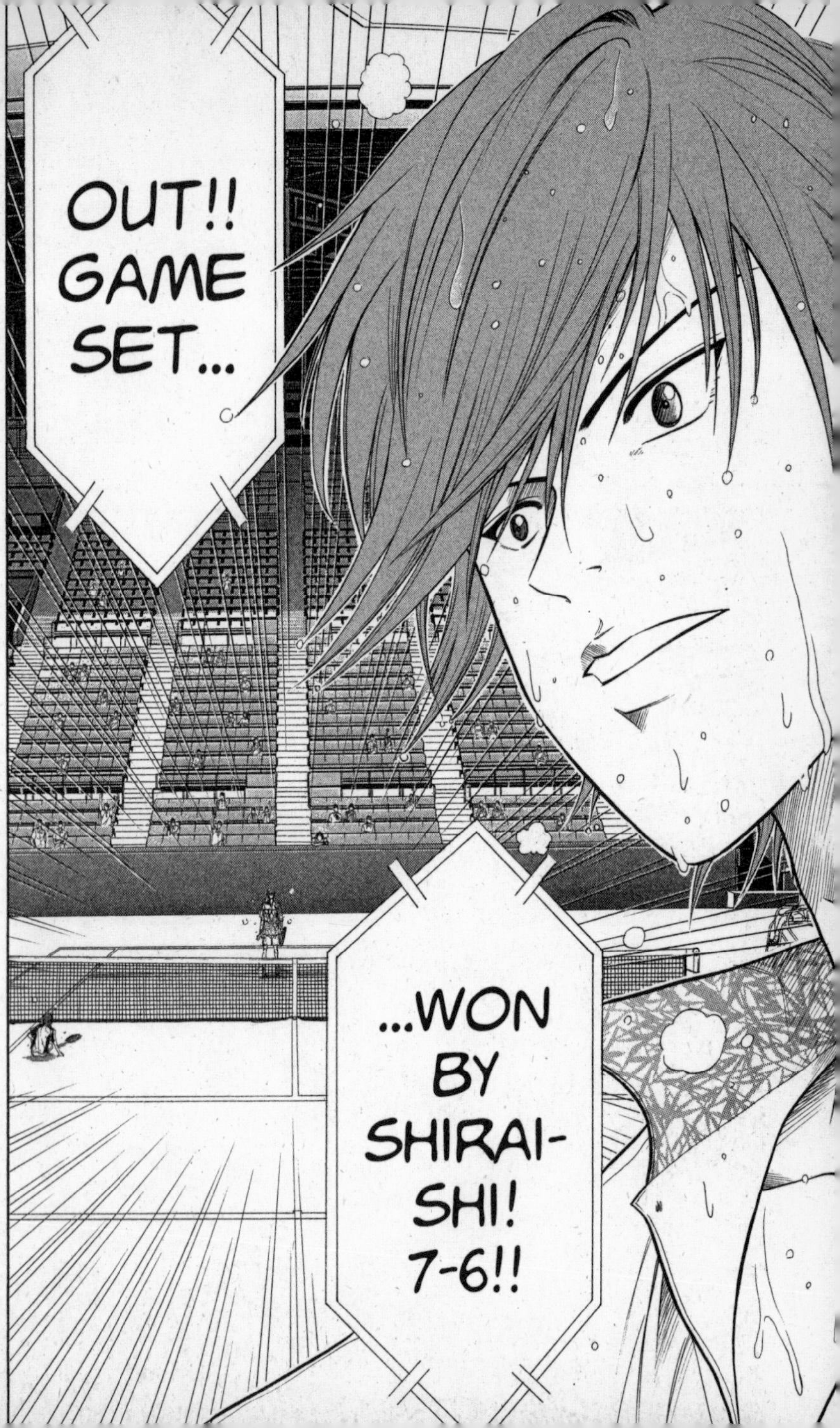
OUT!! GAME SET...
...WON BY SHIRAI-SHI! 7-6!!

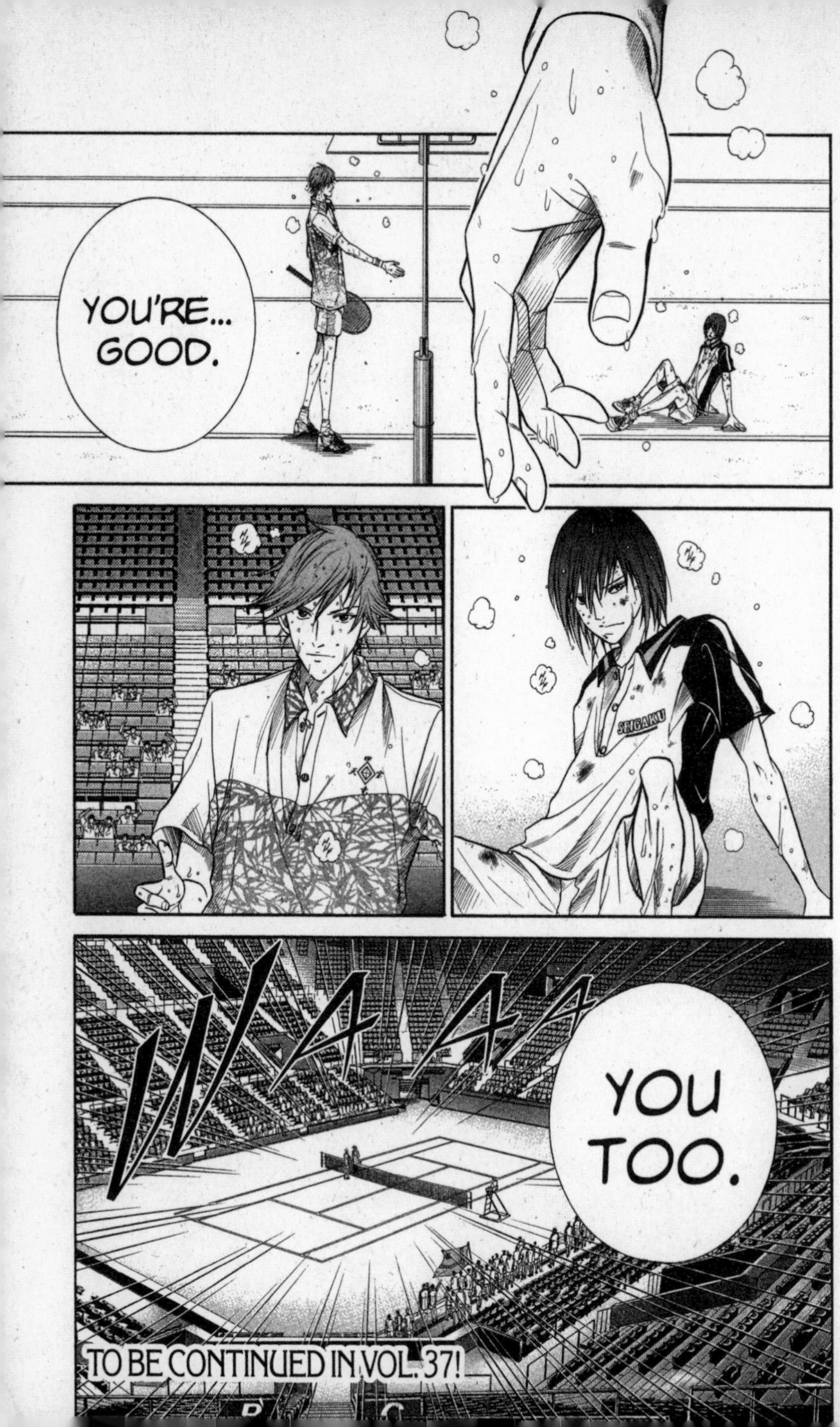
YOU'RE... GOOD.
WAAA
YOU TOO.
TO BE CONTINUED IN VOL. 37!

In the Next Volume...

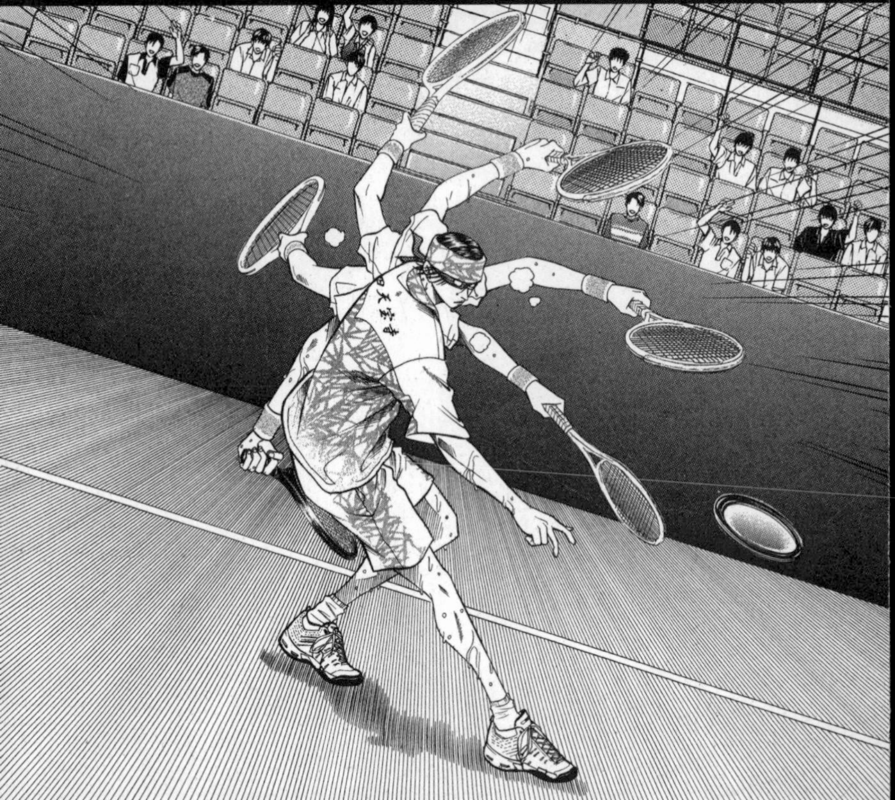

The Terror of Comic Tennis

Seishun's semifinal matches against Shitenhoji continue, and now it's Kaoru and Momo's turn in No. 2 Doubles. Their opponents, Koharu Konjiki and Yuji Hitoji, are highly skilled players but have a style that's a little...unusual. Next, two power players step onto the court for No. 2 Singles: Taka and Gin Ishida, the originator of Taka's Hadokyu shot. In this match of Hadokyu vs. Hadokyu, it's the last player standing who'll win!

Available May 2010!

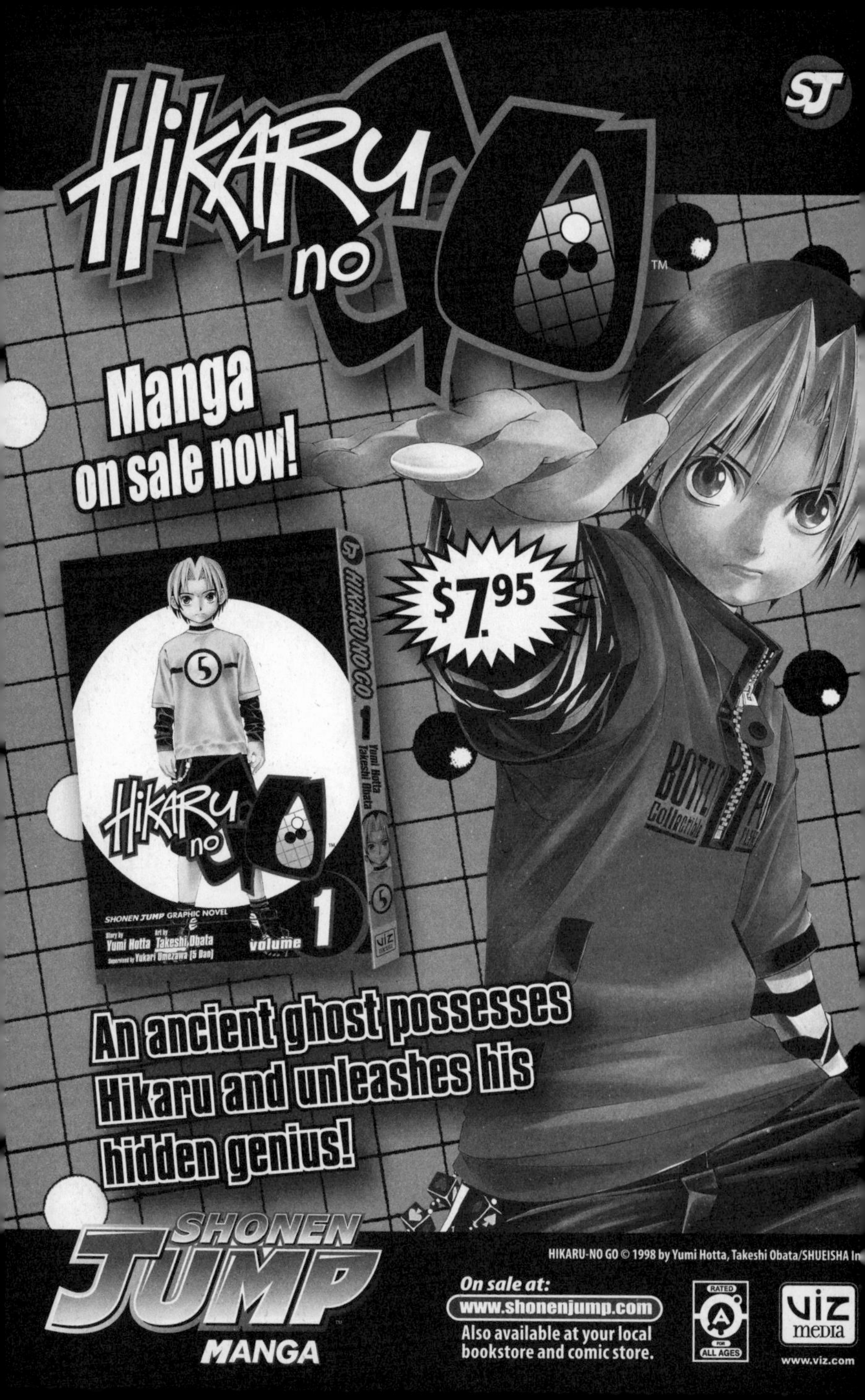
SJ
Hikaru no Go™
Manga on sale now!
$7.95
SHONEN JUMP GRAPHIC NOVEL
Story by Yumi Hotta Art by Takeshi Obata
Supervised by Yukari Umezawa (5 Dan)
volume 1
HIKARU NO GO 1 Yumi Hotta Takeshi Obata
An ancient ghost possesses Hikaru and unleashes his hidden genius!
SHONEN JUMP MANGA
HIKARU-NO GO © 1998 by Yumi Hotta, Takeshi Obata/SHUEISHA In
On sale at:
www.shonenjump.com
Also available at your local bookstore and comic store.
RATED A FOR ALL AGES
viz media
www.viz.com

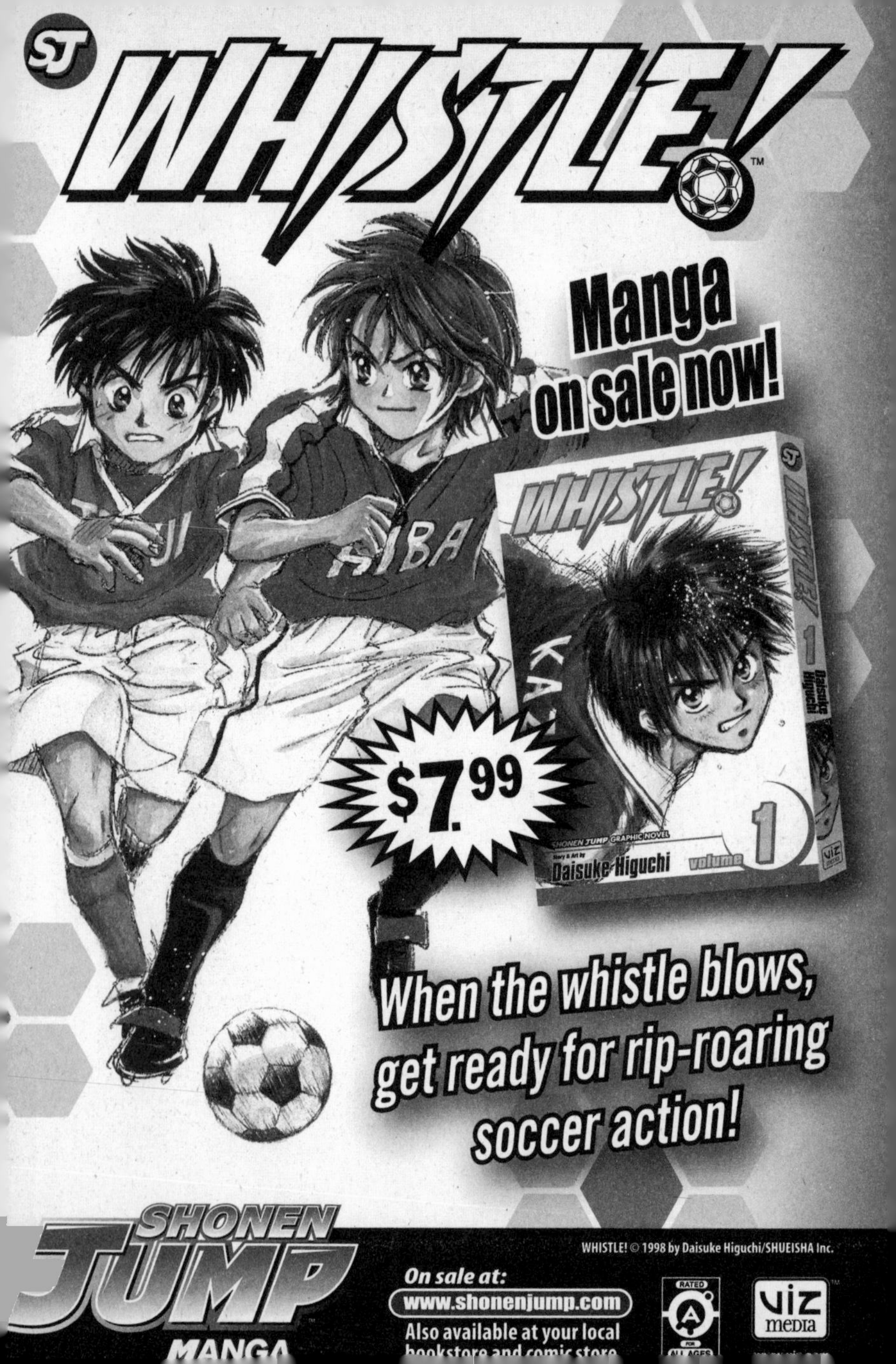
SJ
WHISTLE!™
Manga on sale now!
SJ
WHISTLE!
Daisuke Higuchi
1
SHONEN JUMP GRAPHIC NOVEL
Story & Art by
Daisuke Higuchi
volume 1
$7.99
When the whistle blows, get ready for rip-roaring soccer action!
SHONEN JUMP MANGA
WHISTLE! © 1998 by Daisuke Higuchi/SHUEISHA Inc.
On sale at:
www.shonenjump.com
Also available at your local
RATED A FOR ALL AGES
VIZ media

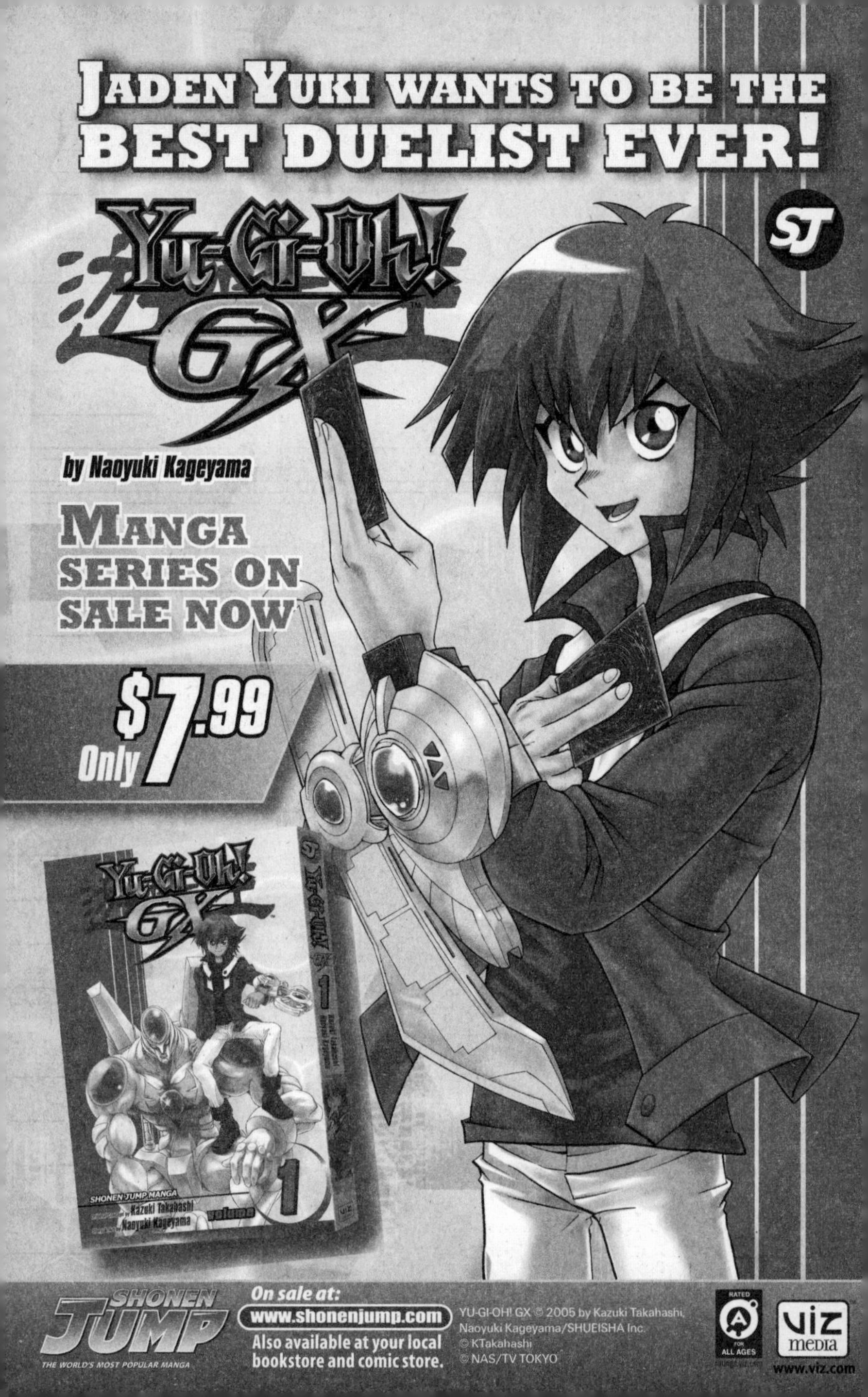
JADEN YUKI WANTS TO BE THE
BEST DUELIST EVER!
SJ
YU-GI-OH! GX
by Naoyuki Kageyama
MANGA
SERIES ON
SALE NOW
Only $7.99
YU-GI-OH! GX
SHONEN JUMP MANGA
Kazuki Takahashi
Naoyuki Kageyama
volume 1
SHONEN JUMP
THE WORLD'S MOST POPULAR MANGA
On sale at:
www.shonenjump.com
Also available at your local bookstore and comic store.
YU-GI-OH! GX © 2005 by Kazuki Takahashi, Naoyuki Kageyama/SHUEISHA Inc. © KTakahashi © NAS/TV TOKYO
RATED A FOR ALL AGES
viz media
www.viz.com